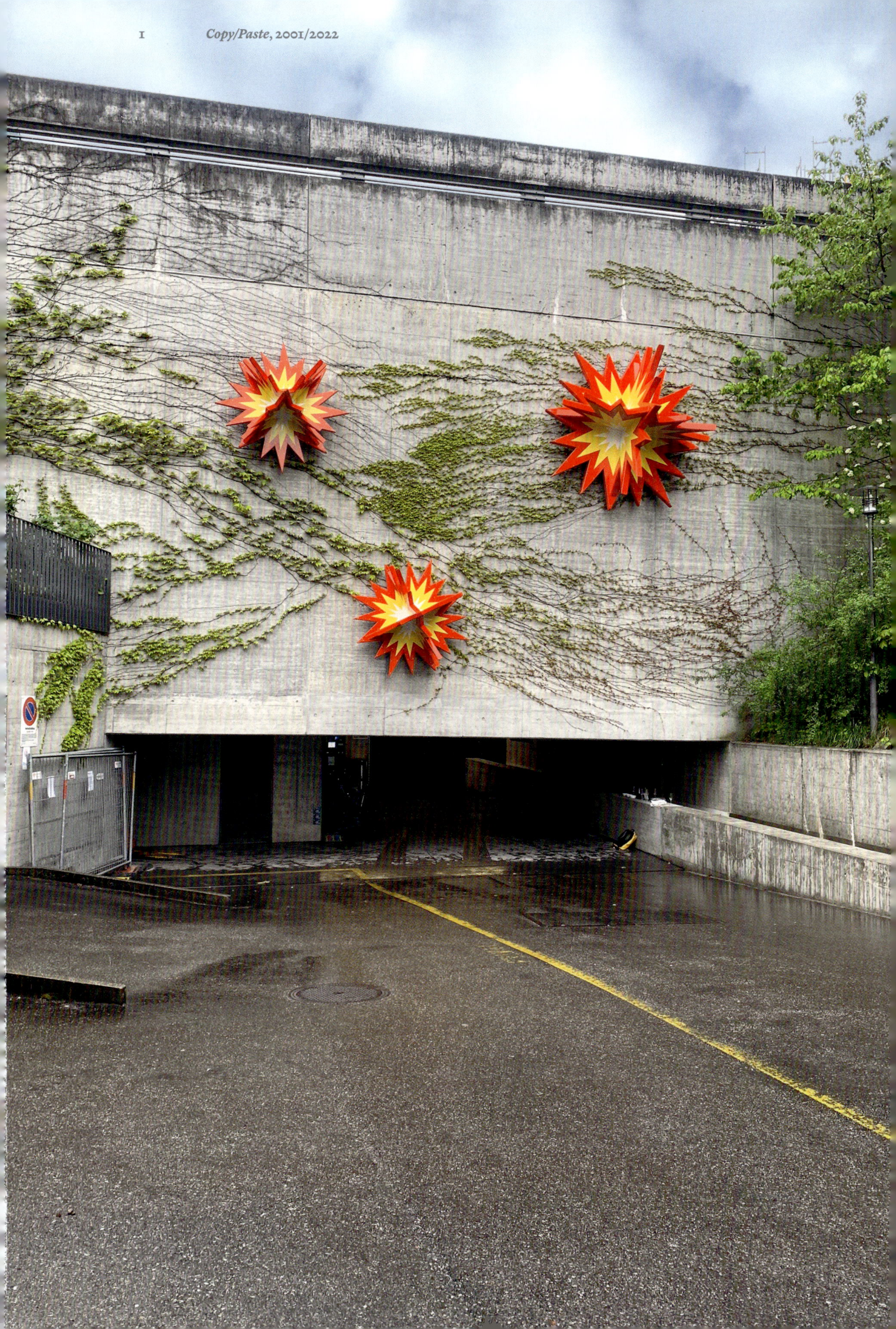

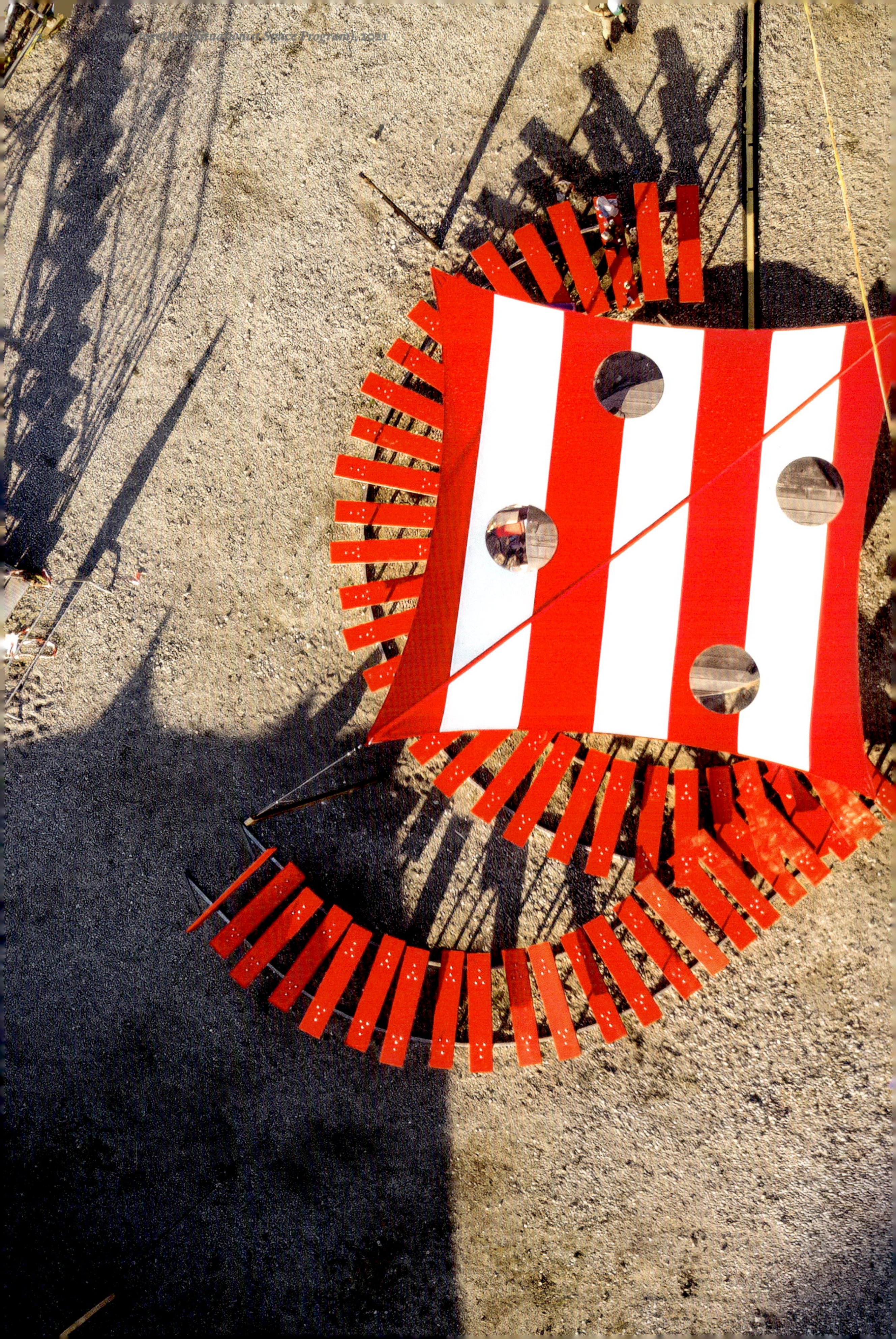

Come Together (Situationist Space Program), 2021

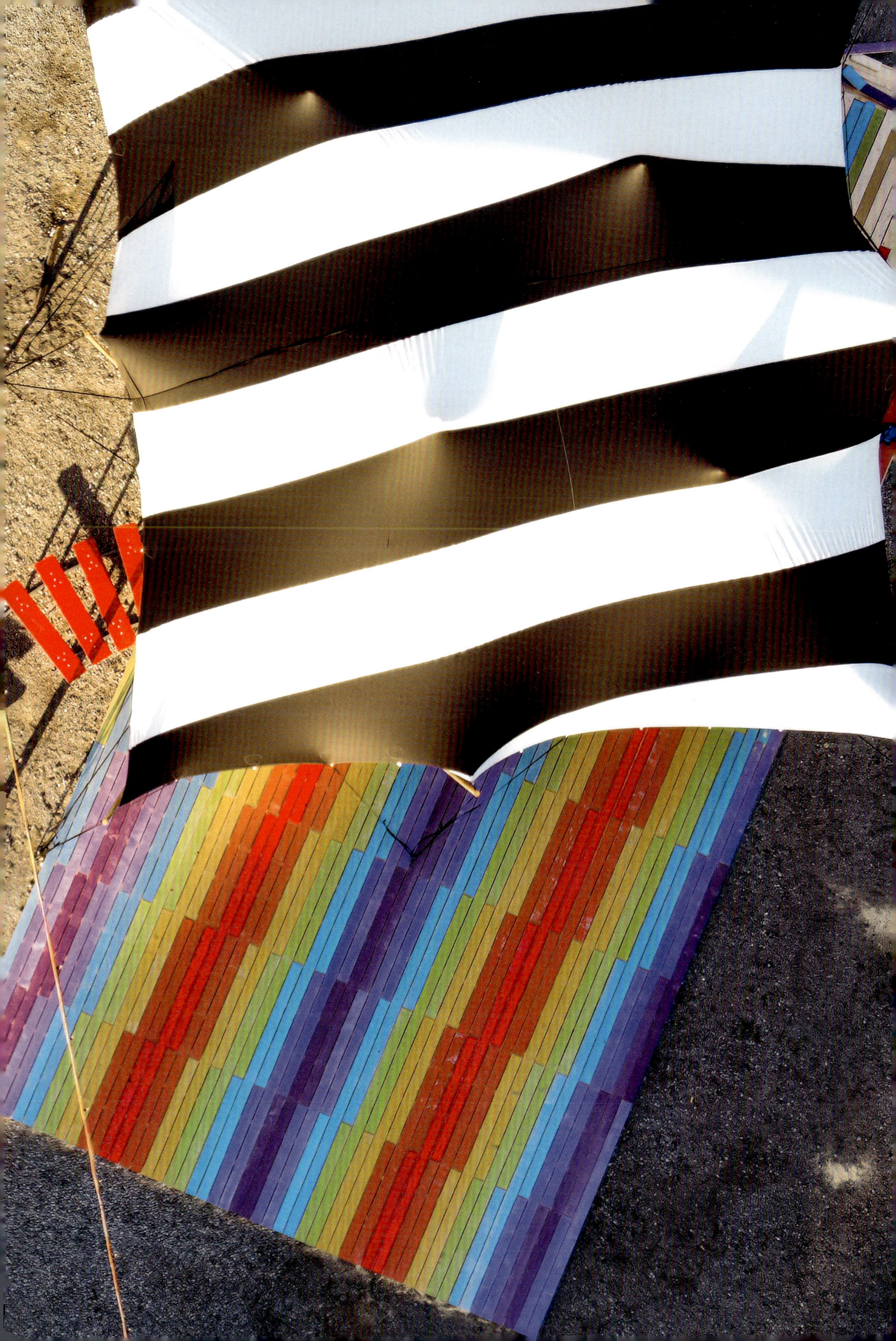

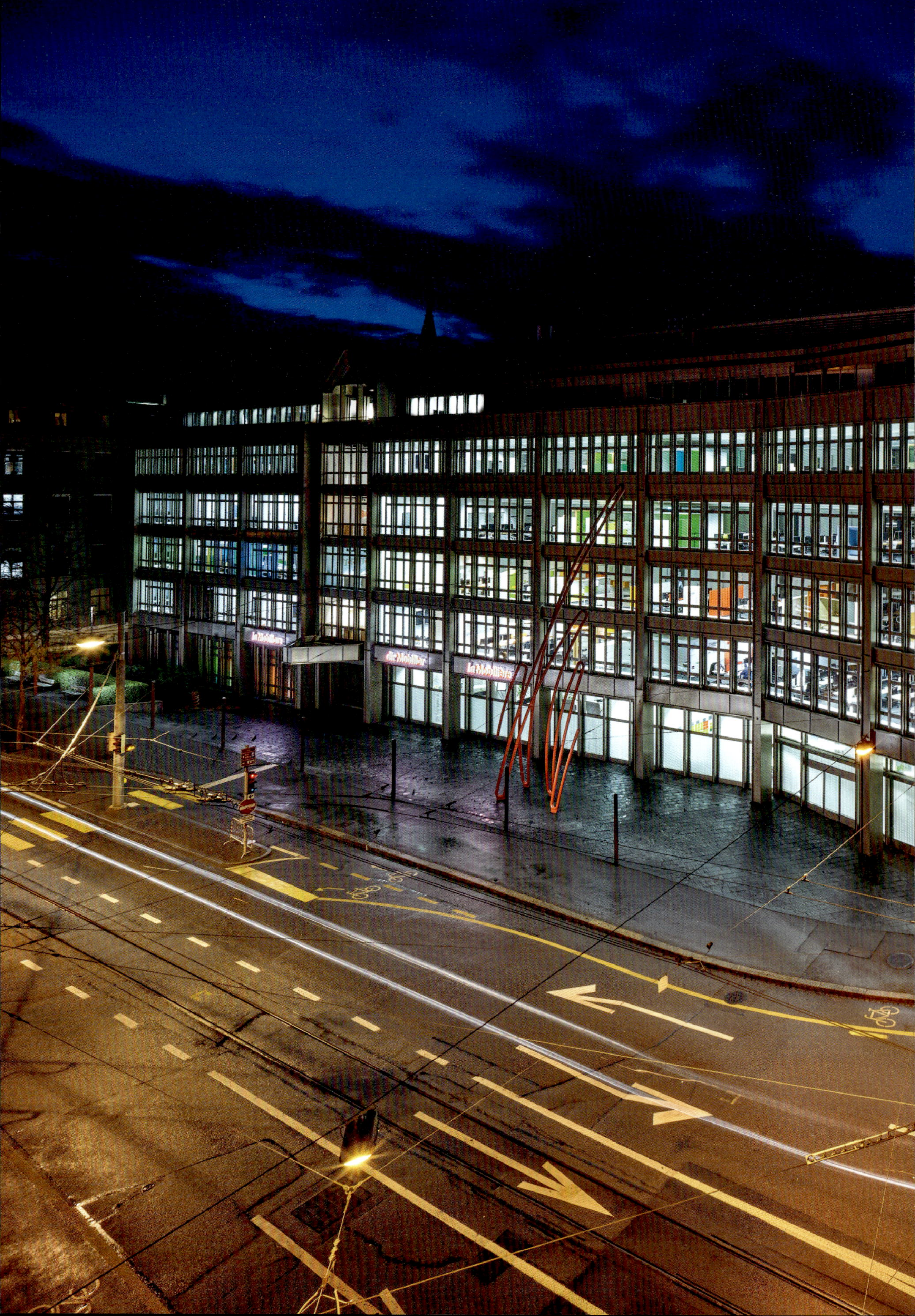
la Mobilière
die Mobiliar
la Mobilière

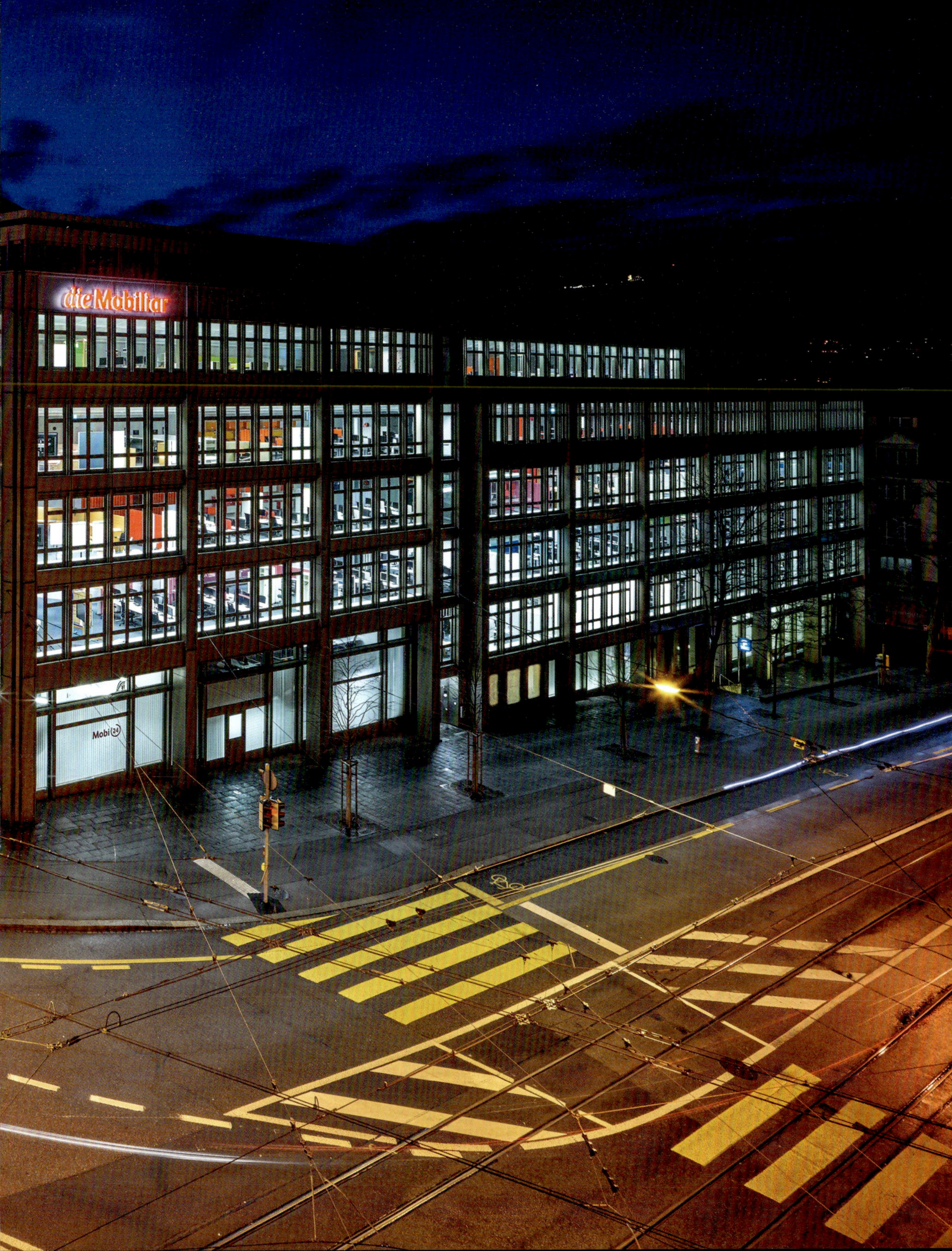
dieMobiliar
Mobi 24

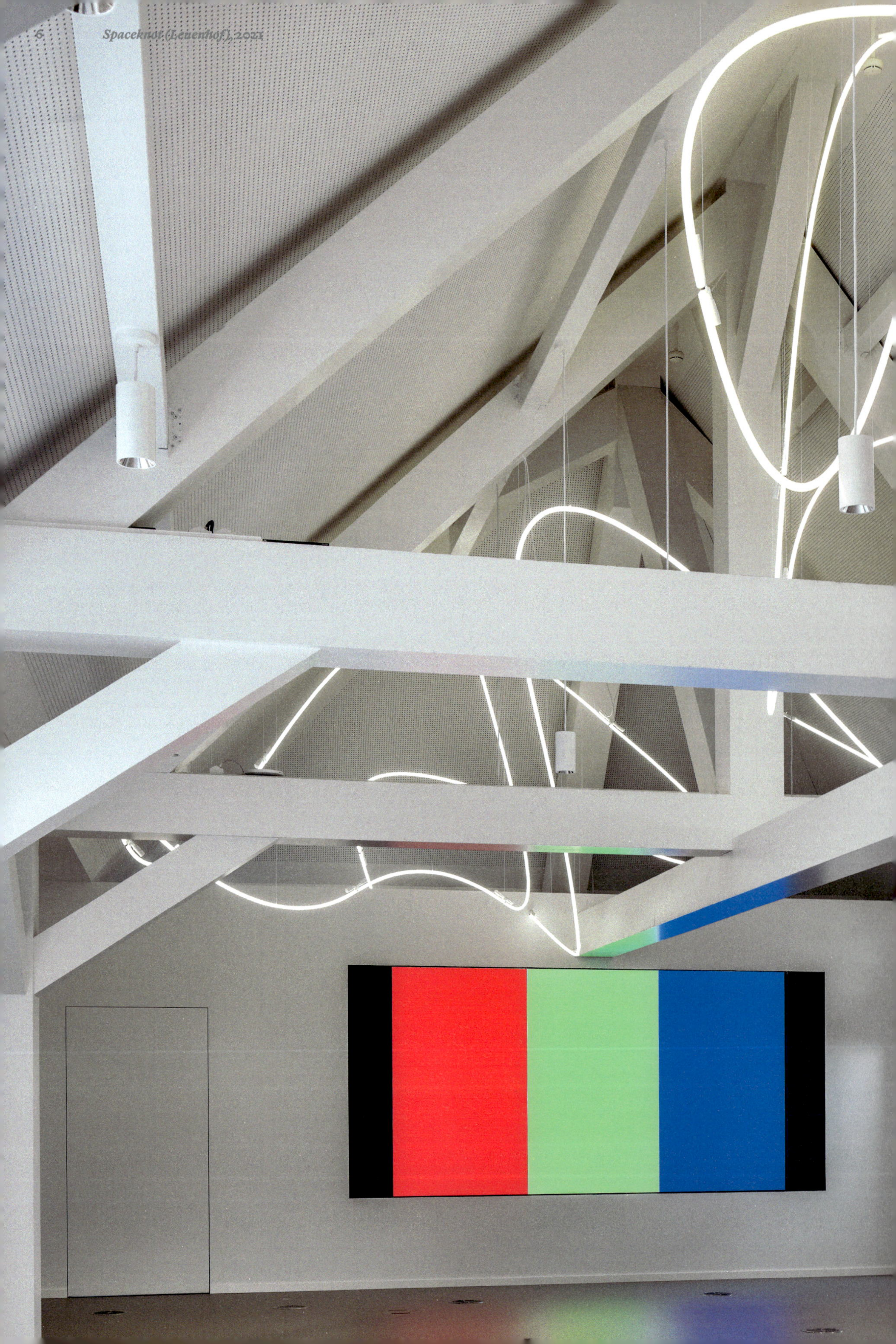

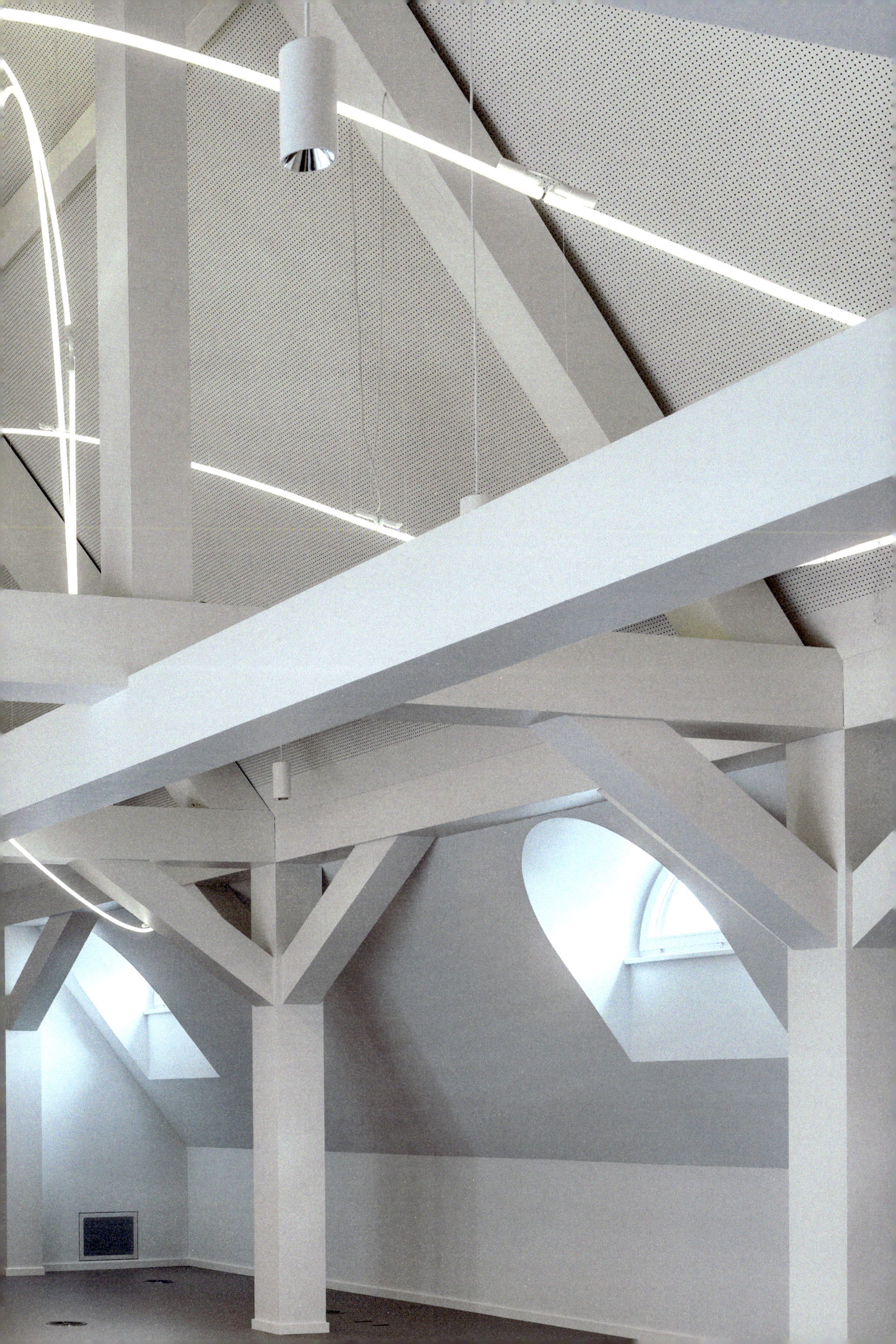

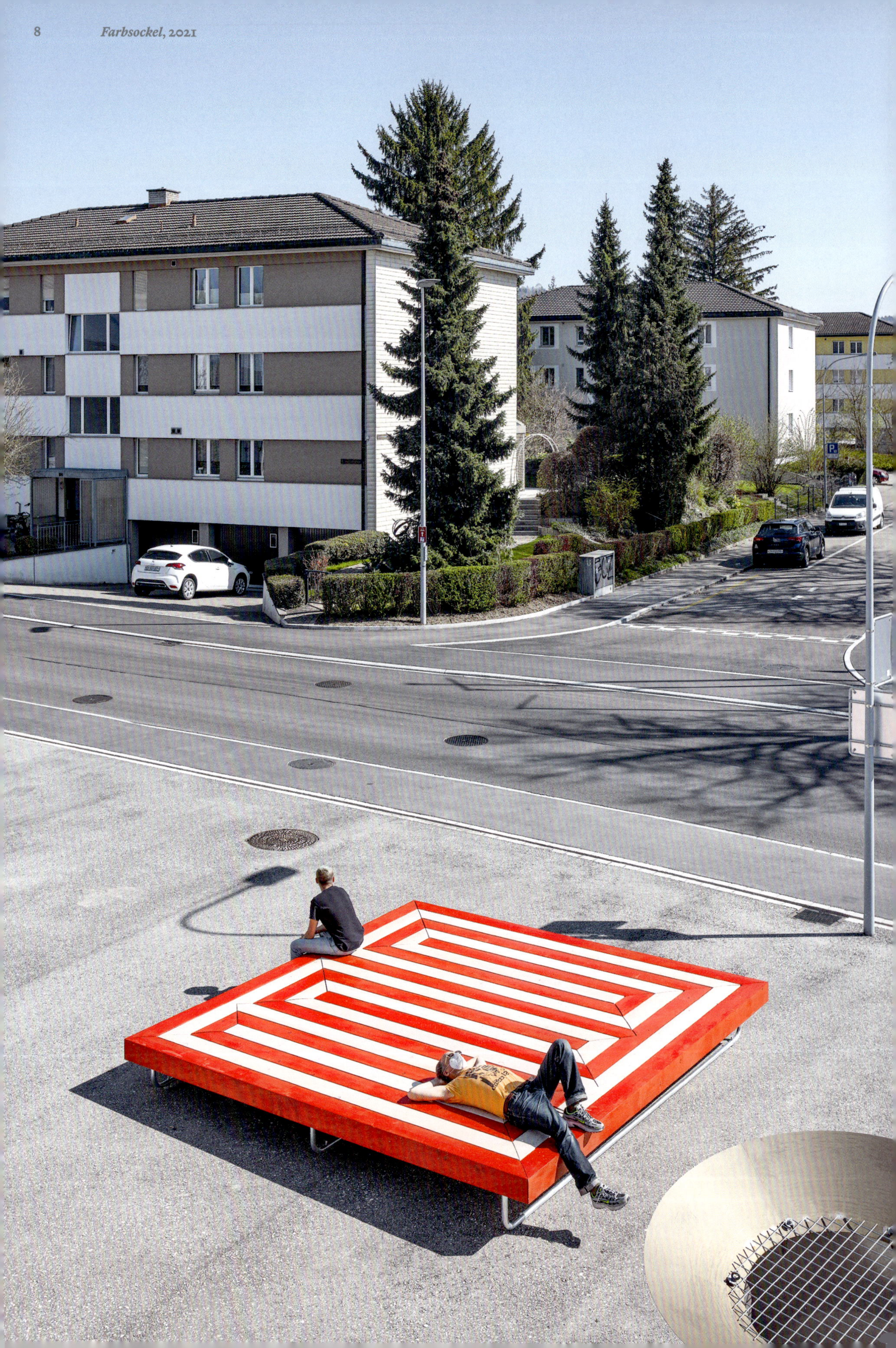

Kerim Seiler

1997–2022

Set and Setting

Editors:
Anne Vieth, Kerim Seiler

Published by:
Verlag der Buchhandlung Walther und Franz König
Ehrenstraße 4, D-50672 Köln

Bibliographic information published by the Deutsche Nationalbibliothek. The Deutsche Nationalbibliothek lists this publication in the Deutsche Nationalbibliografie; detailed bibliographic data available at http://dnb.d-nb.de.

Texts:
Paul Tanner, Anne Vieth, Stefan Zweifel

Translation into English:
Anne Fellner, Ishbel Flett, Susanne G. Seiler

Copyediting:
Clemens von Lucius (German)
Lian Rangkuty (English)

Visual Concept and Graphic Design:
Studio Marie Lusa (Marie Lusa, Alberto Malossi)

Lithography:
Georg Sidler, Samuel Trutmann

Project Support:
Kevin Smullin Brown, Ruben Schneider, Sven Schumann

Printing and Binding:
Offsetdruckerei Karl Grammlich GmbH
Karl-Benz-Straße 3
D-72124 Pliezhausen

Typeface:
ABC Marist, Seb McLauchlan

Distribution:
Buchhandlung Walther König
Ehrenstraße 4
D-50672 Köln
Tel: +49 (0) 221 / 20 59 6 53
verlag@buchhandlung-walther-koenig.de

Printed in Germany
ISBN 978-3-7533-0369-7

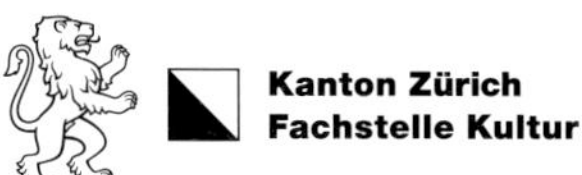

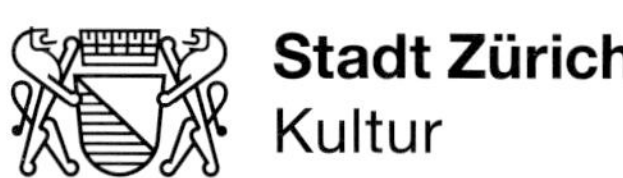

swiss arts council
prohelvetia

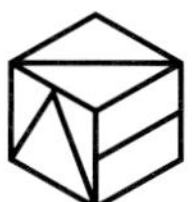

This book is dedicated to Claire Dugan & Edna Seiler, Susanne & Laila Seiler, Peter Stiefel, Dieter Hagenbach, our forebears, children, in-laws and to Natxo, Elio, Charly and Lionel.

In loose order through time: Silvio Ammann & Luisa Dazio, Aaron Henderson & Sophia Moeschlin, Gregor Metzger, Mercedes Villanueva, Kathi von Koerber & Hernando Villa, Diego & Peter Vetter, David Renggli, Antonio Hernandez & Nic Thür, Dölf Bachmann & Lis Broccard, Alvenia Bridges, Robert Meles, Dan Amarel, Miho Hatori, Régine Gallard, Arvild Baud & Iris Minich, Esther Eppstein, Gábor Altorjay & Martina Schiesser, Lin May Saeed, Damian Grieder & Melanie Grieder-Swarowski, Diego Fernandez, Annabelle & Steffen Lemmerzahl, Miet Warlop, Ludwig von Cramer-Klett, Isabel & Nicolas Steele, David Woodard, Marietta & Silvio R. Baviera, Christoph Wenger, Udo Breger, Manuel Hendry, Angela Tomas & Claudio Zier, Andreas Züst, Isa Nogara & Roli Brümmer, David Brunner, Nadja Putzi, Joel Farb, Lo, Lea, Tom & Guy Krayenbühl, Vincent Teuscher, Denis Stoffner, Lukas Meier, Daniel Egli, Urs Fischer, Danielle & Mathis Brauchbar, Beat Krebser, Roger Sonanini, Jürg Tschalèr & Eveline Moser, Urs Lehmann, Peter Wyss, H.G. Hildebrand, Jean-Paul Reichler, Pascal Ulli, Igor Bauersima, Rolf Graf, Daniele Buetti, Katrin Glaus, Nadine Geissbühler, Nathalie Meier, Markus Freitag, Pumel Glarner, Jozo Palkovits, Barbara Weber, Plinio Bachmann, Sämi Fausch, Urs Hirschbiegel, Nik Emch, Dino Simonett, Simon Renggli, David Chieppo, Rudolph Koella, Maurice Béjart, Davide Legittimo, Tjorg Douglas Beer, Bernhard Johannes Blume, Robert A. Fischer, Romeo Grünfelder, Jan Holtmann, David A. Huber, Heinz Spoerli, Olof Kühnholz, Peter Lynen & Ingrid Scherr, Dirk Meinzer, Ulla von Brandenburg, Franziska & Bruno Mancia-Bodmer, Bernhard Martin, Reto Lütscher, Marc R. Richter, Angela Richter, Oliver Ross, Grazia Conti Rossini & Christoph Schifferli, Gabi Steinhauser, Barbara & Niklaus Helbling, Freddy von Escher, Serge Ziegler, Regula & Ruedi Bechtler, Bice Curiger, Jacqueline Burckhardt, Juri Steiner, Dorothea Strauss, Hannes Wettstein, Martin G. Schmid, Rein Wolfs, Alexandra Blättler, Mendes Bürgi, Charlotte von Koerber, Gianni Jetzer, Michelle Nicol & Rudolf Schürmann, Mark Divo, Christoph Doswald, Nic Hess, Patrick Huber, Shirana Shahbazi, Olivier de Perrot, Alain Kupper, L/B, Simon Maurer, Stefan Nikolaev, Agathe Nisple, Nadia Schneider Willen, Jérémie Crettol, Giovanni Carmine, Karin Frei, Guido Magnaguagno, Ursula Rindlisbacher, Renate Jordan, Zuni Halpern, Toni Stooss, Walter Brunner, Christian Herdeg, Alexandra Hopf, Bernd Ruzicska, Andra Ursuta, Christian Wassmann, Lucia Coray & Henry F. Levy, Fabian Marti, Regine Helbling, Jean-Baptiste Felten, Valerie Felten, Barbara Higgs, Martin Jann, Peter Kelting, Basil Kobert, Heike Munder, Basil Nufer, Beatrix Ruf, Dirk Wauschkuhn, Ruedi Gfeller, Meta Kenworthy-Ball, Tobias Madörin, Jacqueline Uhlmann, Jürg Halter, Sabine & Alessandro Parenti, Mirjam Varadinis, Maike Cruse, Matthias Dietz, Lluïsa Sàrries i Zgonc, Bálint Dobozi, Katharina Dohm, Ariel Huber, Susanna Kulli, Bettina Steinbrügge, Flora Schoeller, Nina Weber, Lena Amuat, Christiane & Melanie Dankbar, Bruce Gordon, Bettina Malcomess, Jonathan Garnham, Adrian Notz, Benjamin Sommerhalder, Adina Popescu, Laura Sundermann, Ed Young, Daniel Hug, Jimmy Jung, Caroline Pachoud, Tanja Roscic, Ludger Hovestadt, Benjamin Dillenburger, Fredi Fischli & Niels Olsen, Carmen Tobler, Claudio Gasser, Martin Andereggen, Ramias Steinemann & Gigi Hotz, Fai Baba, Caroline Curtius, Guido Baudach, Alireza Farahmand, Anne Keller & Werner Dubach, Gitti Hug & Martin Bölsterli, Simon Lamunière, Noah Stolz, Vanni Bianconi, Magnus Bischofberger, Melis Bischofberger, Nina Baier-Bischofberger & Florian Baier, Nele Dechmann, Christian Keller, Lukas Kueng, Anna Leader, Andreas Steiger, Bekiwe & Wezizwe Sigcau, Melike Bilir, Marie-Christine & Patrick Dreyfus, Sami Eschmann, Patrick Gosatti, Franziska Kessler, Jonathan Liebmann, Noji Matutu & Joseph Gaylard, Andreiana Mihail, Frédéric Post, Thomas Thiefs, Matthias Valance, Jasper Walgrave, Veli & Amos, Anja Brogan, Bheki Dube, Małgorzata Gołębiewska, Fidi Hamann & Amadeus Gerlach, Dirk Bell, Rafael Horzon, Sebastian Hoffmann, Bruno Margreth & Zoë Meyer, Reiner Opoku, Marie Sacconi, Jo Sollich, Reto Thüring, Esther & Heinrich Baumann, Ion Grigorescu, Kicki & Heinrich Hohenlohe, Fubbi Karlsson & Nella Rieken, Hiroshi Matona, Markus Ott, Loa Pictet, Ulf Saupe, Wendelin Kammermeier, Anne Naundorf, Nicola Ruffo, Ralph Hug, Martin Joos, Ulrike Lorenz, Joaquin Luzoro, Ernst Scholl, Isabella Retter, Leocadia & Markus Hongler, Anita Kapraljevic, Oliver Mansaray & Daniel Scheppan, Manuel Schubbe, Raphaël Brunschwig, Salomé Coninx, Solynka Dumas, Anne Fellner & Burkhard Beschow, Maria Larsson, Attila Saygel, Lorenz Schreiber, Anna Rosa Thomae, Yulia Belousova, Kurt Compagnoni, Silvia Gioberti, Barbara Pfyffer, Swen Dornig, Corinne Gautier, Bálint Liptay, Jan-Philipp Sexauer, Lorenzo Metzler, Vincent Rebers & Dagny Revera, Albert Mauerhofer

A special thank you to Grieder Contemporary and Sexauer Gallery.

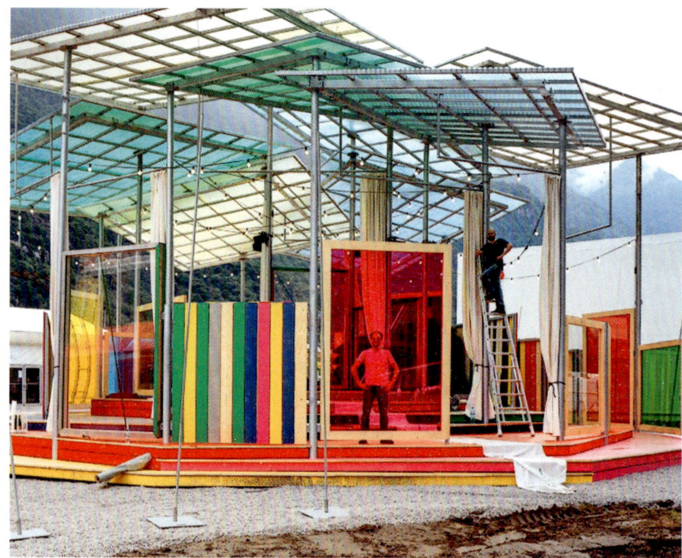

1 *What If (Situationist Space Program)*, 2016
Acrylic lacquer, colored float-glass, neon tubing, corrugated polyester sheets, fabric, galvanized steel, perspex, pillows, rivets, screws, silicone, thread, wood; 8.5×19×19 m; Production still *Gottardo 2016*, Pollegio

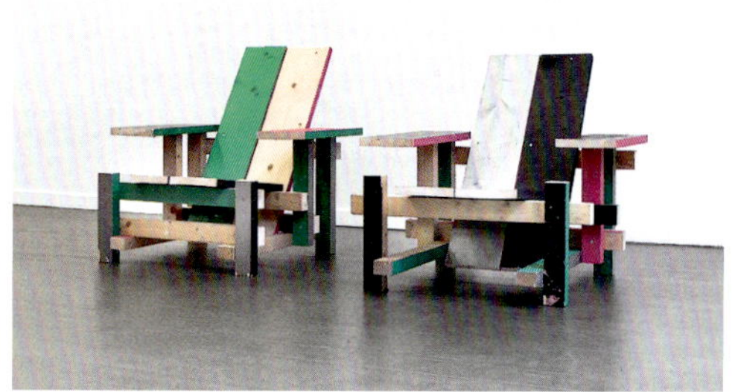

2 *Lolek und Bolek*, 2012
Acrylic lacquer, screws, wood; 75×175×82 cm; Installation view *Freak Magnet*, Galerie Melike Bilir, Hamburg

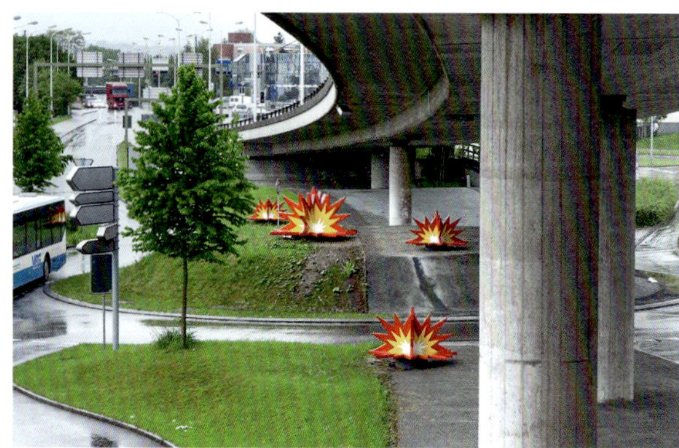

3 *Copy/Paste*, 2001
Calcareous grassland, green Andeer granite, two component lacquer, rivets, steel; Dimensions variable; Installation view Glattzentrum, Wallisellen

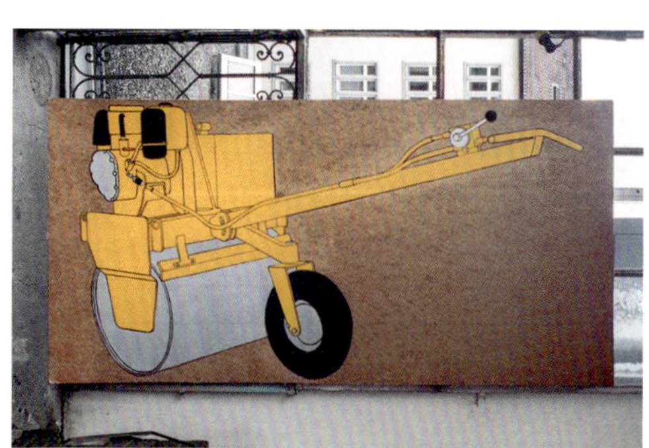

4 *KEIN TITEL IV (Walze)*, 1997
Acrylic paint, pavatex; 99×195 cm; Installation view Goethestrasse 20, Zürich

Set and Setting: Kerim Seiler 1997–2022
Anne Vieth

BIOGRAPHICAL INFORMATION

Kerim Seiler, born in Bern in 1974, is known for his large-scale projects in public space, ones that combine the characteristic aesthetics of rough materiality, stimulating colorfulness, and architectural design (fig. 1). He attended the *Vorkurs* at the Schule für Gestaltung in Zürich and transferred to the École Supérieure des Beaux-Arts in Geneva in 1993. From 1997 he studied at the Hochschule für bildende Künste Hamburg and graduated in 2002 from the class of Bernhard Johannes Blume. Both the Bauhaus-oriented *Vorkurs* and his Master of Advanced Studies in Architecture from ETH Zürich in 2011 continue to influence Seiler's thinking and work today. His artwork is characterized by the study of constructed spatial structures and their impact on the individual.

THE AESTHETIC EXPERIENCE IN SPACE

Seiler often moves between disciplines, he thinks and works beyond borders. His oeuvre includes sculptures, installations, performances, drawings, neon works, and prints. Crossovers between art and design are also apparent, as in the series of furniture sculptures entitled *Lolek und Bolek* (2012, fig. 2), which humorously process Gerrit Rietveld's design classic, the *Red and Blue Chair*, by alienating proportions, materiality, and color. His diverse "ArchiSkulpturen"[1] (e.g. p. 82, 84, 98), also transcend genre boundaries and are part of a long history of development in the approach of basic architectural and sculptural questions with reference to space. This began during modernism and reached its first peak with the Environments and Happenings of the 1960s. Since the 1990s it has mostly been subsumed under the collective term installation art, which includes works of art that clearly relate to space. In the continuous crossing of genre boundaries and the refusal of (genre) definition lies a fundamental characteristic of installation art; in addition, there is an awareness of the involvement of context and viewer in the production and reception of art.[2]

Theodor W. Adorno described the softening of genre boundaries since modernism as a "fraying of the arts" ("Verfransung der Künste").[3] This process has lost none of its currency today and artists are still constantly enriching it with new aspects. The consensus here is the knowledge of each categories' cultural construction. For Seiler, playing with genres enables him to continuously explore his utmost artistic interest: the aesthetic experience in space. His credo "Space is my canvas" clarifies, on the one hand, the relevance that space represents as an existential variable for the artist, and, on the other hand, it addresses his engagement with the creation and reception of art. For Seiler, space is the venue for his creative thoughts and realizations. This already begins with the process of developing the works in the studio, which Seiler considers an essential part of an artwork, and is continued in reference to the locations where the individual works are realized. In this, he questions both the functions and concepts of sculpture and architecture, as well as the generation of space and the understanding on which it is based. Seiler describes his concept of space as a "non-hierarchical understanding of space in which all aspects of a situation interact simultaneously." This suggests that Seiler understands space as a social structure where individuals and things meet and their relations create identity, action, and knowledge. The artist transfers this idea into the real space that his works form, as depicted for example in the temporary works *What If* and *Tschutschu* (both 2016, p. 66, 68). For the opening ceremony of the Gotthard Base Tunnel in June 2016, Seiler created these two walk-in installations—a kaleidoscopic pavilion and a picnic area with elements reminiscent of railway tracks. Both works serve as meeting places. The experiences made possible for the visitor are strongly oriented towards the specific site and situation and can at the same time lead away from corporeal moments to the realm of associations, irritations, memories, and utopian ideas. Seiler seeks both the world of bodies and the world of ideas in his art. There resounds quietly and remotely a stimulus from the artist. A yearlong engagement with the ancient philosopher Plato during a study trip to Cairo encouraged Seiler to initiate his quest into the visible and invisible.

THE STUBBORNNESS OF IMAGES

What do we actually need to see in order to understand or rather to imagine a car accident or an explosion as an event? Seiler approaches this question in a series of early works, the results of a preoccupation with the medium of video during his studies in Geneva. In video, an enormous number of individual images are strung together as sequences to create a moving image. The medium is ideal for depicting a course of action, i.e. an event. But can something similar be achieved with a single image? The young Seiler is driven by fundamental *pictorial questions*, which revolve around the effect and obstinacy of images, around reproduction and representation, the linguistic nature of images, the collective pictorial memory, and the power of images. Here he sees the art of comics as a kind of stirrup: in works such as *Copy/Paste* (2001, fig. 3; p. 1, 195) Seiler transforms an event into a frozen state by creating a suggestive image. Herein also lies the difference to a comic-strip, which visualizes the process in a sequence of images. The artist limits himself to the single image that captures the explosion at the moment of the bang. In the comic-like, strongly graphic aesthetic, the validity of signs is revealed, as is the repertoire of images associated with them. This is also demonstrated in the work series *KEIN TITEL* (1997, fig. 4; p. 224). Furthermore, Seiler questions the function of everyday objects. What remains when their function is abolished and they are transferred into images?

The installations in Serge Ziegler's gallery, *Ohne Titel* (1998, fig. 6; p. 158, fig. 50), and in the exhibition *Freie Sicht aufs Mittelmeer: Junge Schweizer Kunst mit Gästen und Gastmahl* at the Kunsthaus Zürich and the Schirn Kunsthalle Frankfurt, *Ohne Titel (Tex Avery)*

(1998, fig. 5; p. 223), unite Seiler's early approach to work and thought and expand it to include the component of space. The central image and object—a dump truck at Ziegler's, a VW New Beetle at the Kunsthaus Zürich—is positioned in the space as an anamorphosis, a depiction that can only be seen undistorted from a certain viewpoint, and is embedded in a fictitious street situation that is manifested in common road markings on the ground. The interplay of object, image, real space, and (optical) fiction culminates in the figure of the recipient, because it is they who walk through the installation and see the ambiguous figure from a certain view point in a form that is familiar to us and therefore tangible.

> In the mid-1990s, the examination of these everyday objects also led to a fascination for construction sites and especially for road markings. Suddenly it became clear to me that we live within a large-scale composition.[5]

Considering the described works, it is conclusive that Seiler directed his attention to everyday visual signs and their variety of meaning and impact, but also to their formal nature. The work *Manöver I für Barbara* (fig. 7; p. 222), created in 1998 in Appenzell, brings together two forms of sign language: common road markings and façade painting characteristic of Appenzell. Most visitors might consider the latter to be very old, but the earliest of these decorations date from 1932: "These houses were certainly painted earlier, but simply in discrete shades of white and grey, meant to simulate plaster and stone [...]."[6] For his intervention in the public space, Seiler chose a pedestrian zone in the center of the village, where he installed a floor work. The lines of the piece are, on the one hand, reminiscent of traffic markings and, at the same time, deeply confusing in their heavily ornamental appearance. In his "traffic garden" the artist displays the tire tracks of a turning car and a greatly enlarged fragment of a façade painting. "The work Kerim Seiler created for Appenzell is a well-ordered disorder that doesn't lead to a destination, but rather astray."[7] The alienation of both of these sign systems and the resulting irritation is thought provoking, and, in the case of some Appenzell residents, inspires them to implement Seiler's ornaments in the design of their carnival costumes (fig. 8).

With the works from 1998, Seiler explored a thematic area, which continues to fascinate him to this day and inspires new reflections. Thus, the speech bubble works (1999–2005, fig. 9–10) and the series *Clones* (2005–2008, fig. 11; p. 156, 168, 171) can be read in the same context as the neon works, which the artist began to realize in 2010 (p. 36, 48–58, 70, 102, 107–113, 120, 130). These deal with visual symbolism and its scope of meaning as well as analogies in marking and drawing processes. In the tradition of many artists working with neon, Seiler conceives the writing works as drawings in space. In addition, works such as *ego sum pauper* (2012, fig. 12; p. 110) and the lettering "NE TRAVAILLEZ JAMAIS" in the work *Relay (St. Moritz)* (2013, fig. 14; p. 100) allude to two of Seiler's main references: to the American artist Bruce Nauman, whose spiral-shaped neon work *The True Artist Helps the World by Revealing Mystic Truths* (1967, fig. 13) makes a comparably ironic self-statement on the artist's myth like Seiler's *ego sum pauper* work; and to the Situationist International with its inspirational credo "Never work" ("Ne travaillez jamais").

PERFORMATIVE INSTALLATIONS

With the installation *Analemma* (2003, fig. 15; p. 198) Seiler develops his first work of the *Mindspace* series. With these grandstand-like wooden constructions the artist draws on his experiences in theater. From 1996 to 2001, he created several theater sets and acted as lighting director on a tour by the influential ballet dancer and choreographer Maurice Béjart, whose concept of the *spectacle total* strongly influenced Seiler. In the *Mindspaces*, the recipients are placed in a theatrical situation. Here, however, no performance in the conventional sense takes place. The artist merely offers the possibility of an action that can take place at the respective location. Whether the recipients *step into the ring* in front of the seats, or they linger in the stands, observing the scene or being observed—one way or another, their actions turn into performance and they become an integral part of the artwork. The architecture built by the artist plays a central role in this.

> The constitution of architecture is left to the subject, who is aware of the shiftability—of the architecture, of their own position, and thus also of the boundaries, allocations of space and representations—at every moment. Outside can mean inside, the spatial stratifications no longer provide information about where one ends and the other begins. The subject is thus placed in an active role: on the one hand, by visualizing their multiple possible positioning in space, as imago, as reflection, and as physical reality, and, on the other hand, by a permanent request to establish connections of meaning.[8]

The processes of imagination and the creation of meanings, as addressed by the art historian Barbara Steiner, are alluded to in the title of the series: *Mindspace*—space for the mind that enables and stimulates the work. The *Mindspaces* also make it clear that Seiler does not attribute neutrality to sites and situations, but rather understands them in the context of sociocultural practices, which become tangible and visible in his installations.

Analemma was conceived by Seiler in 2003 as part of a public art competition for the outdoor area of the Zürich schoolhouse Lachenzelg/Imbisbühl. This work, as well as the work *Rampensau* (fig. 16; p. 194), created in 2001, combines different performance architectures. While *Rampensau* forms a synthesis of stage and skateboard ramp in the Theater an der Winkelwiese in Zürich, the construction of *Analemma* is a mixture of antique amphitheater, circus ring, sports grandstand, and staircase. The markings in red, yellow, and white on the floor in front of the four rows of seats reflect the system of a sundial. The shadows cast by the grandstand construction in conjunction with the floor markings function accordingly. Another important basis of the work is the staircase as a space of action and specific setting for a school. The stairs are for sitting around, for seeing and being seen, though in the form of an open staircase outside the school building. The artist writes in his project sketch for *Analemma*, which also outlines the intention of the work:

> The result should activate, invite to use. The art should help forget art, understand art. It should find space in the lives of the students, be available. It lives from its use. And maybe one day the students will even remember it.[9]

This inviting aspect, which encourages the recipients to become just as aware of their own actions in a specific (spatial) situation as of their interaction with others, i.e. their effect on the collective, also characterizes the other *Mindspaces*. To this day, these are still installed in the most diverse locations—in the interior of a museum (fig. 17), with a picturesque view over Rome (p. 166), on the roof of a parking lot (fig. 18), or in front of a house façade with numerous passers-by (fig. 19)—and in varying dimensions and color designs. These and all other *Mindspaces* have the inherent performativity as an identity-constructing strategy in common as well as the creation of an open situation, which does not demand participation, but makes it possible and thus recognizable.

This is a fundamental difference to Bruce Nauman, who also directs his installations towards the recipient, but precisely calculates the participation

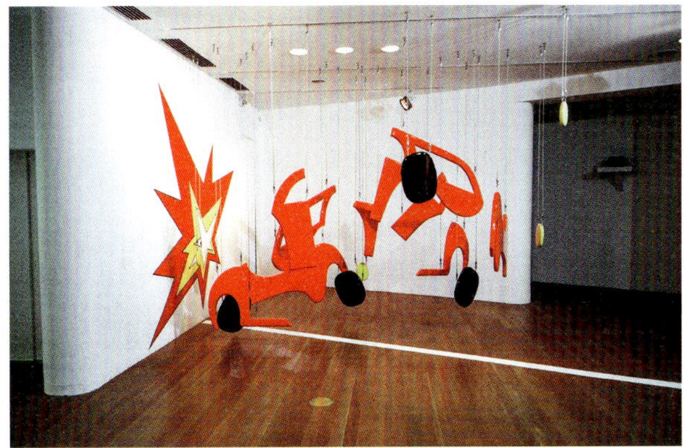

5 *Ohne Titel (Tex Avery)*, 1998
Acrylic paint, pavement marking tape, screws, silicone, two component lacquer, wire rope; Installation view *Freie Sicht aufs Mittelmeer*, Schirn Kunsthalle Frankfurt

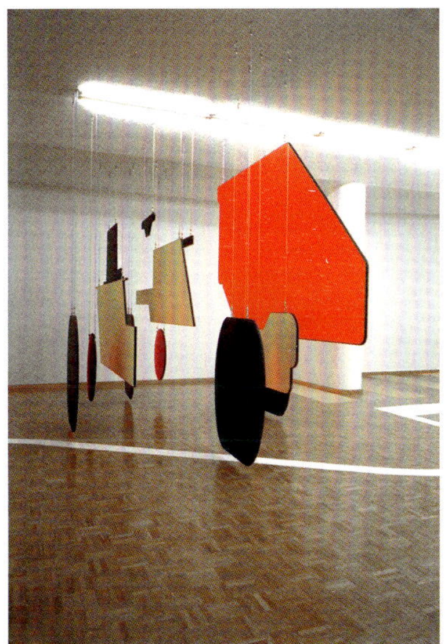

6 *Ohne Titel*, 1998
Acrylic paint, hot-melt marking paint, medium-density fiberboard, screws, wire rope; Dimensions variable; Installation view *Ohne Titel*, Serge Ziegler Galerie, Zürich

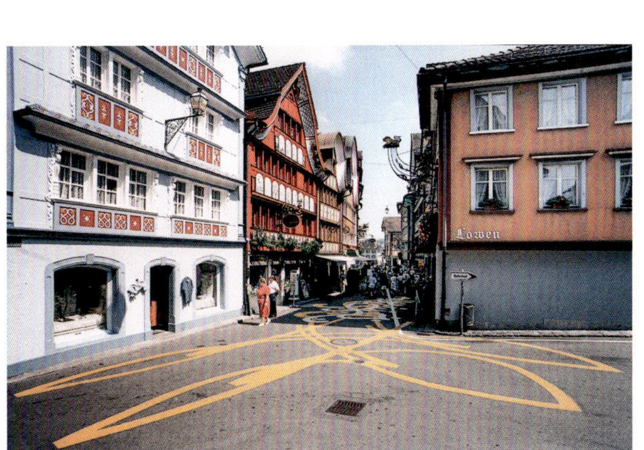

7 *Manöver I für Barbara*, 1998
Hot-melt marking paint; c. 25×25 m; Installation view *Art and Appenzell*

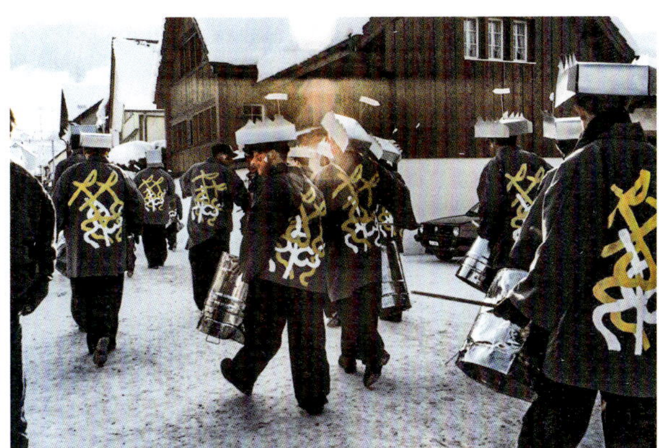

8 Carnival group *Funkebaabe* quoting *Manöver I für Barbara* on their costumes

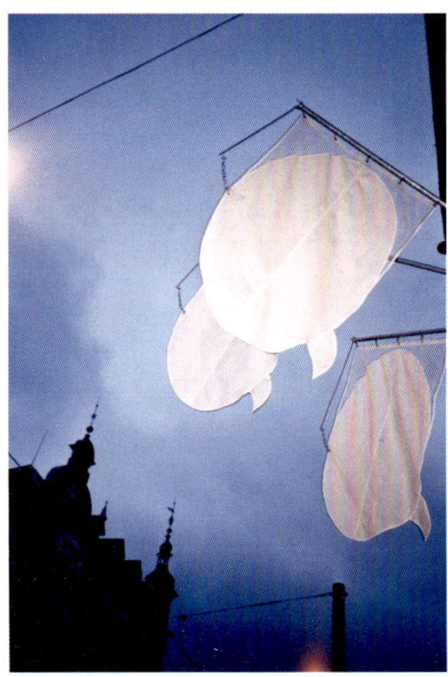

9 *Ohne Titel (Sprechblasenfahne)*, 2002
Fabric, galvanized steel; 2×2×1.5 m;
Installation view *Baustellenromanze mit Bier und Tanz*, message salon, Zürich

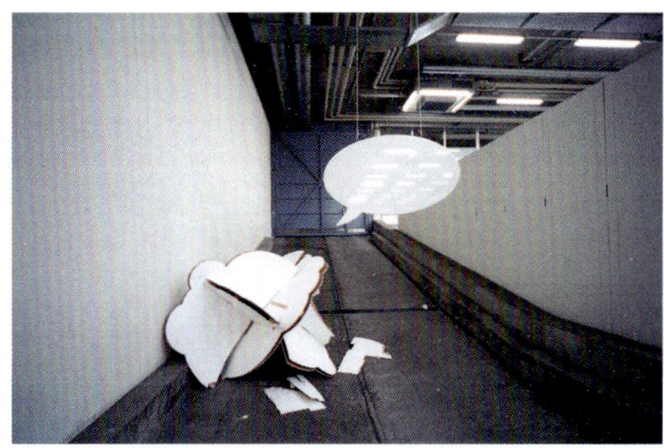

10 *Wolke, Sprechblase*, 1999
Cotton cord, medium-density fiberboard, screws, two component lacquer, white paint, wood; Dimensions variable; Installation view *Swiss Art Awards*, Basel

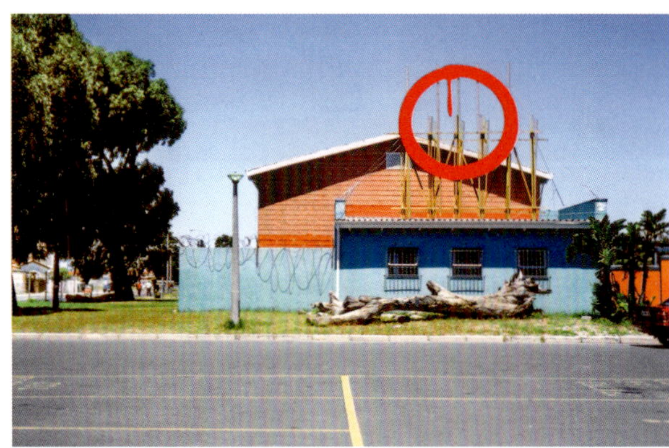

11 *Clone (Guguletu)*, 2005
Acrylic lacquer, concrete masonry unit, plywood, screws, wood; 5.5×6×3 m; Installation view *Clones International – Stop 1: Africa*, Ikhwezi Community Centre, Guguletu

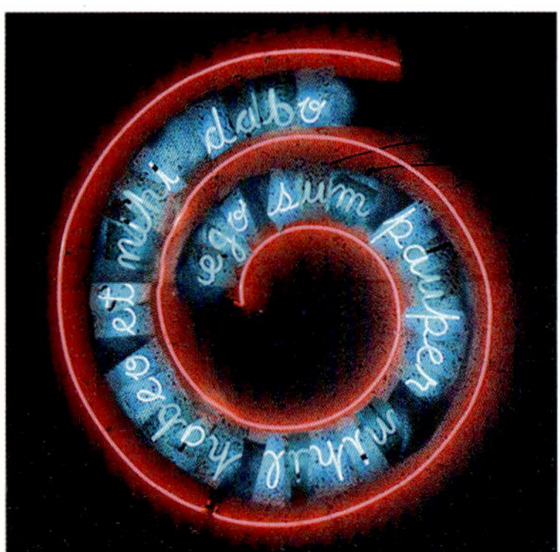

12 Study for *ego Sum Pauper*, 2012
Digital collage

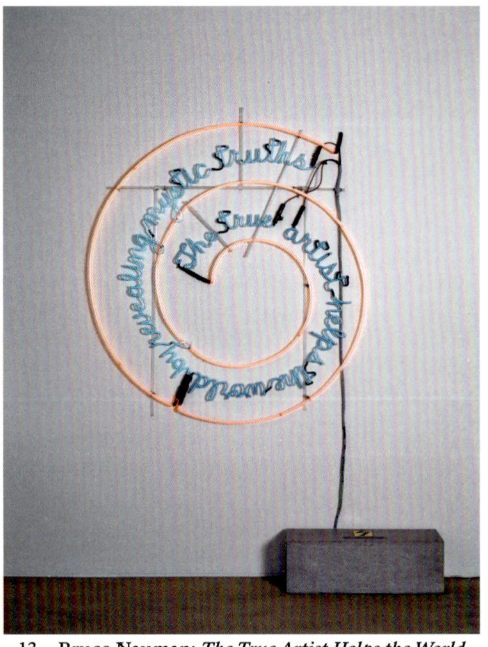

13 Bruce Nauman: *The True Artist Helps the World by Revealing Mystic Truths (Window or Wall Sign)*, 1967
Glass, neon tubing; 150×140×5 cm

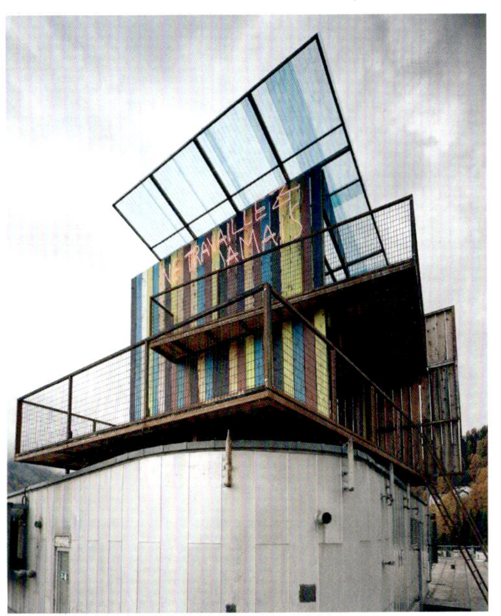

14 *Relay (St. Moritz)*, 2012/2013
Acrylic lacquer, neon tubing, corrugated polyester sheets, steel, perspex, rivets, screws, wood; 5.5×8.2×6.4 m; Installation view *St. Moritz Art Masters*

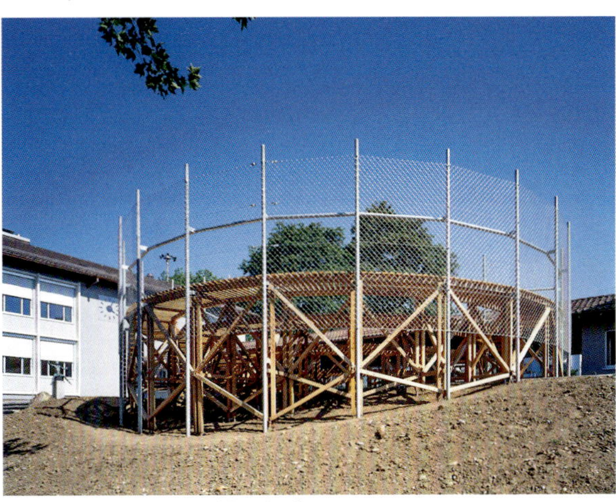

15 *Analemma*, 2003
Chain-link fence, galvanized steel, hot-melt marking paint, screws, wood; 3.2×⌀10.6 m; Installation view Imbisbühl/Lachenzelg, Zürich

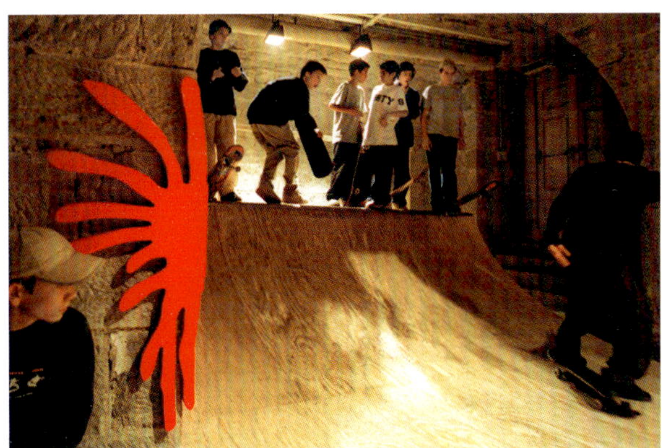

16 *Rampensau*, 2001
Medium-density fiberboard, plywood, screws, steel, two component lacquer; 260×412×484 cm; Installation view *Rampensau*, Theater an der Winkelwiese, Zürich

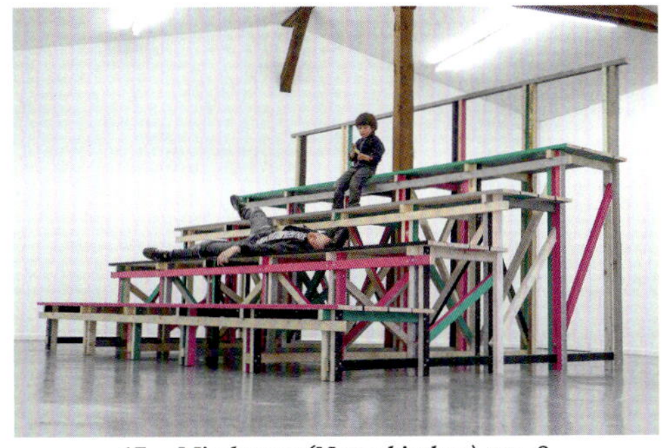

17 *Mindspace (Neuenkirchen)*, 2008
Acrylic lacquer, neon tubing, screws, wood; 244×294×416 cm; Installation view *Diskurs im Grünen*, Springhornhof, Neuenkirchen

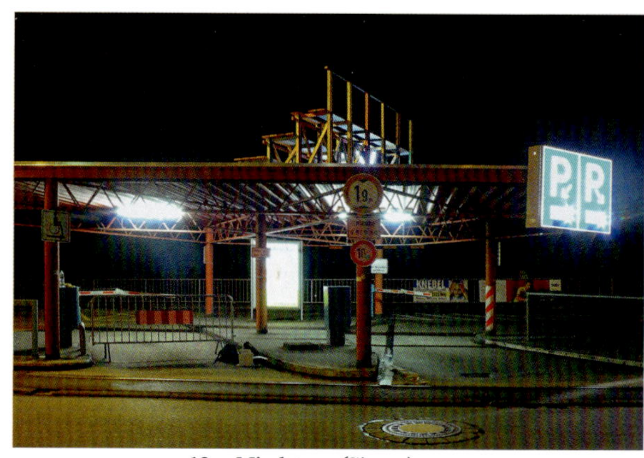

18 *Mindspace (Siegen)*, 2010
Acrylic lacquer, neon tubing, screws, wood; 244×294×416 cm;
Installation view *Blickwechsel*, Parkhaus Rathaus, Siegen

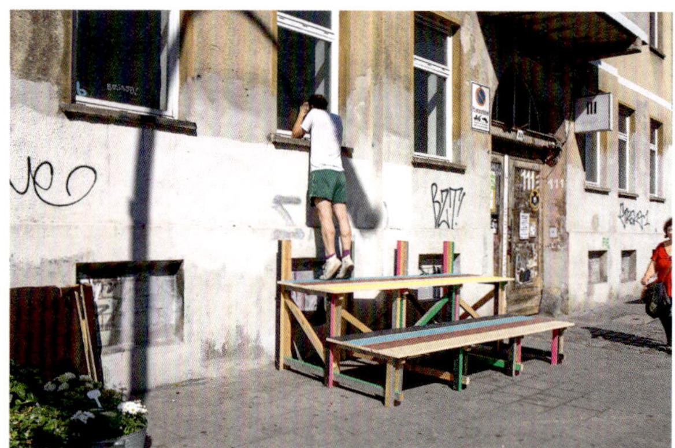

19 *Mindspace (Tarantula)*, 2013
Acrylic lacquer, screws, wood; 120×168×260 cm;
Installation view *Tarantula*, Berlin

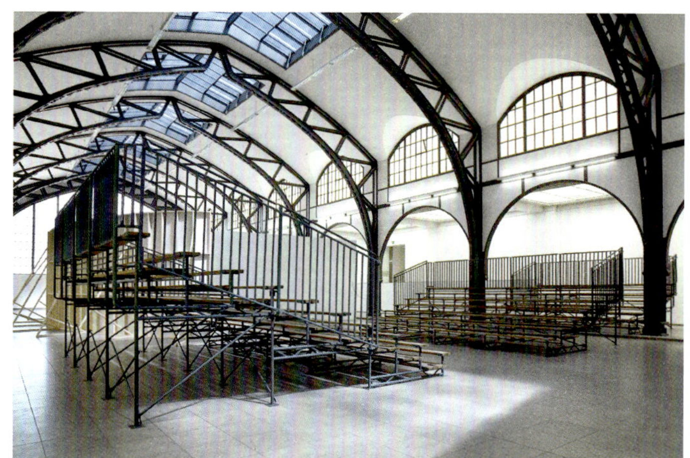

20 Bruce Nauman: *Indoor Outdoor Seating Arrangements*, 1999
Steel and wood seating bleaches; Dimensions variable;
Installation view Nationalgalerie im Hamburger Bahnhof, Berlin

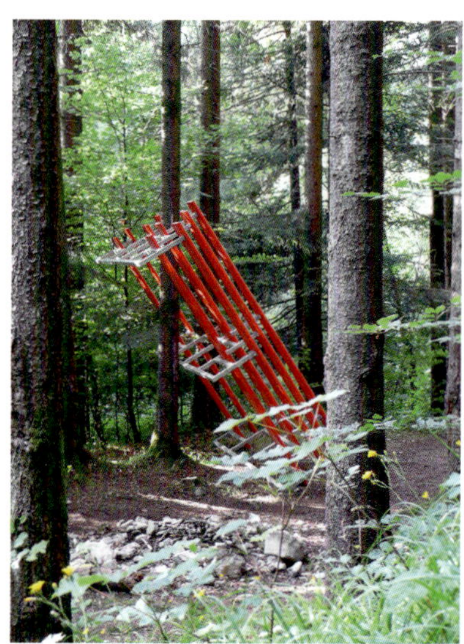

21 *Fusionsobjekt*, 2006/2007
Acrylic lacquer, galvanized steel, screws, wood; 111×400×324 cm;
Installation view *Art en plain air*, Môtiers

of the recipient.[10] In the *Corridor* installations, it becomes apparent that Nauman wants to control the actions of the exhibition visitors as much as possible by means of the created situation. In a 1996 interview, he expresses his skepticism towards the recipient and their role in experiencing the artwork:

> The first *Corridor* works were about having someone else make the performance. My problem was figuring out how to narrow down the work so that the performance would be what I wanted. In a sense, it was about control. I didn't want anyone else to do the performance.[11]

Nauman usually aims for a strong physical irritation of the recipient. To achieve this, he develops spatial events that can cause discomfort, anxiety, and even panic. The effect—the heightened awareness of the interplay of certain spatial circumstances and individual or collective actions—is comparable to Seiler's approach and serves him as a role model. In Nauman's work *Indoor Outdoor Seating Arrangements* (1999, fig. 20), however, we discover the striking difference in the two artists' approaches. In the work, two sets of bleachers are placed opposite each other. The recipients sit facing each other, with the distance between the bleachers kept so small that the spatial situation of observing and being observed becomes uncomfortable in all movements, actions, and gestures. The constellation is designed in such a way that the framework of action is determined and the experiencers are offered little room for decision, action, and thought. Seiler proceeds differently as described. He is aware of the authoritarian gesture of his role model and consequently adapts Nauman's approach (fig. 21).

The common denominator of numerous works by Nauman and Seiler is the developing of a performative installation. This places Seiler within the history of a specific form of installation, integrated in the so-called performative turn in the arts.[12] It began in the 1970s with artists including Nauman, Dan Graham, Carolee Schneemann, and Allan Kaprow. If a performative moment is inherent in every work of installation as a forced movement through space, then there are installations that intensify this aspect or even declare it to be the content of the work. The art historian Angelika Nollert writes as follows:

> The performative installation is not about the dissolution of the work into an event, but about the event as the constituent force of the installation, about the symbiosis of event and work. It is about the performative character of installation art, which can itself also be fleeting. The performative installation addresses the visitor directly and immediately, inviting them to participate. This shifts the relationship between subject and object, and the subject becomes integrated in the work. The exhibition institute becomes a place for the presentation of situationist interventions and social practices known from everyday life. [...] In this process, interaction becomes an integral element of the works, which only reveals its character through the intervention. The exhibition space is transformed into a place that is characterized by communication and cooperation between subject and object; it thus mutates into a social construct. The actions of the persons arise from the artistic impulse.[13]

The *Lattenwald* series, which Seiler developed from 2002 to 2004, also falls into the realm of performative installations (fig. 22; p. 186–188). While the *Mindspaces* open up space for the audience, the *Lattenwald* unfolds a completely different effect, here space is closed off and difficult to access. "Seiler has forced the viewer to reclaim the space for themselves and at the same time physically engage with the work," write Katharina Dohm and Bettina Steinbrügge.[14] In addition, this series also hints at the examination of the artist as performer. The installations focus on the process of the work's creation, as the shape and arrangement of the slats suggest a vigorous yet exhausting act by the artist. In *Lattenwald* (2002, fig. 22) this is further emphasized by exhibiting the tools and remains of the production process. The artist is essentially an absent attendant. This indirectly performative artist persona is also contained in the work *Seelenzentrifuge,* (2000, fig. 23) and other affiliated works (fig. 24–25; p. 172–174). For the exhibition visitor, the installations are the result of the destructive drive of an excavator. The vehicle, formerly operated by the artist, is left driverless and stands like his alter ego in the exhibition space. Once again we see Seiler's fascination in creating theatrical situations.

There are also a number of performances in which Seiler appears as the protagonist. For example, the rented bumper cars, which the artist and his colleague David Renggli set up on a 30-centimetre high white pedestal during the *Lange Nacht der Zürcher Museen* 2003, accompanied by live bands. Although it is primarily intended for the use of visitors, Seiler himself participates in the situation as a driver (fig. 26). The action *Space Is My Canvas* (fig. 27; p. 74–79), which has been repeatedly performed since 2014, can be cited as a performance in the conventional sense. Seiler has presented this performance at different locations such as the Campo di Sant'Agnese at the 56th Venice Biennale or the ABC art fair in Berlin. In the performance, the bare-chested artist irons a mountain of sheets for hours on end that have been bleached by the sun, as a reference to the famous photograph of an ironing James Rosenquist from 1981 (fig. 28). The sheets resemble pieces of canvas and are hung on a clothesline after they are ironed. The iron is connected to a microphone and the resulting sound is transmitted to the audience. The iron hisses, steams, and glides over the fabric, as can be heard on the vinyl edition of the performance after the event (p. 83). While performances always question the categories of space and time, *Space Is My Canvas* explicitly brings the temporality of performative actions to the fore.

Adrian Heathfield writes in his publication on performance art:

> Such experiences in and of performance make us aware that time itself is a product of structures of thought, that our perceptions and understandings of time are cultural construct, and as such open to revision and change. [...] In its attention to and playful subversion of the orders of time, performance gives access to other temporalities: to time as it is felt in the body, time not just as progression and accumulation, but also as something faltering, non-linear, multi-dimensional and multi-faceted.[15]

In *Space Is My Canvas*, Seiler not only takes clichéd ideas of the artist qua persona ad absurdum, but also those of gender roles. This sense of humor and (self-) ironic perspective appear in numerous works by the artist. Other examples include the photo series *Honeymooners* (2005–ongoing, fig. 29–32) and the sculpture *Springbrunnen*, conceived as a public fountain in Chur (2003, p. 180). Once again, Seiler draws on antique notions:

> [...] humor is a very special juice, within which, from antiquity to the Baroque, the temperaments of phlegmatic, sanguine, choleric, and melancholic are mixed so well that the mood for laughter is prepared or is in effect. Humor is thus either active or passive. If you possess it, you can create this mood through comedic practices in the hope that the comedy will reach someone who has a sense of humor.[16]

A NEW NEW BABYLON

The tower-like sculpture *New Babylon* (2015, p. 82) is conceived for the public space. Here, with its colored surfaces and glass, it engages passers-by in a playful

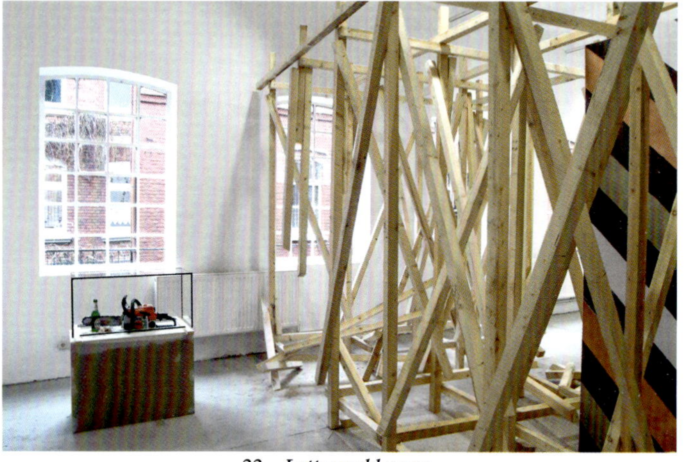

22 *Lattenwald*, 2002
Beer, bread, chainsaw, cheese, forest helmet, white paint, particle board, perspex, screws, wood; Dimensions variable;
Installation view *Handlungsräume*, Halle für Kunst, Lüneburg

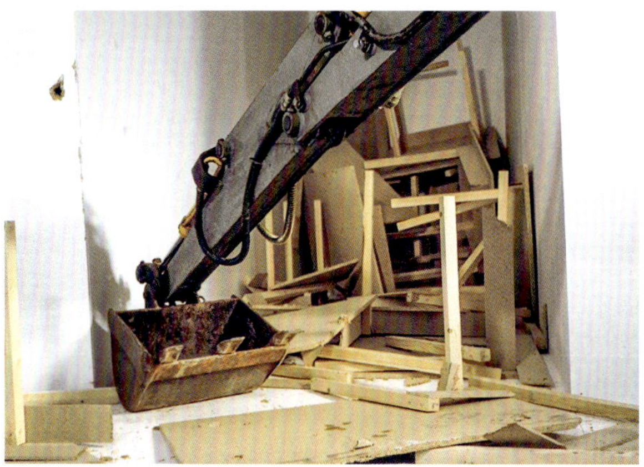

23 *Seelenzentrifuge*, 2000
Excavator, one-way mirror film, white paint, particle board, screws, spotlights, tripods ; Dimensions variable;
Installation view Horten Out bei Bochynek, Düsseldorf

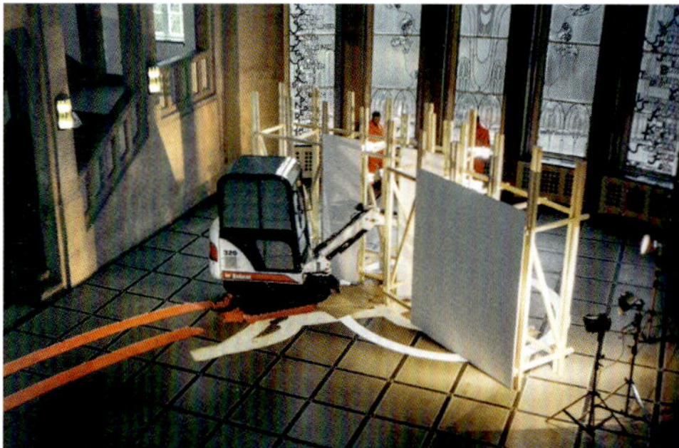

24 *Wilibalds Traum / Wilibalds Morgen*, 2002
Excavator, one-way mirror film, hot-melt marking paint, particle board, screws, spotlights, tripods, white paint, wood; Dimensions variable;
Installation view HFBK, Hamburg

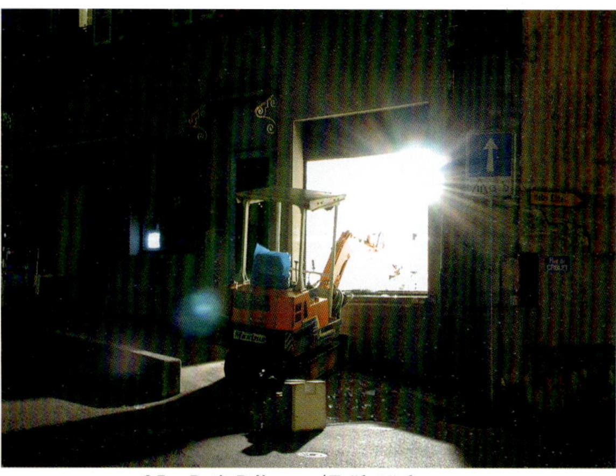

25 *Petit Déjeuner / Frühstück*, 2000
Excavator, one-way mirror film, hot-melt marking paint, particle board, screws, spotlights, tripods, white paint, wood;
Dimensions variable; Installation view *Petit Déjeuner / Frühstück*, message salon caravan & PAC, Fribourg

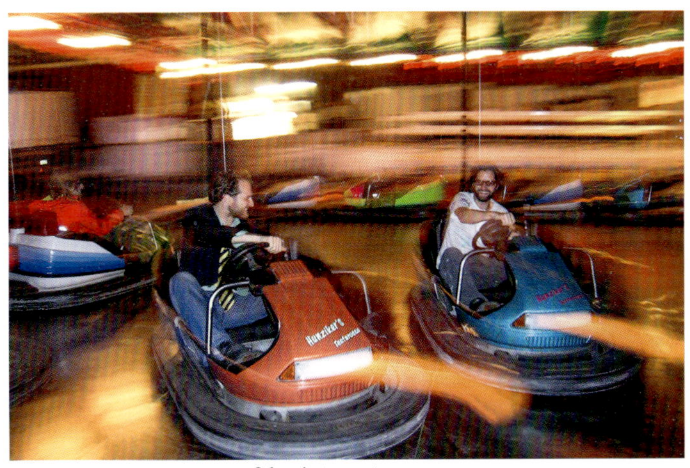

26 *Autoscooter*, 2003
Collaboration with David Renggli; Bumper cars, white paint, particle board, screws; Dimensions variable; Installation view Löwenbräu Areal, Zürich

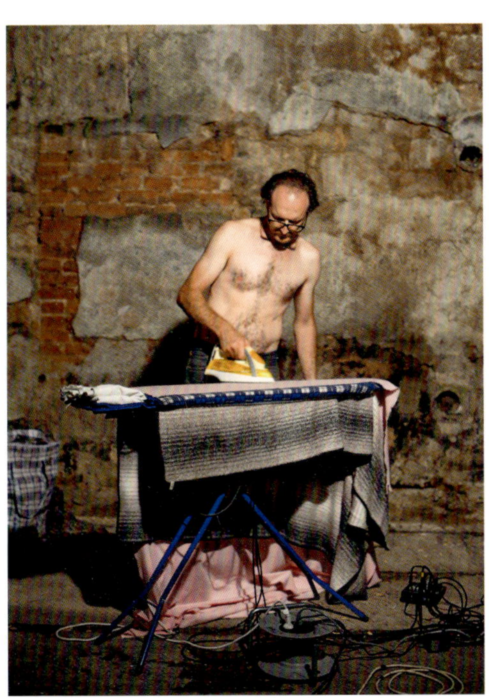

27 *Space Is My Canvas (Performance)*, 2014
Amplifier, clothes line, clothespins, contact microphone, flat iron, ironing board, mixing console, sheets, sound system; Dimensions variable; Performance view *International Contemporary Art Festival*, Bomb Gallery, Mostar

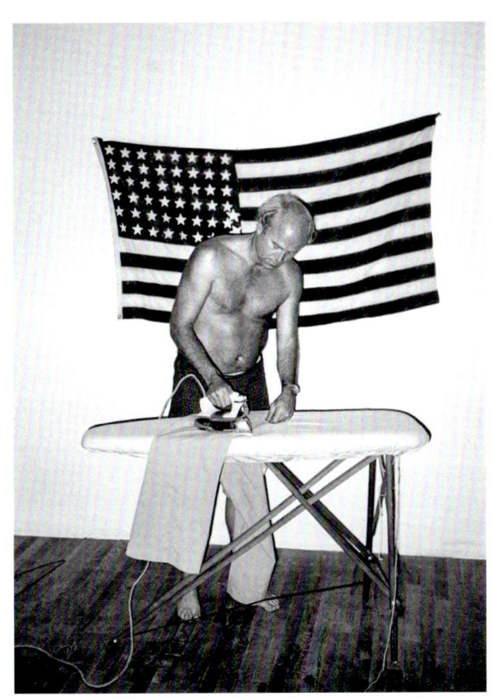

28 Chico Aragão: *James Rosenquist Ironing His Trousers*, 1981
Black and white photograph; 43,2×30,5 cm

dialog. By allowing the gaze to pause and arousing curiosity, the artwork breaks the visual habits and behavioral patterns of everyday life. *New Babylon* is a continuation of the works *Birdhouse I* (fig. 36) and *Birdhouse II* (p. 86), whose structure is reminiscent of *Hangende Sector (Hanging Sector)* (1960, fig. 33) by the Dutch artist Constant. The title *New Babylon* refers directly to Constant's large-scale project of the same name, which he worked on from 1956 to 1974. In the context of the Situationist International (SI), Constant developed a model for a new society, starting with a concept for new cities. These are divided into different sectors and levels. Traffic and transport are placed away from the areas where the actual public life was to take place, which should be characterized by freedom and creativity. The inhabitants of these cities should be able to evolve from *Homo faber* to *Homo ludens*. Everyday life should no longer be determined by work and profit. Moreover, this newly gained leisure time should sensitize the awareness for togetherness and promote the exchange of the collective. Constant devised a specific architecture for this purpose. Laura Stamps explains:

> That architecture would be a global network of sectors supported by pillars, common open spaces in which life would be subject to constant change. Movable architectural components such as walls, floors, stairs, bridges, and ladders would allow the New Babylonians to continually build new environments and create new routes. Color, light, texture, temperature, and air quality could also be adapted to the mood of the moment. Individuality would be banished.[17]

Constant visualized his ideas in numerous drawings, paintings and collages. We can see clearly, especially in his models (fig. 33, 35), some of which were placed on Seiler's installation *Minotic Neocolor Mindspace (Second African Color Circle)* in 2007 (fig. 34), how much Constant's visions shape Seiler's thinking. Apart from formal similarities, parallels in content are striking. Seiler also strives to create atmospheres in his works that evoke movement, participation, and conscious perception, and in which the individual can experience him or herself, as part of the collective. This can be seen in *Shrine* (2007, p. 154) as well as in *Effetto Barnum (Situationist Space Program)* (2009, p. 140) and *Hypnos* (2010, p. 142). While *Shrine* still clearly refers to a living space in the structure of a house, the other works bring Constant's sectoral idea more to the fore. *Hypnos* includes, in addition to the architectural structure, an inflatable sculpture that reproduces the molecular structure of morphine and evokes another of SI's beliefs: "There will be rooms that make you dream better than drugs, and houses where you can only love."[18] The reference to mind-expanding substances recurs in Seiler's work, for instance in the sculpture *Alice* (2008, p. 150), which the artist temporarily installed on the roof of the Kunsthaus Zürich as part of the exhibition *Shifting Identities*. The LSD molecule sits on the roof of the museum's extension, financed by the controversial patron Emil G. Bührle, and protrudes into one of the exhibition rooms. The molecule stands for a different perspective of the world, for the probing of unbounded states of consciousness. In addition to the charged content, Seiler is attracted to the contradiction that arises from the sober, brutalist architecture and the sculptural intervention.

Seiler creates situations of encounter and interaction in public space. Here, the term *situation* can also serve as an objective description. However, since Kerim Seiler's reflections refer back to the concepts of the SI, the programmatic definition is also invoked.[19] Like Constant, Guy Debord hoped to unleash creativity and sensitivity in created situations, thus integrating the potential of cultural production into urban space. Both took as their point of departure a directly experienceable concept of space in which the question of the connection between social order and space is at the forefront. This refers to the core ideas of social theories of space,[20] such as those written by Henri Lefebvre, Pierre Bourdieu, and later Martina Löw, among others, which understand space as a condition and product of social practice.[21]

> I understand spaces as relational arrangements of bodies and social goods in places. The concept of an (arranged) order emphasizes that spaces are based on the practice of arranging (the performance of the perceptually synthesizing connection as well as a practice of placement), but that spaces also provide a social order. This order in the sense of social structures both precedes action and is a consequence of action.[22]

Here Martina Löw sketches an understanding of space that finds an echo in Seiler's work and is made comprehensible there. In the encounter with his works, the processes of arrangement in relation to one's own actions, as well as with regard to the other present bodies and objects, becomes accessible for the recipient. They experience themselves as a component within the formation of spaces. When Seiler himself speaks of a "non-hierarchical understanding of space," both his unabated idealism and his fascination with utopian models of life, such as *New Babylon*, become apparent. This interpretation also results from his approach to site-specificity. The work *Relay (Situationist Space Program)* (p. 114–118) is installed by the artist in Johannesburg, in 2012. The rudimentary structure made of colored boards is used by local artists as a studio and meeting place. Here, too, the artist generates a specific situation and, in the clearly performative orientation of the installation, initiates awareness of the inherent potential for action and experience. In 2013, he builds the second *Relay* (p. 100) in St. Moritz, i.e. in a completely different urban structure. The work is an exact copy of the first *Relay*, but in St. Moritz, Seiler leaves out the toilet, furniture and other elements that guide the user in their actions. In St. Moritz, too, primarily artists use the space as part of a studio grant. Seiler intends to use the built situation to create a living space, be it in South Africa or Switzerland (other places where a *Relay* has been built include the garden of Cuno Amiet (p. 72) in the Bernese town of Oschwand and the park of the Enea Tree Museum in Rapperswil-Jona). It is therefore a less site-specific approach, and it is precisely here that the link to Seiler's "non-hierarchical understanding of space" can be made. He thinks in a kind of universal spatial structure and examines this thought by installing many of his works in different places, sometimes identically, sometimes with slight modifications. It becomes clear that, on the one hand, location- and culture-independent processes are set in motion, and that, on the other, the respective context in all its manifestations (for example, climate, culturally influenced access to materials, the concept of living, practiced actions in public space, dealing with art) emphatically determines the work and its aesthetic experience. Seiler is aware that spaces are not neutral and are never free from power structures. Particularly in large-scale public art projects, such as *Iris* (2014, fig. 37; p. 88), *Tyger Tyger* (2011, p. 132) or the design of recreational and working areas of financially strong companies (p. 4, 84), the artist sees himself as walking a fine line in the sense of his situationist approach to his work. On the one hand, he *serves* those forces that promote public space in its manifestation "as a contested good between hierarchical user groups with different interests," on the other, it is precisely in artistic interventions that the potential lies for breaking through "the ideology of (external) space as an instrument of domination."[23] Uwe Lewitzky aptly describes this dilemma of art in public space:

> Due to these facts, a meaningful or effective artistic practice in public space cannot be determined

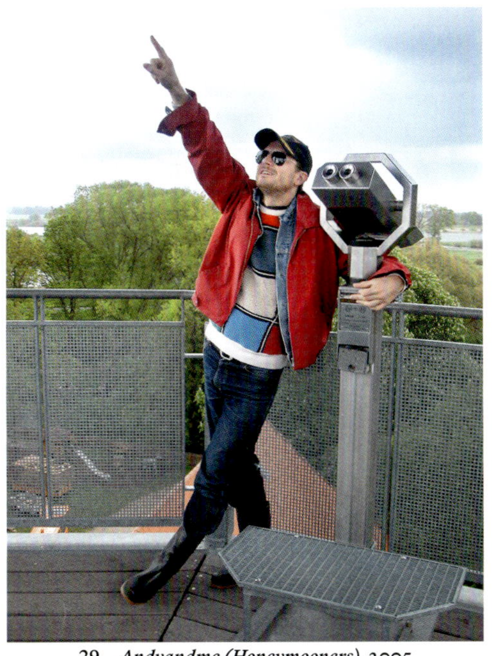

29 *Andyandme (Honeymooners)*, 2005
Digital photography; Dimensions variable

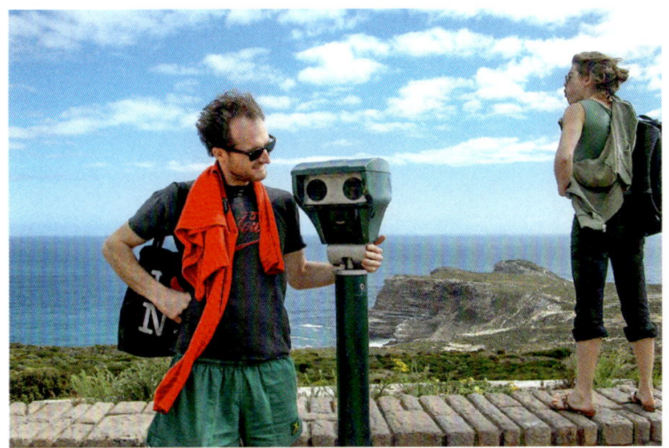

30 *Daisyandme (Honeymooners)*, 2006
Digital photography; Dimensions variable

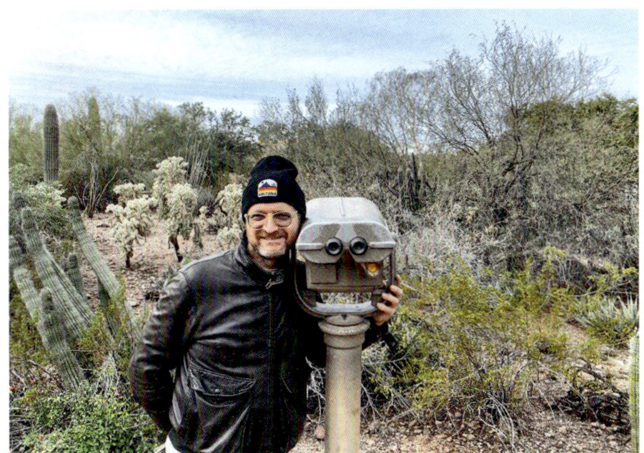

31 *Saving the Desert (Honeymooners)*, 2022
Digital photography; Dimensions variable

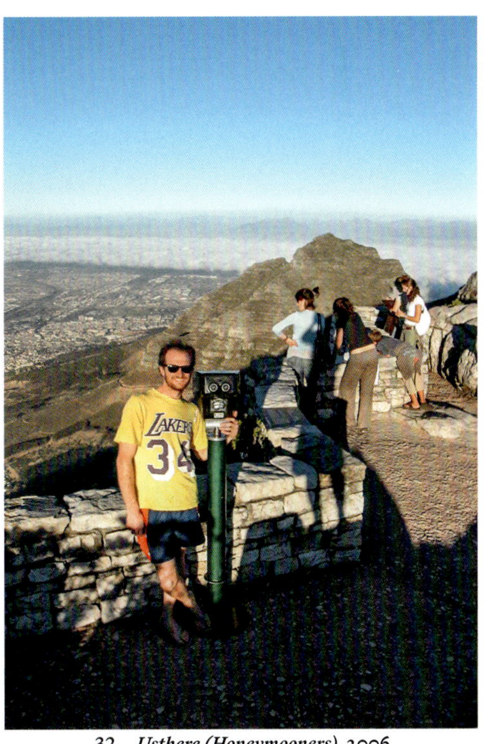

32 *Usthere (Honeymooners)*, 2006
Digital photography; Dimensions variable

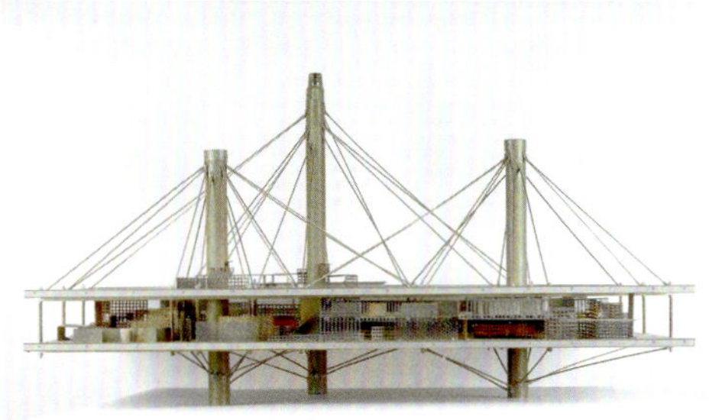

33 Constant: *Hangende Sector (Hanging Sector)*, 1961
Aluminum, copper, iron, oil paint, steel; 76×130×99 cm

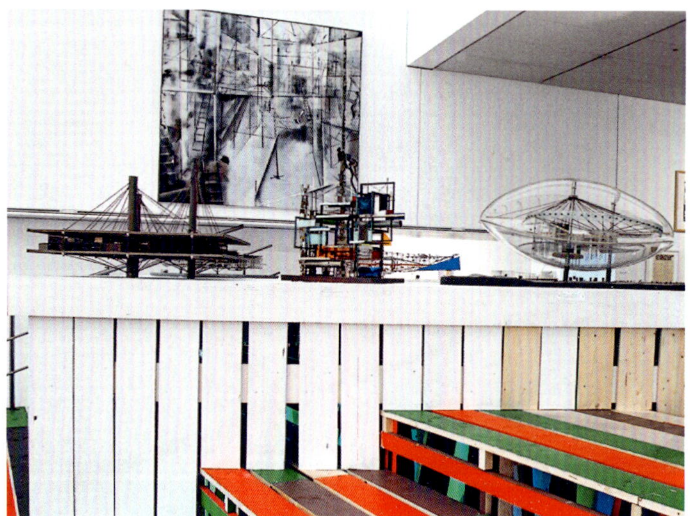

34 *Minotic Neocolor Mindspace (Secondary African Color Circle)*, 2007
Installation view with various models of Constant;
The International Situationist: 1957–1972. In girum imus nocte et consumimur igni, Museum Tinguely, Basel

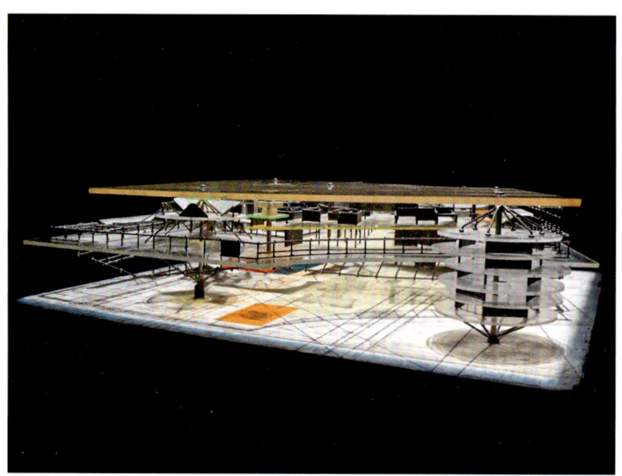

35 Constant: *Gele sector (Yellow Sector)*, 1958
Blotting paper, copper, ink, iron, lead, metal, oil paint, plexiglass, wood; 21×87.3×77.5 cm

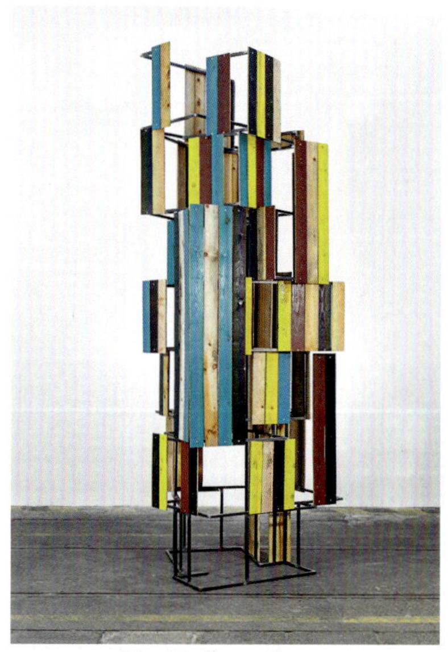

36 *Birdhouse I*, 2014
Acrylic lacquer, perspex, rivets, steel, wood; 400×143×139 cm

per se by assigning it to categories such as New Genre Public Art (intervention) or institutional art in public space (representation). Rather, a meaningful practice functions as an interplay of these two approaches, since representation in an institutional framework makes it possible to accumulate the necessary capital for an effective interventionist practice. The potentiated capital can then be transferred to a group objective and thus serves, for example, to create differential spaces that oppose a logic of economic exploitation and exemplarily create an alternative urban situation in which heterogeneous user groups have the right of entry and integrative participation.[24]

Seiler's two-stage work *118 minus 11 (Kerims Lampenladen) / Gestik des Verschwindens* (2010–2019, fig. 38; p. 120) at Zürich Main Station, created over several years, puts these considerations into practice in several aspects. The work, initially conceived for the closure of the station at night, morphs in a second step into a construction wall of a large building site, freely accessible to all passers-by and thus, in principle, to all groups of the community. Especially for the people who regularly visit the Main Station, such a created atmosphere and situation will be a constant companion and actually become part of everyday life. This is promoted by the constant changes that Seiler has made over the years together with a team of several people. At times, the installation extends over 750 meters and eliminates the usual product advertisements on comparable walls. At the same time, the vista of the installation site—namely the construction wall of a large building project associated with gentrification processes—raises awareness of the capitalist forces at hand. These have manipulated public space for decades and are becoming increasingly dominant. In addition to the enormous influence of digitalization, art theorist Nina Möntmann sees the examination of social spaces as being characterized, above all, by the fact that the "redefinition of the social under the influence of neoliberal competitive logic" has become even more acute, and that "direct as well as abstract social relationships have established themselves as economic forms."[25]

With the project *Carwash (New Babylon) / NEW/NOW* (since 2013, fig. 39; p. 106), which began with the Relay series, Seiler addresses this predominance of the economic by expanding his idea of the inhabitable sculpture into differentiated residential units and approaches real estate investors with the corresponding plans. As is often the case, Seiler works with a team of various experts to realize his vision. Architects, engineers, and specialists in digital construction technology work together with the artist to develop a sculptural project of architectural dimension that puts people and community first—rather than capital interwoven with a given property. *NEW/NOW* is about a change of perspective that shows the way to new concepts of living through the synergy of artwork and residential property.

> Site-determined, site-oriented, site-conscious, site-responsive, site-related. These are some new terms that have emerged in recent years among many artists and critics to account for the various permutations of site-specific art in the present.[26]

In 2004, Miwon Kwon described the extreme diversity of site-specific work that can still be observed today. The term *site-specific* is enriched by new aspects, especially in reference to the changing perspectives in the category of space. In addition to *vaguely site-specific* works, Seiler also develops works with a clear reference to the location. *Tyger Tyger* (2011, p. 132) not only gives a new face to the façade of a minimalist concrete architecture, in fact, the colorful wooden frame on the roof of the building is transformed into a jungle gym for the local day care center. Seiler has created a colored structure that is directly aligned with the architectural features and at the same time reacts to the function of the place. The work *gelf, rôt unde blâ* (2015, p. 80) highlights the history of the site. In Würzburg's Lusamgärtchen, an unusually colorful bench attracts the visitor's attention and invites them to linger. The colors refer to a song of the minstrel Walther von der Vogelweide, who is buried there. The artist uses the contemplative atmosphere of the site to sensitize the visitor to the place, its history and its impact on contemporary urban life. At the same time, this work evokes the spiritual space already mentioned, which is one of many golden threads in Seiler's oeuvre.

NOMADIC WORKFLOW

With the project *Clones International* (2005–2008), Seiler concretizes the approach of continuation that he has incorporated in his work from early on—the continuation of ideas, of forms, of materials, and ultimately, of works of art. The *Clones* are exhibited at numerous locations, from Cape Town and New York to Zürich and Lüneburg (fig. 11; p. 156, 168, 171). They find a temporary home and illustrate both the unique features of the respective location in the interaction of work and context and the parallel phenomena that can be identified when comparing the different installations.[27] The artist himself describes this procedure as a "nomadic workflow." At the center of this lies the non-sedative existence of the works.

In *Nomadic Structures* (2010), Seiler continues this train of thought. He realized his first *Pneuma* (Greek for "spirit," "breeze," "air," "breath") in Trogen in 2005 (fig. 40). In 2010, the sculpture, which consists of beanpoles, color gel, fluorescent lamps, ropes, and the necessary electrical wiring, travels to Southern Africa, taking on a different form each time. In the form of a diary, Seiler records the experiences of his trip, during which he realized the *Nomadic Structures* (p. 134–138) ten times together with Gregor Metzger.[28] In his notes, he describes not only the discussion with the customs officer when the material is to be imported at Cape Town airport, but also the arduous climb up Lion's Head, one of Cape Town's local mountains. Seiler, Metzger, and a group of friends climb the mountain, each bearing a bundle of stakes on their backs to realize the first *Pneuma* (fig. 41) of the trip in front of an impressive panorama.

> [...] we tied pole to pole [...], the operation was a complete success. More and more people arrived. [...] And droves of them came to see the view. A magical evening, the night of the non-occurring leap day [February 28, 2009] and almost full moon. Warm and simply brilliant. Questions rain down on us, Gerald [Machona] has the best answer: *Because we can*. That truly sums it up. Why are you doing this? *Because we can*.[29]

But there are also less carefree moments on this journey, moments when "because we can" is doubted. When the *Pneuma* is to be built in the wilderness of Lesotho, the artist hires a guide, several workers and six horses. The colonial aspect of this action makes him uneasy.

> How important is production? Isn't it enough to imagine something and describe it, maybe even paint it? Does all this material have to be dragged around? And if so, does it call for documentation? What for? As proof that you've done it? So here, at the edge of our world and our time, where archaic life forms are lived, I ask myself the crucial question. *Where is this all going?*[30]

In Mpondoland on the Eastern Cape, Seiler shows the sculpture at the construction site of the new royal palace of the AmaMpondo, the Qaukeni Great Place (fig. 42). "The tubes glow, the twilight turns into night and with that the people come to *Qaukeni*. The *Pneuma* is reflected in a puddle [...]. It's magic."[31]

In the context of the *Nomadic Structures* project, Seiler experiences ambivalent situations that are characteristic of globally active artists. Especially when it means leaving the (cultural) comfort zone, one's own convictions start to waver, need to be reconsidered, and are enriched by the experiences made. Looking back, Seiler speaks of a sharpening of the senses, not least for the significance of art:

> In addition, in South Africa, the meaning of art outside the Euro-American context became clear to me: It's about freedom, and this freedom is especially valuable when you live in a system of oppression or have freed yourself from one.[32]

Both works that were further developed in South Africa, *Nomadic Structures* and *Relay*, have, above all, encouraged Seiler to understand art not as a static structure but as a process that is decisively shaped by the contextual conditions and the recipients.

The "nomadic workflow" can also be observed in numerous other works by Seiler. Either he erects installations that are virtually identical or they take on a new orientation within the formal framework of the original installation. The works *What If* and *Tschutschu*, after being temporarily installed at the Gotthard tunnel, found a new home at the Locarno Film Festival in 2018–2019 (p. 46). The strategy of continuation is also reflected in the consistent use of already used materials. In almost every work by Seiler, one encounters an already familiar element, whether related to material, form or content. This also applies to the color systems he implements. Be it red, yellow, and blue, the dominant primary colors in Johannes Itten's theory of color, which has accompanied the artist since his education, or the free color circle composed by Seiler himself, as it first appears in *Minotic Neocolor Mindspace (Secondary African Color Circle)* (2007, fig. 34, 43; p. 152–153), or his ongoing engagement with the RAL system—all these colors appear again and again in his work. This is also the case in the large-format monochrome paintings, *Flag of Mars* (2018, fig. 44; p. 40) and the experiments with computer-based painting, *Flag* (p. 32–33). The starting point is the examination of the thematic field of the primary colors of light (red, green, and blue) and the primary colors of painting (red, yellow, and blue) and their juxtaposition. The resulting compositions reflect a way of dealing with color that is only partially based on physical facts and is mainly culturally influenced. In these works, Seiler is particularly interested in the influence of the screen on the understanding of color. The screen allows for a moving painting of hitherto unknown luminosity. The shifting and mixing of different color systems—such as the primary colors of light, painting, and the screen—results in supposedly conventional compositions, which, however, expand the viewer's viewing habits and pose a fundamental question: How much information is needed to see a certain color? Comparable considerations on the interaction of information, seeing, and recognition led Seiler to a short period of painting as early as 1997.

Looking at Seiler's work over time, the image of a network comes to mind, both because of the connecting golden threads in content and aesthetics, and because of his "nomadic workflow" method. At the same time, however, this overview tempts me to turn to another important source of inspiration for Seiler: the architect R. Buckminster Fuller and his visionary ideas for new human life forms in harmony with nature. Fuller became known, among other things, for his *Tensegrity Spheres* (fig. 45) and *Domes*, which he developed in 1948 together with Josef Albers and the students of the Black Mountain College. I find their structure of intersections, connections and ramifications to be an interesting image, which abstracts Seiler's past work. An association that arouses curiosity about future intersections in Kerim Seiler's oeuvre.

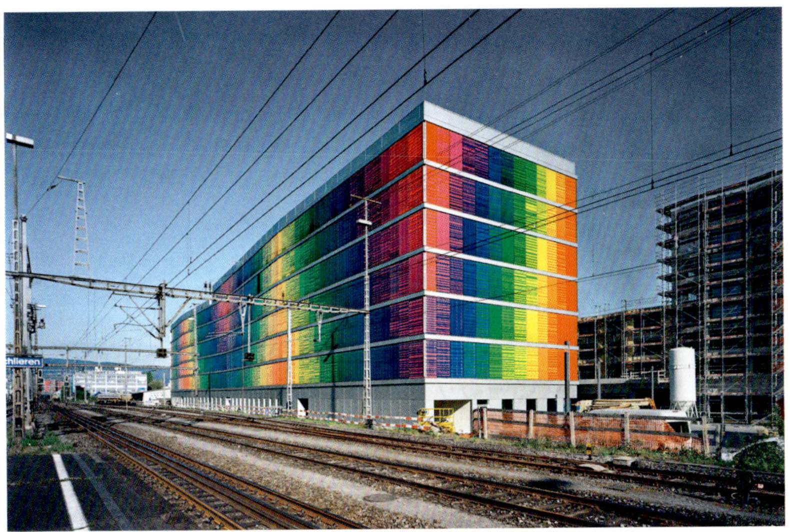

37 *Iris*, 2014
Aluminum blinds, two component lacquer; 36×85×20 m;
Installation view Wiesenstrasse, Schlieren

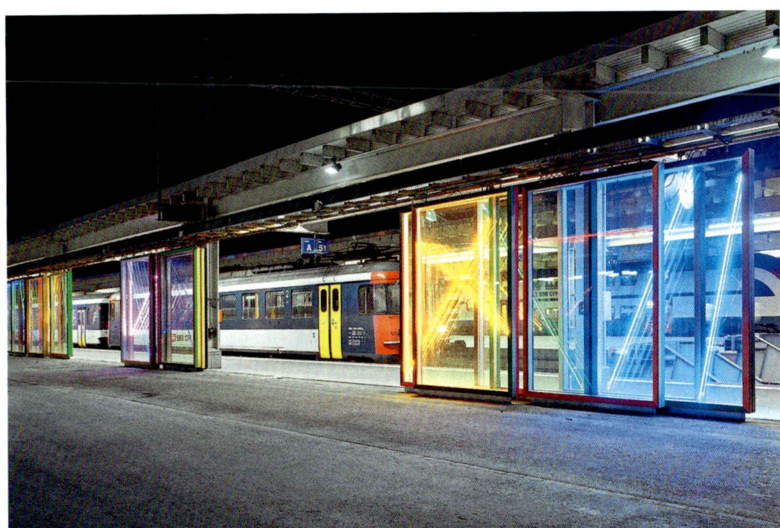

38 *118 minus 11 (Kerims Lampenladen)/Gestik des Verschwindens*, 2012–2019
Acrylic lacquer, aluminum, neon tubing, galvanized steel, perspex, screws, silicone, wood; Dimensions variable; Installation view Europaallee / Zürich Hauptbahnhof

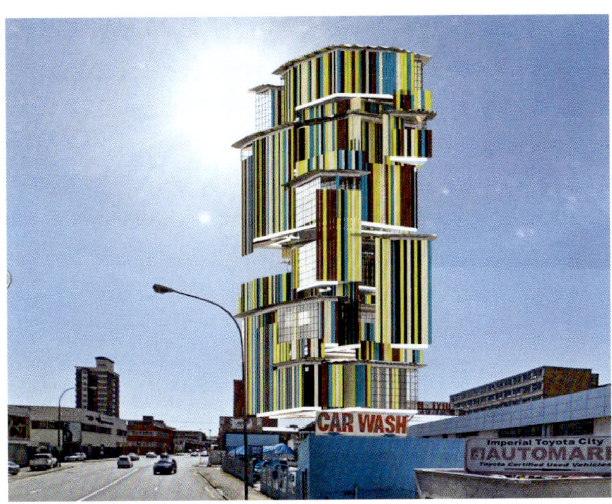

39 *Carwash (New Babylon)/NEW/NOW*, 2013–2016
Collaboration with Benjamin Dillenburger and Steffen Lemmerzahl, Rendering

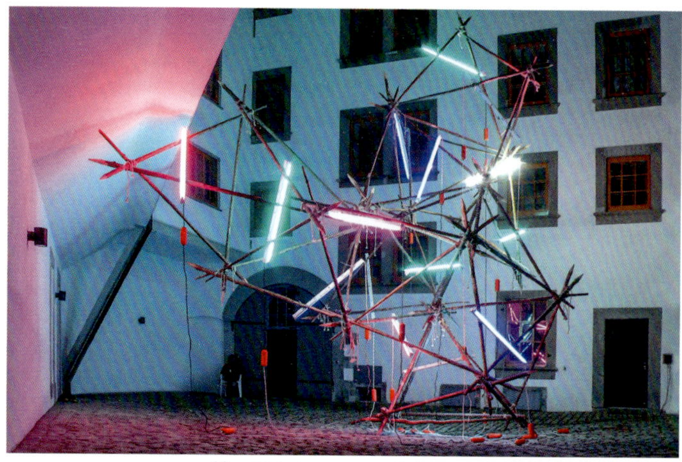

40 *Pneuma, somnambul*, 2005
Beanpoles, color gel, electrical wiring, fluorescent lamps, power generator, ropes, timer; Dimensions variable; Installation view *För Hitz ond Brand*, Fünfeckpalast, Trogen

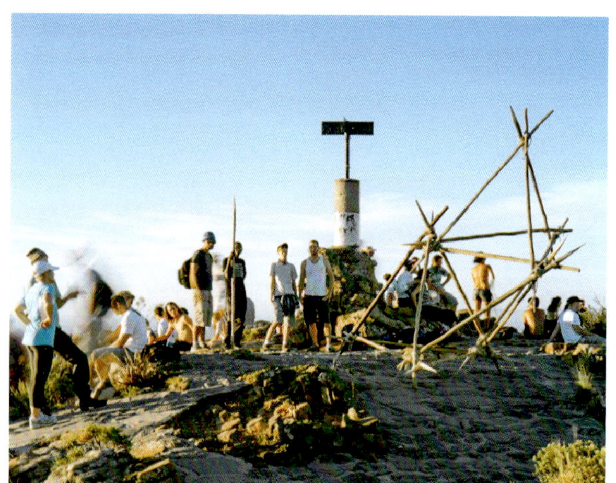

41 *Nomadic Structures (Lion's Head)*, 2010
Collaboration with Gregor Metzger
Performance still Lion's Head, Cape Town

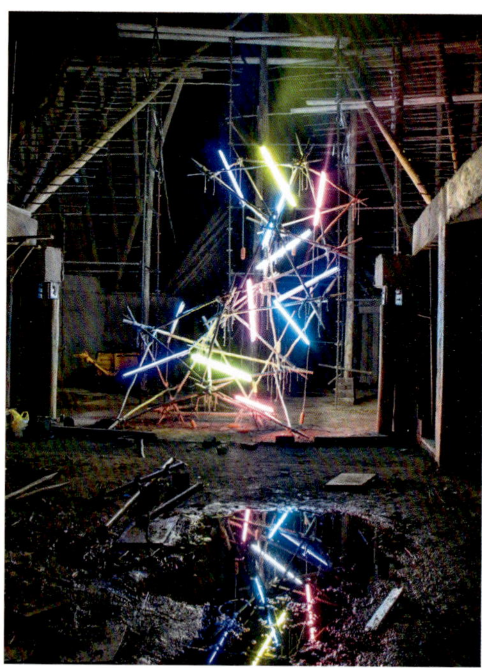

42 *Nomadic Structures (Qaukeni)*, 2010
Beanpoles, color filters, electrical wiring, fluorescent lamps, power generator, ropes, timer; Dimensions variable; Installation view Qaukeni Great Place, Mpondoland

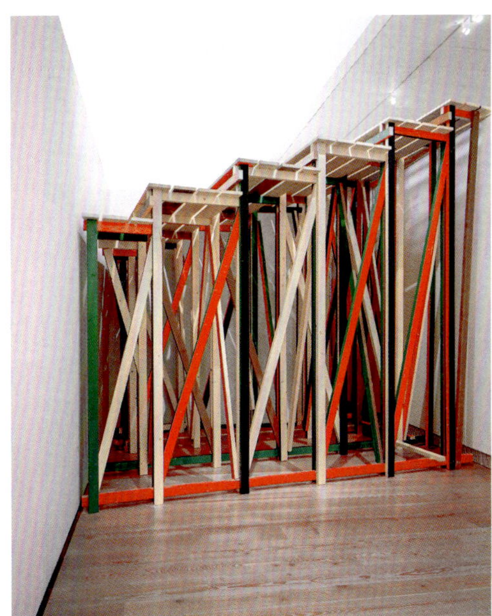

43 *Minotic Neocolor Mindspace (Secondary African Color Circle)*, 2007
Acrylic lacquer, color filters, fabric, fluorescent lamps, white paint, timer, screws, wood; Dimensions variable; Installation view *The International Situationist: 1957–1972: In girum imus nocte et consumimur igni*, Museum Tinguely, Basel

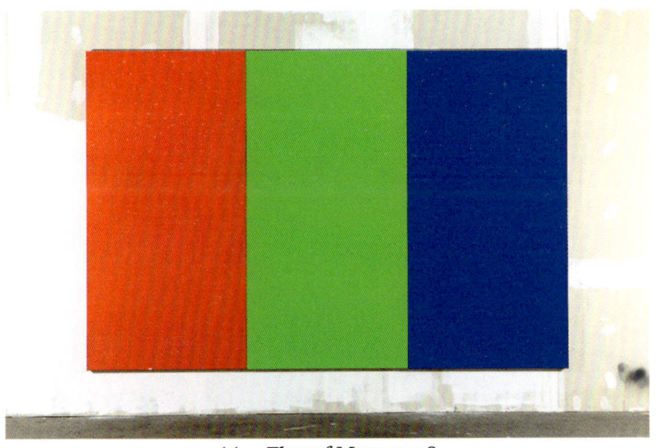

44 *Flag of Mars*, 2018
Canvas, oil paint; 226×339 cm

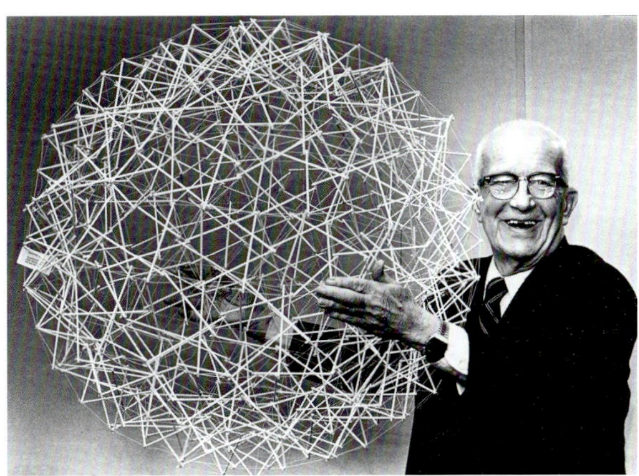

45 R. Buckminster Fuller holds up a *Tensegrity sphere*, 1979

1 See Markus Brüderlin (ed.), *ArchiSkulptur. Dialoge zwischen Architektur und Plastik vom 18. Jahrhundert bis heute*, ex. cat., Fondation Beyeler, Riehen/Basel, (Ostfildern: Hatje Cantz, 2004). The German term "ArchiSkulptur" is shaped by: Eva Kraus, "Plaidoyer pour une archisculpture," in: *Aujourd'hui*, Nr. 53, 1966, 88–89. As further reference literature, Brüderlin cites the following: Sigfried Giedion, *Space, Time and Architecture: The Growth of a New Tradition*, (Cambridge, MA: Harvard University Press, 1941); Carola Giedion-Welcker, *Contemporary Sculpture: An Evolution in Time and Space*, (New York: Wittenborn, 1955). For a far-reaching overview on the interaction of art and architecture see also: Germano Celant (ed.), *Architecture & Arts 1900/2004: A Century of Creative Projects in Building, Design, Cinema, Painting, Sculpture*, ex. cat., Palazzo Ducale, Genoa, (Milano: Skira, 2004).

2 See Juliane Rebentisch, *Ästhetik der Installation*, (Frankfurt/M.: Suhrkamp, 2003).

3 See Theodor W. Adorno, "Die Kunst und die Künste," in idem., *Ohne Leitbild: Parva Aesthetica*, (Frankfurt/M.: Suhrkamp, 1977), 432–453.

4 Kerim Seiler, "Relay (Situationist Space Program) – Crystal Hotel," 2012, unpublished manuscript.

5 Kerim Seiler in conversation with the author in June 2019.

6 Rudolf Koella, "Kerim Seilers Appenzeller Verkehrsgarten," in: *Wahlverwandtschaften*, (Appenzell: IG Art & Appenzell, 1998), 75–78, here p. 77.

7 Ibid., p. 78.

8 Barbara Steiner, "Performative Architektur," in: Angelika Nollert (ed.), *Performative Installation*, ex. cat., Galerie im Taxispalais, Innsbruck, et al., (Cologne: Snoeck, 2003), 180–215, here p. 190f.

9 Kerim Seiler, 2001, unpublished application documents.

10 "In numerous works, Nauman repeatedly strives to manipulate the viewer, so that the latter must constantly redefine their own standpoint, especially in relation to the work of art. In most of the corridor and tunnel installations, the freedom of movement of the viewer is reduced to an extreme minimum. To a certain extent, the visitor is conditioned for the process of perception, i.e. their behavior is made dependent on various predetermined conditions." In: Jörg Zutter (ed.), *Bruce Nauman: Skulpturen und Installationen 1985–1990*, ex. cat., Museum für Gegenwartskunst, Basel, Städtische Galerie im Städelschen Kunstinstitut, Frankfurt/M., (Cologne: DuMont, 1990), 30.

11 Bruce Nauman and Christine Hoffmann (eds.), *Interviews 1965–1986*, (Dresden: Verlag der Kunst, 1996), 161.

12 For a detailed account of the developmental history of performative installations, see the dissertation by Judith Plodeck, *Bruce Nauman und Olafur Eliasson. Strategien performativer Installationen*, (Potsdam: Universitätsverlag Potsdam, 2010). Plodeck not only explains different performativity strategies of installation art, but also devotes extensive attention to the definitions of performativity that are effective in these approaches, which she calls a "figure of discourse." According to Plodeck, early performative, spatial arrangements and installations are characterized by a number of features that are still valid in current examples of this conception of work—also in Kerim Seilers performative installations: "Moreover, they designed specific spatial situations and experimental arrangements that demanded an aesthetic experience—one that lay in the mode of perception of the recipient. These methods, which can be described as performative, extend into contemporary art. [...] This is based on the assumption that the traditional, institutionally established status of the work of art as something to be contemplated was already being questioned and critically reflected upon in the 1960s and 1970s. Not only the status of the work itself, but also the role of the artist as a creative genius and the question of the function of the recipient are up for discussion and disposition. The stipulated assignments of roles were disrupted and attempts were made to reformulate them anew." Ibid., p. 11f.

13 Angelika Nollert, "Performative Installation," Nollert (see note 8), 8–29, here p. 14 and p. 21.

14 Katharina Dohm and Bettina Steinbrügge, "Von mehreren Versuchen sich einen Raum zu erobern," in: *Lasso #1*, (Frankfurt/M.: Revolver, 2004), 58–63, here p. 60.

15 Adrian Heathfield, "Alive", in: idem. (ed.), *Live. Art and Performance*, (London: Tate Publishing, 2004), 6–13, here p. 10.

16 Michael Glasmeier, "Einbrüche des Deplacierten," in idem. (ed.), *Anarchie des Lachens: Komik in den Künsten*, (Munich: Silke Schreiber, 2011), 7–20, here p. 10f.

17 Laura Stamps, "Constant's New Babylon. Pushing the Zeitgeist to Its Limits," in: *Constant – New Babylon: To Us, Liberty*, ex. cat., Gemeentemuseum, Den Haag, (Ostfildern: Hatje Cantz, 2016), 12–27, here p. 13.

18 The Situationist International, cit. from: Uwe Lewitzky, *Kunst für alle? Kunst im öffentlichen Raum zwischen Partizipation, Intervention und Neuer Urbanität*, (Bielefeld: Transcript, 2005), 72.

19 "Our main principle is the construction of situations—that is, the concrete construction of short-term living environments and their transformation into a higher quality of passion." Guy Debord, *Rapport zur Konstruktion von Situationen*, (Hamburg: Edition Nautilus, 1980), 41.

20 For an overview see Martina Löw, *Raumsoziologie*, (Frankfurt/M.: Suhrkamp, 2001).

21 Lefebvre "adopts the project of a short-circuit between representation and living space from the avant-garde Situationist movement around Guy Debord, to which he is at times close." Jörg Dünne and Stefan Günzel (eds.), *Raumtheorie: Grundlagentexte aus Philosophie und Kulturwissenschaften*, (Frankfurt/M.: Suhrkamp, 2006), 298.

22 Martina Löw, "Von der Substanz zur Relation. Soziologische Reflexionen zum Raum," in: Jürgen Krusche (ed.), *Der Raum der Stadt*, (Marburg: Jonas, 2008), 30–44, here p. 35.

23 Lewitzky (see note 18), 121–122.

24 Ibid., p. 126.

25 Nina Möntmann, "Vorwort zur Neuauflage," in: *Kunst als sozialer Raum*, (Cologne: Walther König, 2017), 8.

26 Miwon Kwon, *One Place After Another: Site-Specific Art And Locational Identity*, (Cambridge, MA: MIT Press, et al., 2004), 1.

27 Cf. Andrea Glauser, *Verortnete Entgrenzung. Kulturpolitik, Artist-in-Residence-Programme und die Praxis der Kunst*, (Bielefeld: Transcript, 2009), 167.

28 Kerim Seiler, in: idem. and Patrick Huber (eds.), *Kerim in the Sky with Seiler: LSD – Fluxus – Konkret*, 3 vols., (Zürich: Nieves, 2012), vol. *LSD*, no page.

29 Ibid., Entry 03.01.2010, no page.

30 Ibid., Entry 03.09.2010 – Sani Pass, no page.

31 Ibid., Entry 03.29.2010 – Chintsa, no page.

32 Kerim Seiler in conversation with the author in June 2019.

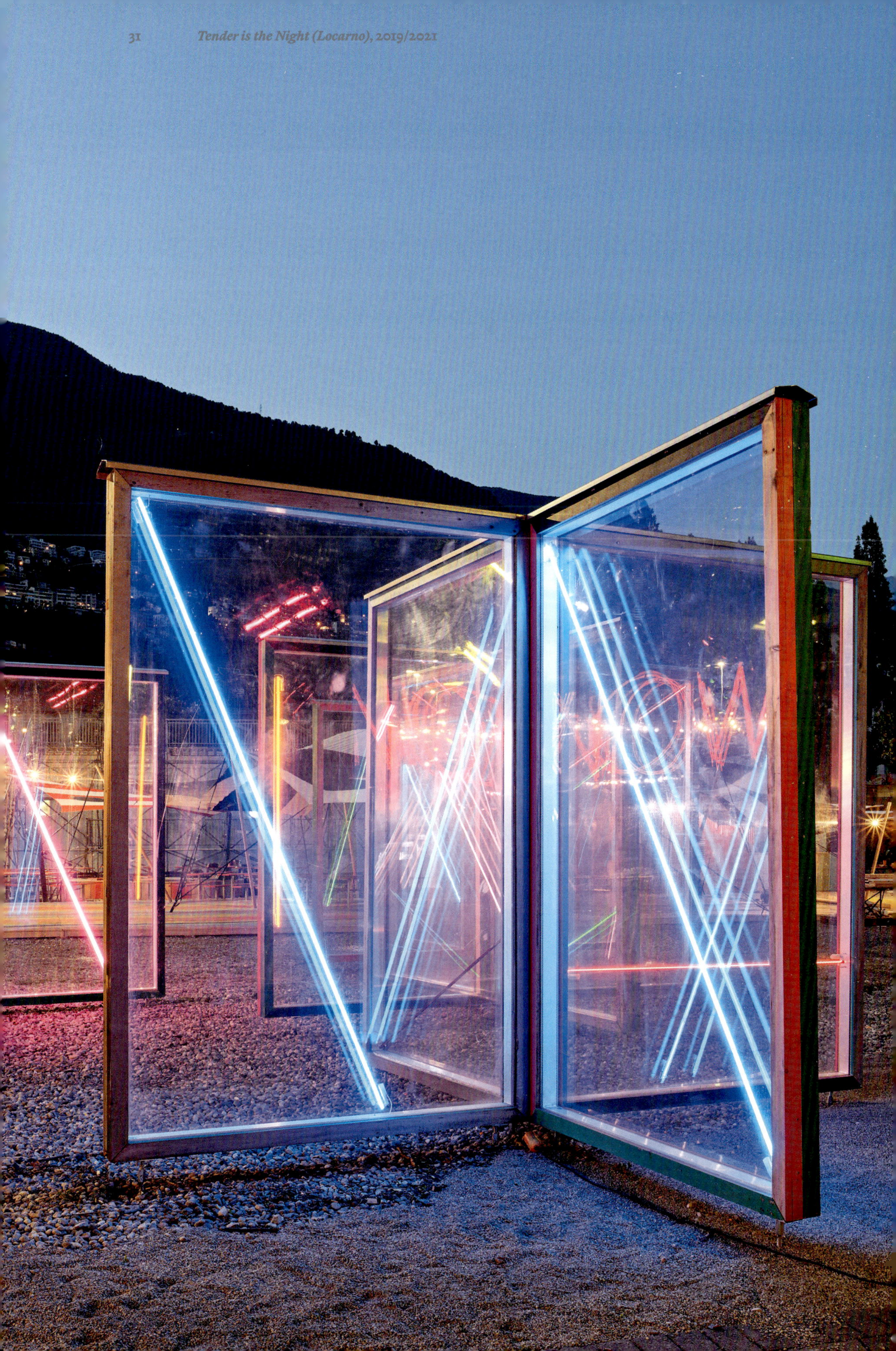

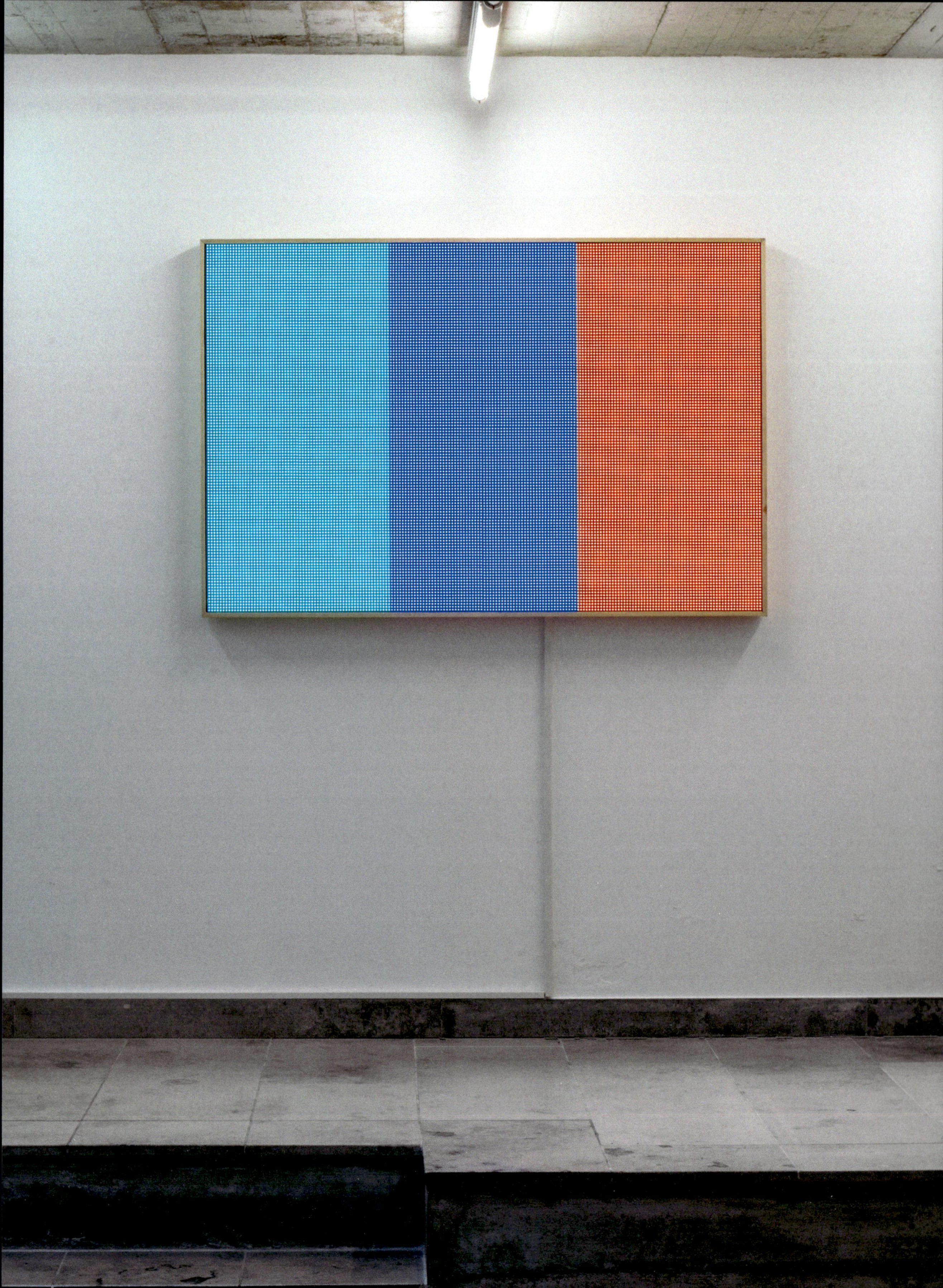

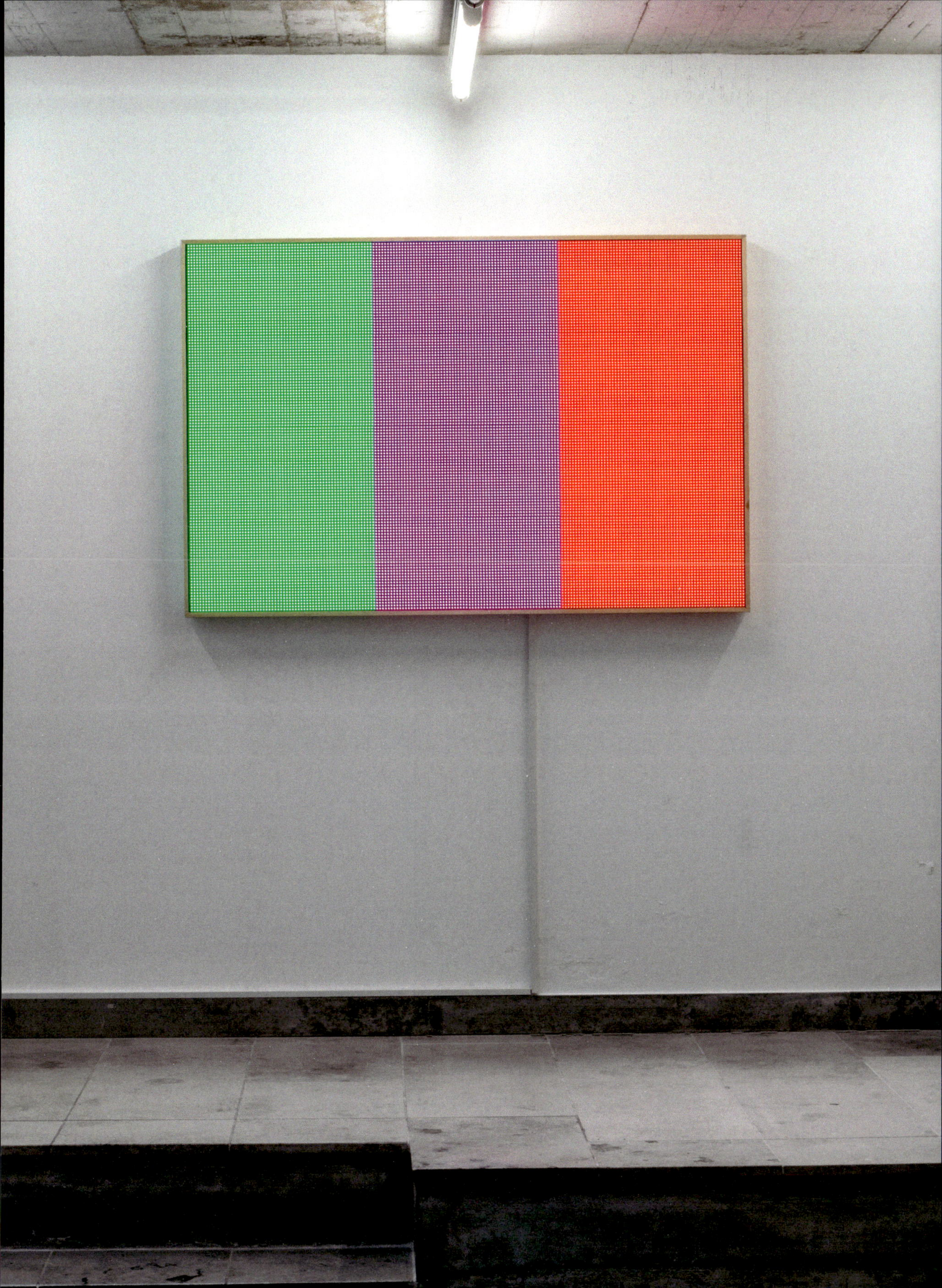

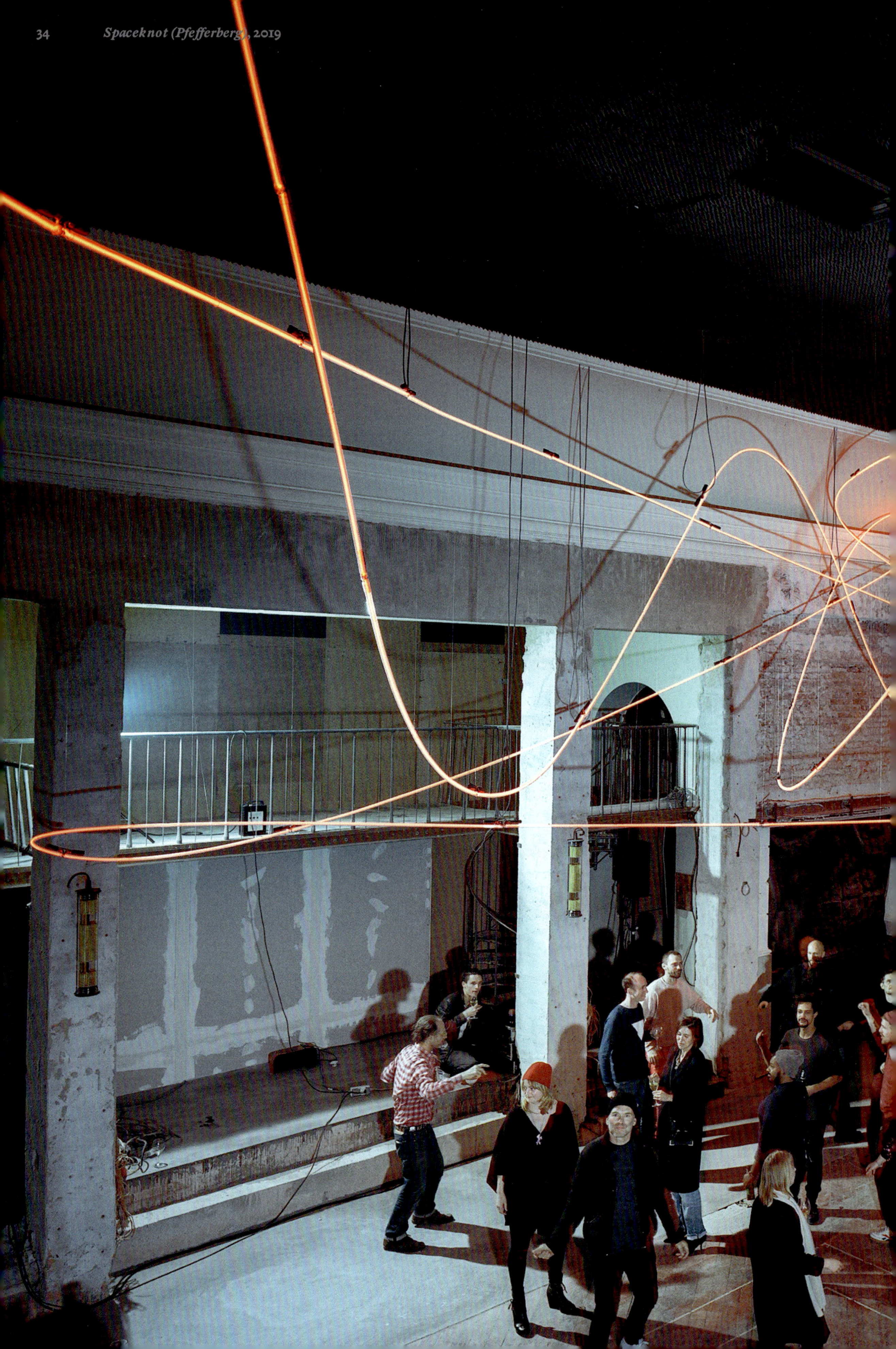

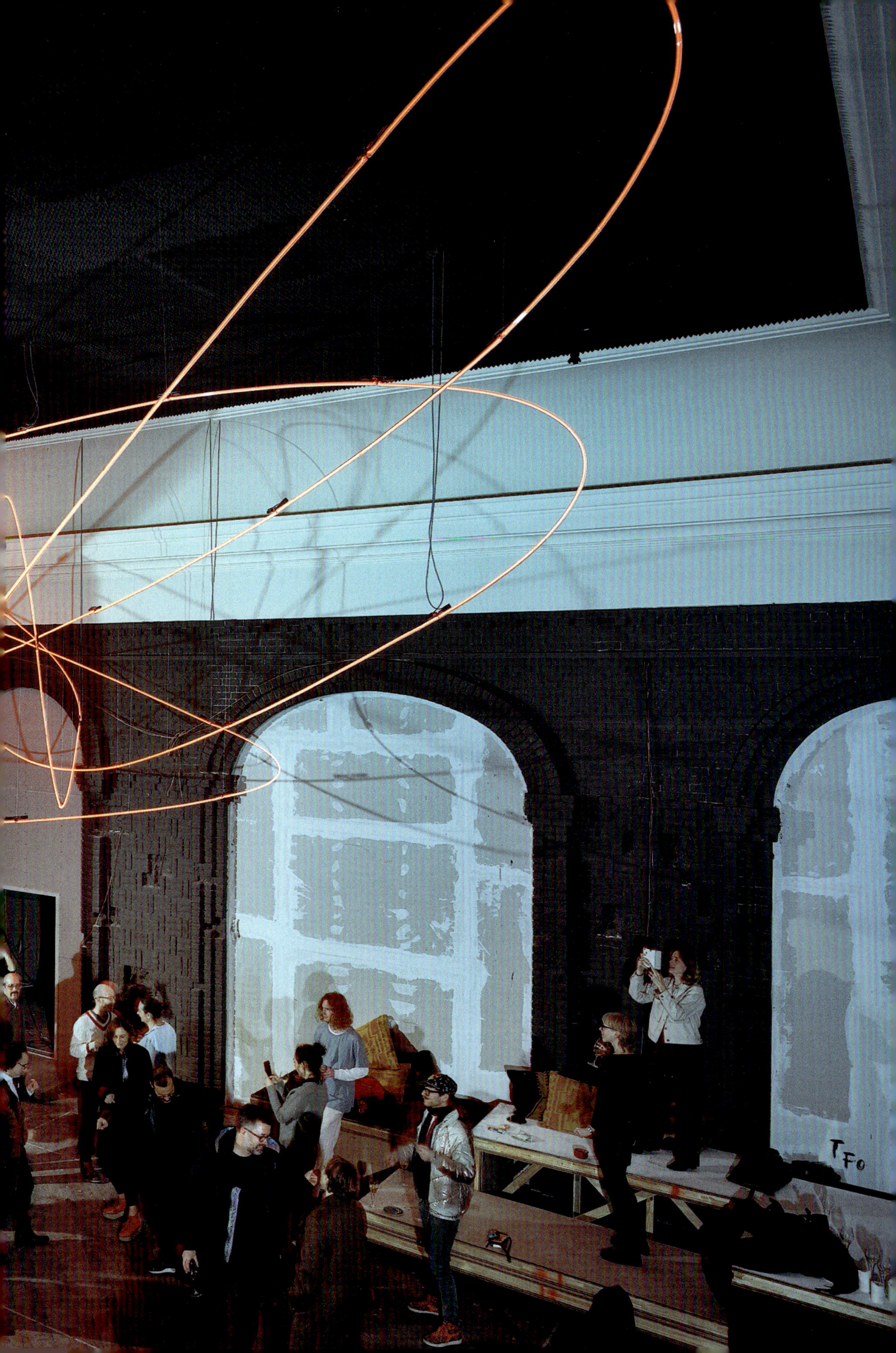
TFo

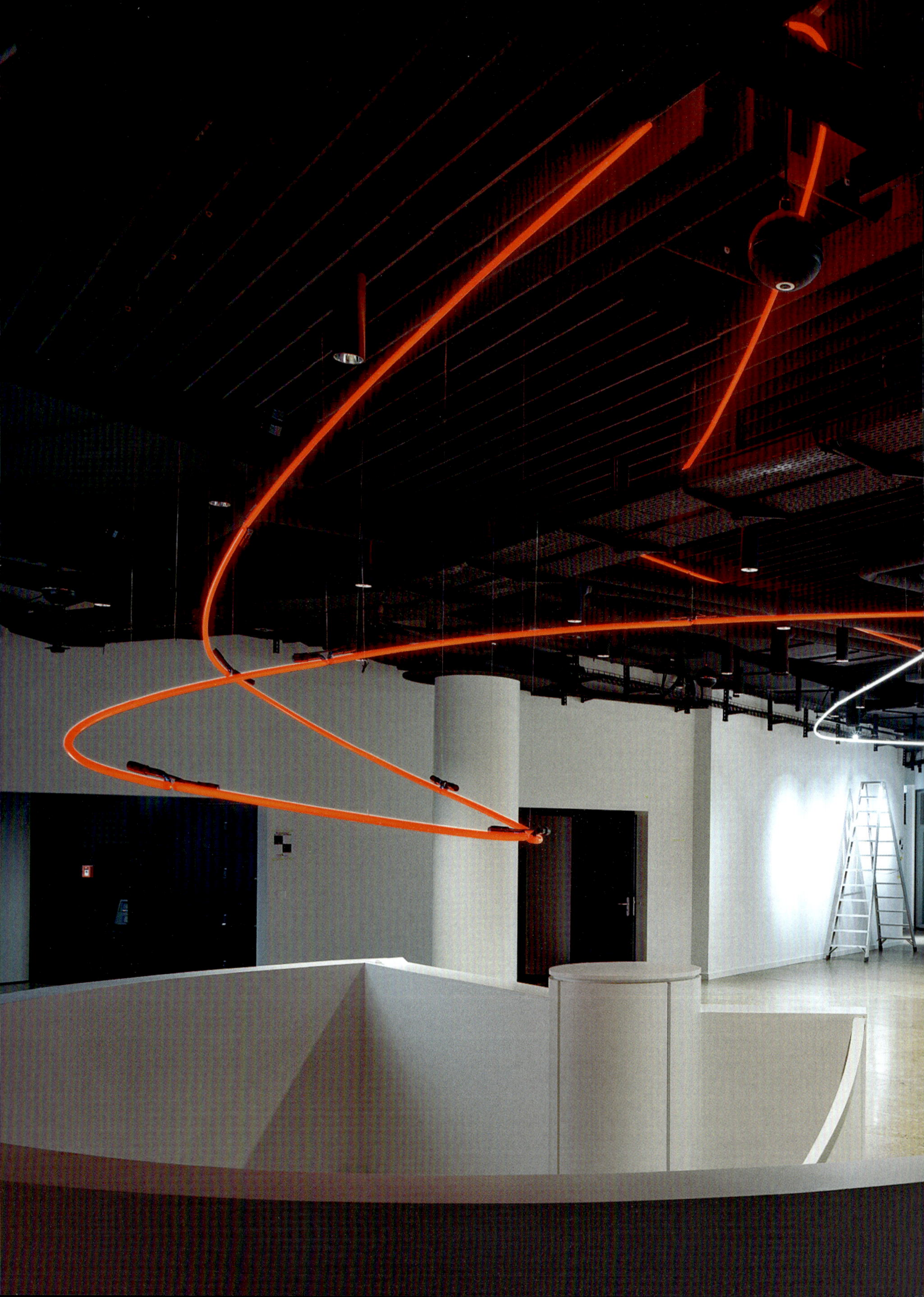

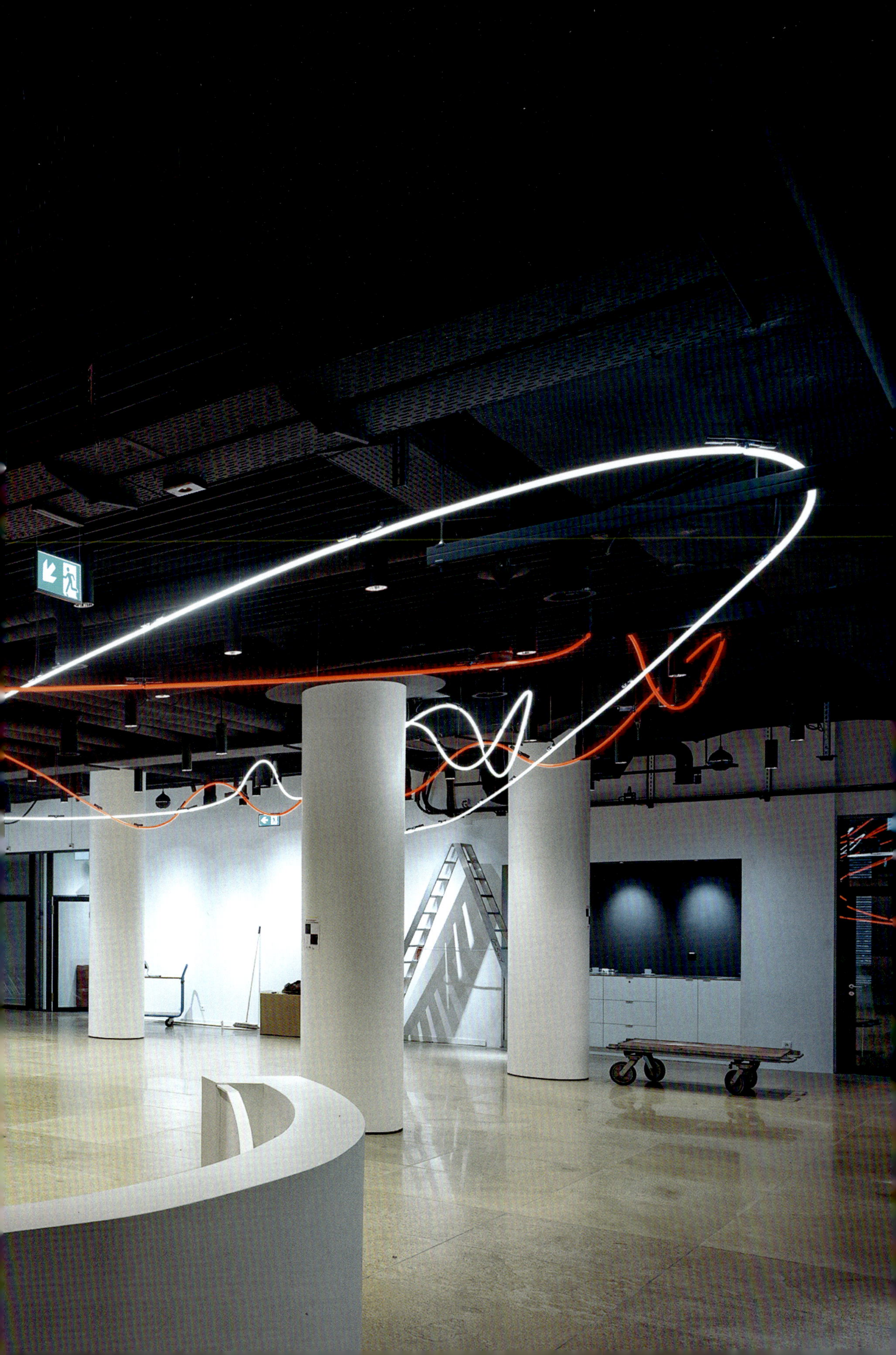

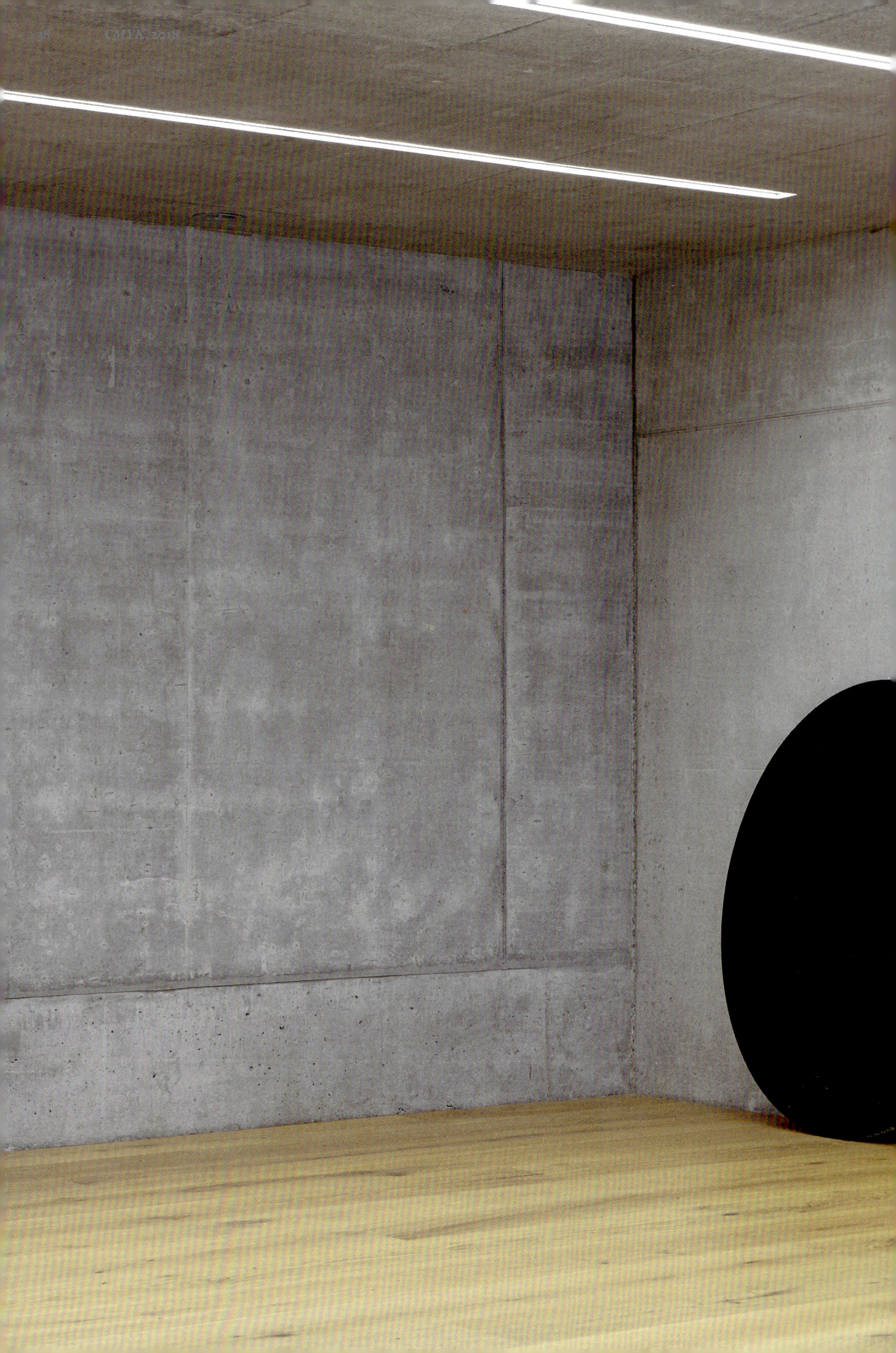

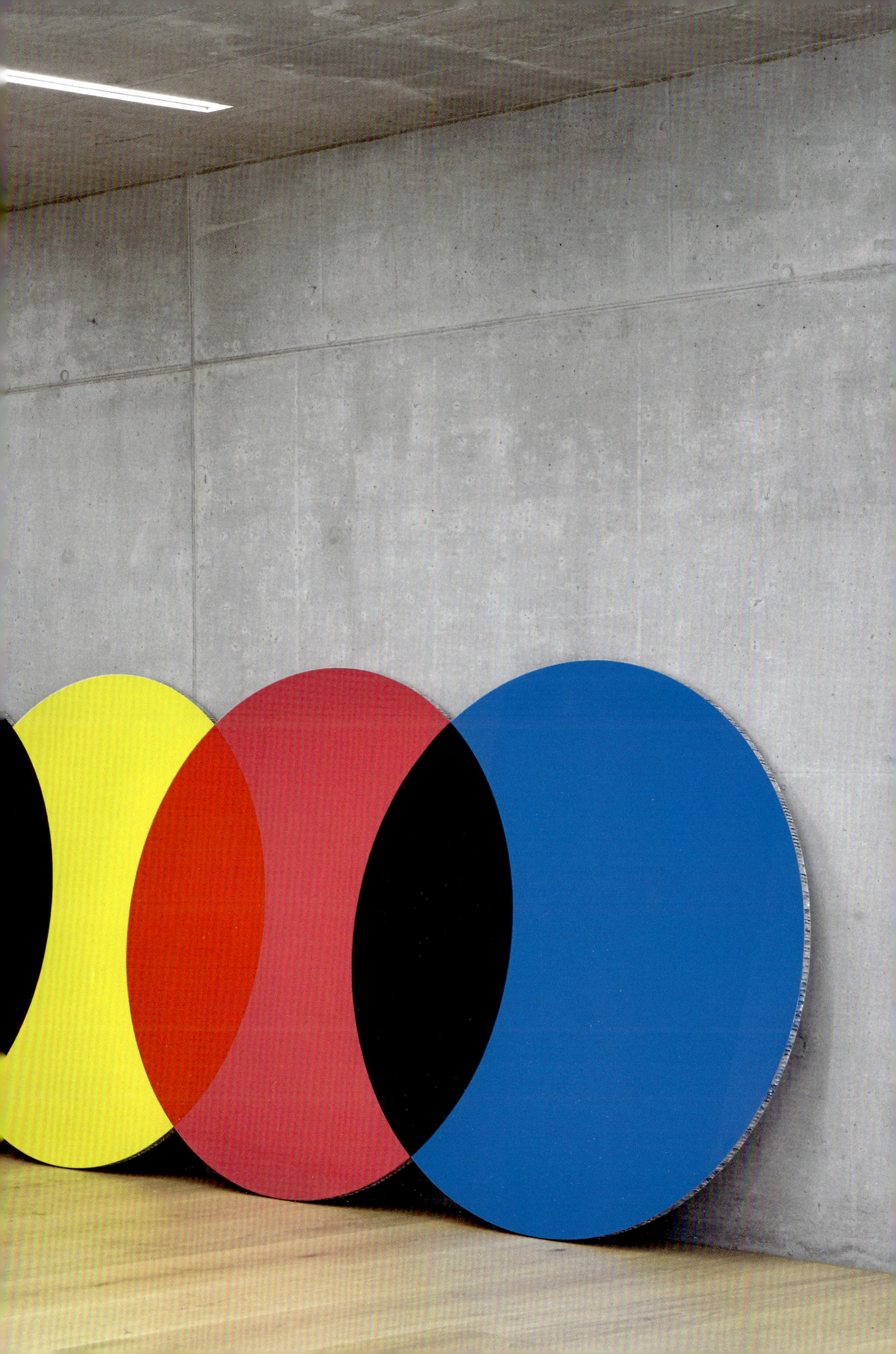

Flag of Mars, 2018

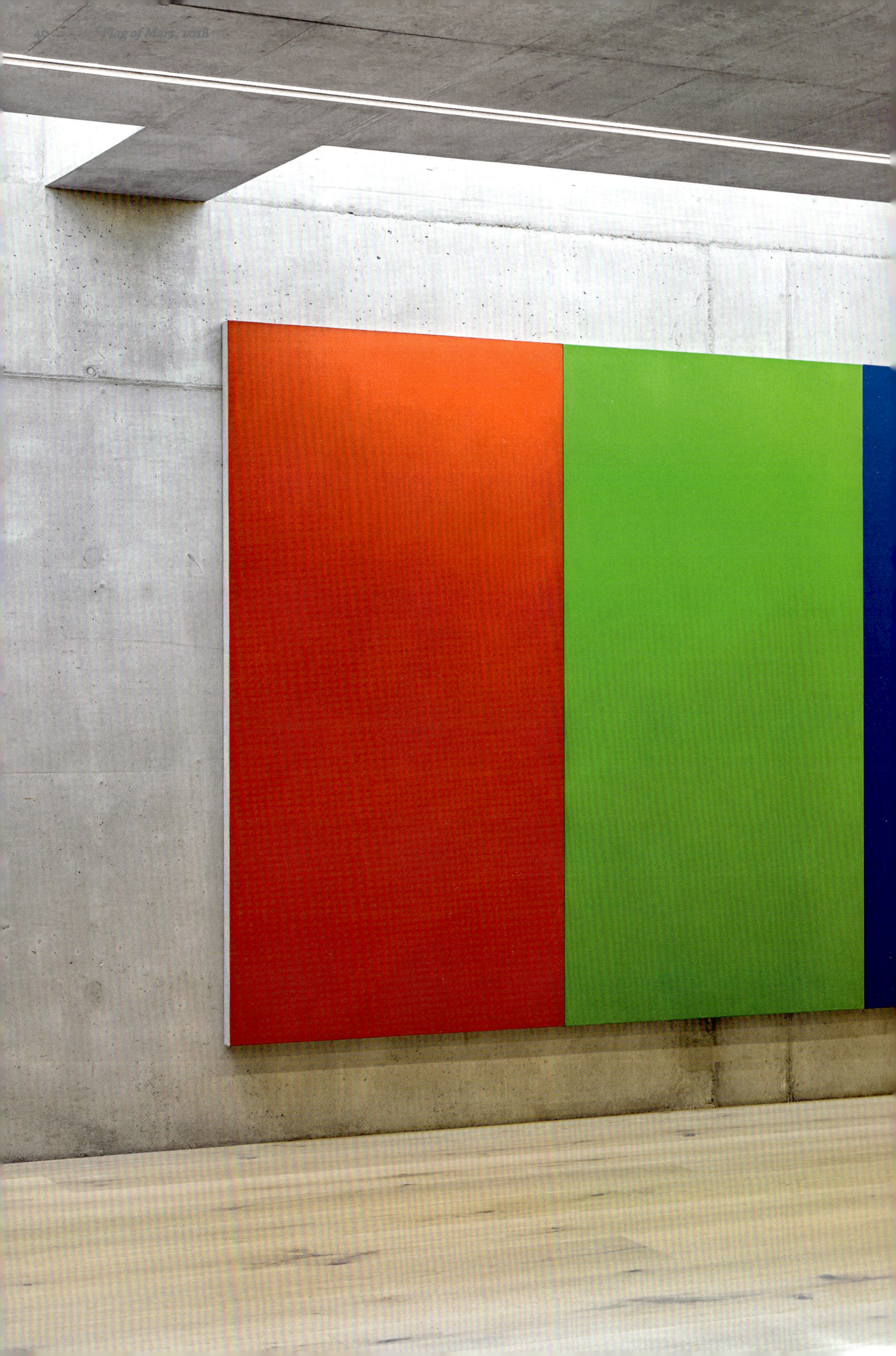

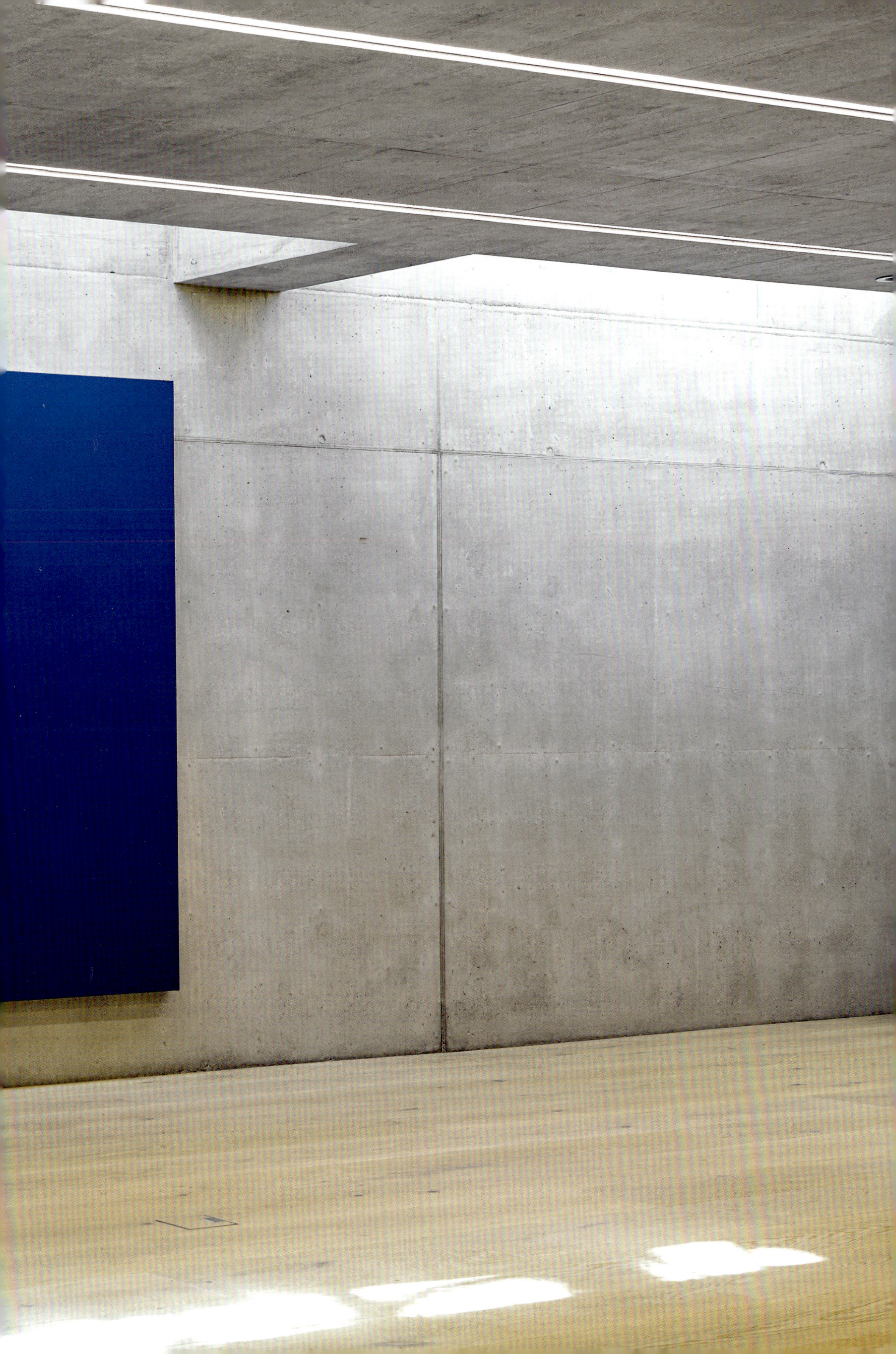

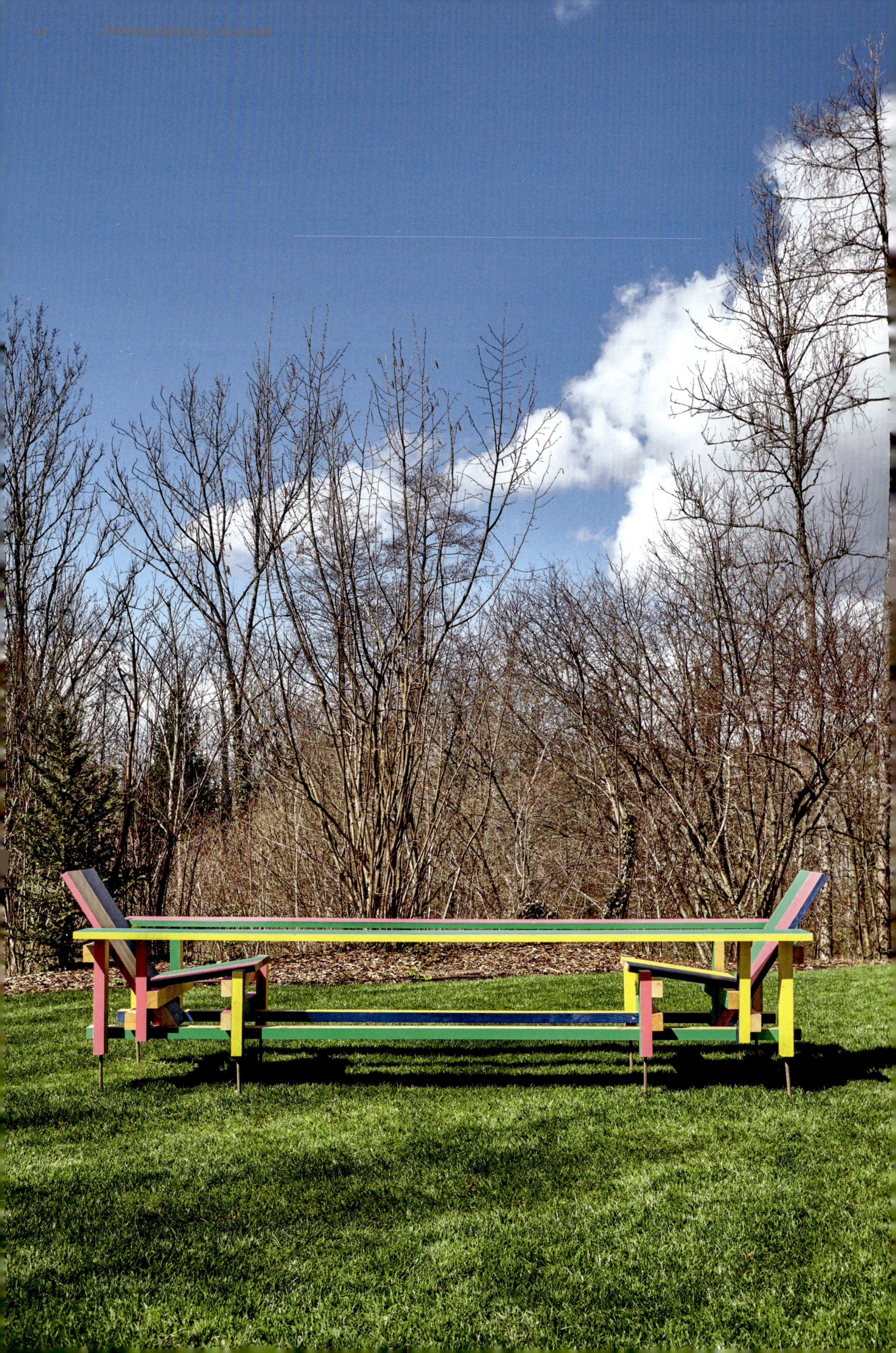

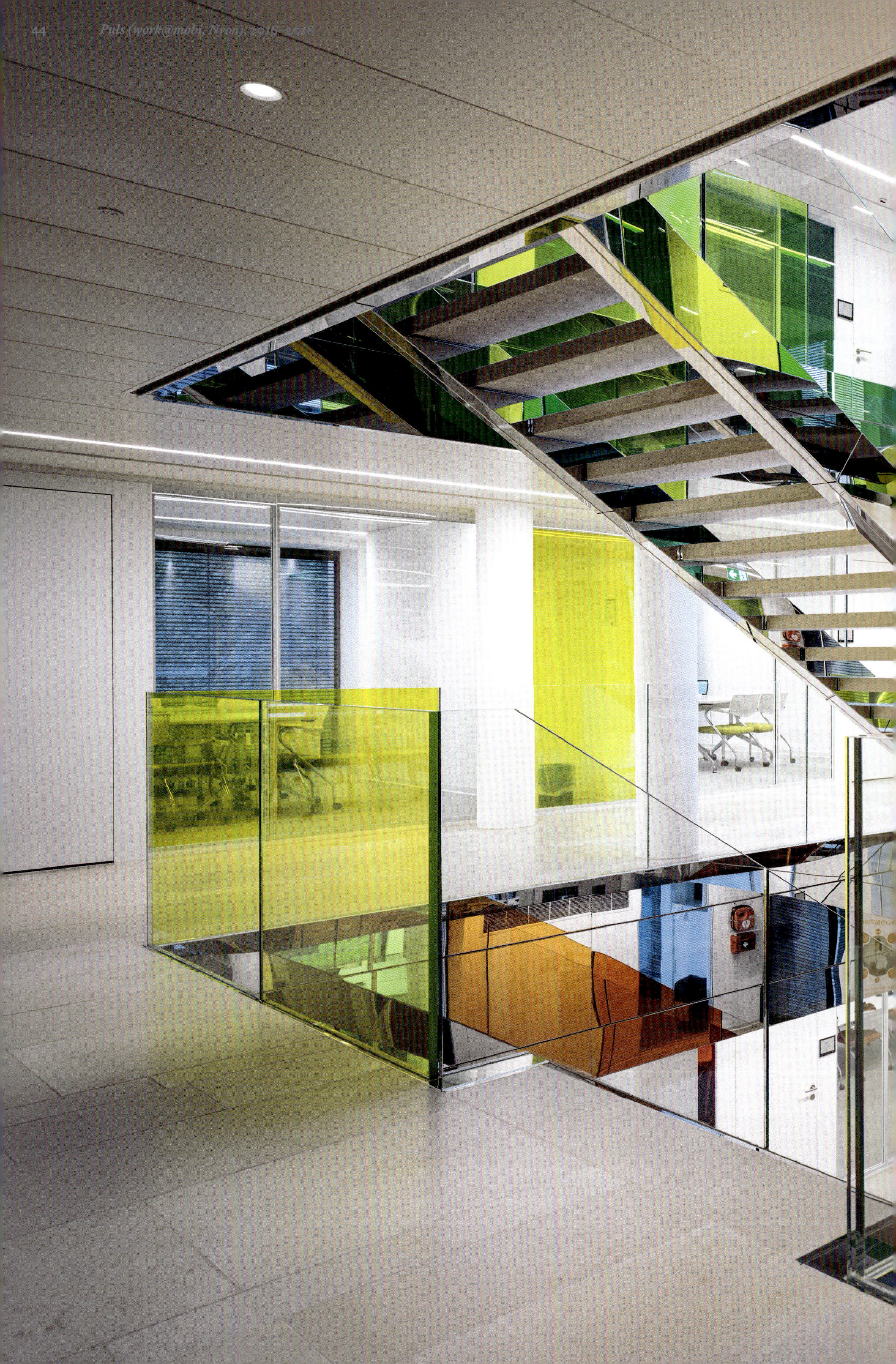

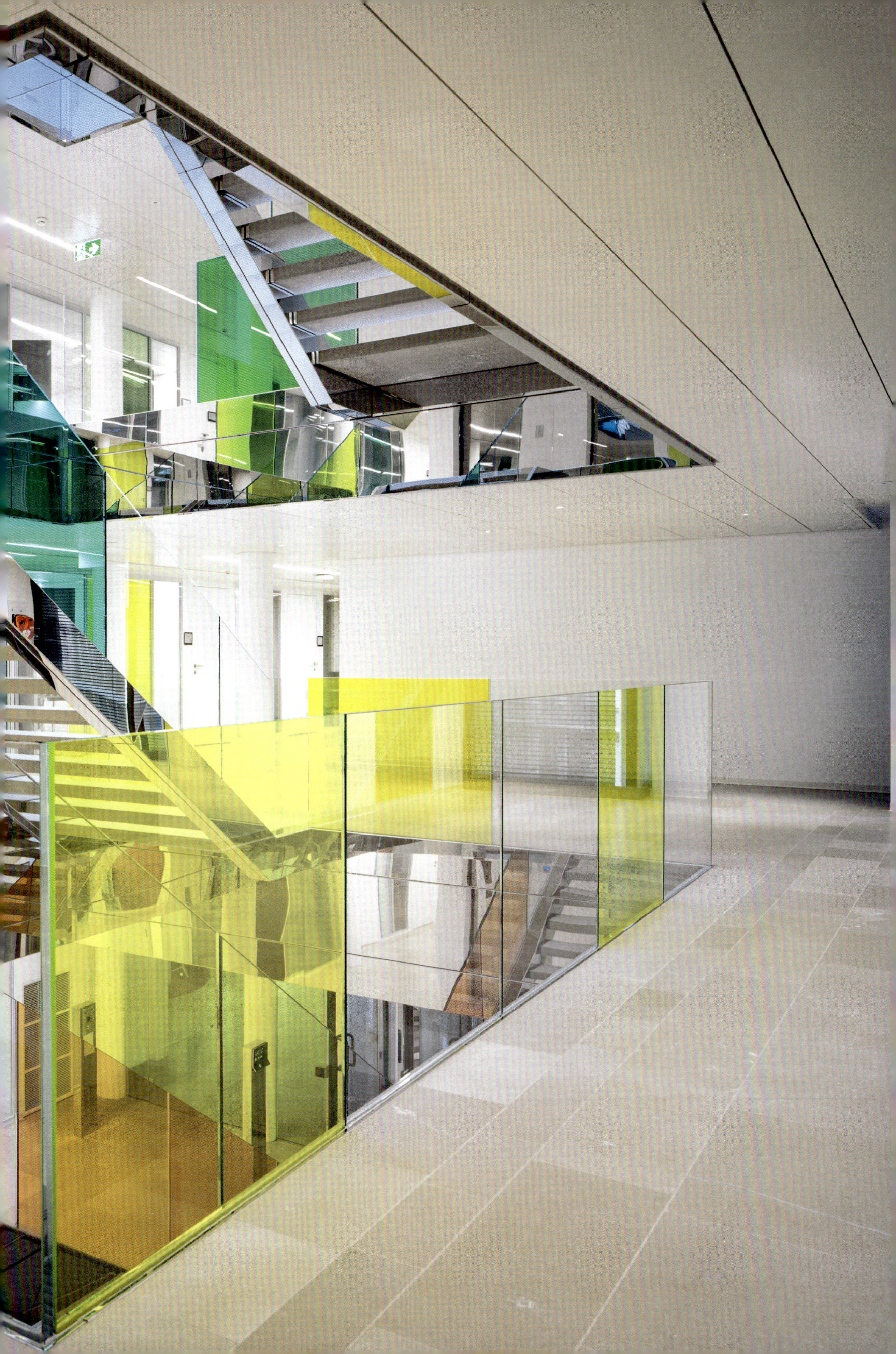

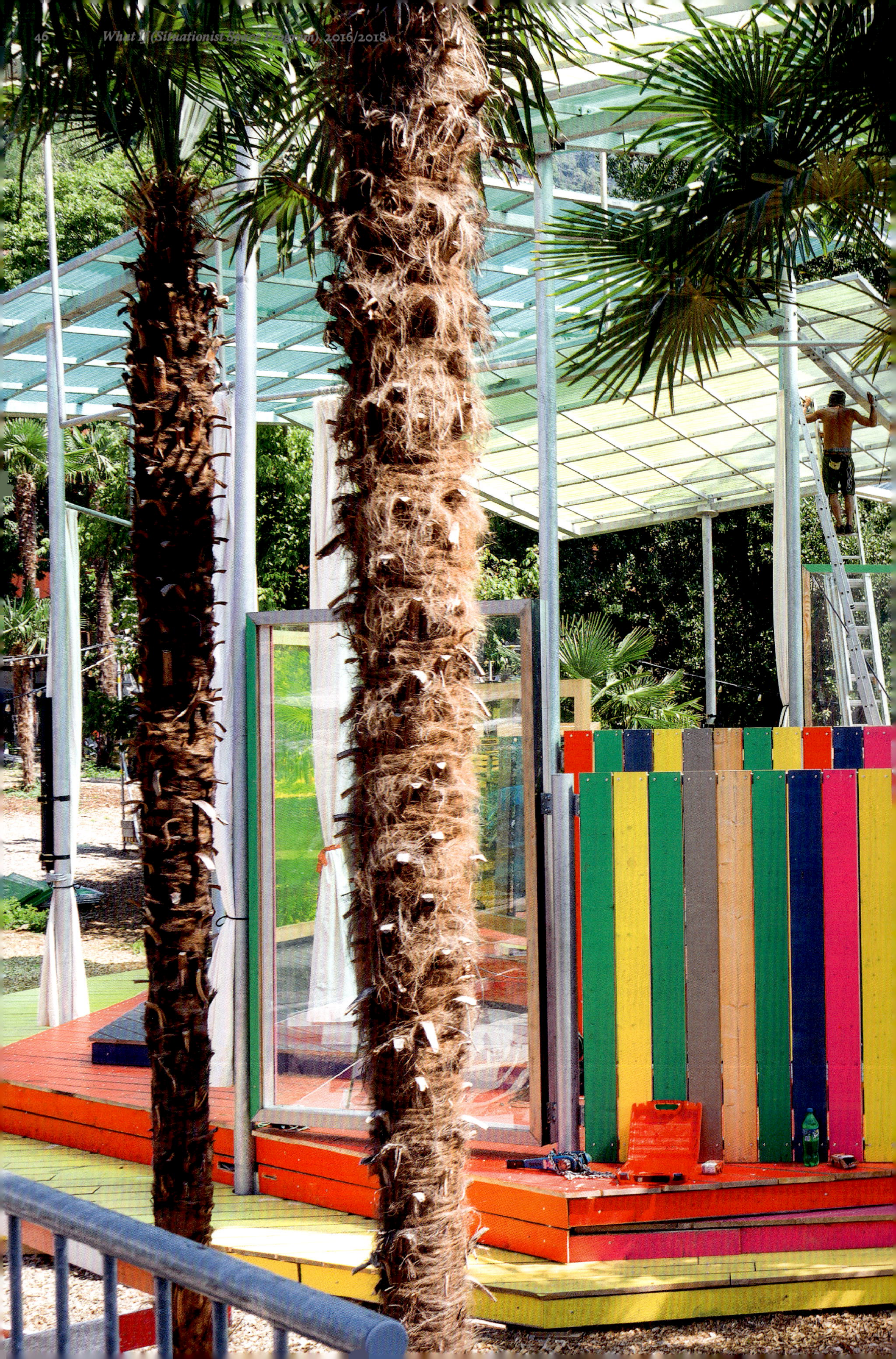

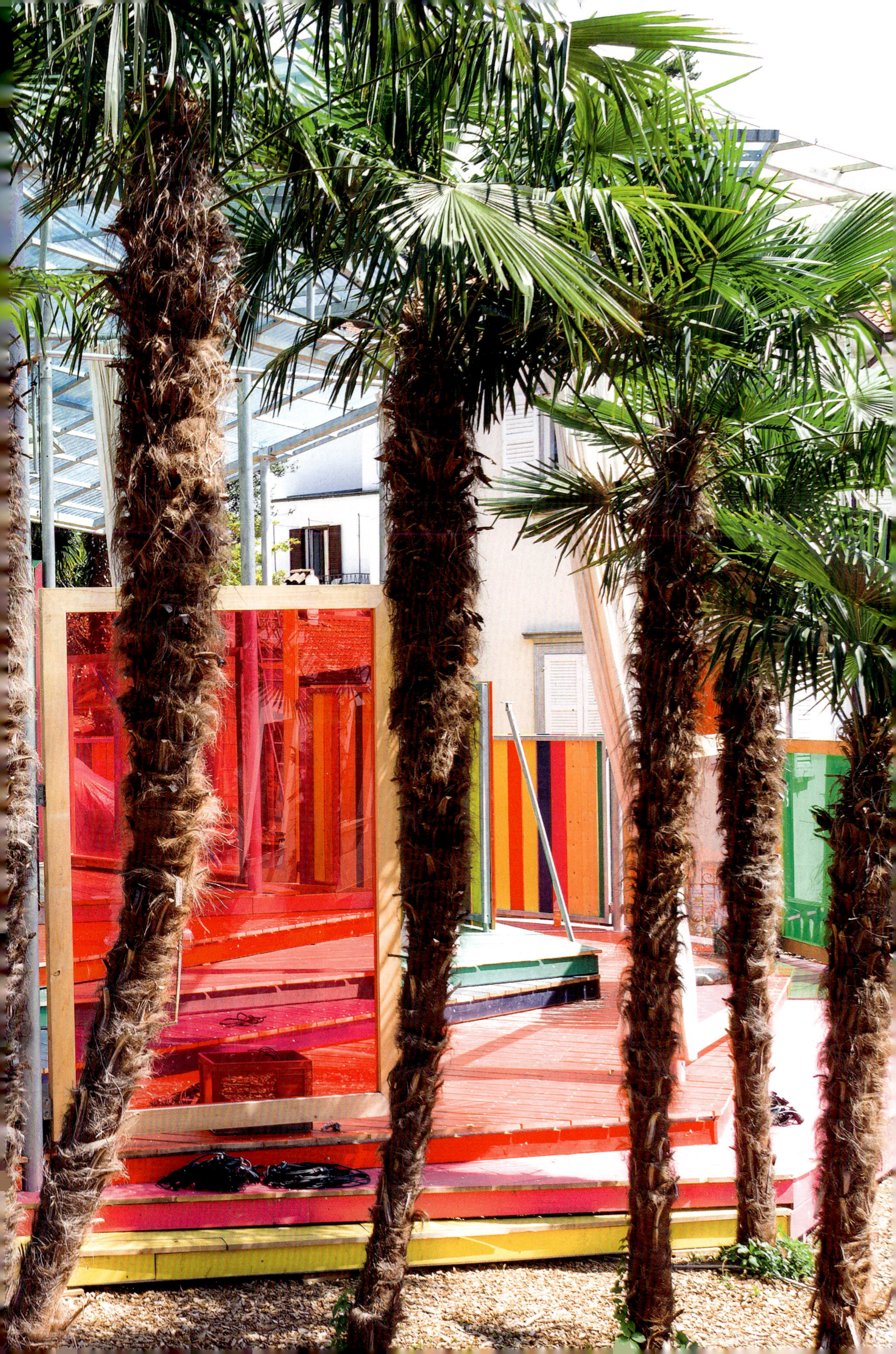

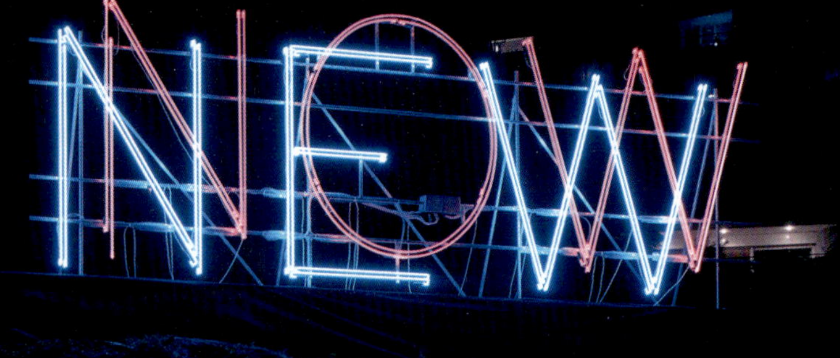
NEW
NOW

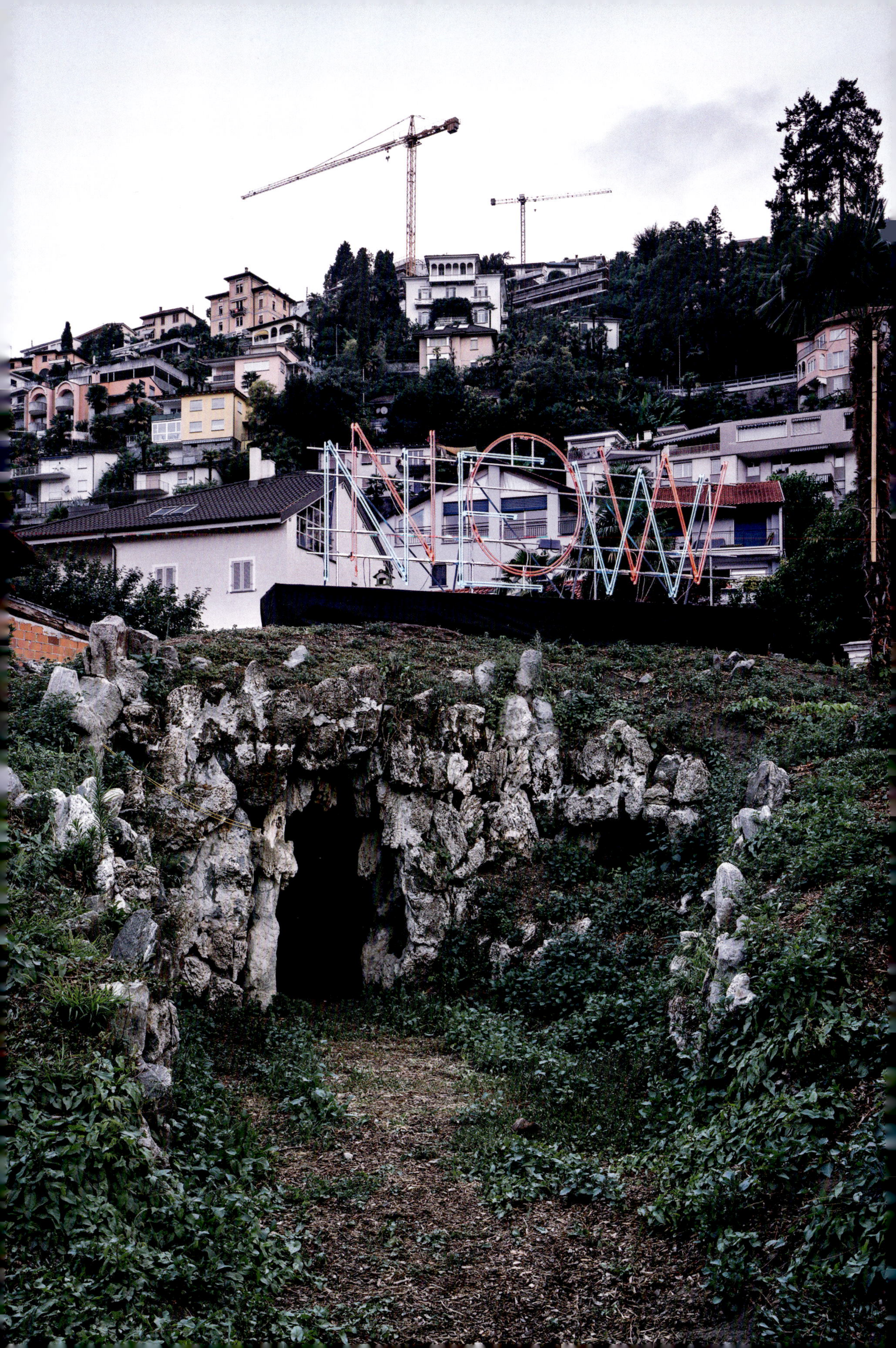
NEW
NOW

Power (Chäshalde), 2018

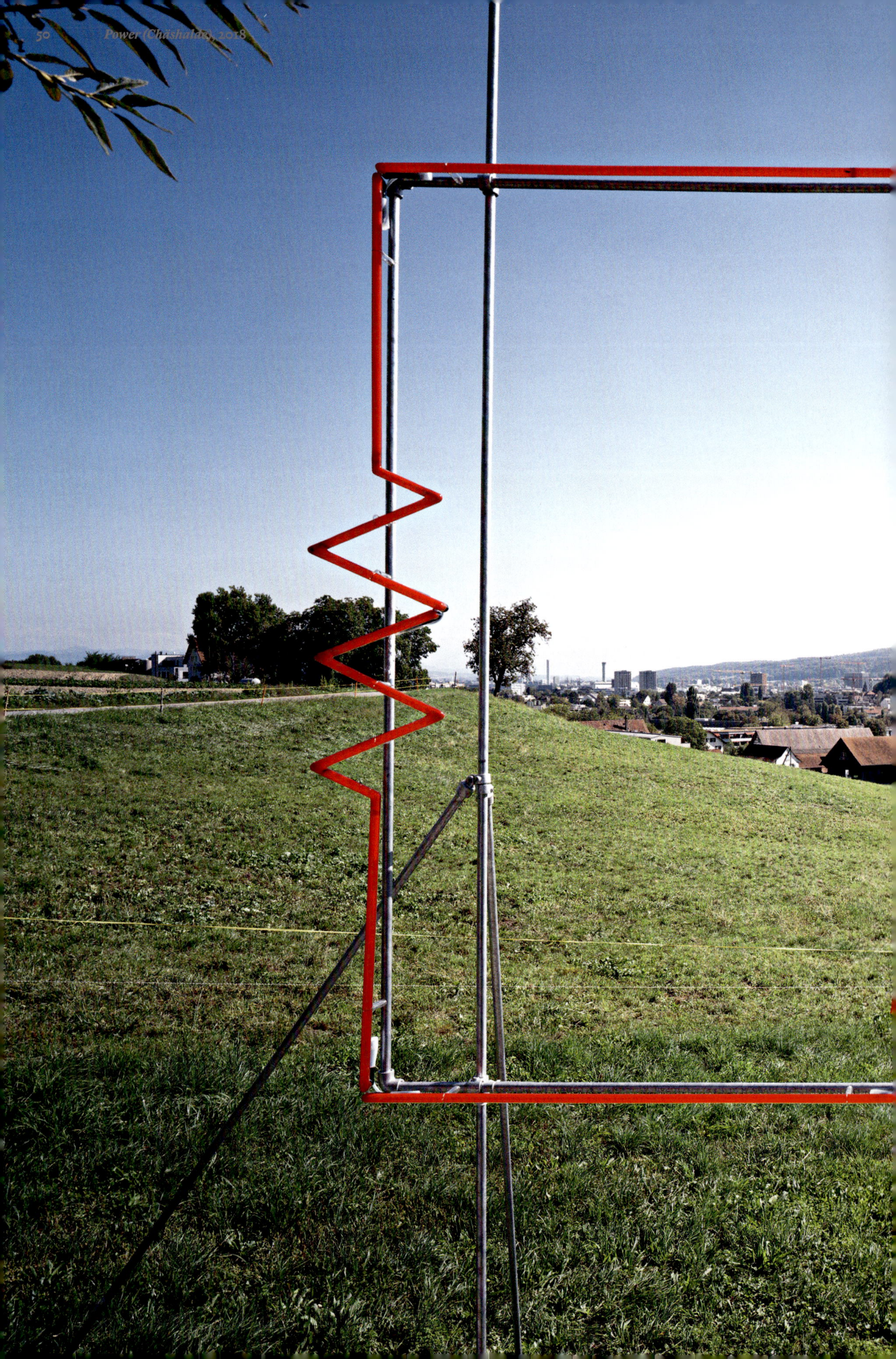

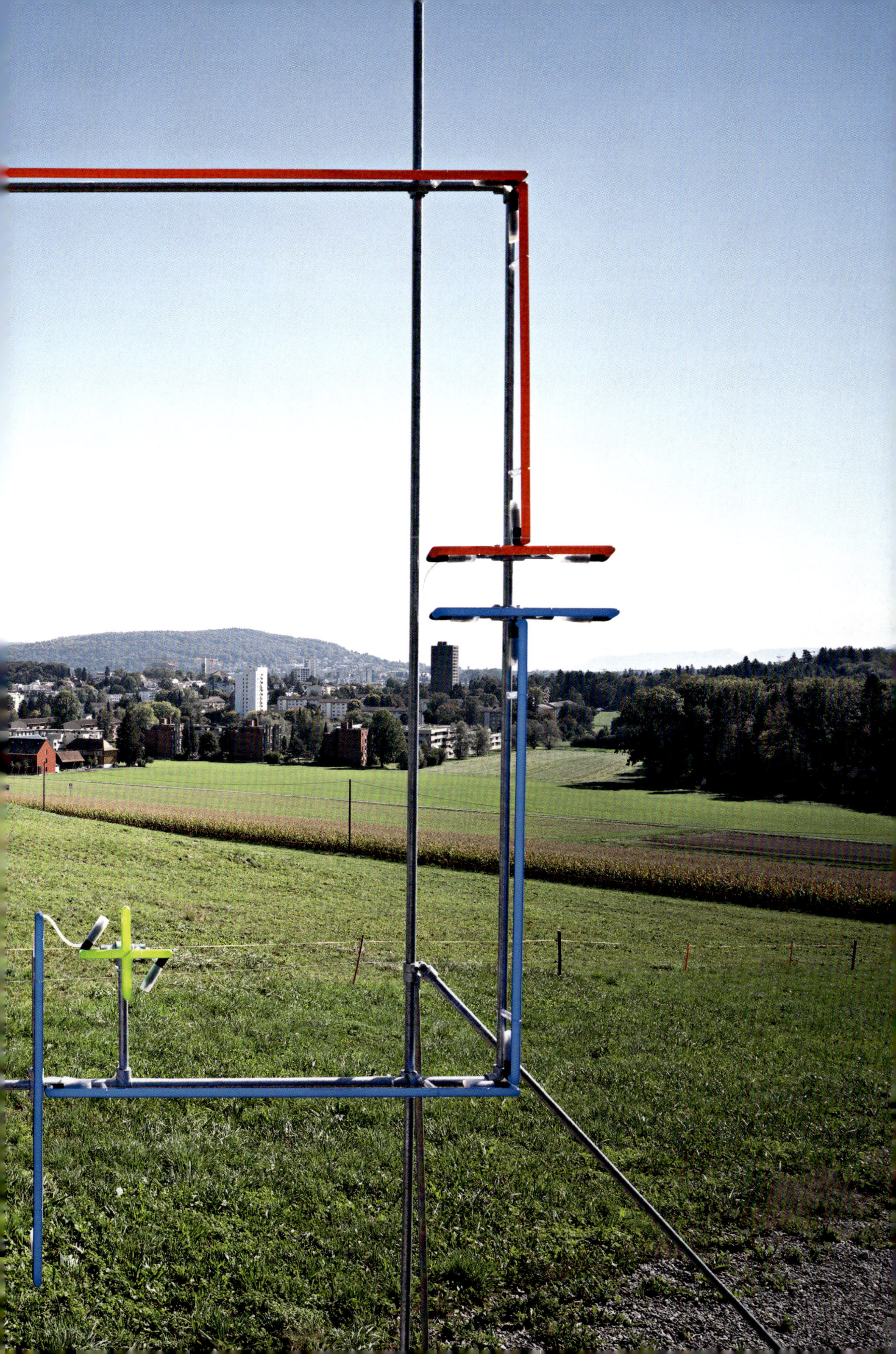

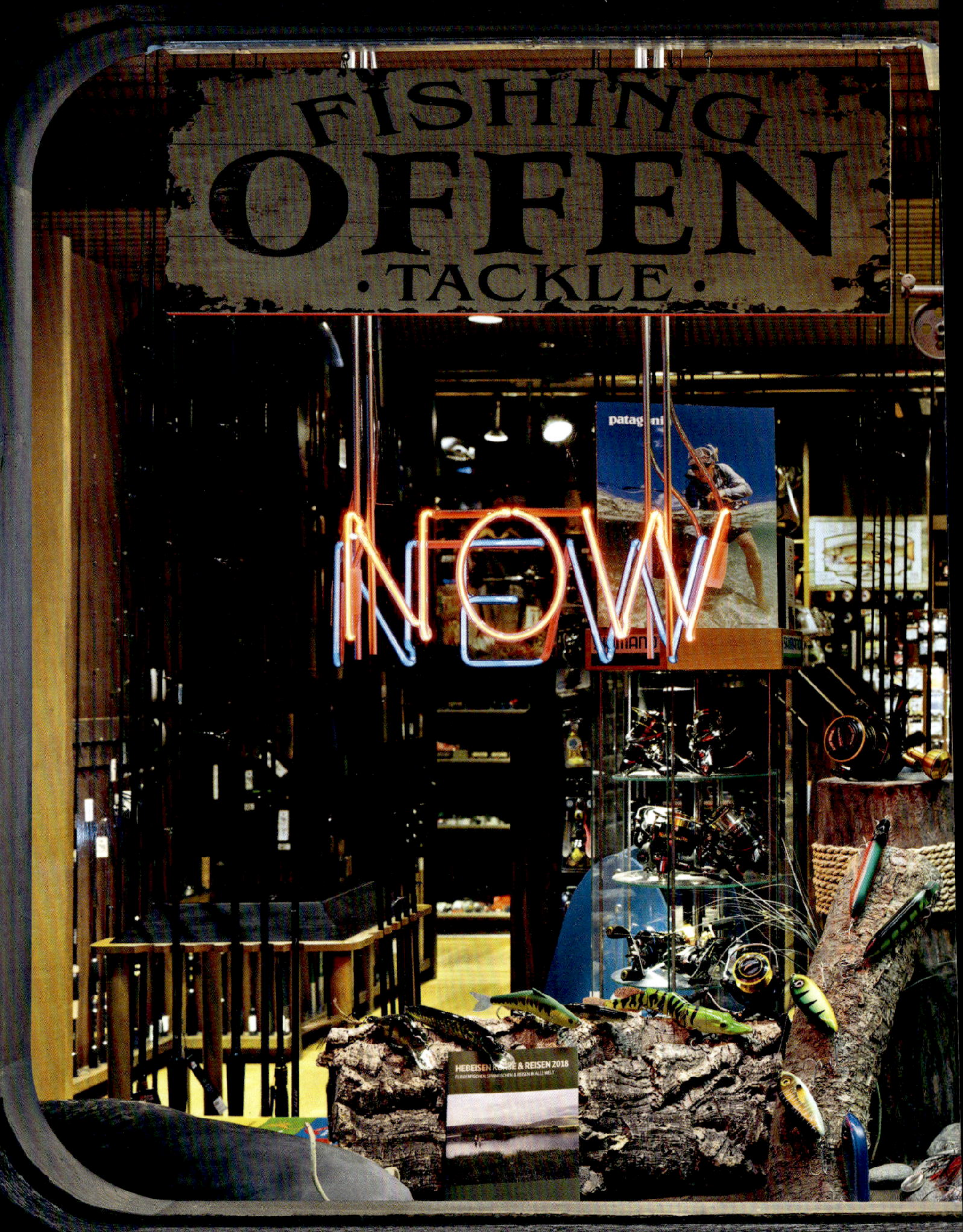
FISHING
OFFEN
·TACKLE·
NOW
NEW

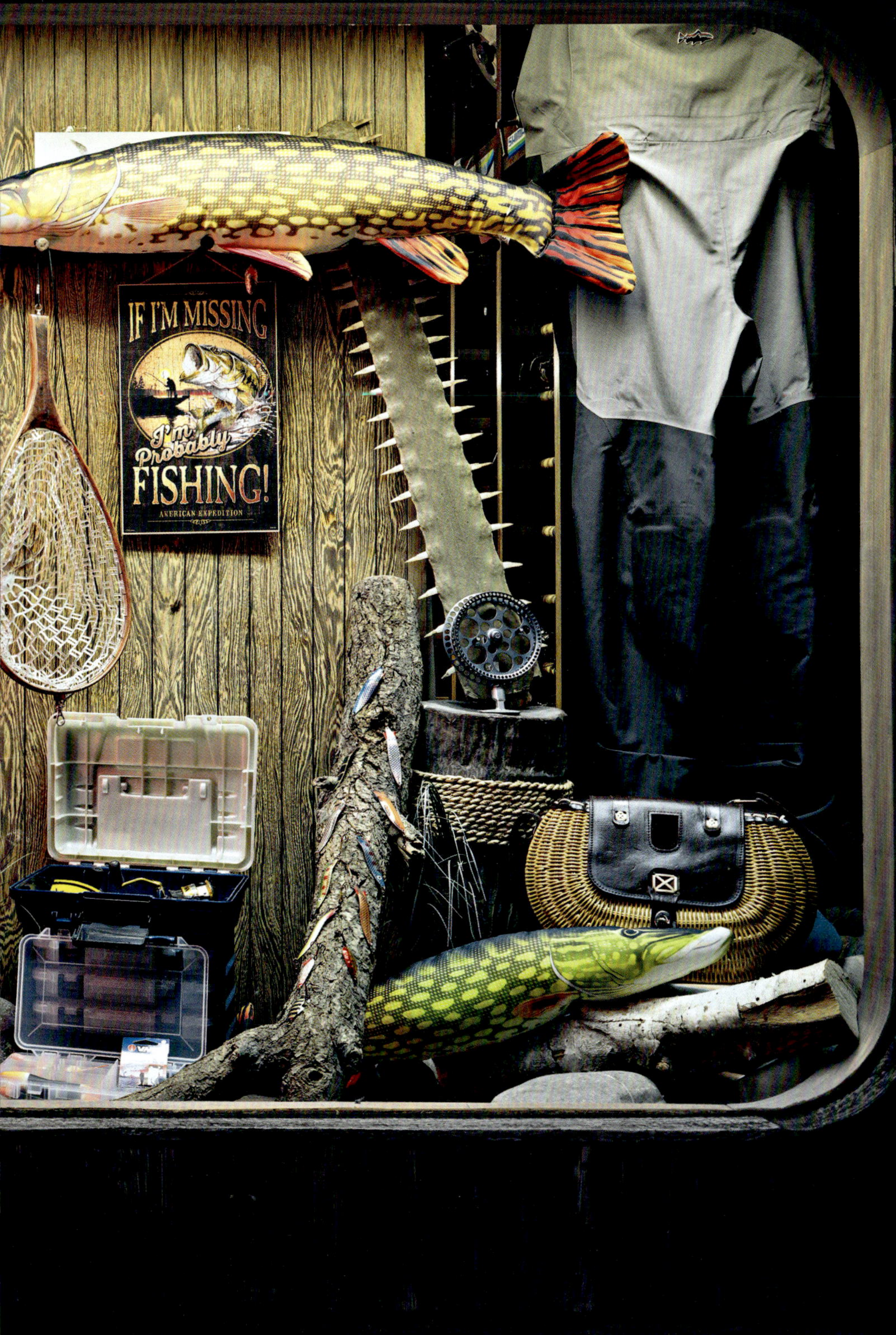
IF I'M MISSING
I'm Probably
FISHING!
AMERICAN EXPEDITION

NE TRAVAILLEZ JAMAIS (Hürstholz), 2018

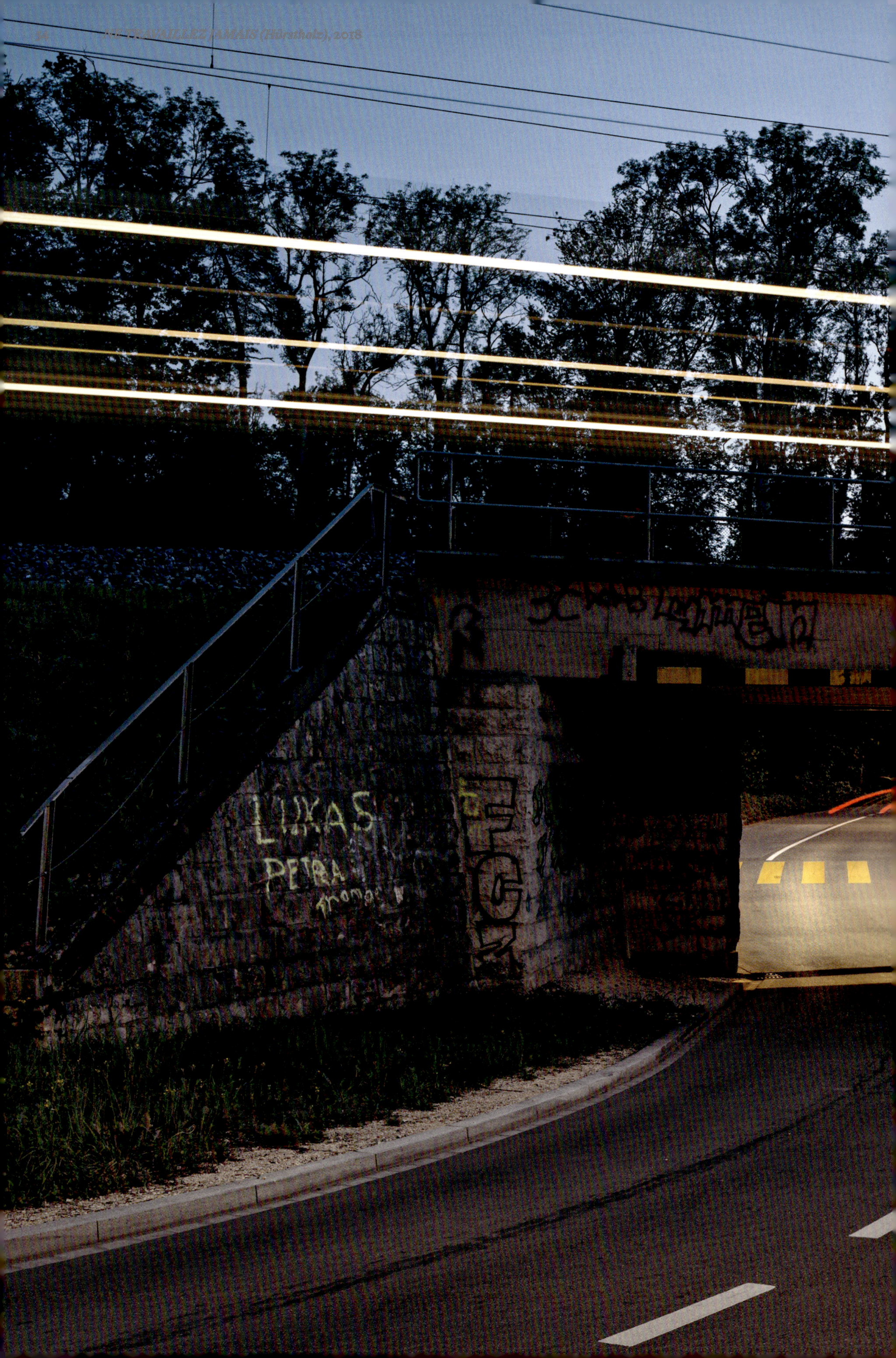

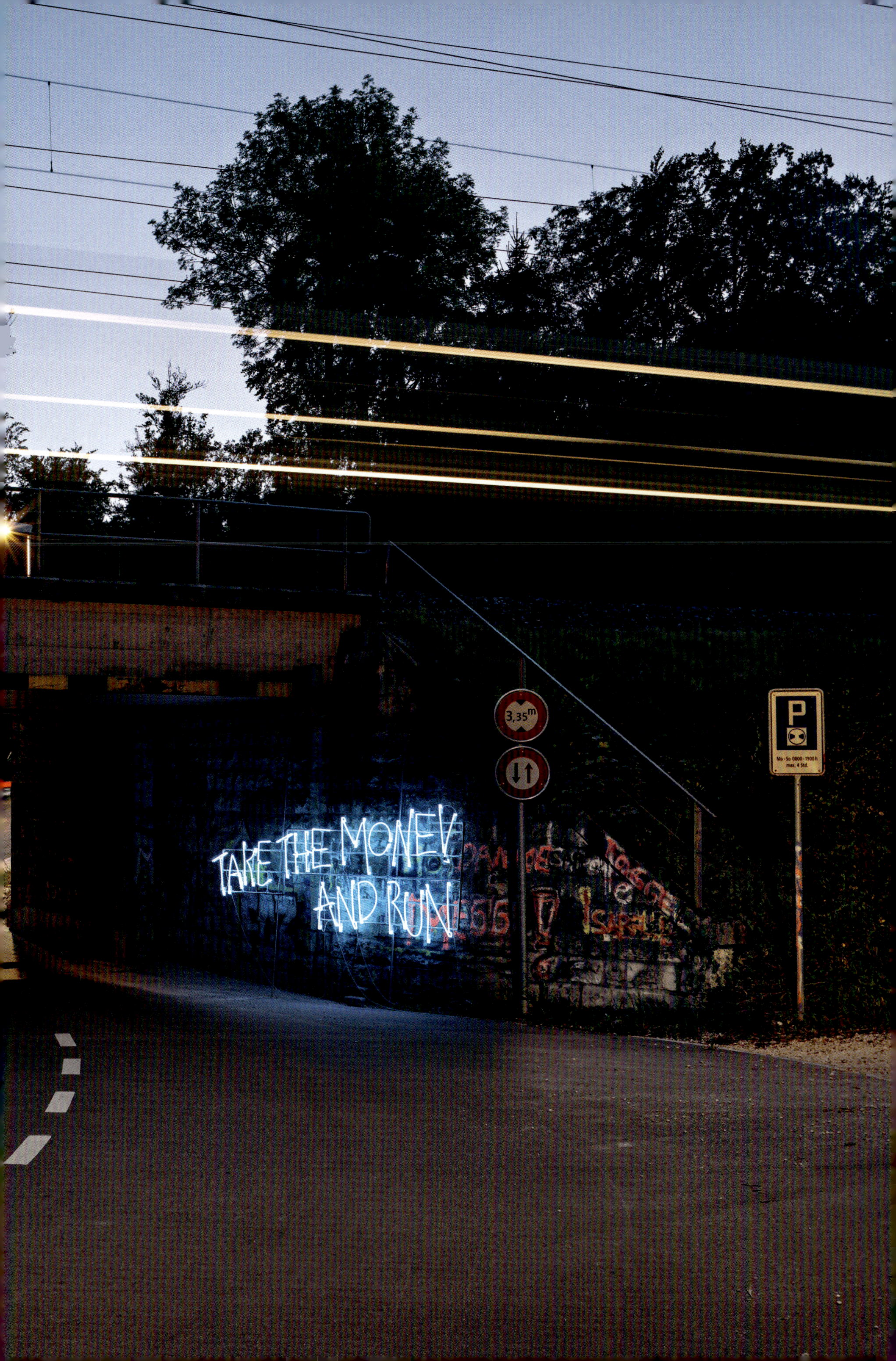
TAKE THE MONEY
AND RUN
3,35m
P

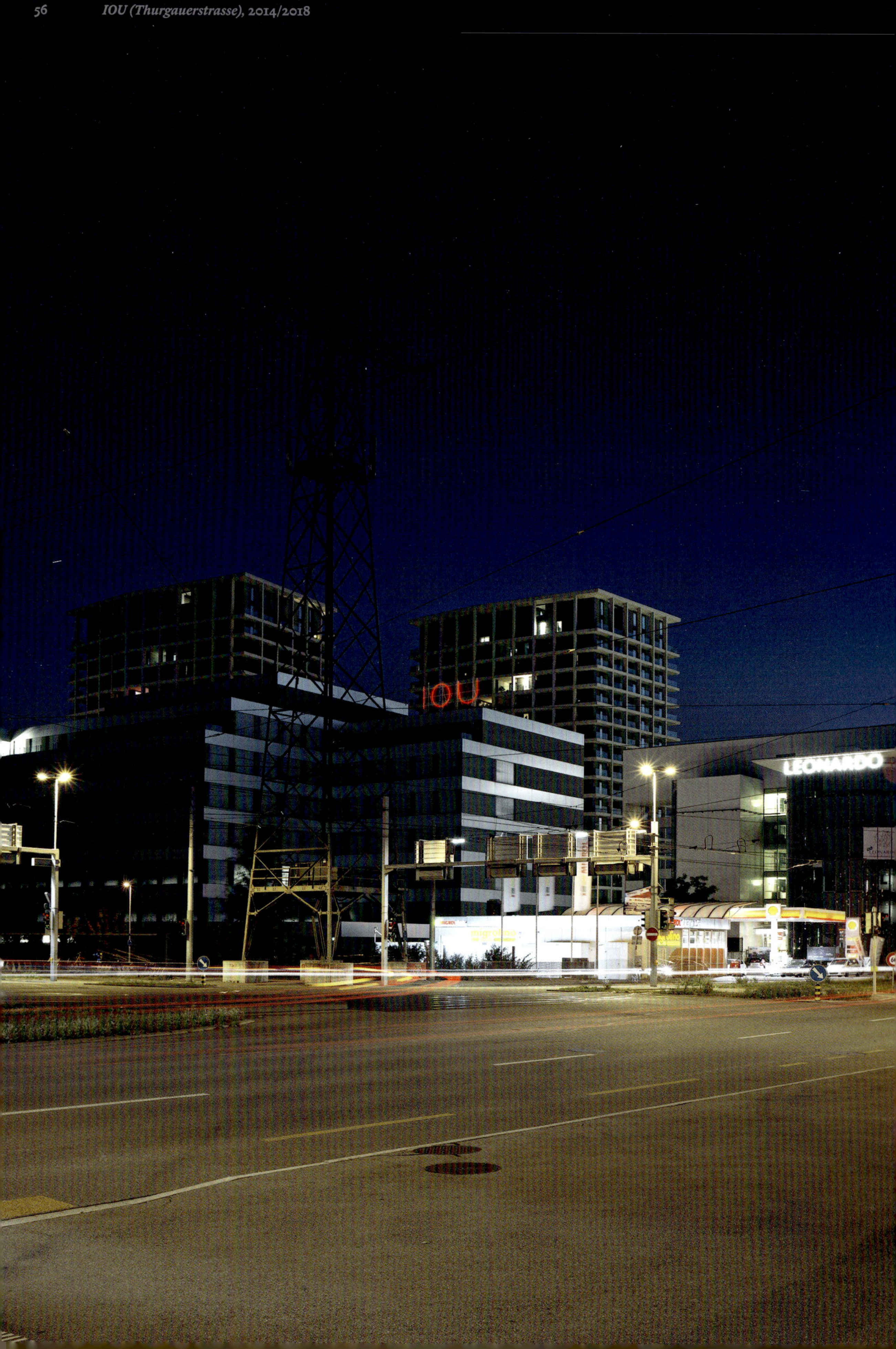
IOU
LEONARDO

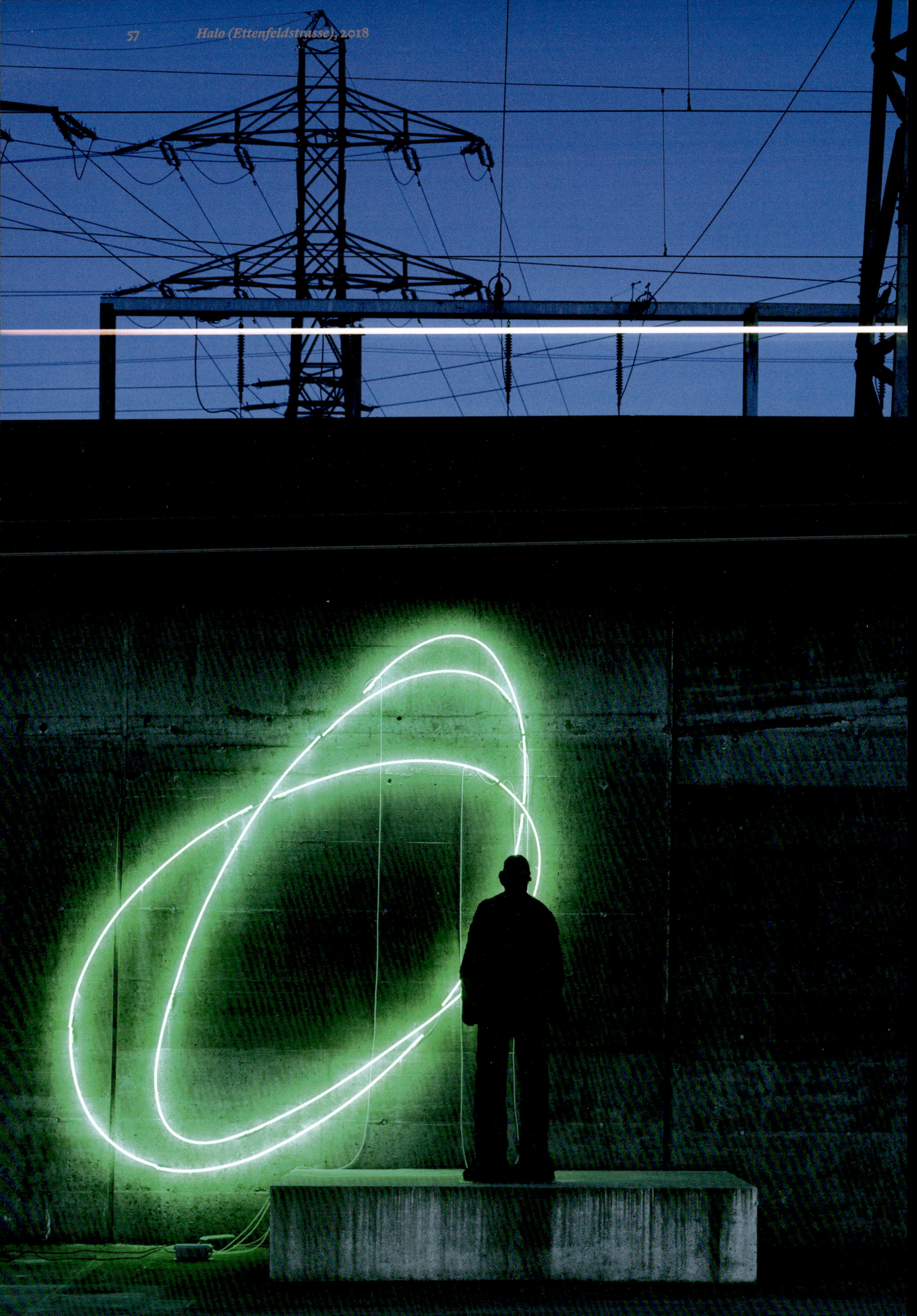

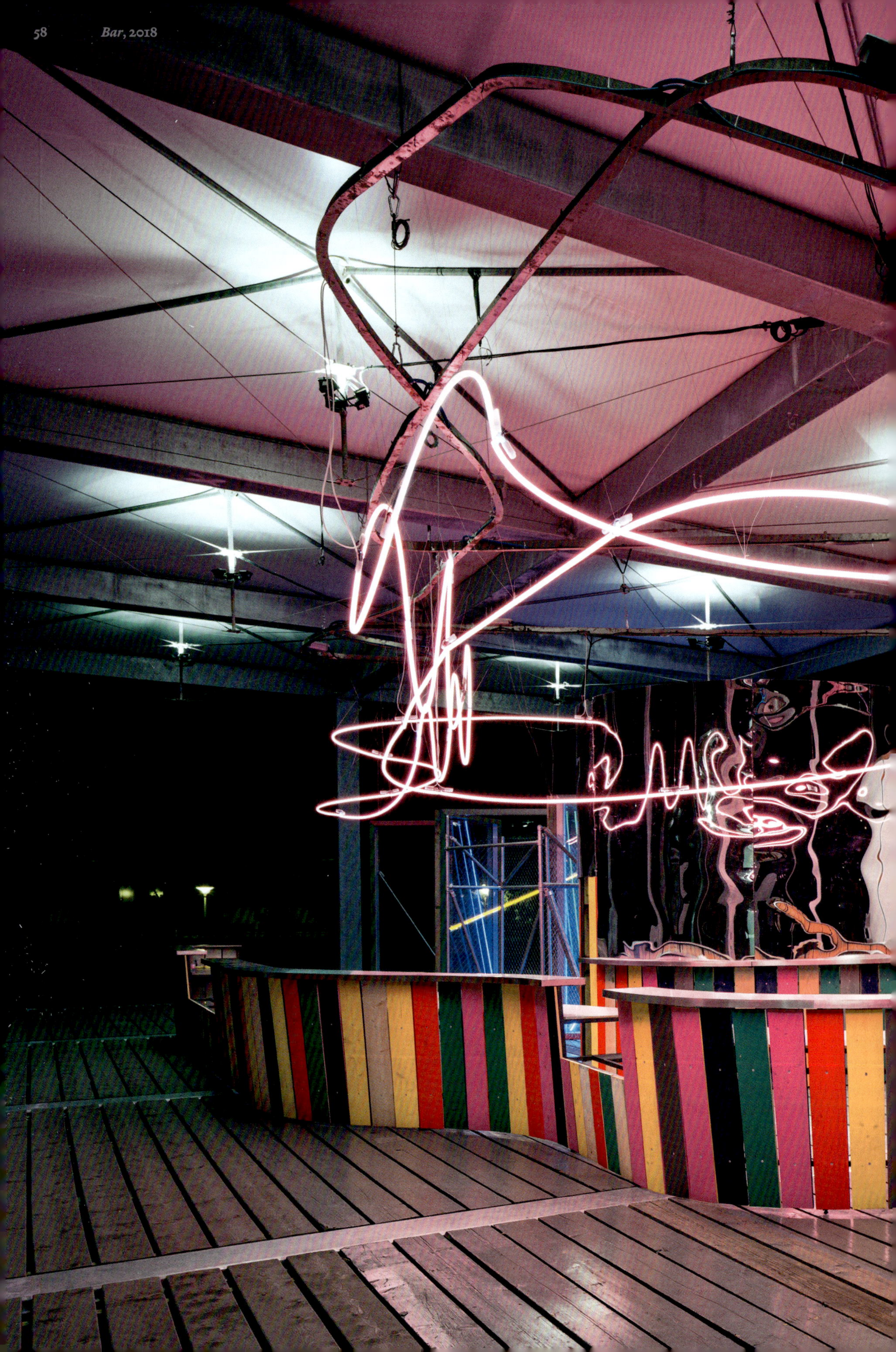

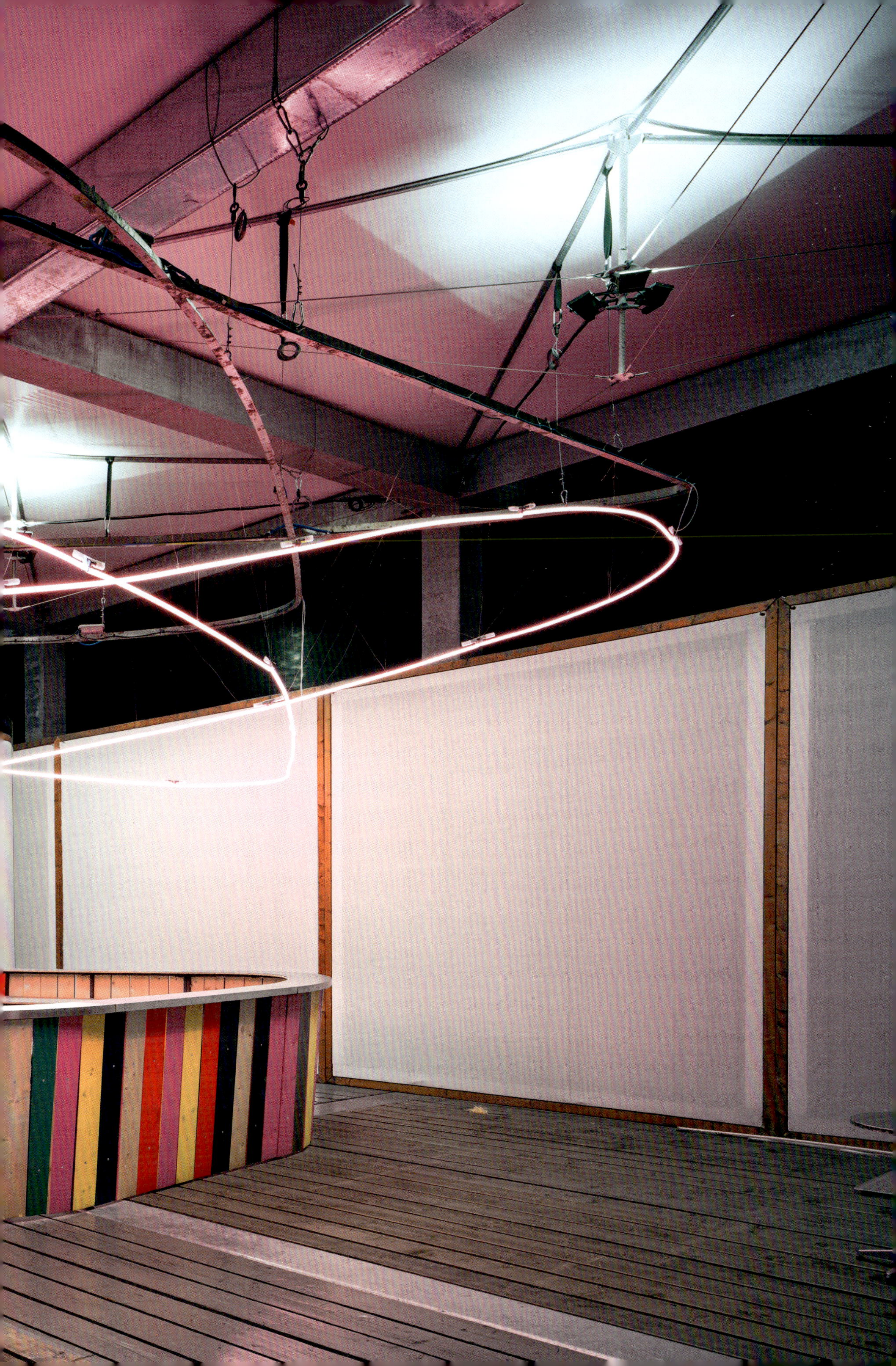

61 Ours d'après Régine Gallard (Paradeplatz), 20[illegible]

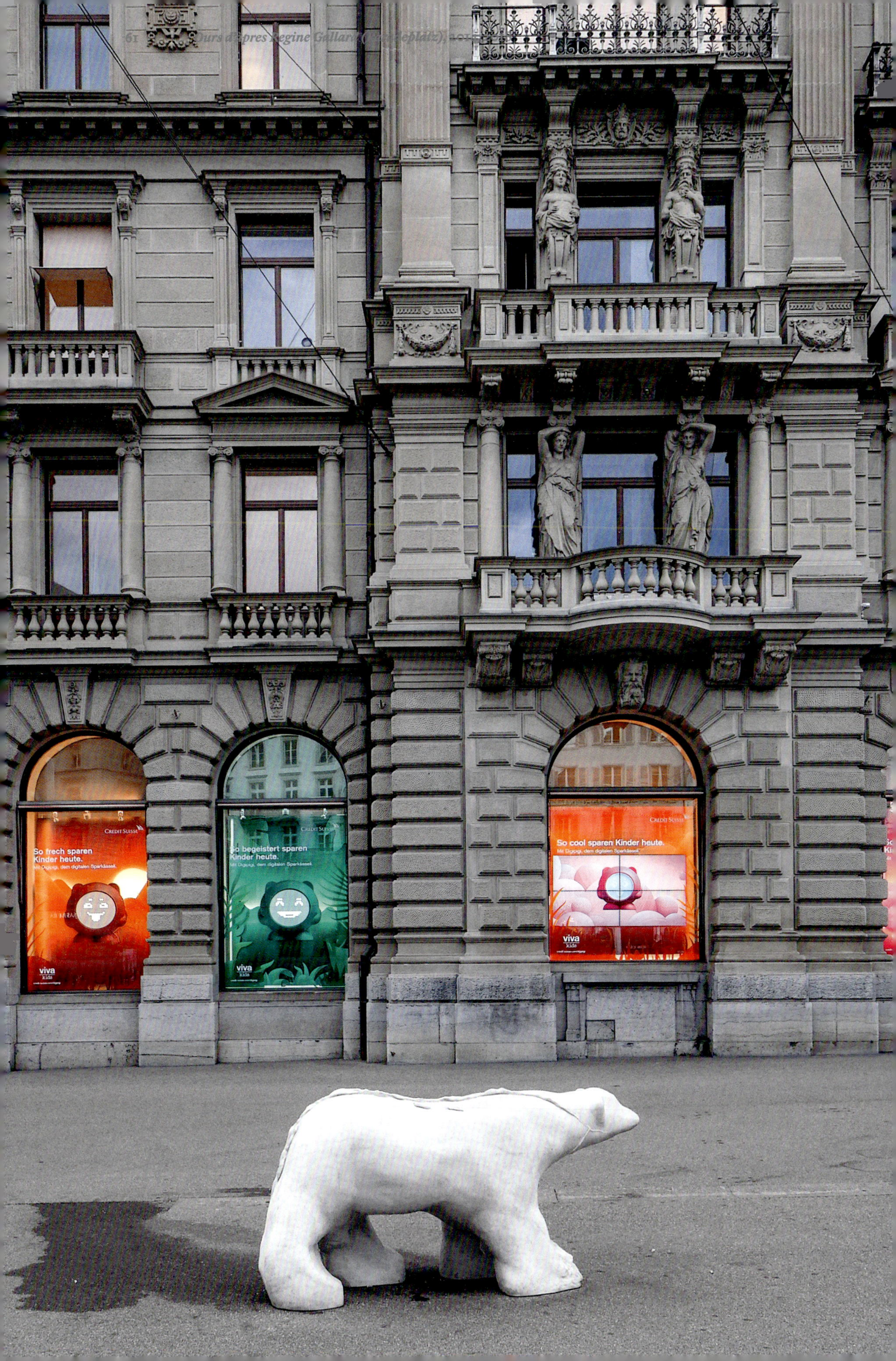

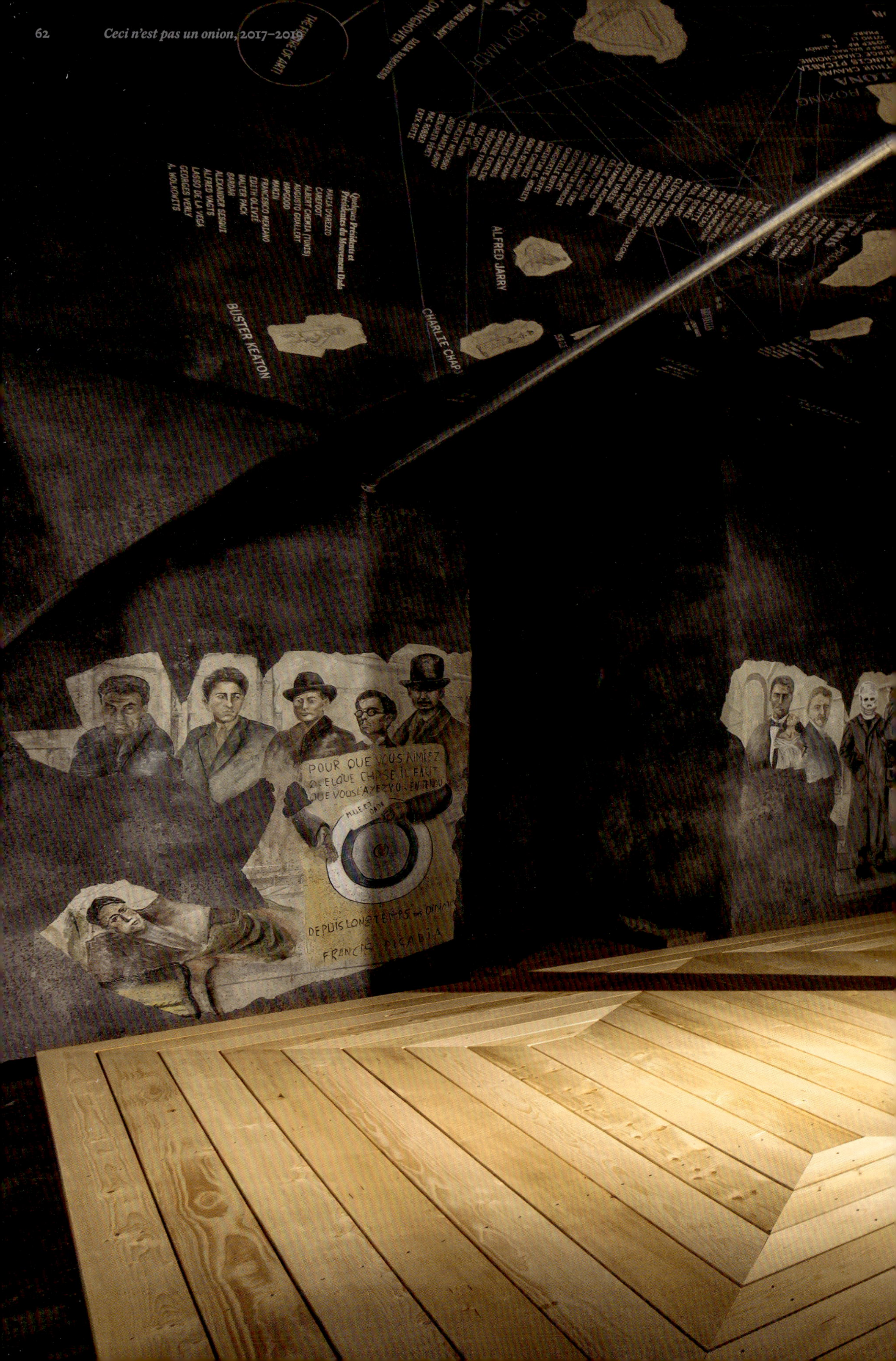
READY MADE
ALFRED JARRY
BUSTER KEATON
CHARLIE CHAP
POUR QUE VOUS AIMIEZ
QUELQUE CHOSE IL FAUT
QUE VOUS L'AYEZ VU ET ENTENDU

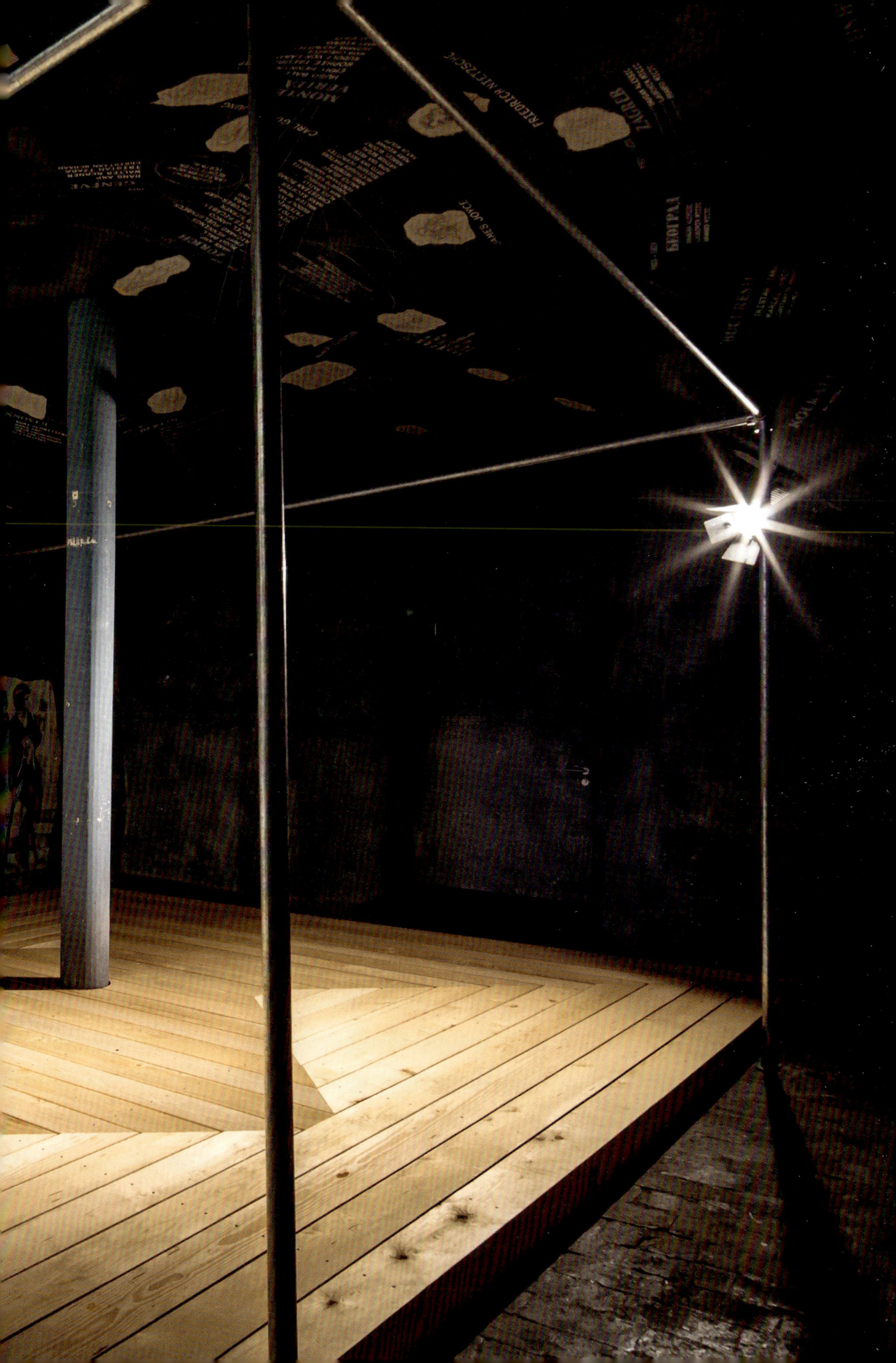
FRIEDRICH NIETZSCHE
ZAGREB
JAMES JOYCE

Labyrinth (Mos_Espa), 2012/2017

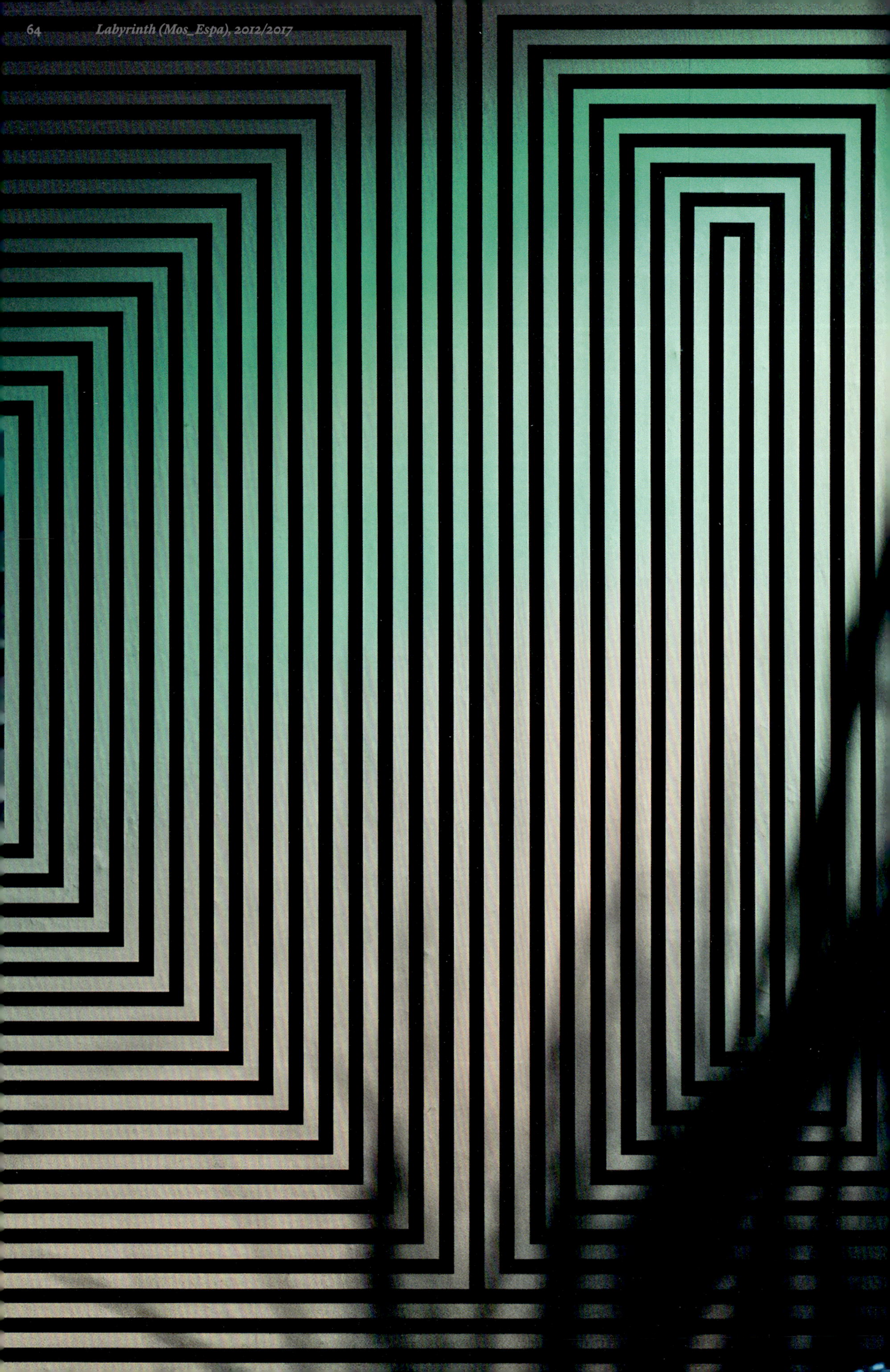

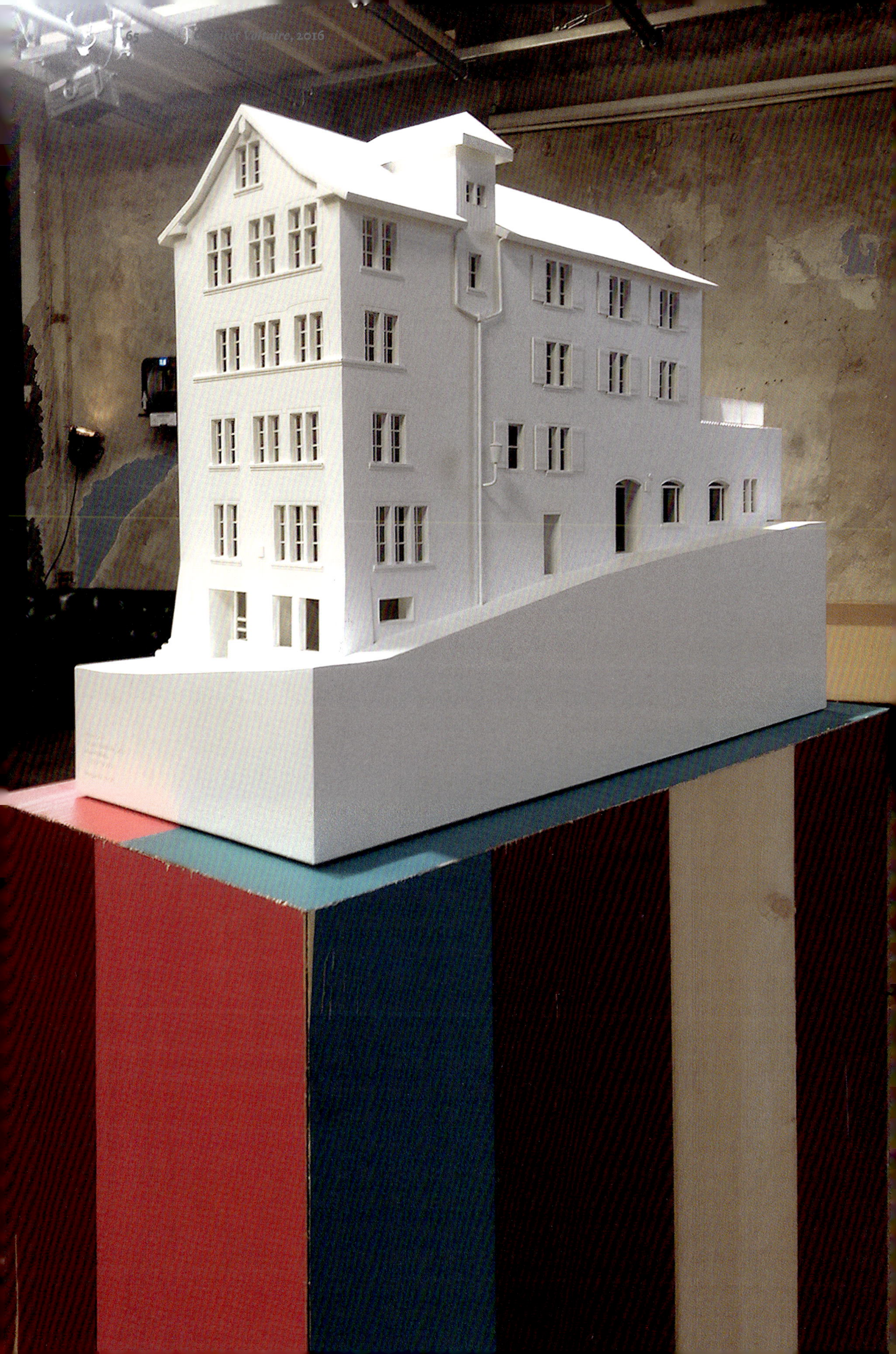

Voltaire, 2016

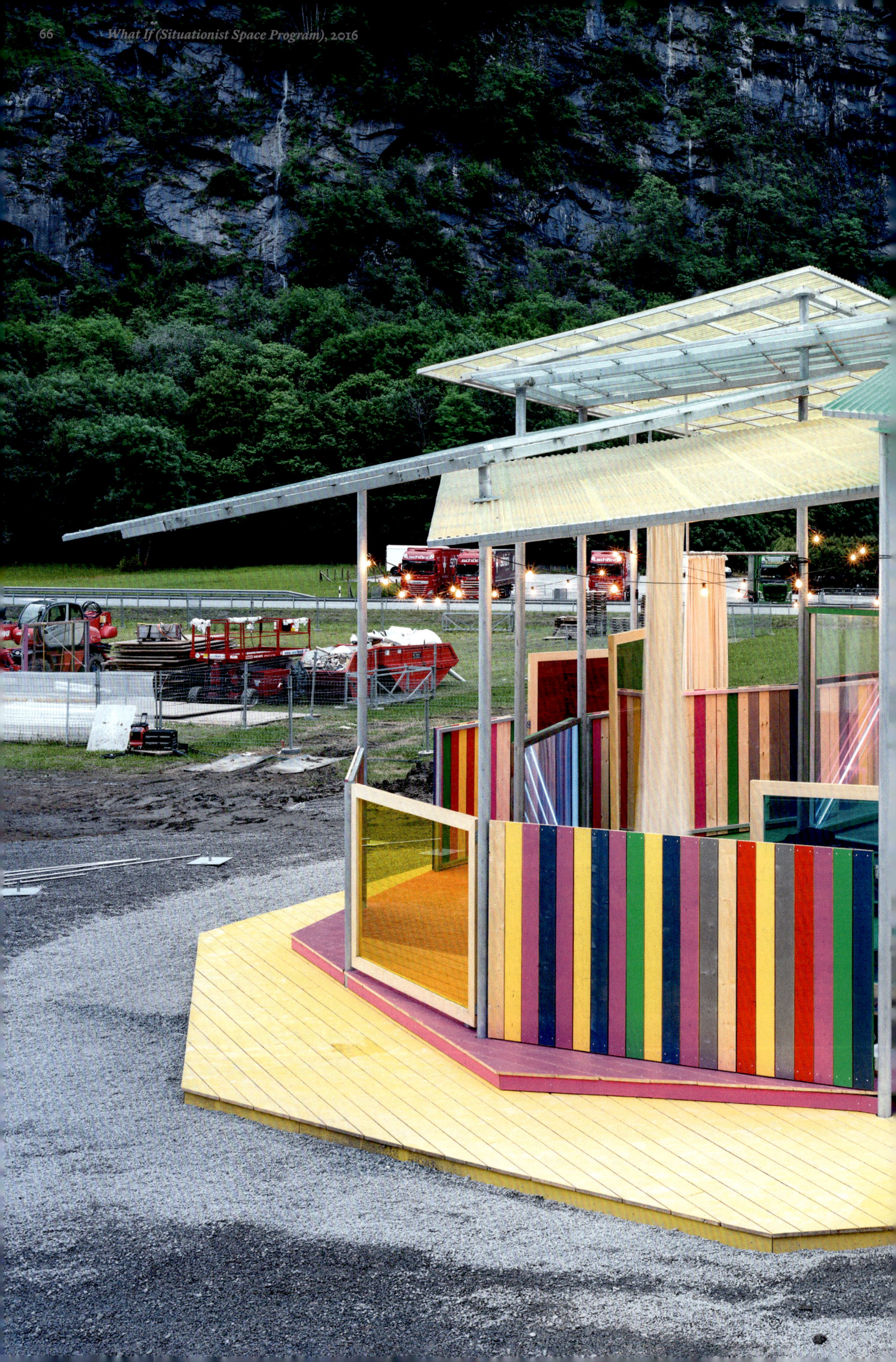

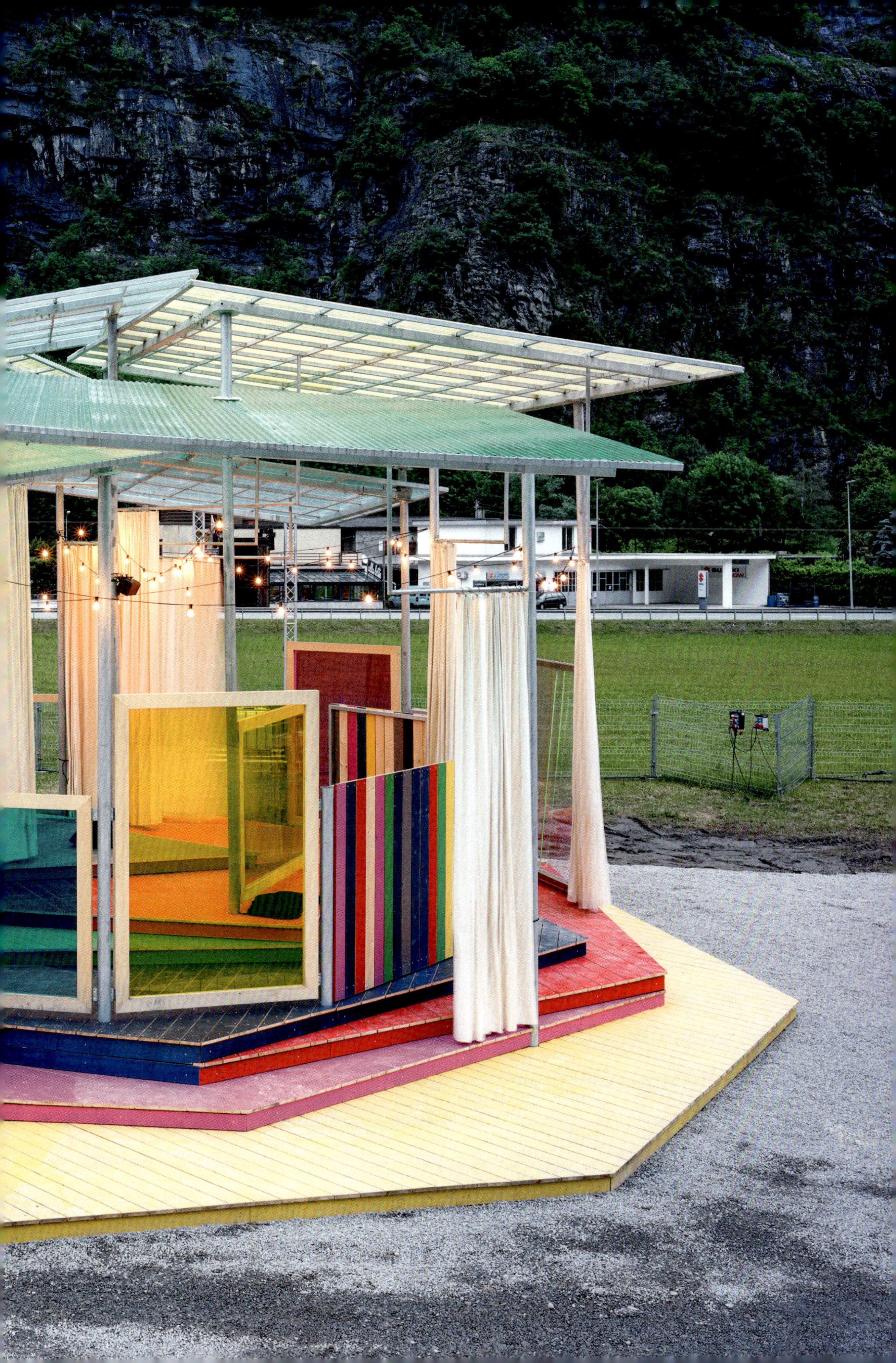

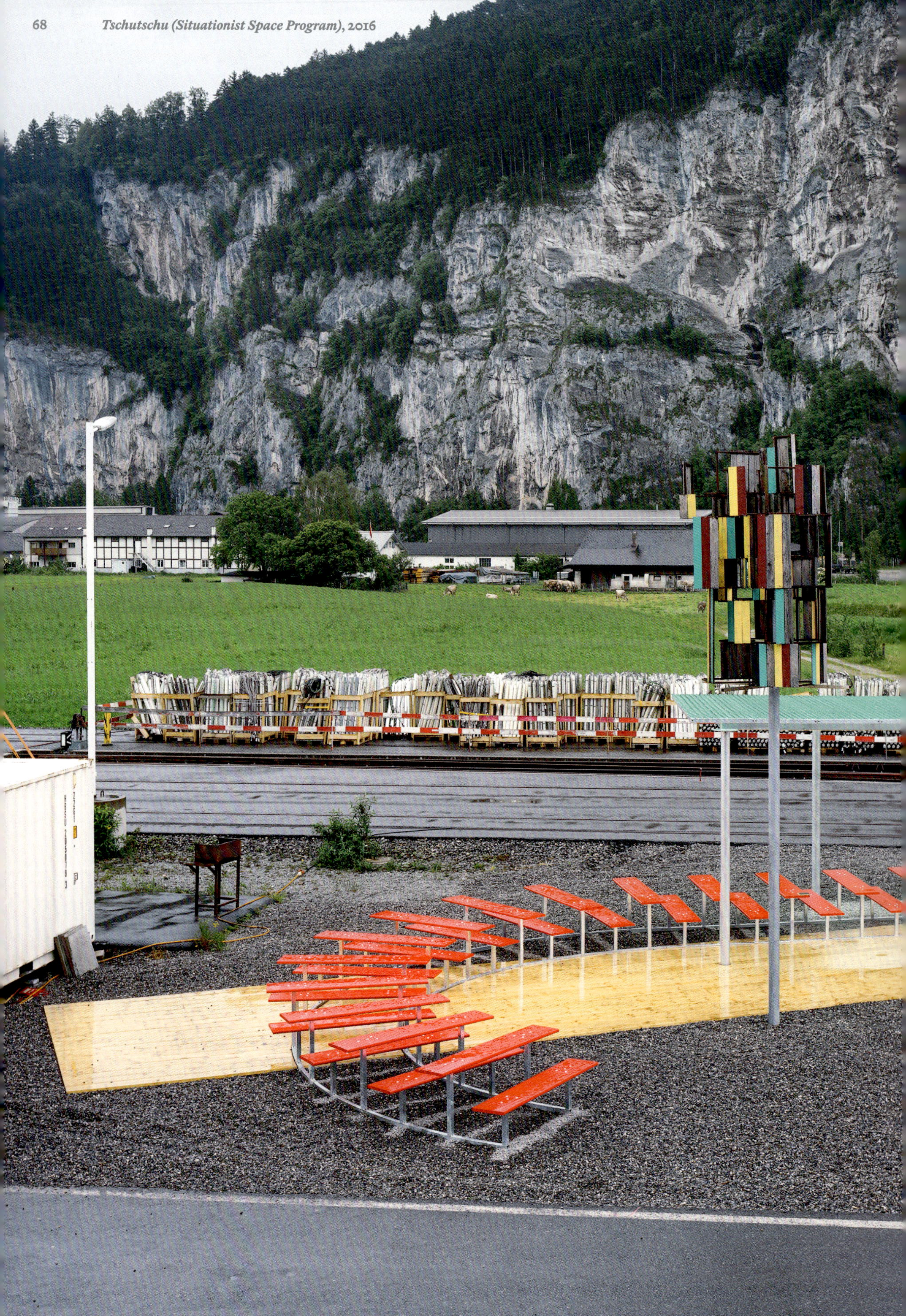

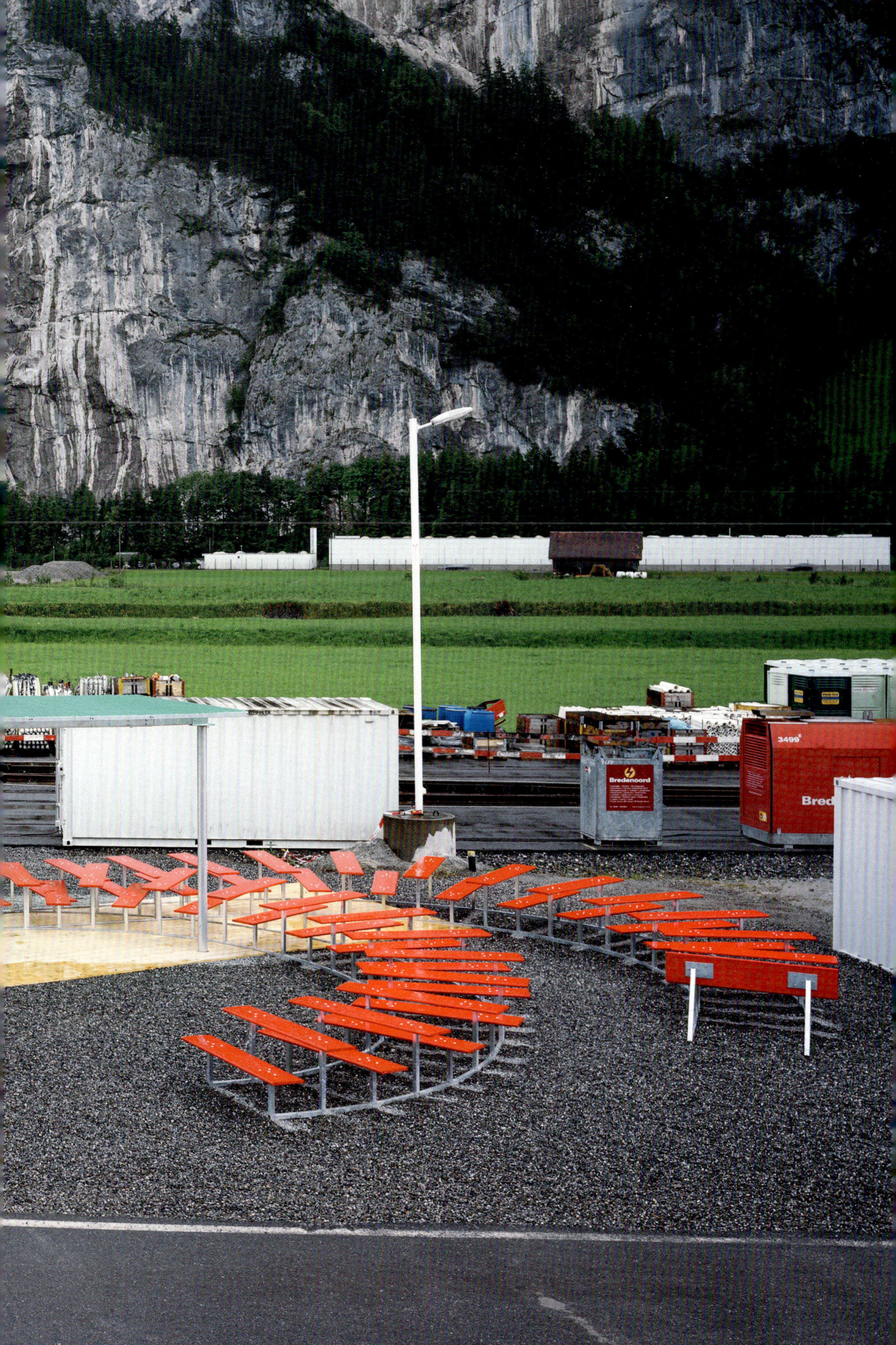
3499
Bredenoord

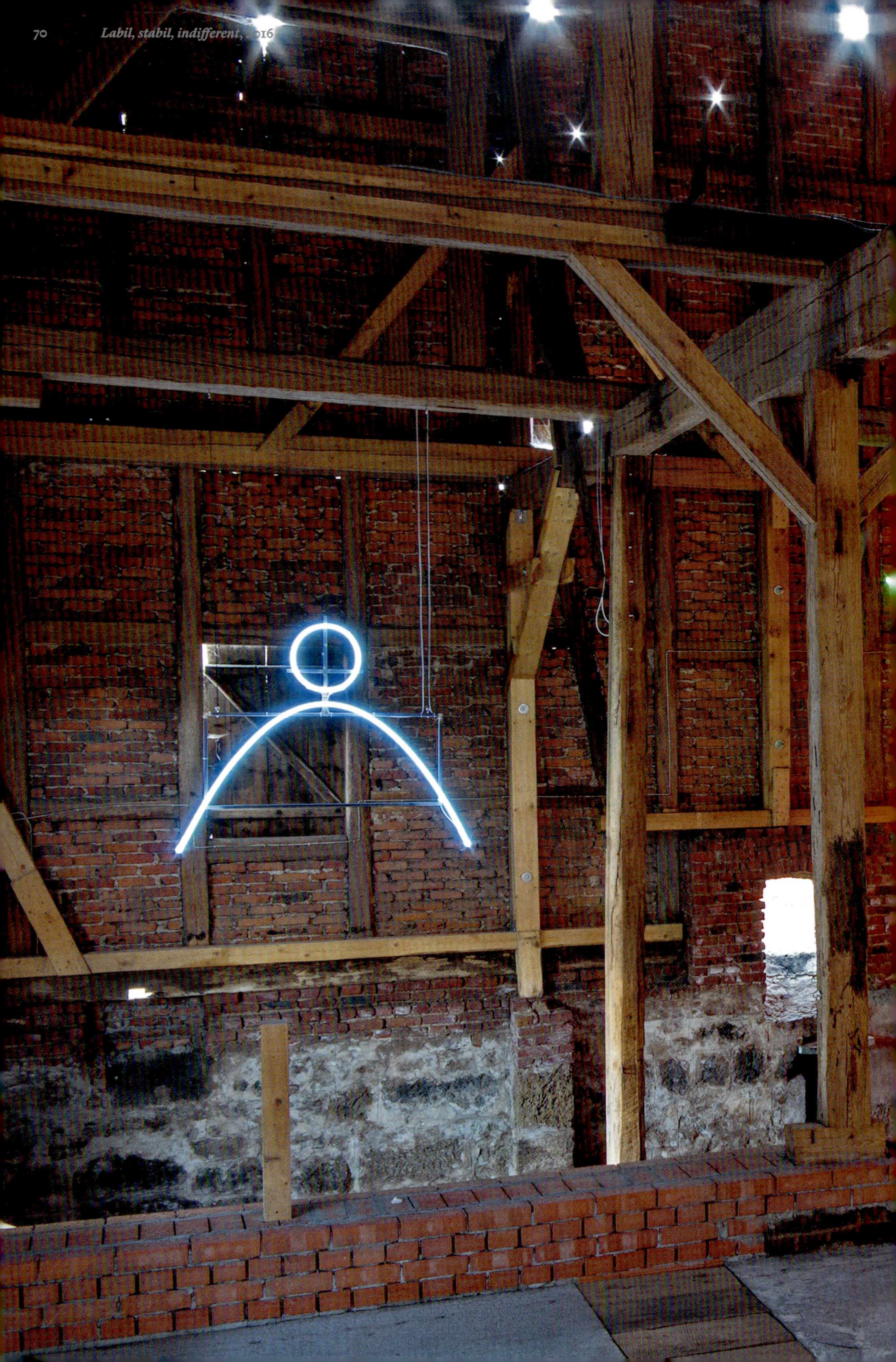

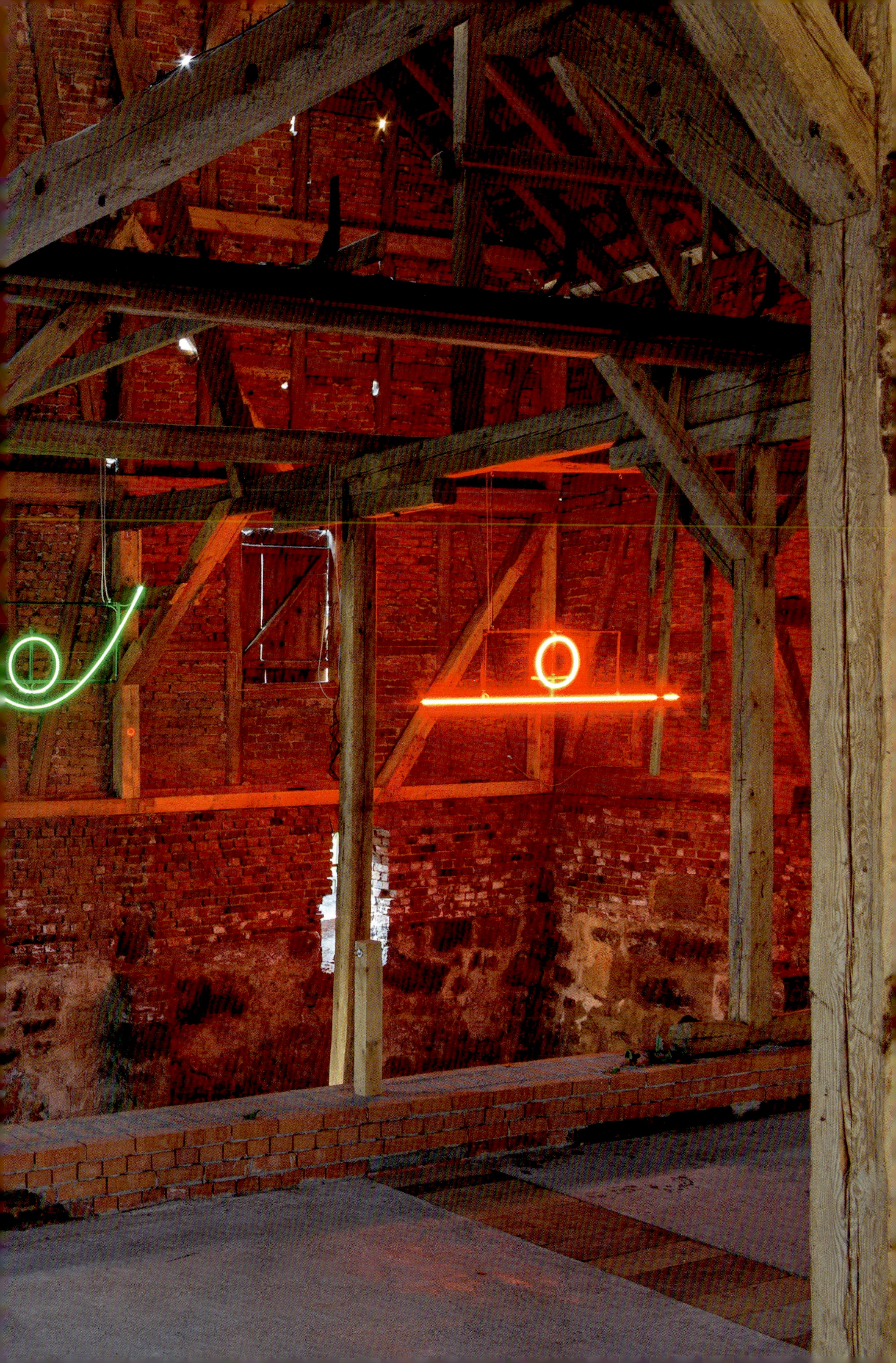

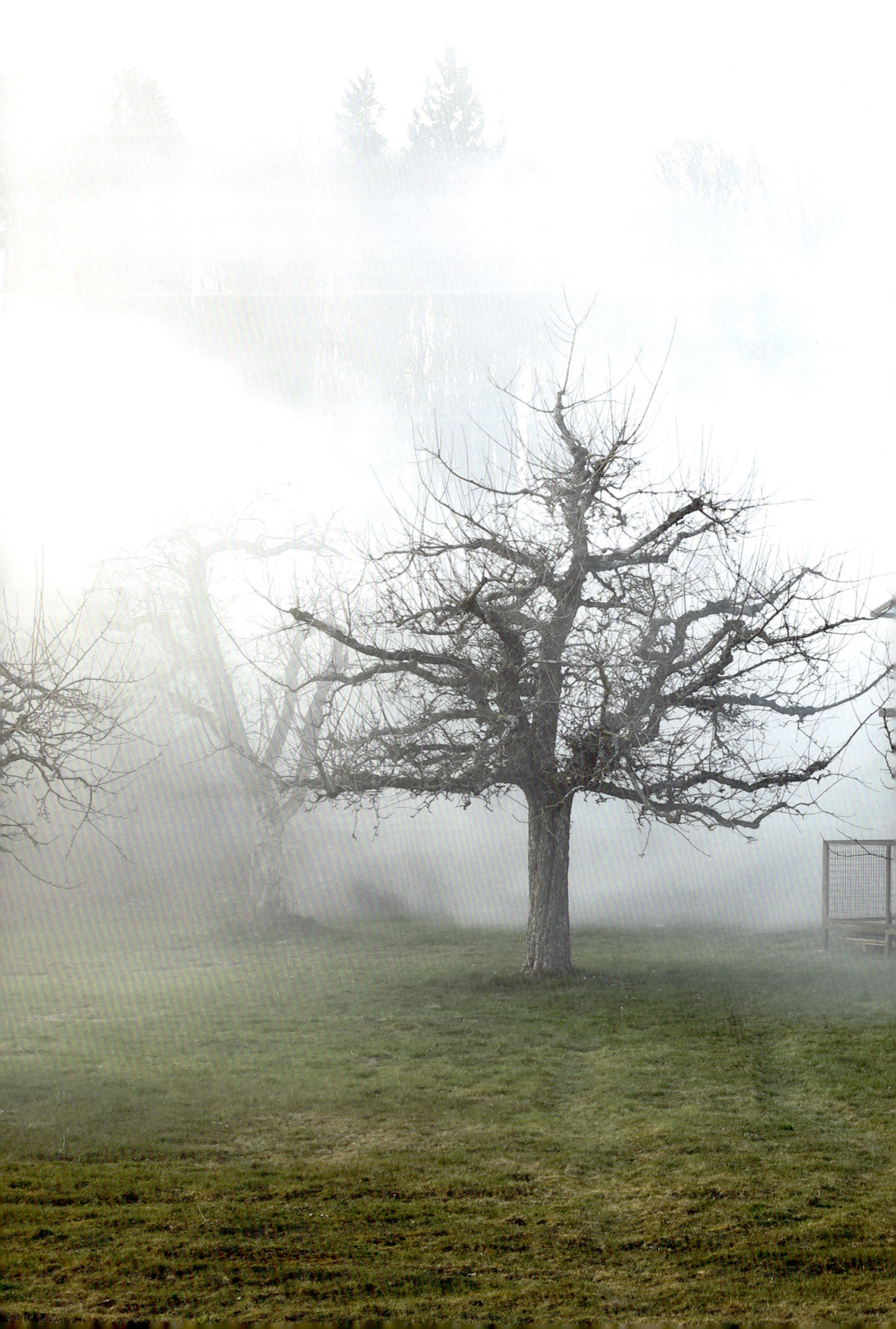

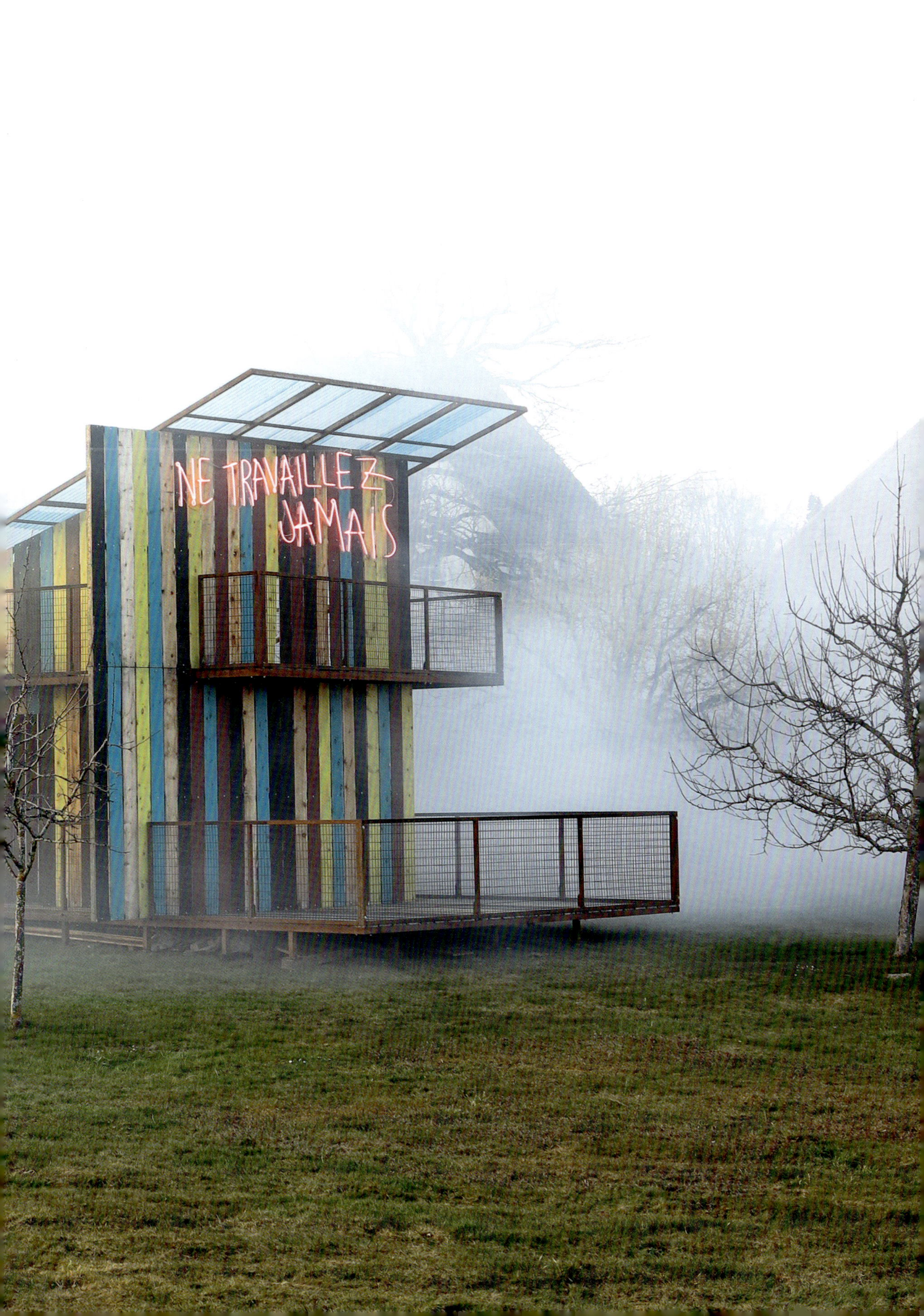
NE TRAVAILLEZ
JAMAIS

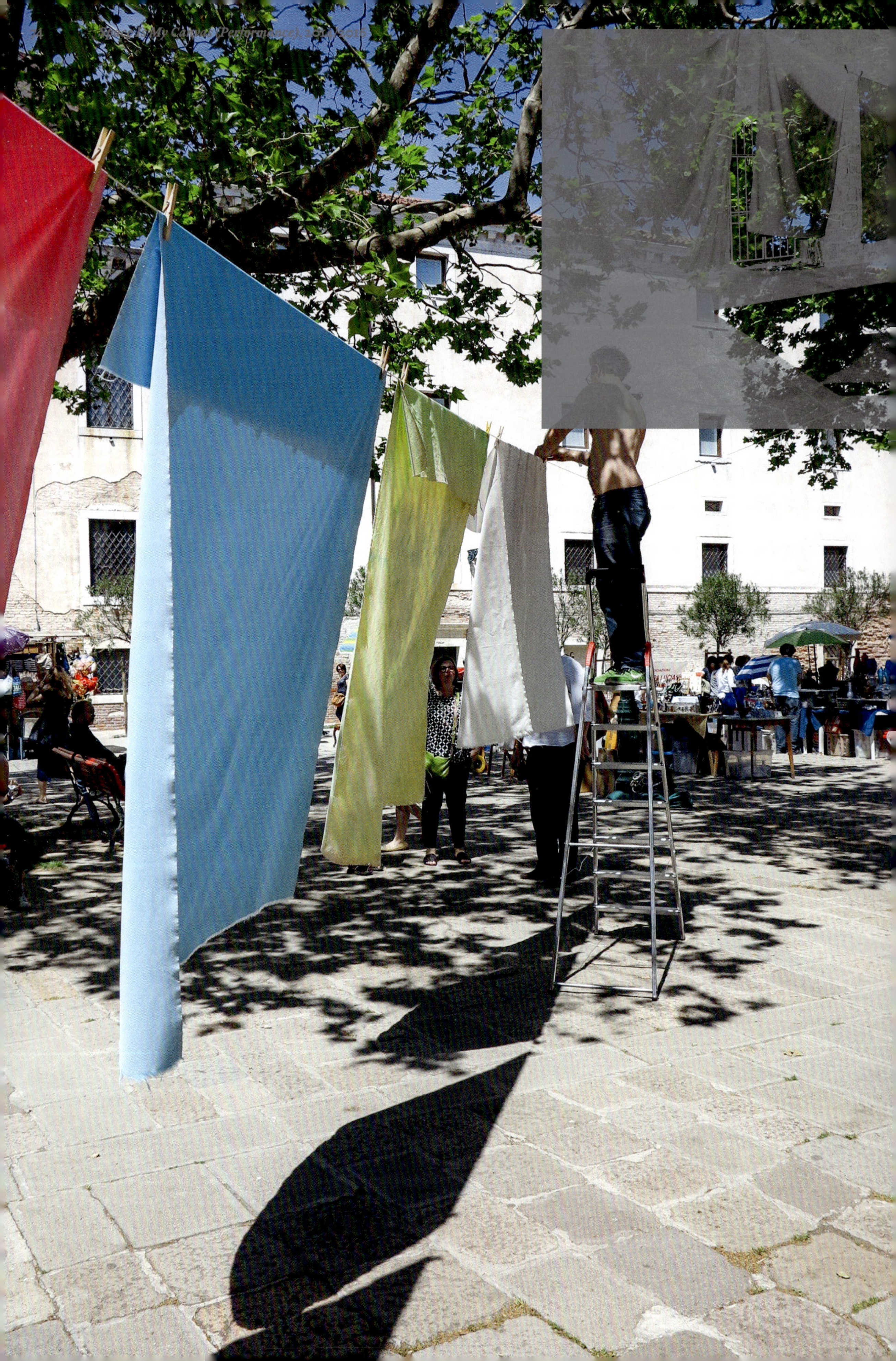

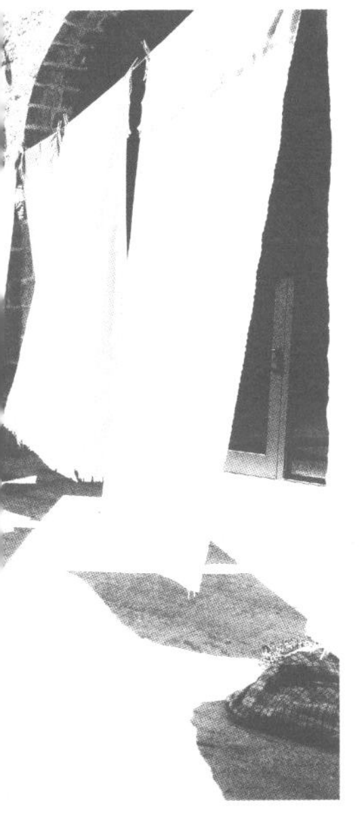

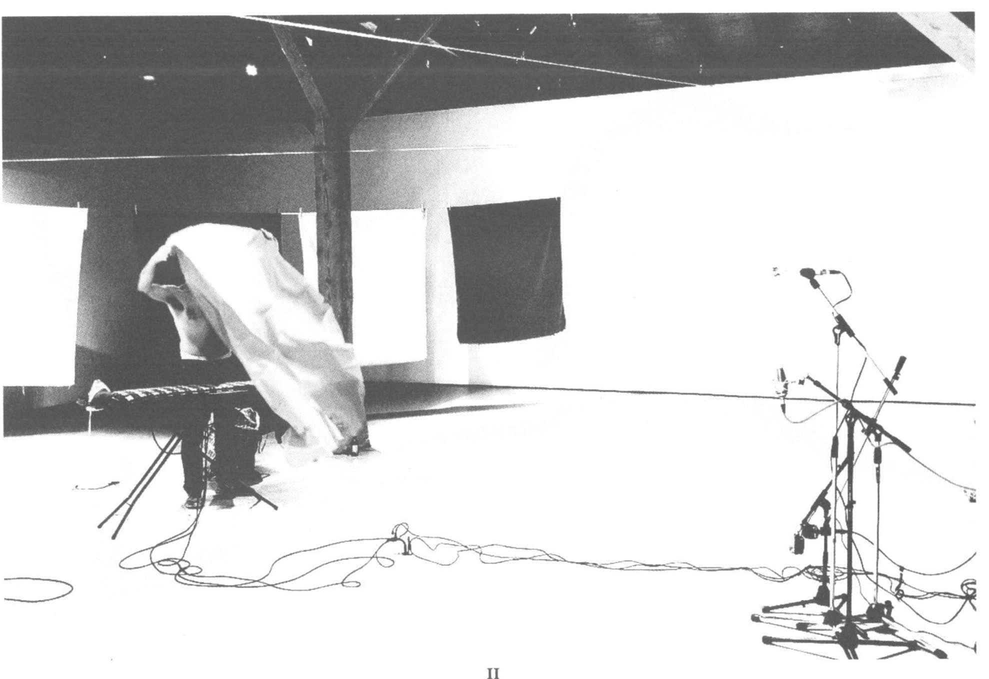

II

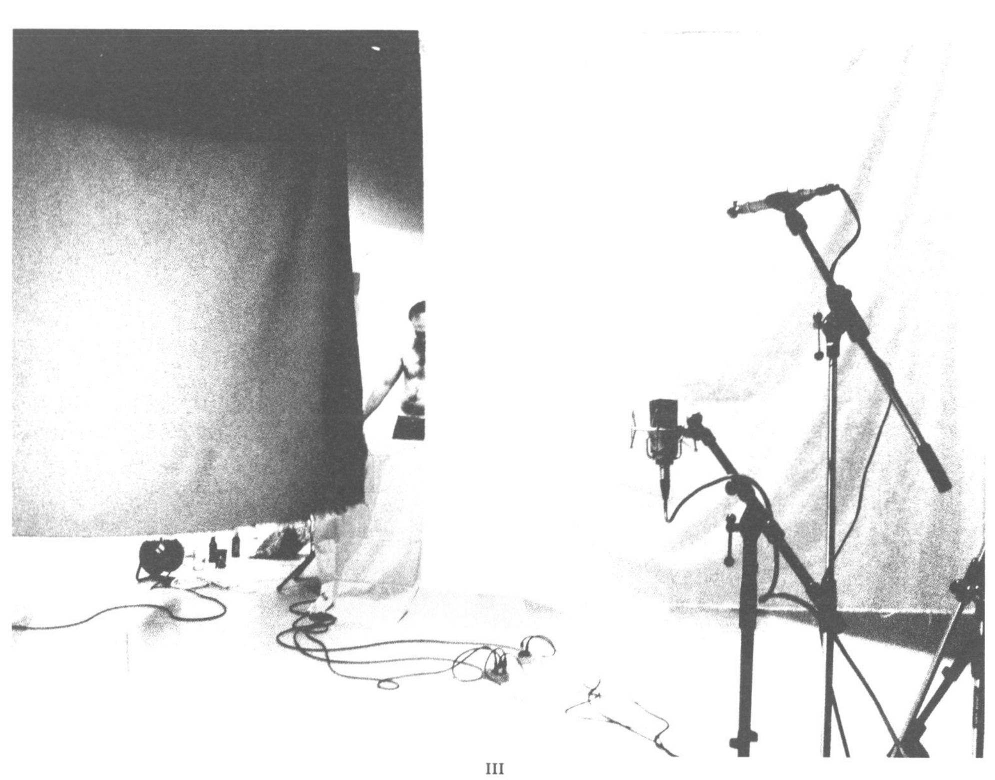

III

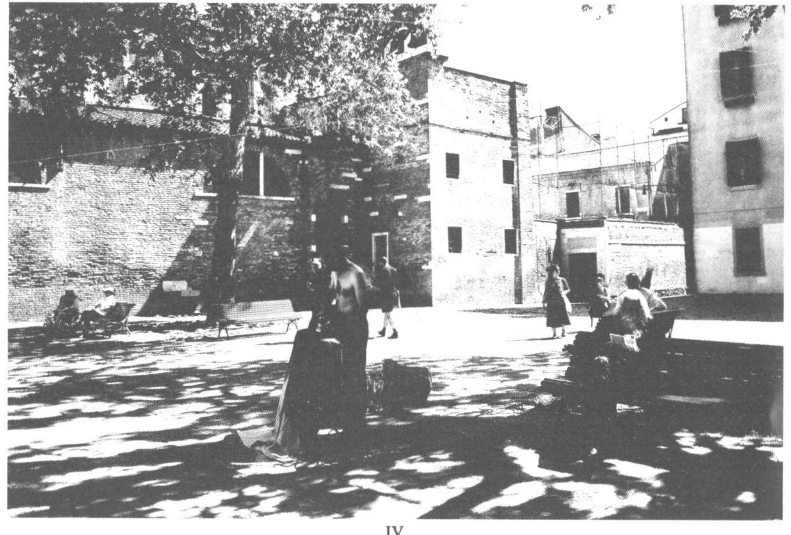

IV

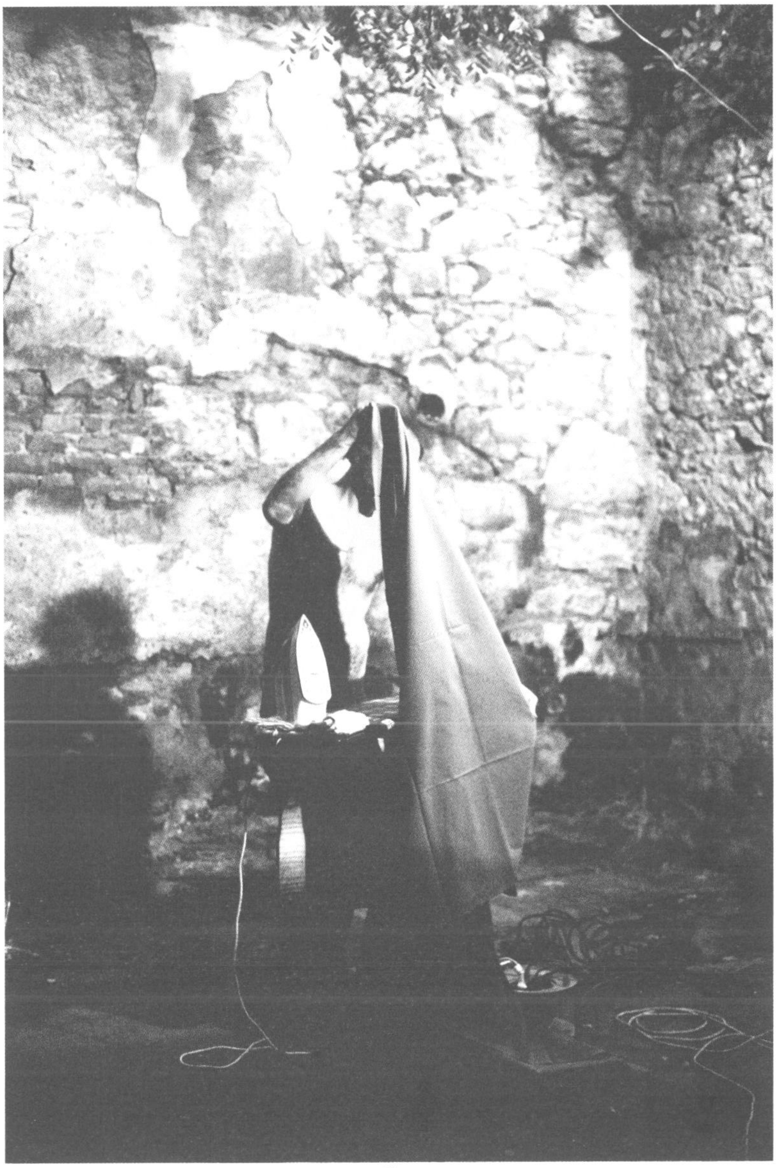

V

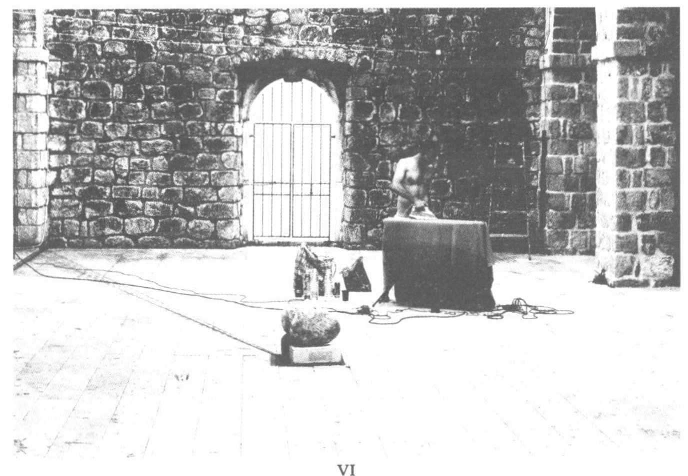

VI

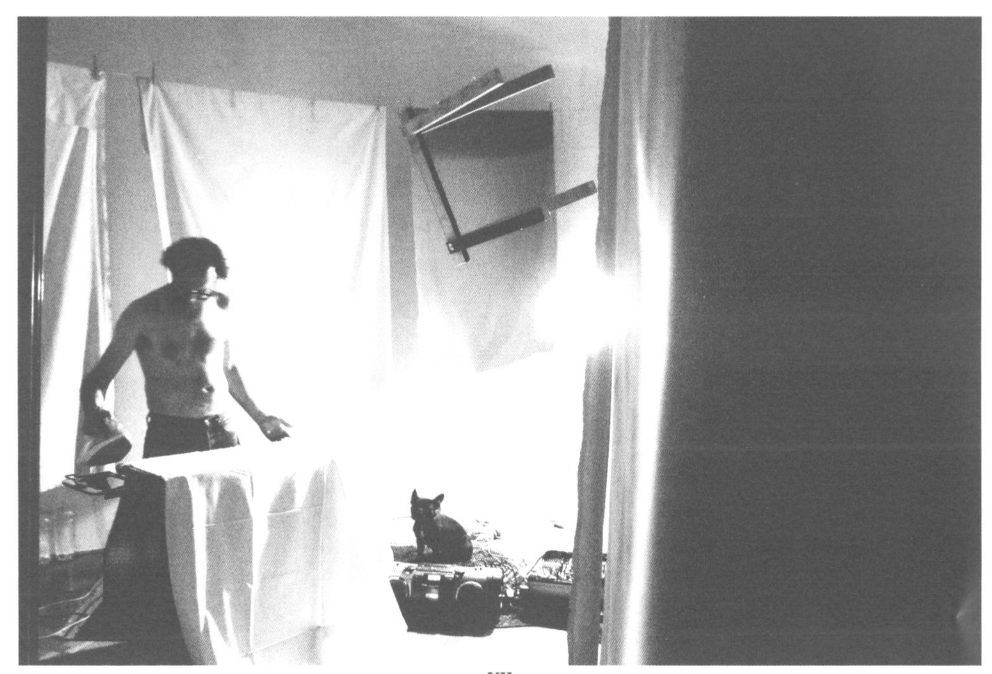

VII

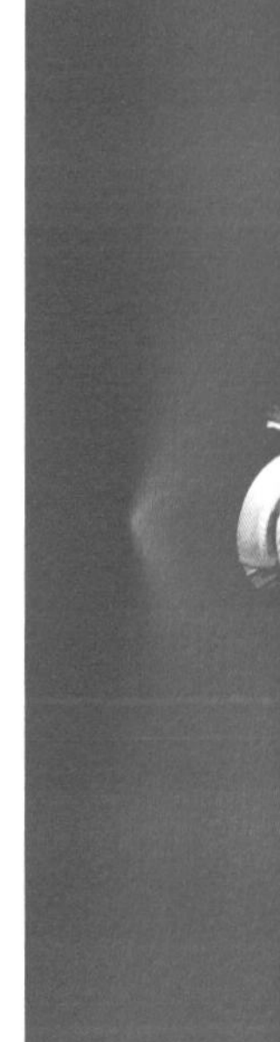

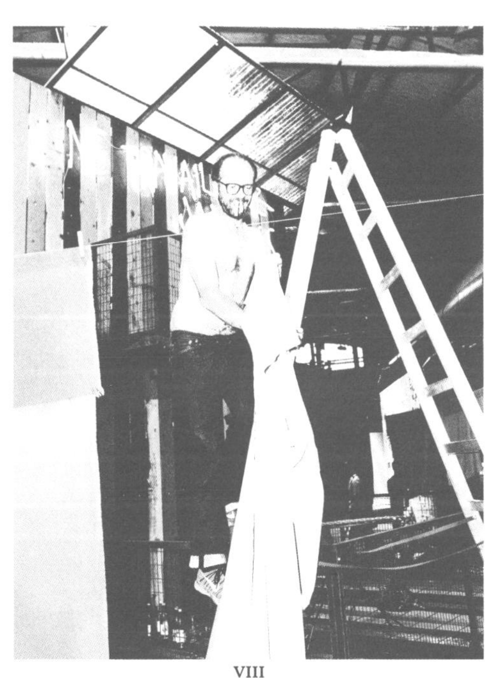

VIII

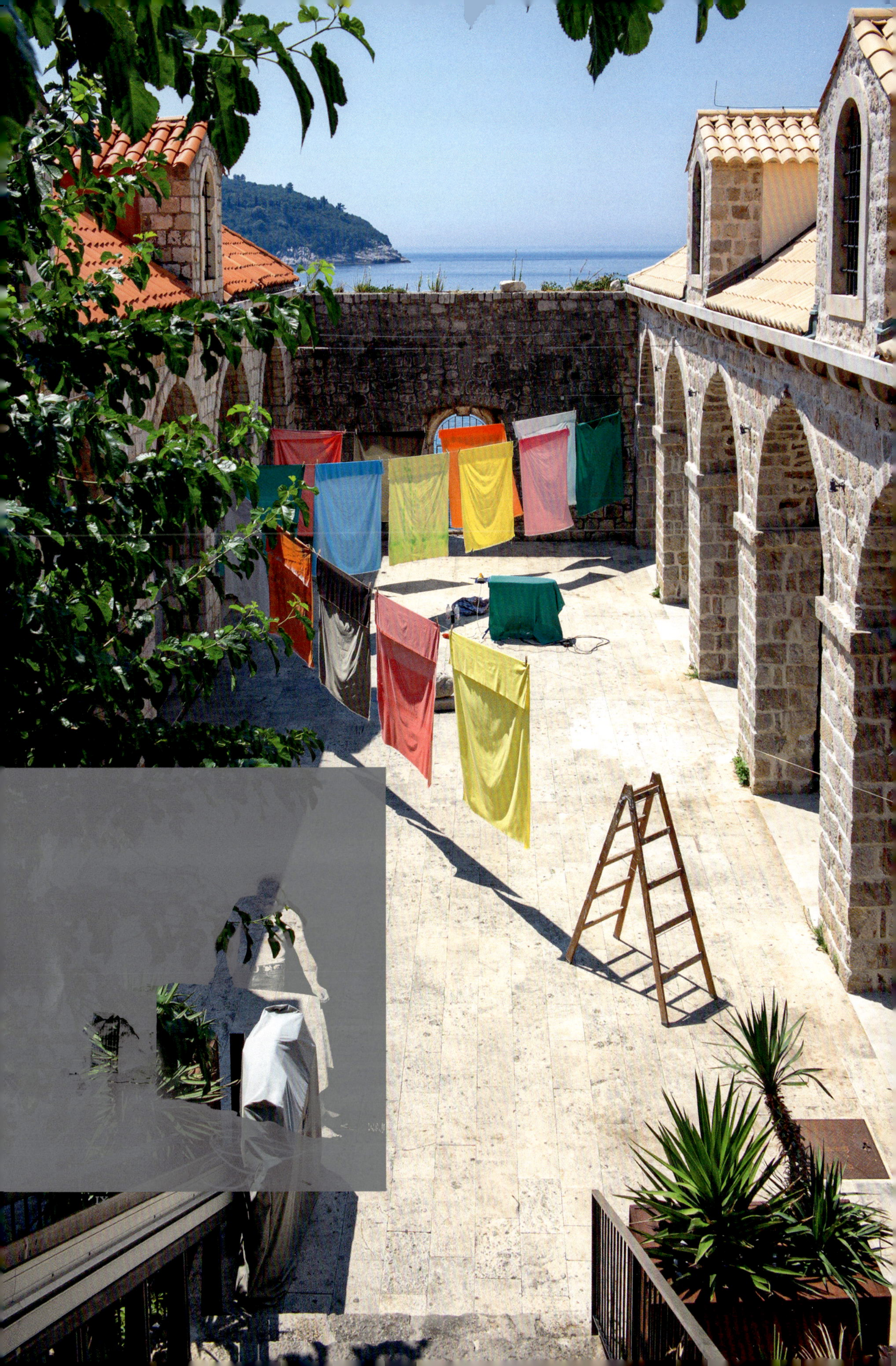

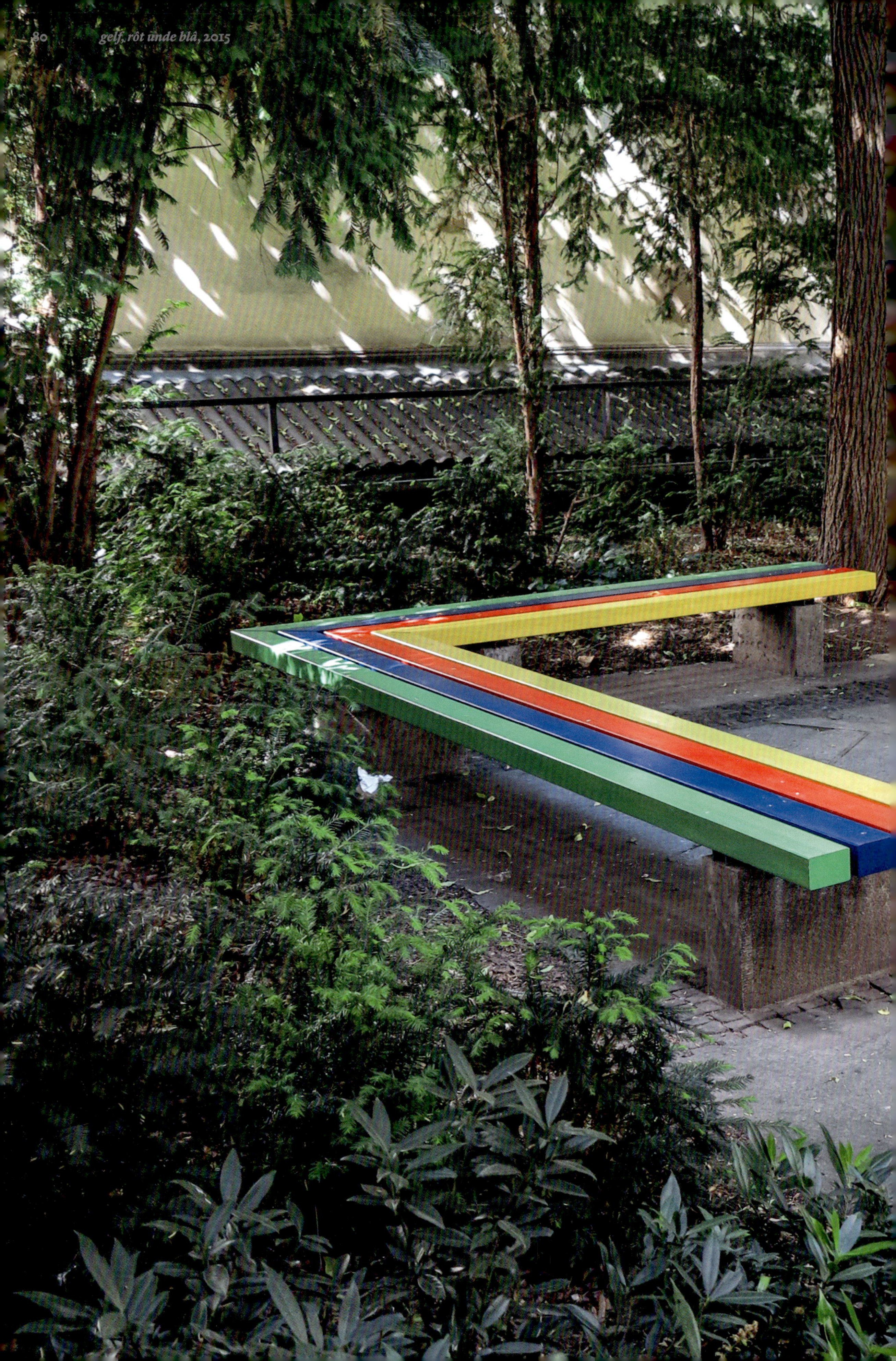

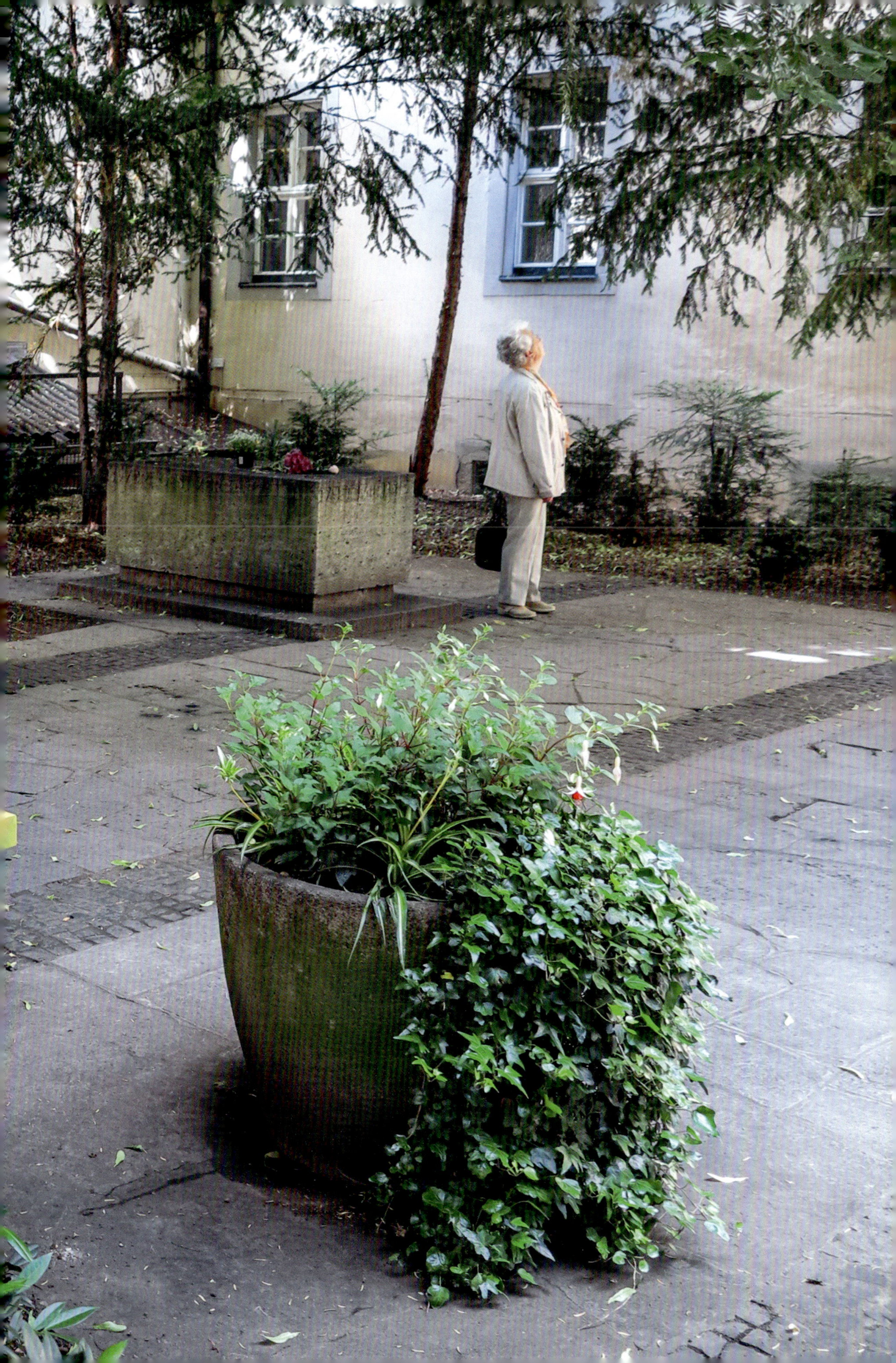

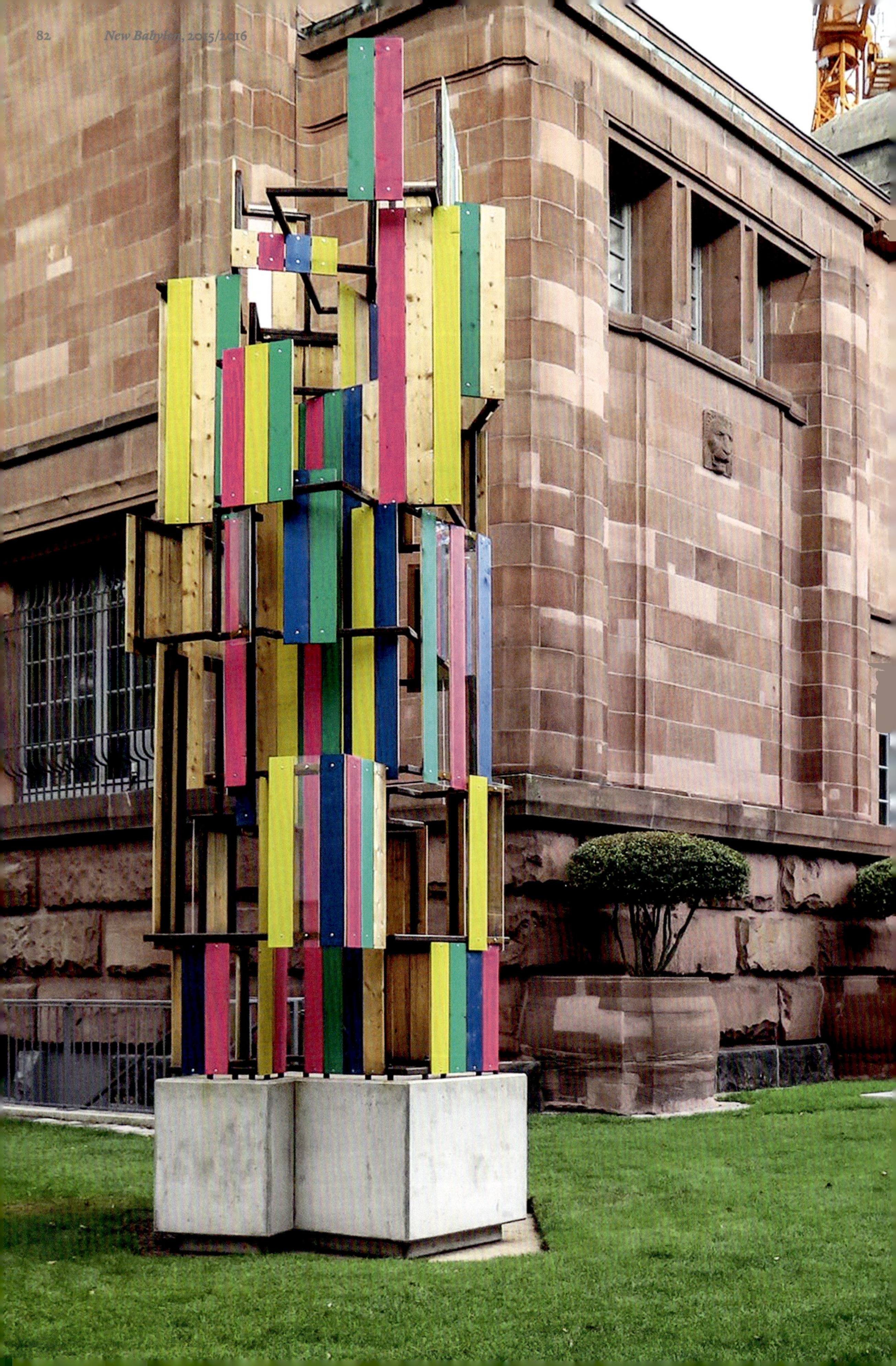

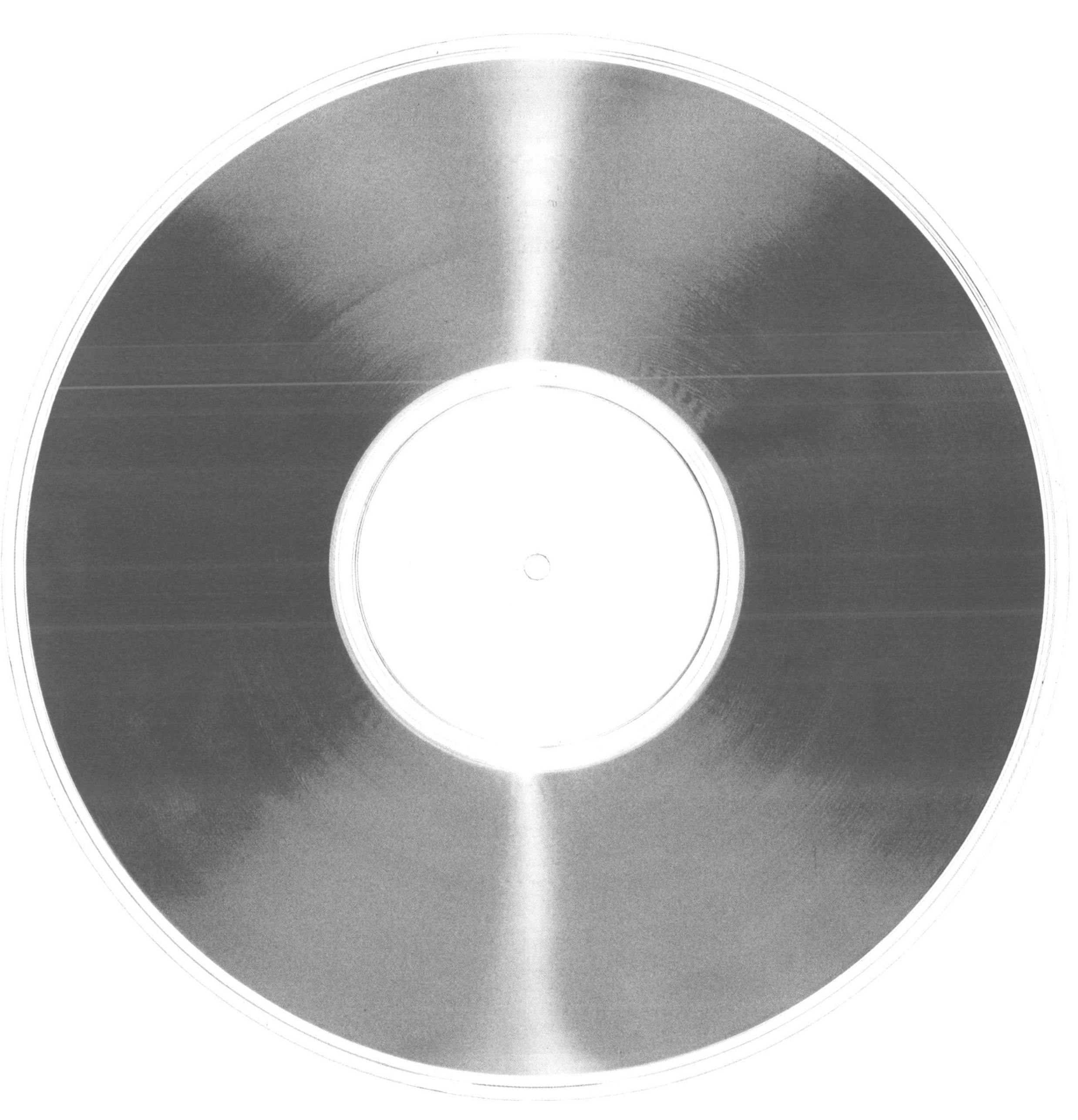

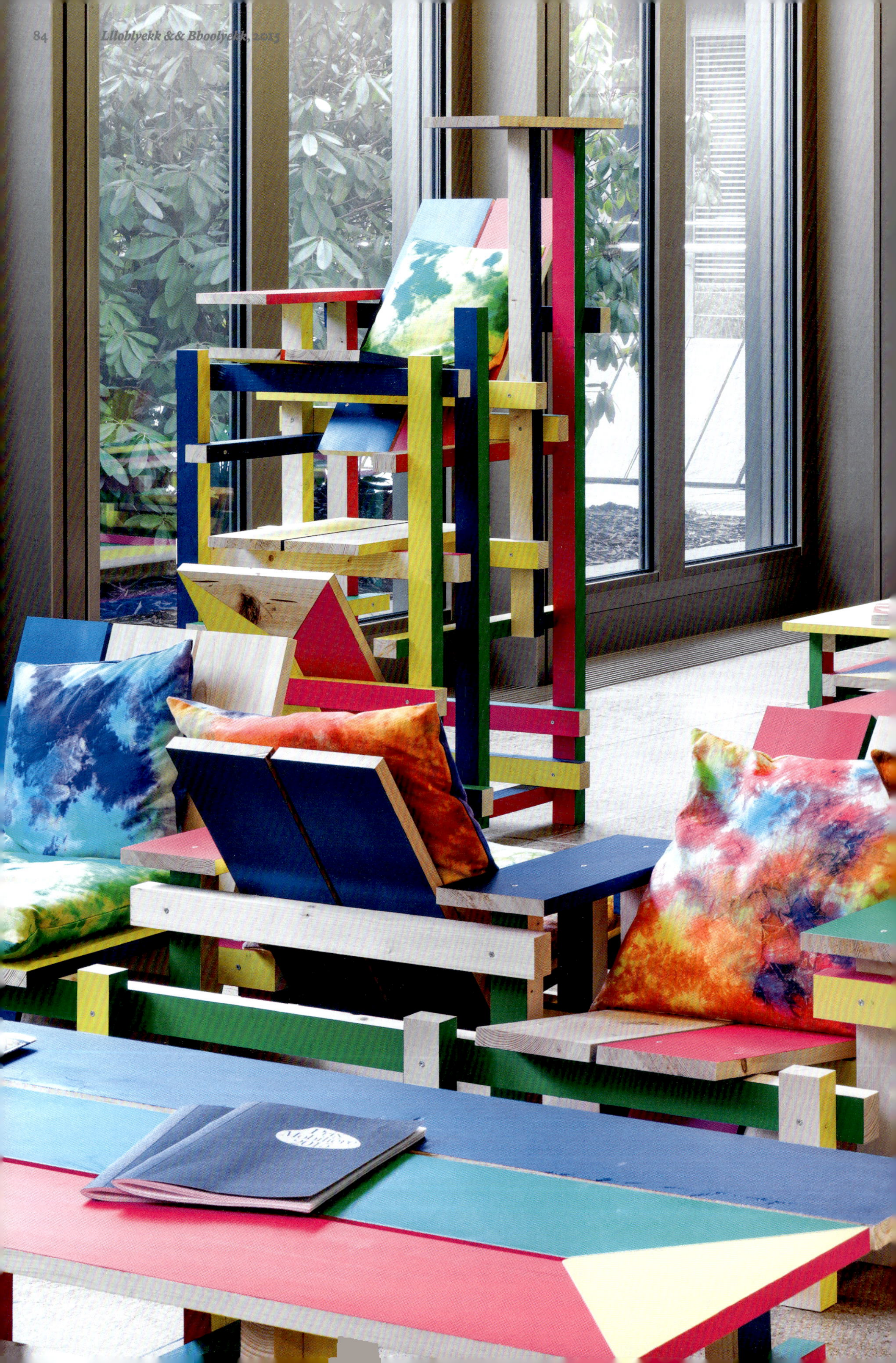

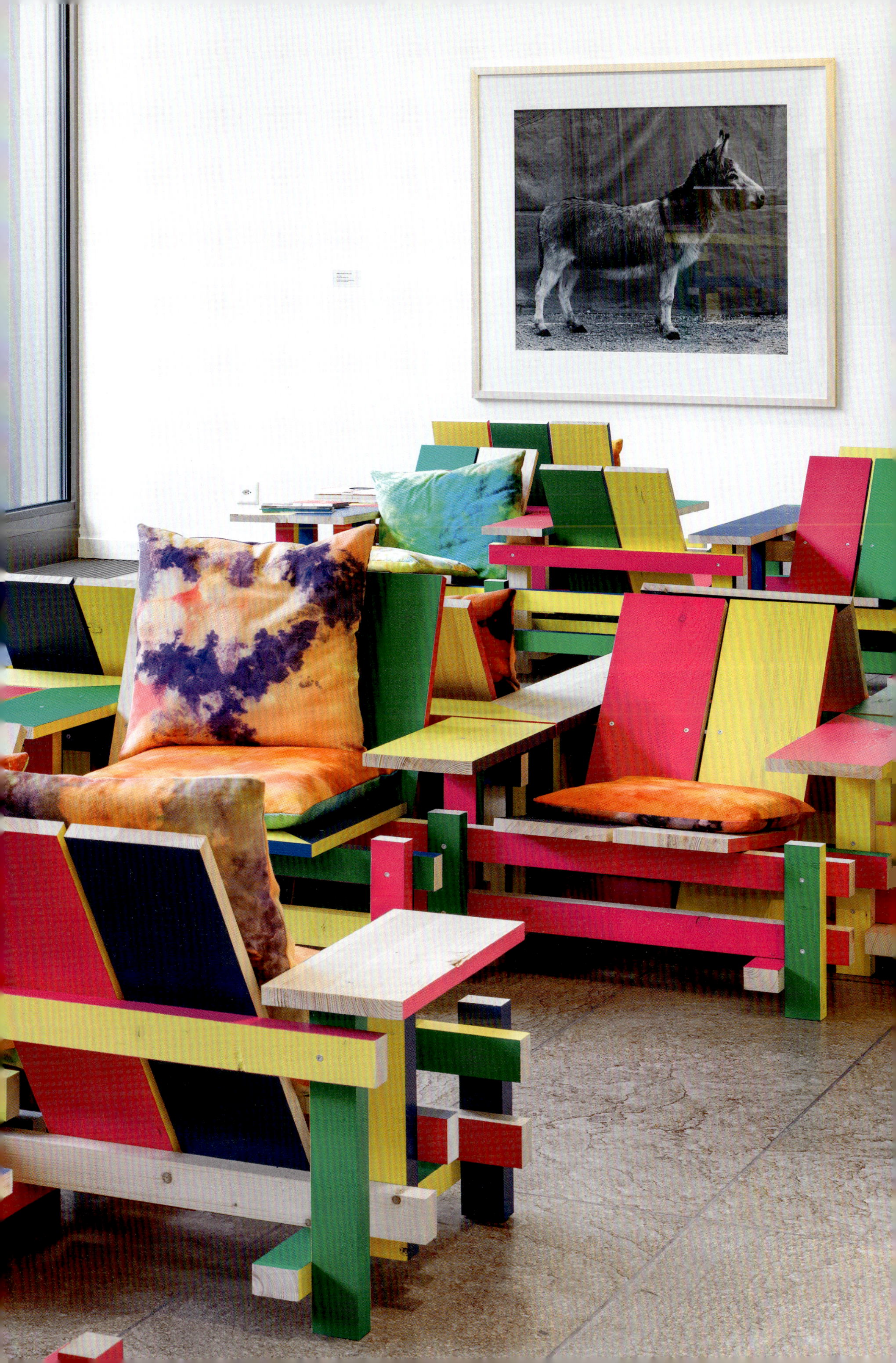

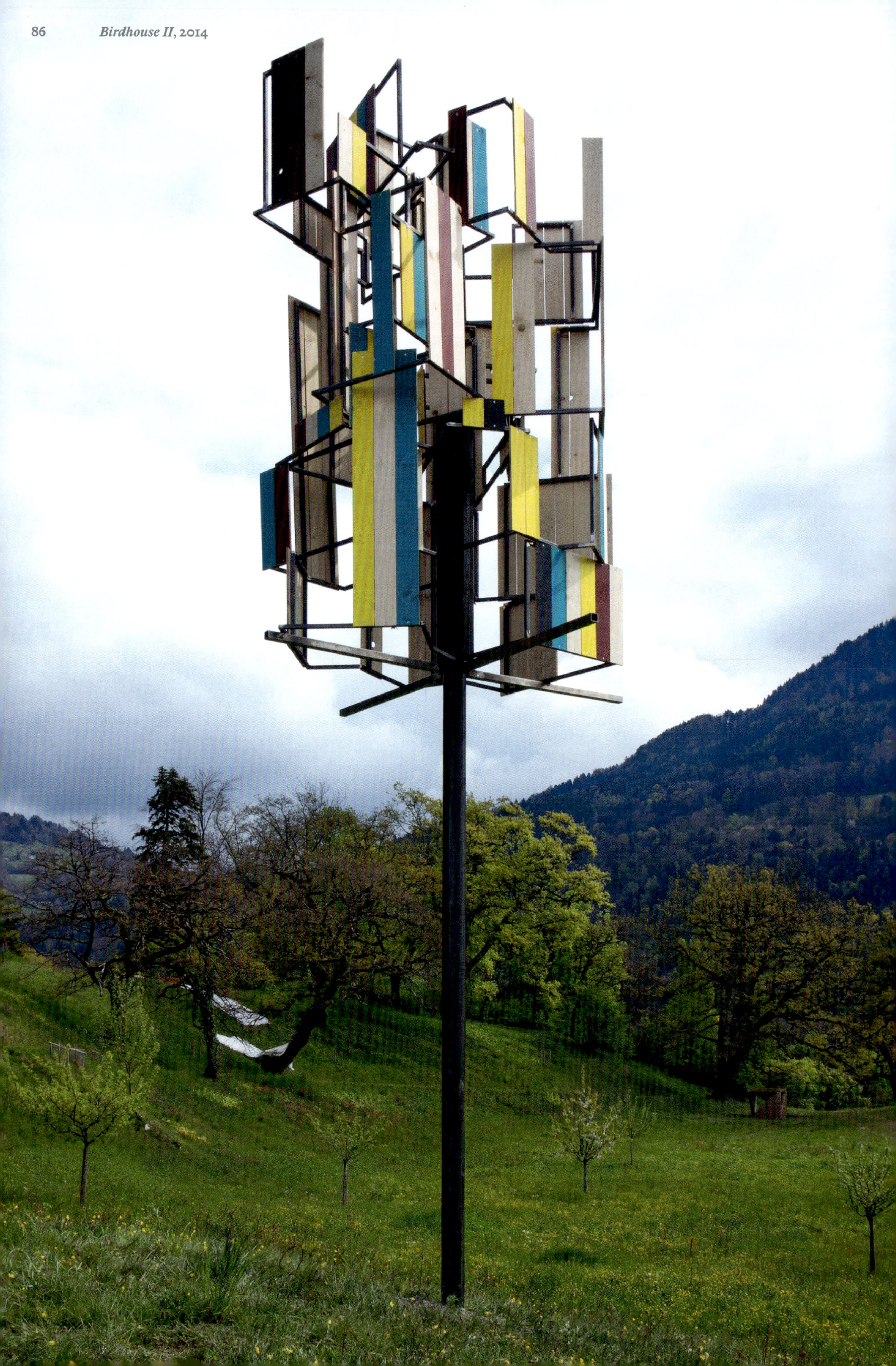

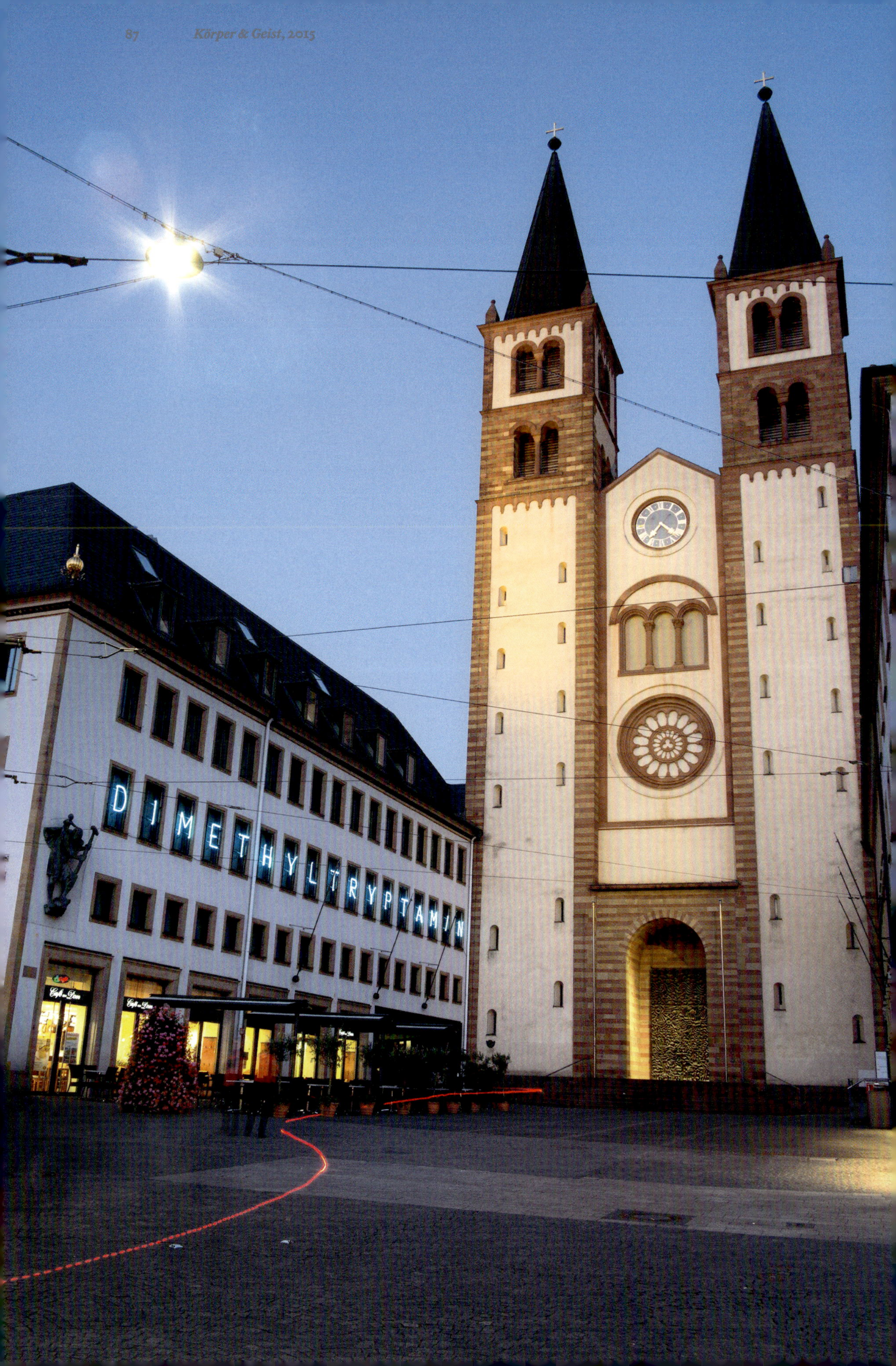
DIMETHYLTRYPTAMIN

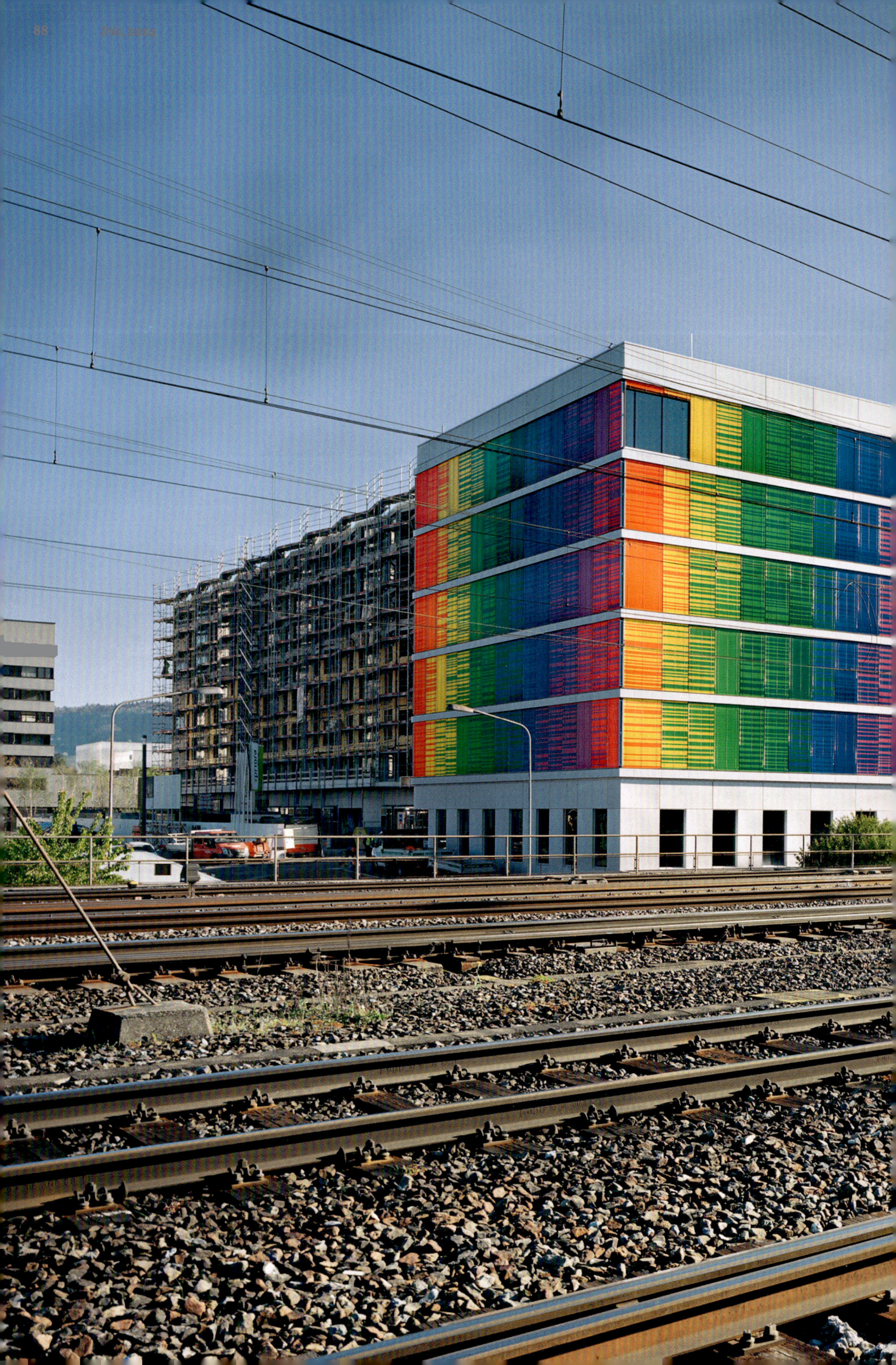

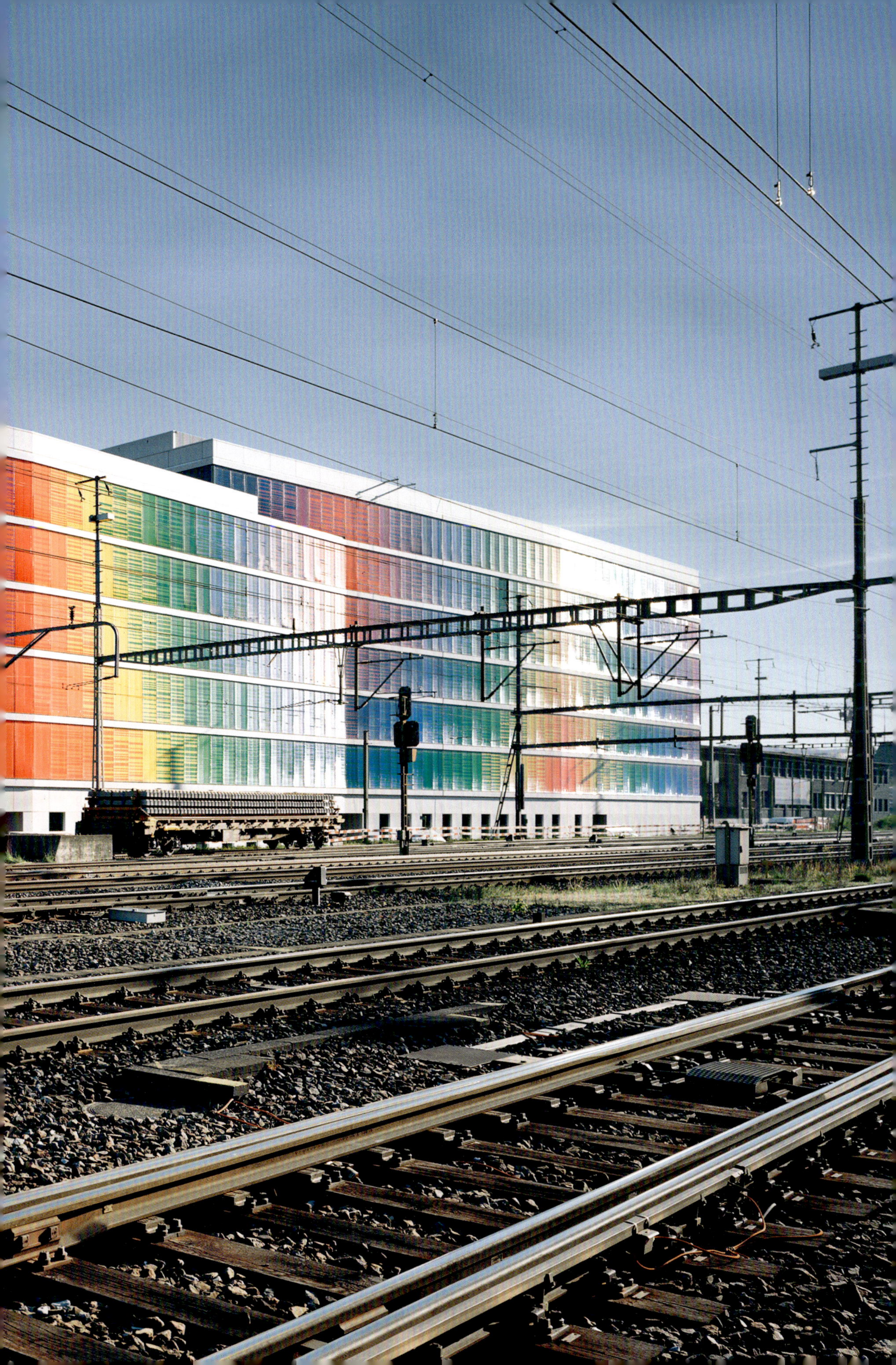

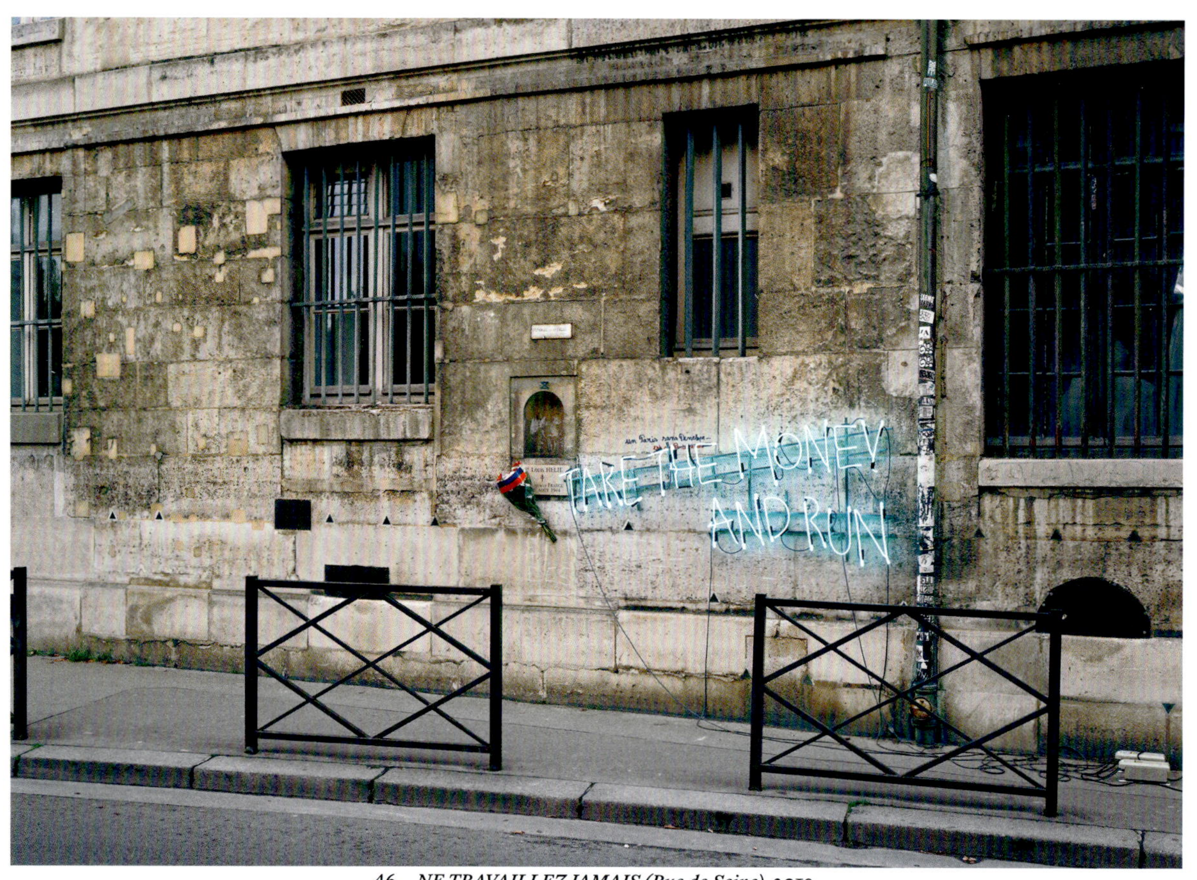

46 *NE TRAVAILLEZ JAMAIS (Rue de Seine)*, 2019

Drifting into Freedom
Trails of Tension between Dada and Situationism
Stefan Zweifel

We can drift far off with Kerim Seiler and his work. As the Paris Situationists drifted on their *dérives* through the psychogeographic hubs of Paris, Venice and London, Kerim Seiler's work explores those creative hubs that transpose certain fixed points in the history of art and literature from the historical to the present—the new and the neon forming points of light like landing strips, where the ideas of the future touch down—winking and blinking, in our midst. From Dada to Situationism, from Bruce Nauman to Gordon Matta-Clark: in the great game of senselessness and sensuality, historical positions span an arc delineating our own existence and present. This can at times involve collisions that send sparks flying, and sharp-edged stars, as I witnessed back in 2000 at his second exhibition at Galerie Serge Ziegler, and shortly afterwards, with one of his first collectors, in the collector's kitchen. After spaghetti bolognese and a bottle of Primitivo, I looked up at the star bent into the corner of the kitchen and recalled the words of Friedrich Nietzsche—"One must still have chaos in oneself to be able to give birth to a dancing star." ("Man muss noch Chaos in sich haben, um einen tanzenden Stern gebären zu können.")

Indeed, the traces that Seiler's collisions leave on the retina are bright and blithe, as when his wooden structure *Effetto Barnum (Situationist Space Program)*, like an Aby Warburg "after-image" of Le Corbusier's pavilion set on the lake-side Zürichhorn, precariously deconstructs the illusion of a new measure to the human scale. Or when his liberal borrowings from the color sequences of the Zürich Concretists shine a light on compositions that capture the concepts and slogans of the Paris Situationists (1957–1972), though even at the time they were disdained and disparaged, by none more vehemently than Max Bill. When Bill, who maintained an acerbic and witty exchange of correspondence with the Situationist Asger Jorn about the reorientation of the Bauhaus, left the Hochschule für Gestaltung in Ulm in 1956, the Situationists rejoiced, "The first stone has fallen!" On the ruins of those fallen stones, they built the Bauhaus Imaginiste.

With dazzling lightness their jubilation rolls and tumbles through Kerim Seiler's neon tubes in a St. Moritz installation that spells out the Situationist slogan "Ne travaillez jamais" above a wooden shack, a place where one can never feel at home. And in 2019, on the wall of a house in Paris where Guy Debord had painted that very same slogan in 1952, Seiler presented a version, translated into the here and now of capitalism, "Take the money and run." Thus, the system's hermetic realms of thought, be they delineated philosophically or aesthetically, are transformed and torn down by Kerim Seiler, so that a paintbrush on the arm of an excavator can merrily inscribe its blood-red traces into the ruined landscape, in his work *In Cold Blood* (2005).

In 2007, in the middle of the Situationist International exhibition *In girum imus nocte et consumimur igni* at the Museum Tinguely in Basel, the artist constructed a colorful stairway, on which Kerim placed Situationist writings and installed large fans blowing air through the room. The Latin title of the exhibition, borrowed from a film by Debord, is a palindrome that roughly translates as: "We drift in circles through the night and are consumed in fire." At the time, I did not fully grasp the deeper meaning of Seiler's stairway, but it was a convenient place to sit and watch Debord's films or leaf through the Situationists' writings. It is only now that I realize how this stairway intuitively positioned the role of Situationism within the history of the avantgarde.

The stairway of the avantgarde, heightening, step by step, the breach of taboos, rises from those Piranesian dungeons of the imagination that the Marquis de Sade explored during his imprisonment in the Bastille in 1785. In *120 Days of Sodom,* de Sade set out 600 human perversions, laying the foundation for *les chocs* that pulse like a *basso continuo* beneath the history of the avantgarde from Charles Baudelaire and Arthur Rimbaud to Guillaume Apollinaire and Dada, through the pamphlets of the Surrealists and Georges Bataille's obscene *Story of the Eye* (1928), only to implode in Guy Debord's film *Hurlements en faveur de Sade.* Debord showed the film at Cannes in 1952 before an audience expecting the ultimate in breaches of taboo, only to be met with a black screen and a soundtrack of quotes by Lautréamont and James Joyce, together with complex sociological thoughts on the misery of the present day, that later morphed into the Situationist treatise on the sexual misery in student circles, and heralded the May 1968 revolts that would, at last, see the rise of *imagination au pouvoir.* As Debord later commented, "we made Paris dance." That, at least, they did.

Debord had come onto the scene in the postwar years with the aim of furthering the spiral of the avantgarde. At first, he intended to seek advice from the Surrealists in the circle of André Breton, who, in their works, had sung the praises of de Sade as *divin marquis* and celebrated him in their art. But he soon realised that Surrealism had defused the nihilistic power of the Dadaist "no" and given it consumer appeal. Breaking taboos, especially erotic taboos, had been appropriated by the power of capital and the galleries and had degenerated into a system-immanent inducement to consume.

Through their actions, the Situationists sowed unrest in the minds of Paris: they dressed as police; they misdirected traffic on the Mabillon intersection right in the middle of Saint-Germain-des-Prés; they dreamed of altering train schedules so that the passengers would not arrive at their destination, but at a place where they had no home. Instead of returning home as usual from a life spent framed and regulated by the commute between shopping malls, industrial estates and suburban housing blocks in the familiar rhythm of *métro, boulot, dodo,* they would end up in Milan instead of Lyon, only to discover that there the espresso tasted much better and that, just perhaps, they could start a new and better life far from their families.

They dreamt of houses that would glide by night on smooth rails into other spheres where people could let themselves go completely: to have an experience like an acid trip, and more besides, as Ivan Chtcheglov put it in his *Formulary for a New Urbanism:* "There will be rooms more conducive to dreams than any drug, and houses where one cannot help but love." It was in this same spirit that the architect Constant designed his major *New Babylon* project (1960–1970) for those "New Babylonians" who, as Peter Sloterdijk put it, "frolic in the *hanging gardens of madness*—combative, ingenious, co-delirious."

With his huge *Carwash* project in Johannesburg's Central Business District, Kerim Seiler sought to create a vast, sprawling, utopian life-space in the spirit of Constant's *New Babylon*, where pure functionality would give way to poetic foresight: a *détournement* materialized. There is a nod to Constant as well in Kerim's sculpture *Alice*, conjuring an LSD molecule over the roof of Kunsthaus Zürich—the Bührle wing on acid.

Guy Debord, in the end, excluded all fine artists from his movement. No more artworks, anywhere. The concept of the artwork was replaced by the utopia of an art that leaves nothing but fleeting traces in the cities and landscapes, and instils in the casual observer a yearning to leave the life lived so far and become open to the unpredictable. With this very thought in mind, Seiler went to South Africa in 2010. In delirious diary entries, collected in the publication *Kerim in the Sky with Seiler*, he tells how, as part of the *Nomadic Structures* project, he and some friends and helpers set up *Pneuma, somnambul* at the top of Lion's Head, using three stakes and twelve ropes per person. He describes this "most Situationist-DADAist experience of all time" with laconic wit. On packhorses, like Antonin Artaud on his horseback journey through Mexico, he felt "a real connection with the south" in spite of the colonial, even imperial, might of the column of horses.

> The Situationist existence, viewed in the long term, is also very strenuous. Ricardo is helping me with the installation. As expected, the whole thing takes a lot longer than usual. But I dare not get stressed out, as I otherwise would, and that is a very good exercise for me. The outside influence generates a different tension in the knots of the *pneuma*. Considerably calmer, my mind shrinks, I write now: my heart expands. And with that, the *pneuma*.

SOS DADA

Such *dérives* of more than a few days were considered dangerous by the Situationists. After all, one of their own, Ralph Rumney, had "disappeared" while exploring Venice. (He had met the daughter of Peggy Guggenheim and was thus firmly in the clutches of capitalism.) And indeed, there we were, in the summer of 2015, sitting in Venice—gigantic cruise ships gliding past, each a colossus of consumption—awaiting the delivery of an LP pressing of *Space Is My Canvas*, only this time the spaghetti was served with vongole instead of bolognese sauce.

After the formal opening of the Salon Suisse under the motto "SOS DADA," Kerim Seiler stood there in the middle of an expansive piazza, surrounded by fluttering linen sheets that were drying out like our lungs in the hot breeze. He stood there as a man ironing sheets—an unusual vision of maleness, not just here in Italy—with the sounds of the iron and the hissing fabric creating a strangely unfamiliar soundtrack. It brought with it the distant echo of a 1972 performance by Judy Chicago at her *Womanhouse,* in which a woman endlessly ironed clothes with the sound amplified. This sizzling ephemerality, in itself, conjured what Hugo Ball might have seen as an ingenious flight *out* of time. Or even *into* time: a demonstration against the cruise liners filed its way past the artist, briefly converging with his performance.

Like the Situationists, Kerim Seiler looks to the legacy of Dada. In the first nights at Cabaret Voltaire, which are likely to remain forever an unfathomable mystery, the didactics of Dada led from the No to WW1, via the No to the bourgeois culture that had made it possible in the first place, and further, in a third step, to the No against the language underpinning that bourgeois culture.

For we rule in each sentence we utter, speakers with subjects, as the German Kaiser over his underlings sent as objects into the trenches of syntax where the verbs express the respective battle slogans. Yet this No, instead of sparing the Self that says No, destroys it—as Hugo Ball was to discover upon the recitation of his first sound poems.

What Hugo Ball experienced when he appeared onstage in a bizarre costume, like a perspiring priest, to recite his poem *Gadji beri bimba* on the 5th of February 1916, was that he was suddenly seized by ancient, almost otherworldly, forces and performed the sound poem like a litany in the singsong cadence of some old liturgical chant, before being carried offstage, emotionally and physically exhausted, and bathed in sweat. Thus, the dialectics of the Dadaist No culminated in self-dissolution; in a No to one's own self. At the re-inauguration of Cabaret Voltaire in Zürich in 2002, Seiler condensed this dialectic into a work called *Arthurs Träne,* showing the boat on which poet and pugilist Arthur Cravan had fled into the oceanic expanses of his dreams, and disappeared in the Gulf of Mexico, leaving behind only the keelwater of his boat in that endlessness that Arthur Rimbaud, father of the avantgarde, had once celebrated as follows:

> Elle est retrouvée.
> Quoi? – L'éternité.
> C'est la mer allée
> Avec le soleil.

This sun's play of light, reinterpreted by night in the constellation Ursa Minor, colored Seiler's wooden boat—while Cravan posed in a portrait, wearing a hat and a fur coat, his face iridescently contorted by a trippily kaleidoscopic riot of color. Yet the cheerfulness of that face is blurred by the sadness at the disappearance of Cravan and the demise of Dada. The teardrop of the title (*Arthurs Träne*) blends with the salty brine of the oceanic. Illuminated by the Little Bear, Ursuta, Ursa Minor, that teardrop causes the rowing boat to overflow and sink.

WITH ARTAUD AND CRAVAN THROUGH MEXICO

The gently melancholic aura of this work would later give way to a crazy light show about the artist's journey through Mexico with Adrian Notz of Cabaret Voltaire in search of traces of Cravan. Kerim Seiler also wrote a diary, as yet unpublished, about this:

> The evening involves a total of some seven fights. By the last one, the crowd is ecstatic. In *lucha* [a form of wrestling] the quality of the competition improves with each fight and the last bout is between the best fighters. It is no different today. None other than Mistico has stepped into the ring for the final fight. And in this fight, we get a taste of the high art of *lucha libre*. What we see is more acrobatics than brawn, more theater than brawl. In this light, *lucha* appears as a ritual, as theater in the classic sense. On the one hand, the good, on the other, the bad, both driven by a superhuman force to overcome the laws of physics. The masks are animal heads, sacred figures. The fighters are mask-wearers, the girls virgins, the referees priests; the whole is a staged catharsis, a modern ritual, uniting and incorporating all aspects of contemporary mysticism. In short: a real discovery. As we leave the arena, we feel overwhelmed—and I, happy.

Of course, this journey, too, was rooted in the old avantgarde; it followed in the footsteps of Antonin Artaud, who, on the failure of his *Theatre of Cruelty,* had abruptly given up heroin and embarked on a pilgrimage in 1936 to the Tarahumara Indians in the high plains of Mexico. There, the clefts and canyons of the rock formations, with their vaginal abysses and phallic peaks, revealed themselves to him as the alphabet of nature that speaks directly to the individual under the influence of peyote, letting him "come flooding back from the other shore of existence." This is one way of finding the wavebeat of eternity and of sensing that the artist's quest for traces returns time and time again, as Nietzsche sensed in his doctrine of eternal recurrence.

To take part in this grand game, however, one must go through the three metamorphoses described by Nietzsche in *Also sprach Zarathustra*. First, one must become a camel, laden with all the ballast of knowledge, and explore the works and worlds of Dadaism and Situationism; then a rampant lion, fighting wildly to create space for new values. Yet when the lion scratches with his claws new values onto the old scales of value, the dependency on what has been negated remains. The way towards the freedom of a new art has not yet been found.

This succeeds only after the third metamorphosis: upon becoming a child, who, like a "self-propelling wheel," creates new worlds in divine innocence, full of playful eagerness, only to discard it all and invent anew. After reevaluating all our values, we have to dream, like a child, of a "childland" that counters a world so disfigured by the wounds and scars of "fatherlands," and instead conjures up a place where we can rediscover and reinvent ourselves.

So it was that I, during the Babel translators' conference in Ticino, stumbled and staggered through a structure that incited me to become a babbling child myself; a self-propelling wheel. The child is entirely at one with itself, like the idiot; living within the self and self-will. Like every great artist, the child develops its own idiom, like the idiot—known in Ancient Greek as *idiotes* (literally "private person") who unfolds the rich tapestry of self-will and of his own simple-minded folly.

IN PRAISE OF FOLLY AND THE FOLD

In this stupor of *Blödigkeit,* in this folly of simplicity, the artist is exposed, unprotected and uncomprehendingly, to the mind-numbing whirl of thoughts and impressions that assail him. However, so as to be less vulnerable and undefended, the idiot usually turns up as a pair: Don Quixote and Sancho Panza, Laurel and Hardy, Bouvard and Pécuchet—or Séraphin and Plume. For a pair, two-fold, can reinvent the world and evade the police, as in the 1967 illustrated children's book by Philippe Fix, *Le Merveilleux Chef-d'oeuvre de Séraphin,* in which Séraphin builds his dream house in the middle of town, with glittering battlements and fantastical wooden structures, as in Seiler's *NEW/NOW* project in Johannesburg. A towering dream-house, sky-high like our childhood wishes. Yet investors move in around Séraphin's house and build highrises, increasingly curtailing his free space. In the end, they send in the police to evict Séraphin and his friend Plume. The two flee upwards, higher and higher, right up to the attic. Then, when the police arrive, they take a few steps and join them together. They place four steps in the air and then quickly dismantle the lower one and place it at the top. In this way, they hover ever higher on their four steps. Carried by the desire for freedom, afloat in the sky, drifting away into freedom, pursued by the envious gaze of the police of reason—there, in the air, Séraphin and Plume planted the roots of our ageless lifelong yearning.

Similarly, perhaps, the staircase in the Museum Tinguely, illuminated by Kerim Seiler's colors, was also a refuge for the imagination. On it one came closer to the sky and thus closer to the labyrinth that the artist had created on a huge cloth sewn from two layers of fabric and strewn across the niches of the museum. This plunges us once more into the labyrinth of references: the

Situationists had, at one point, planned a major exhibition at the Stedelijk Museum in Amsterdam, directed by Willem Sandberg, under the title *Die Welt als Labyrinth*. They wanted to tear down one wall of the museum to open it up to the everyday, to city life, while at the same time bringing urban life into the creative realm of the artists. This idea, though unrealized, as the Situationists cancelled the exhibition, pervades Seiler's many installations. Stairway joins stairway. But what connects the steps, some assemblage or a fold?

TWOFOLD

Kerim Seiler has touched upon this latter question. For an issue of the magazine *Gazetta ProLitteris* in 2000 on the matter of the fold and simplicity, he created a small craft sheet. Three clouds hover above a flat surface broken by the horizon line. Is the horizon line a joint charged with sexual desire, or is it a fold within which the power of simplicity, onefold, expands into the manifold?

The joint fills the interim space between two level strata. The fold, by contrast, as set out by Gilles Deleuze in his book *Le Pli*, is never one: it is not a principle that rests within itself, like the joint, but is always twofold—a *Zwiefalt* that harbors the promise of endless unfolding. Recall Aristophanes in Plato's *Symposium*. Originally, humans were round. They were all-round happy, spherical people who were so contented with their lot, revelling in their smooth skin, that the gods of Olympus became jealous of the happiness these double humans enjoyed, so they cut them in half and over the wounds of the semi-sphere they drew the skin together in the middle and folded it, then they turned the heads around on their necks so that they would gaze lifelong upon the knot of skin—the navel—to remind them of the split and the rupture, the painful wound and the birth, and with that, of their own mortality and death. Those who do not meld symbiotically into the sphere, spend their lives exploring—as humans, as artists—the *Zwiefalt* and, with that, the ambiguous happiness of a disjointed existence. The principle of the fold shatters our faith in the unity and oneness of the all-powerful subject bent on "subjugating nature" or even torturing it, as Francis Bacon would have it, "on the rack." The fold is never one. It is always twofold, doubled, dichotomous, an enigma that cannot be solved by a truth. That enigmatic creature, the human being, lives this twofold existence. And Kerim Seiler unfolds this in his work, in all its manifold diversity.

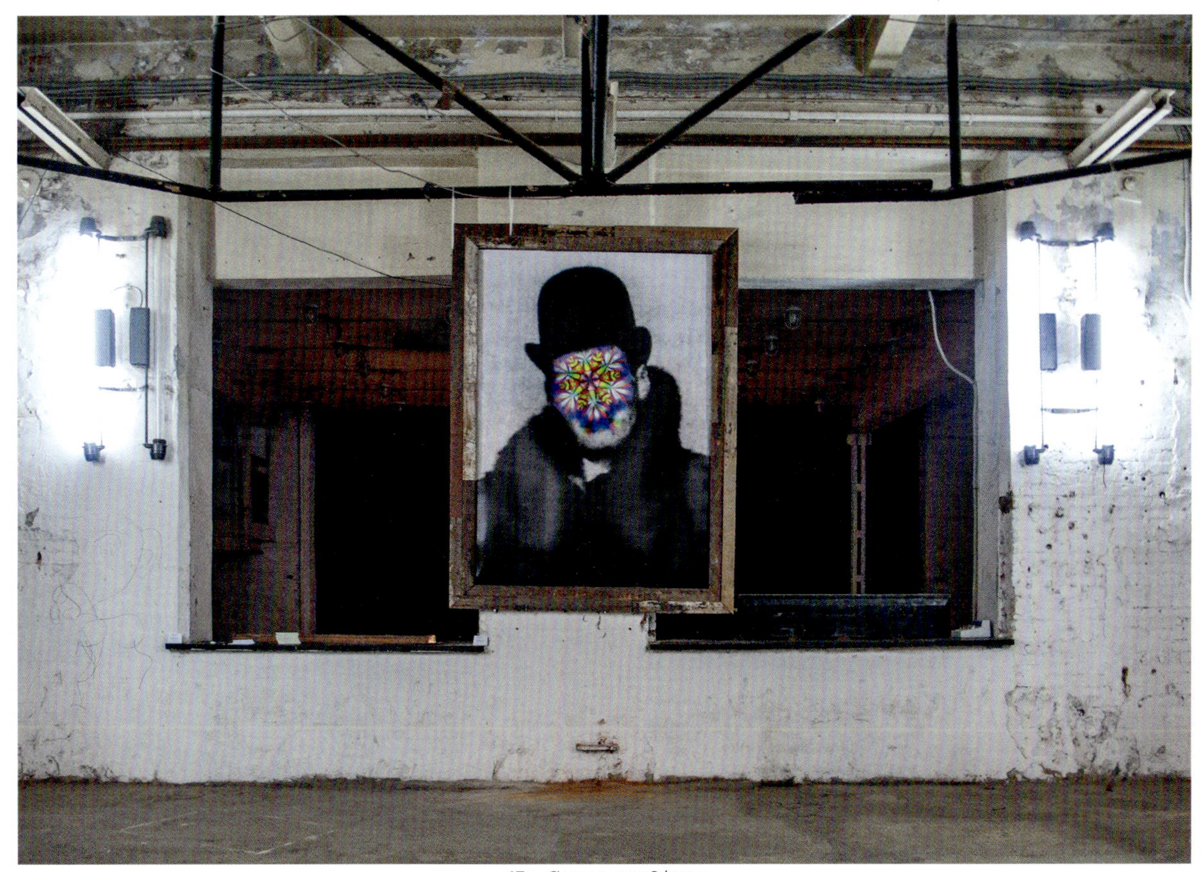

47 *Cravan*, 2008/2012

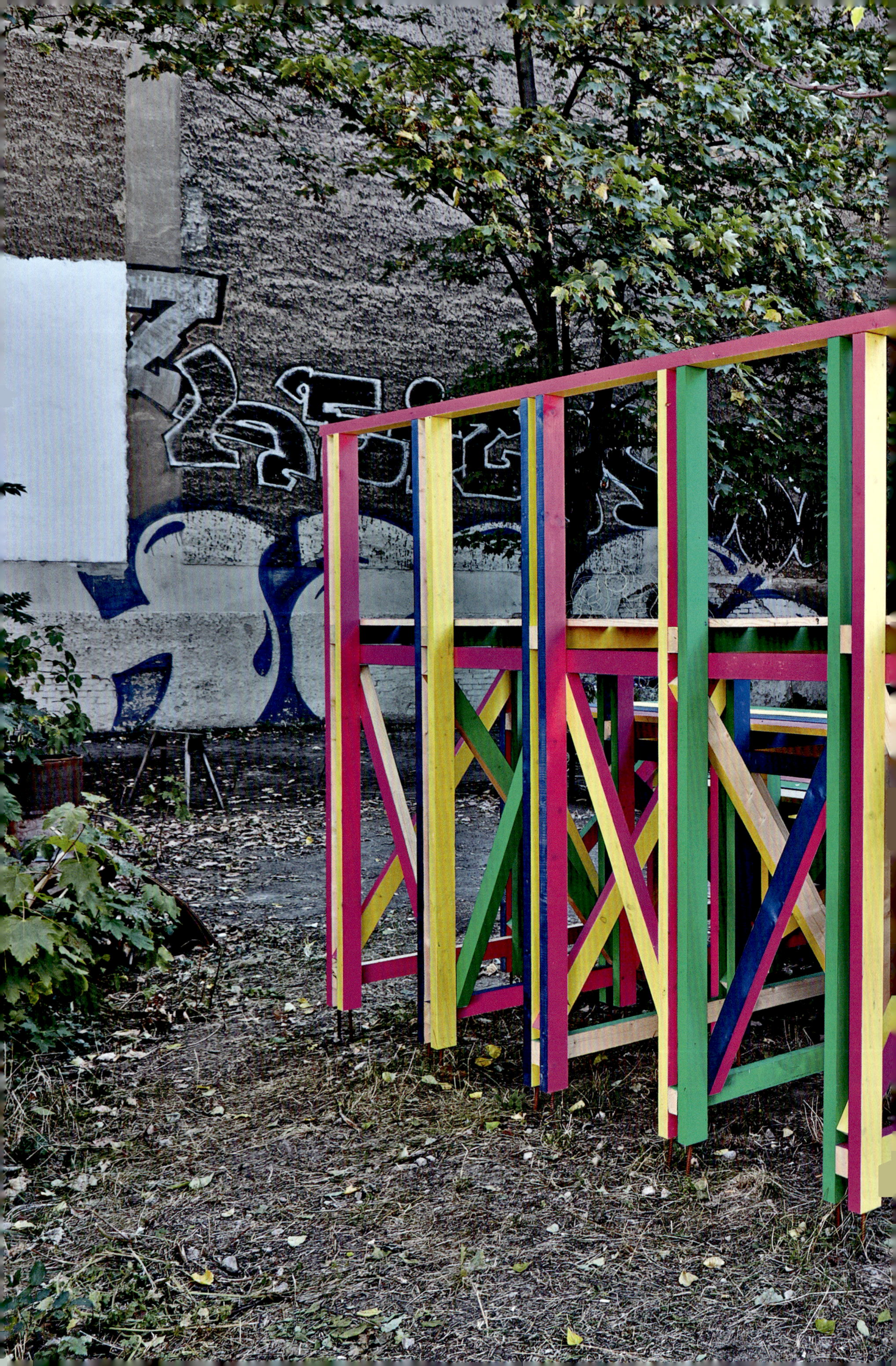

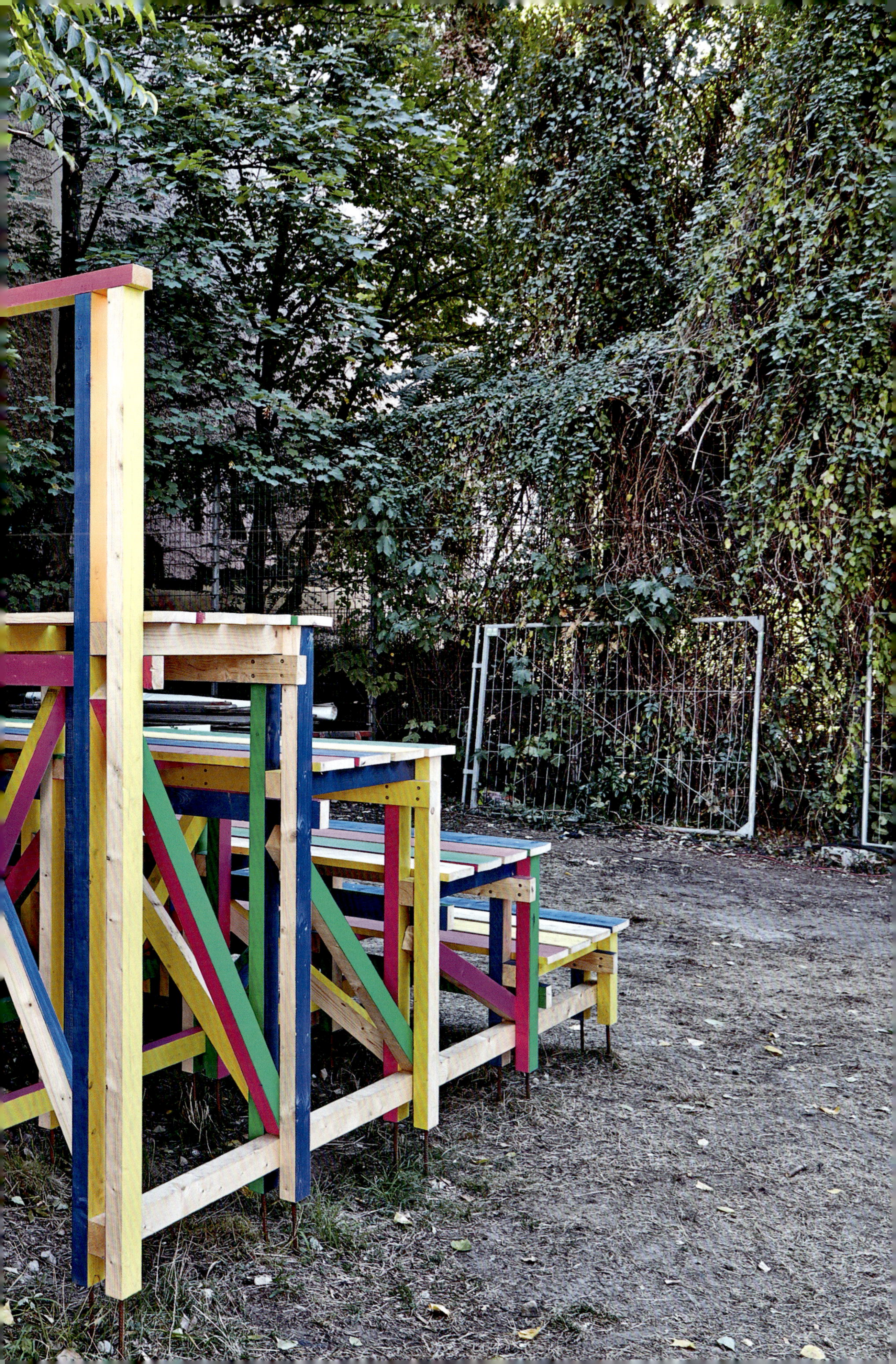

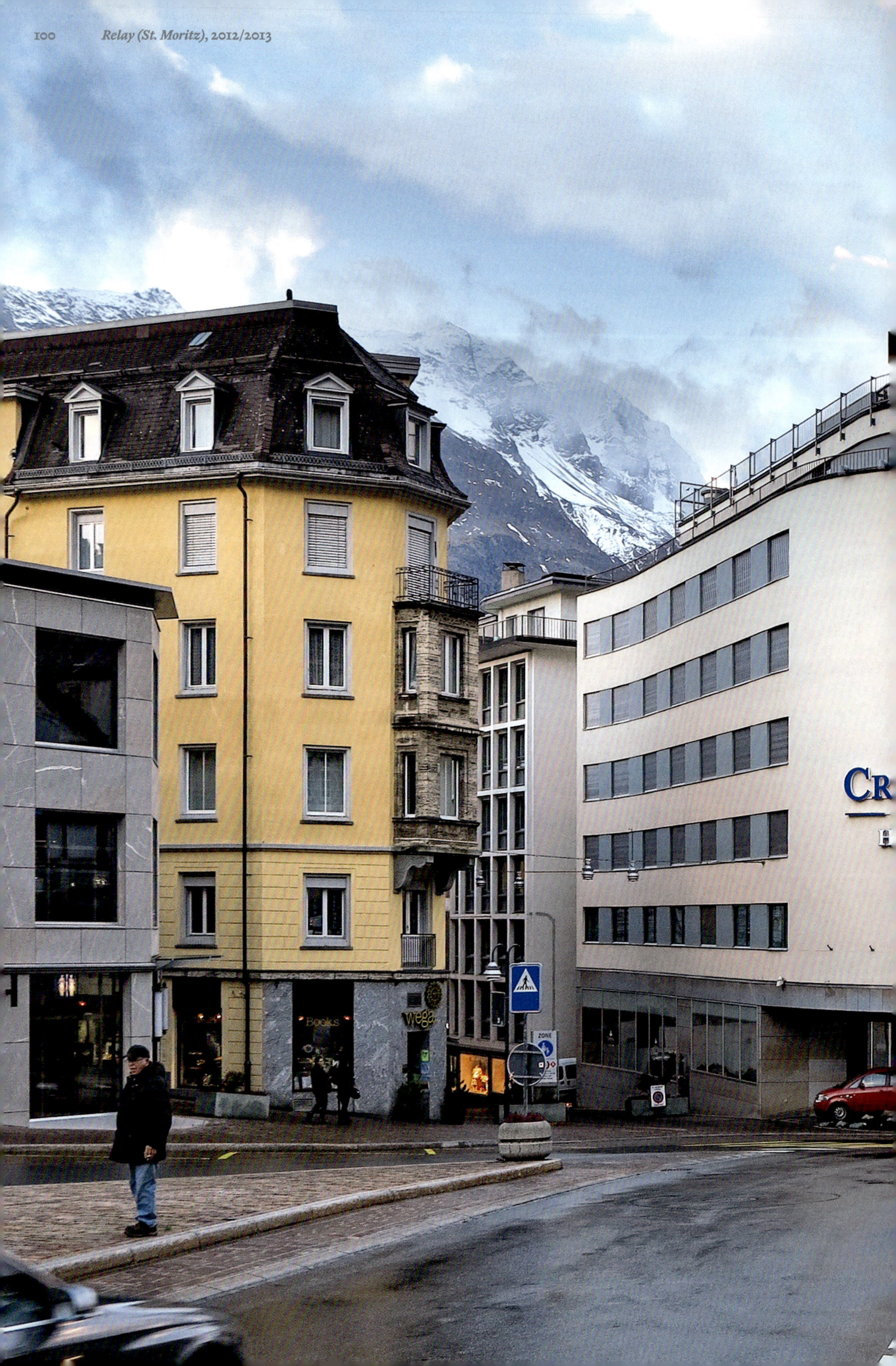
Books
wega

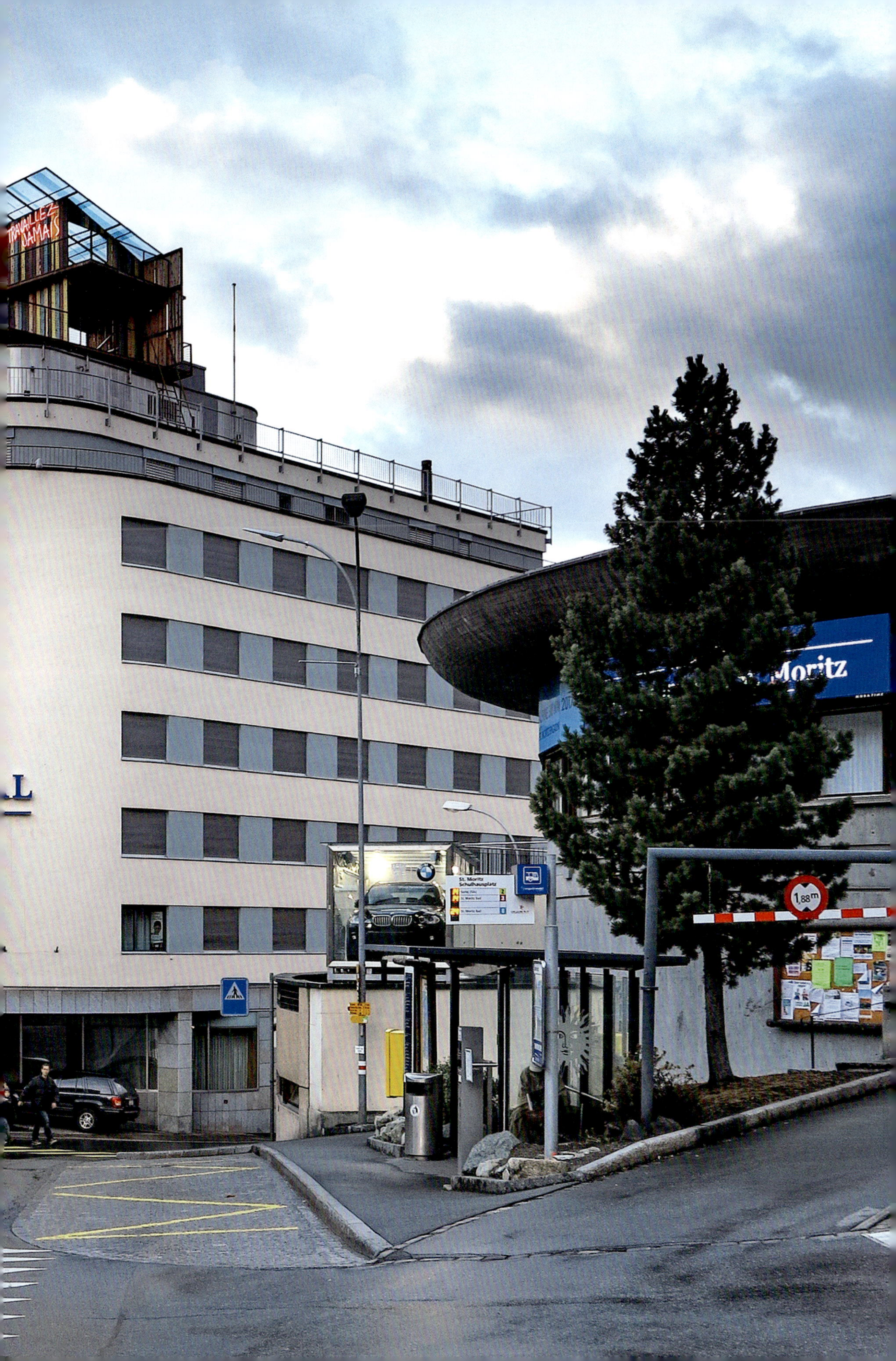
TRAVAILLEZ
JAMAIS
Moritz
St. Moritz
Schulhausplatz
1,88m

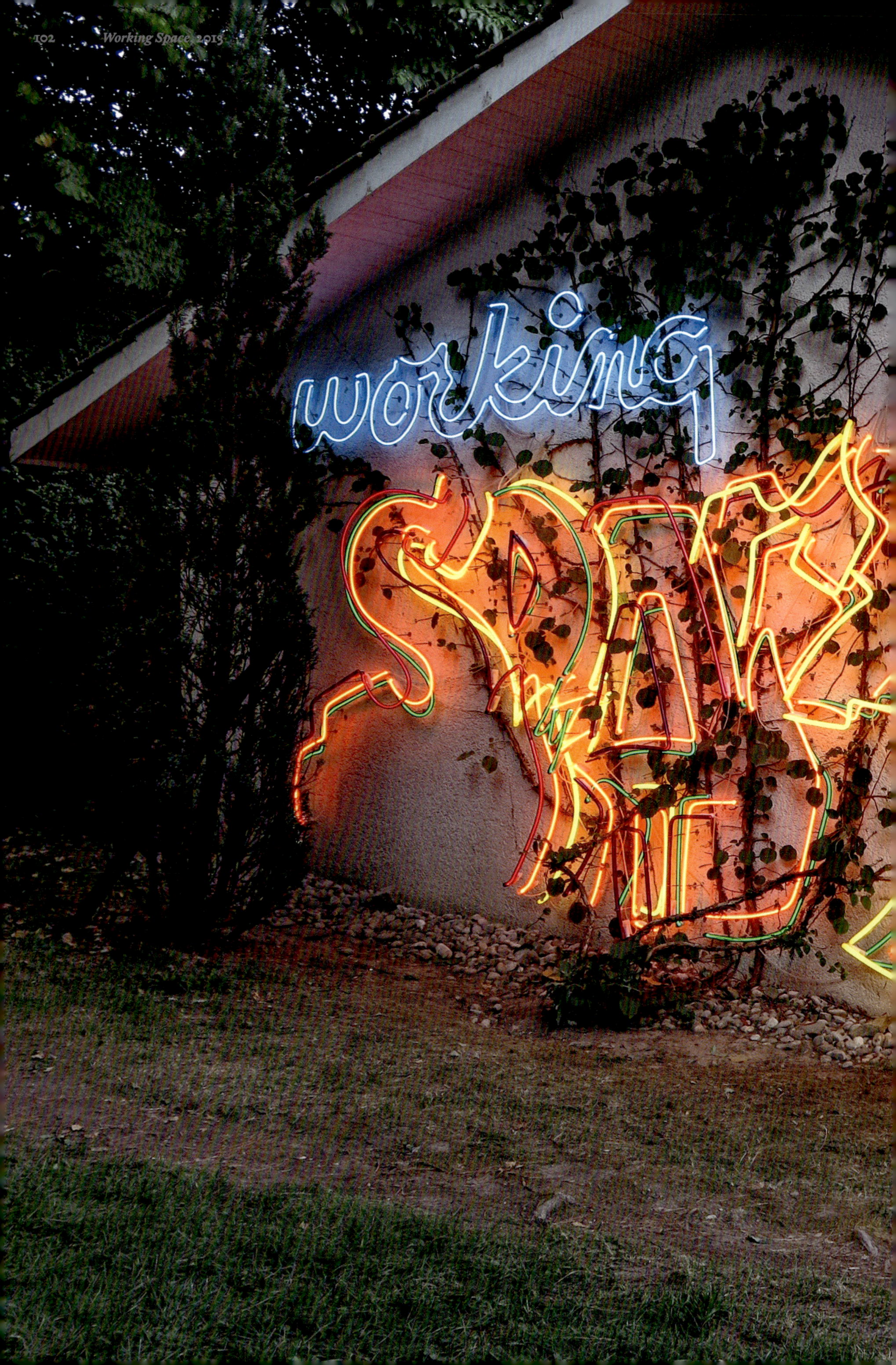
working

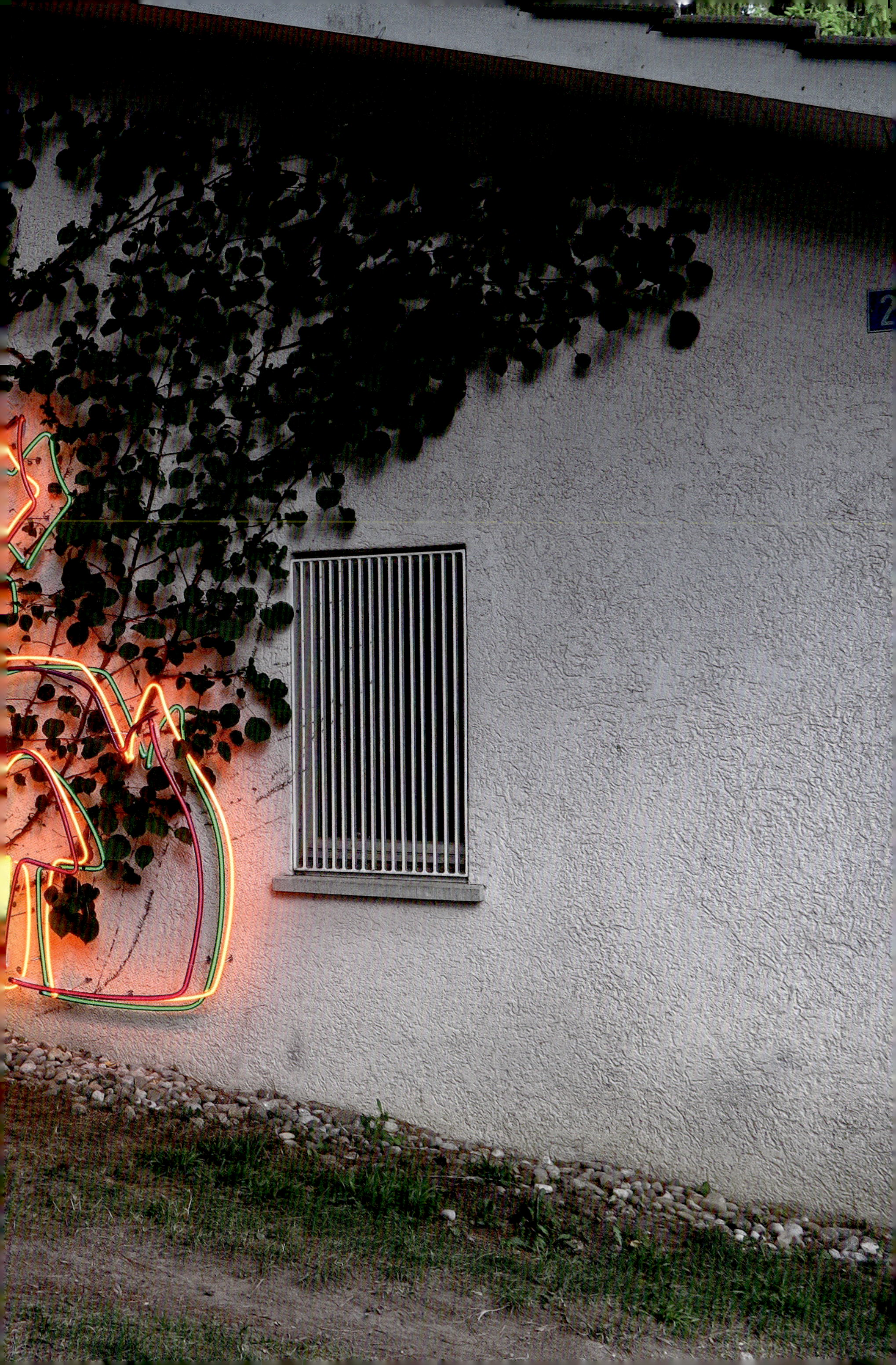

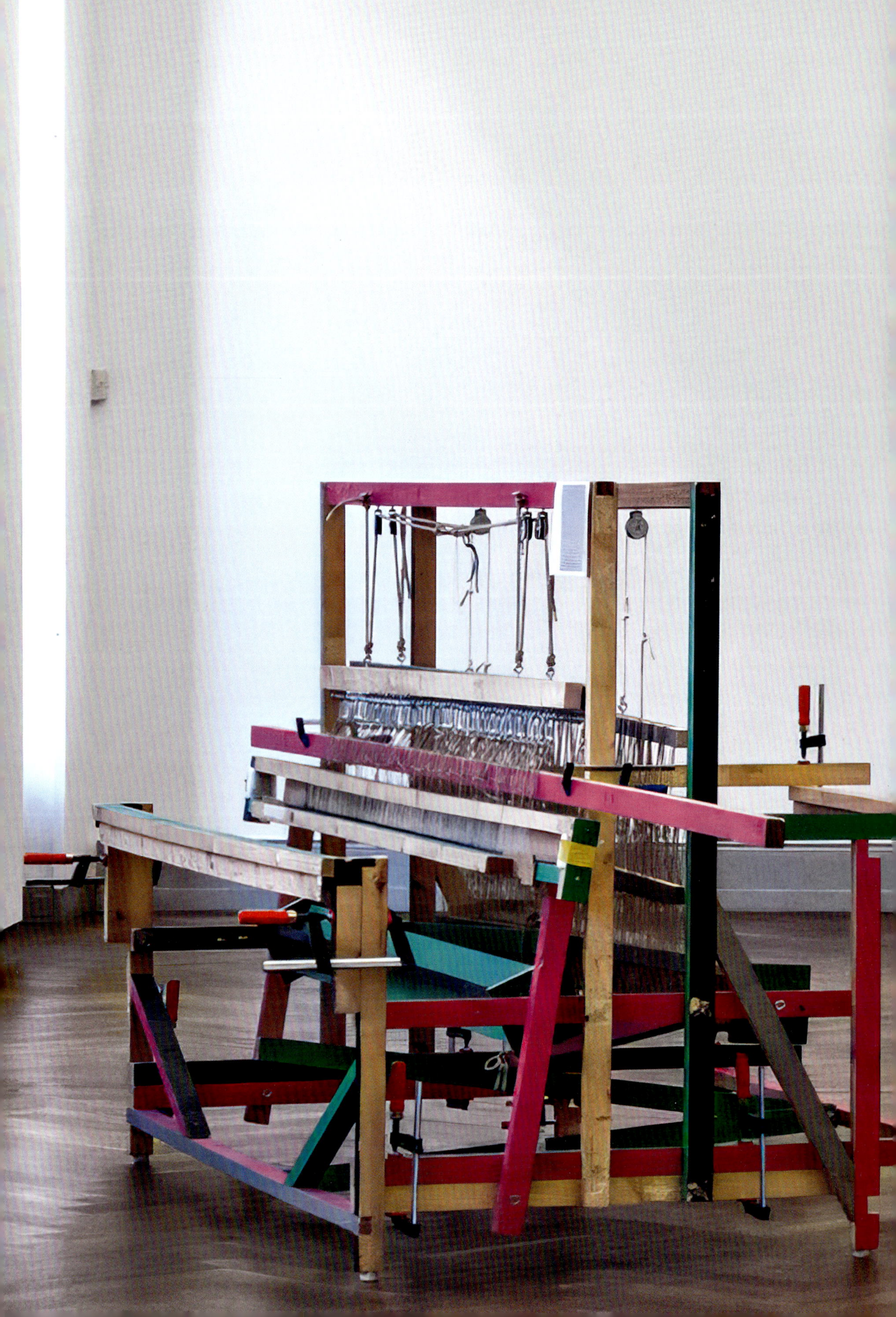

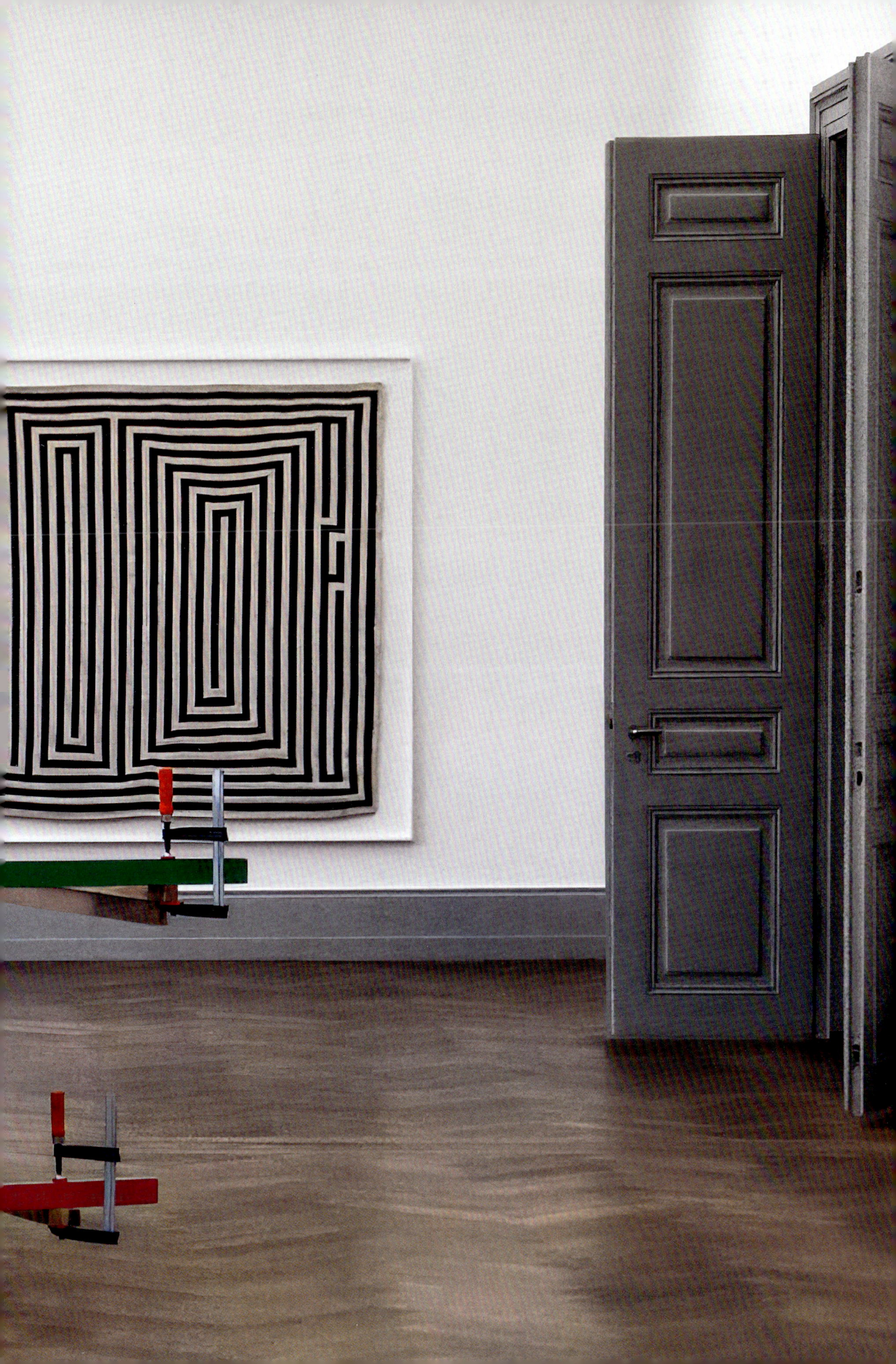

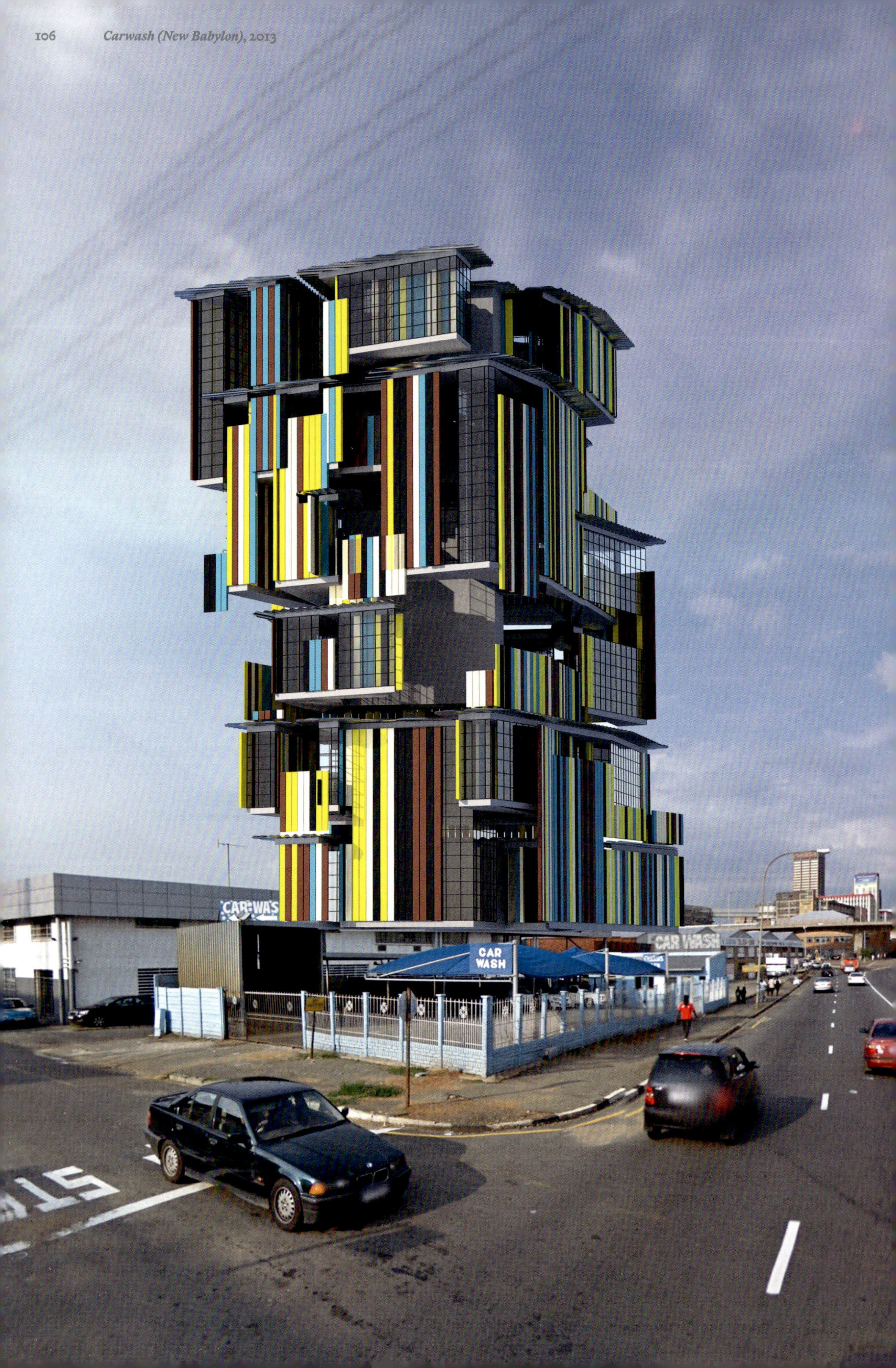

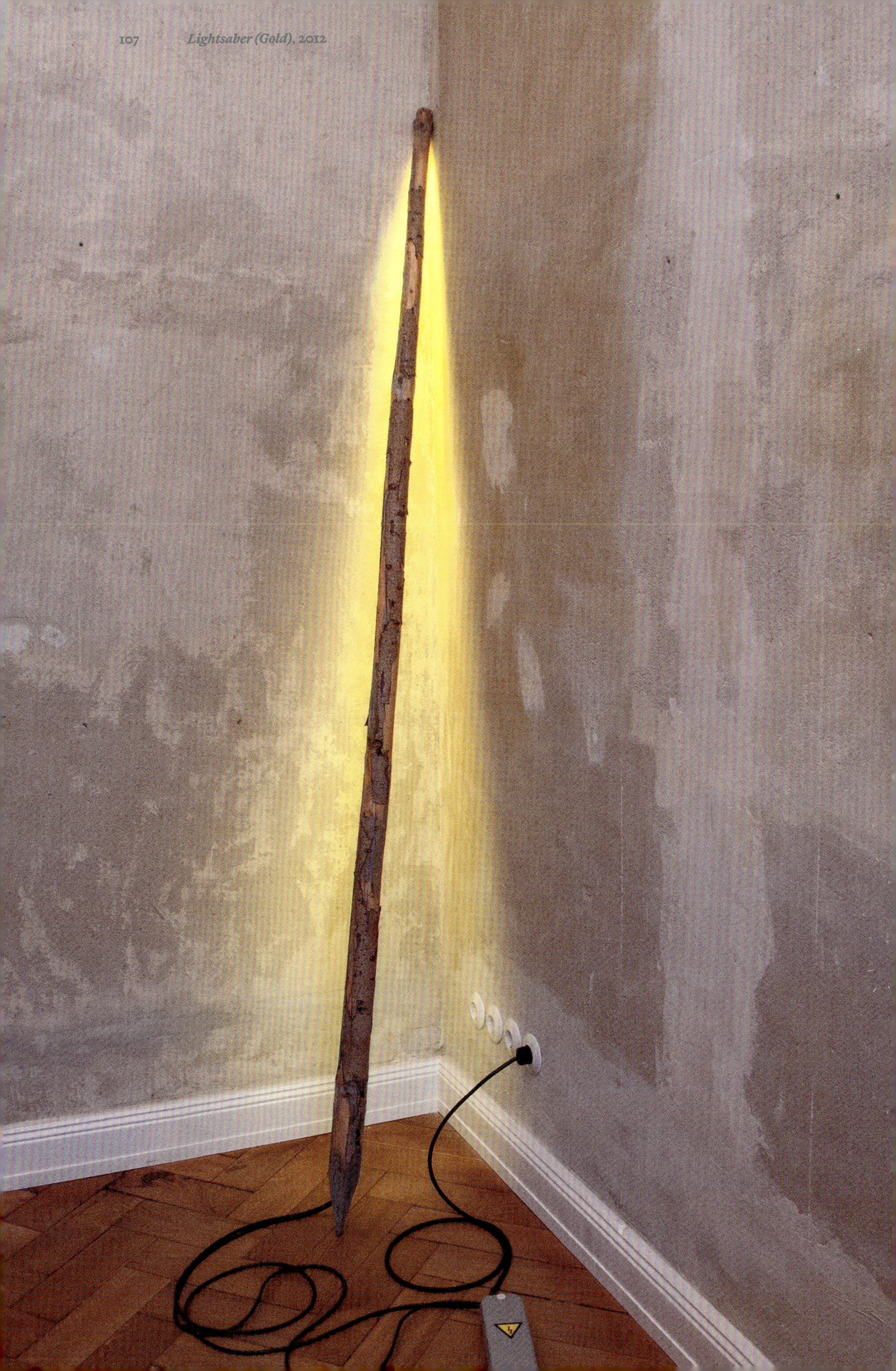

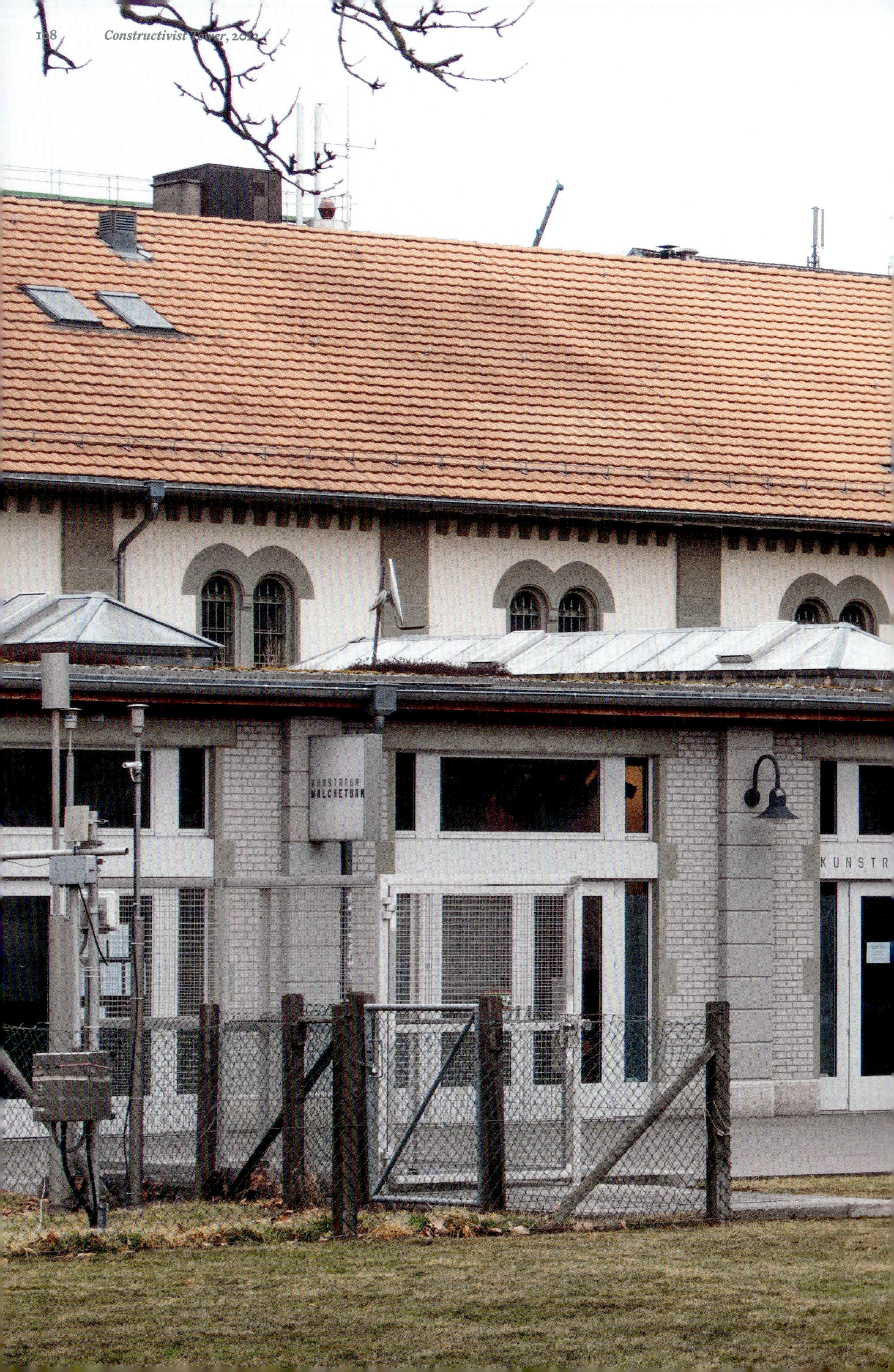
KUNSTRAUM
WALCHETURM
KUNSTR

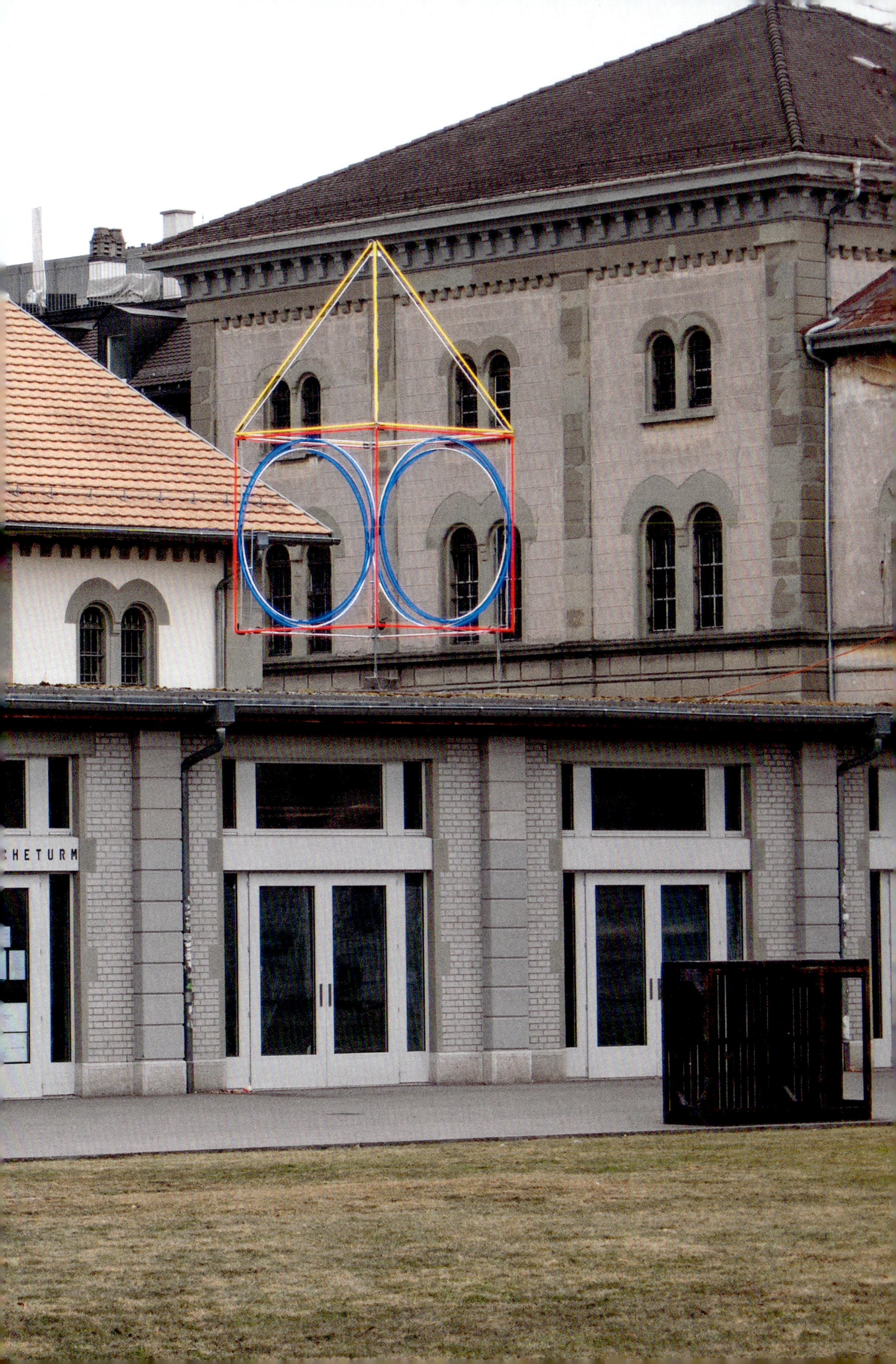
CHETURM

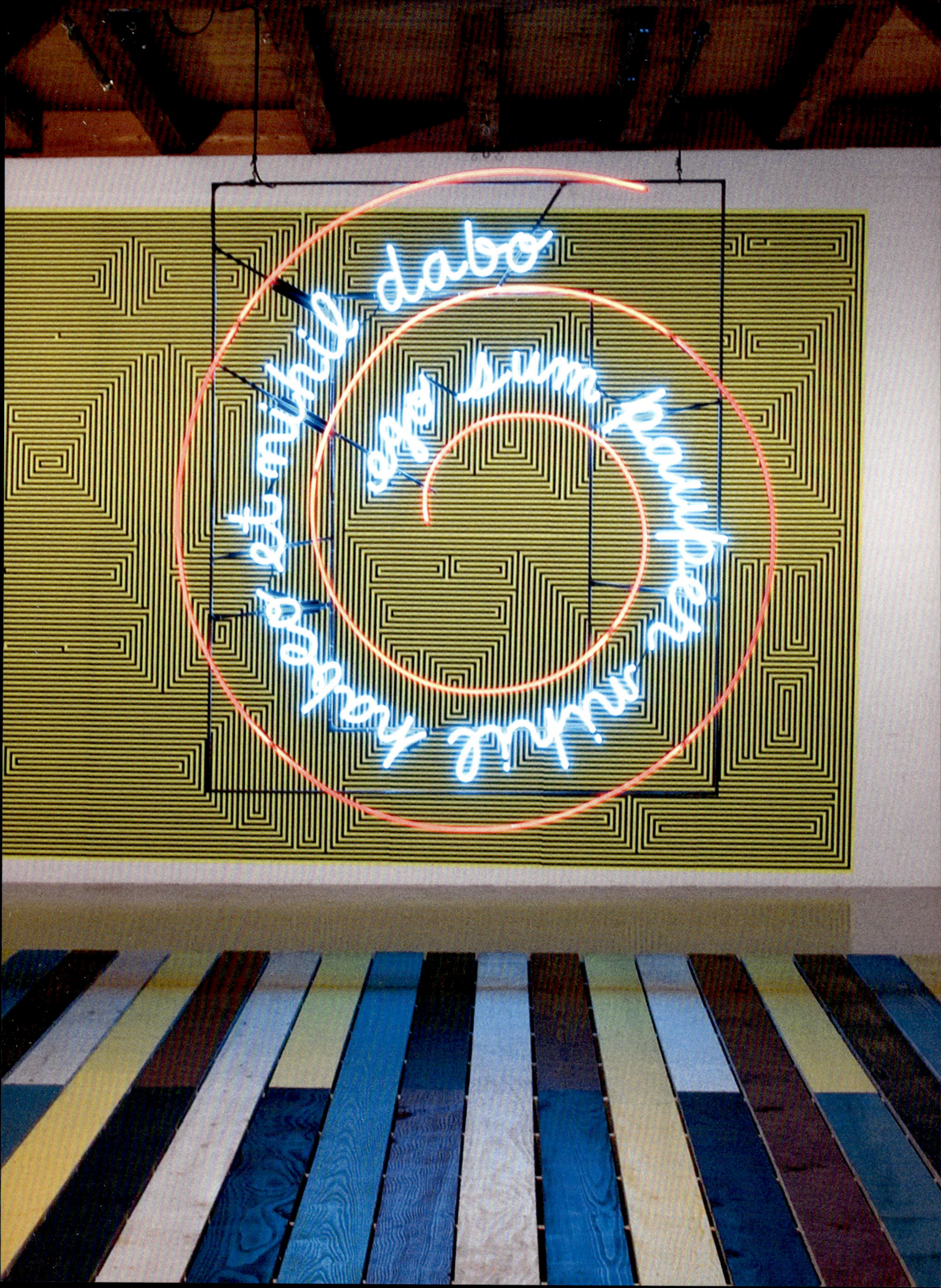
ego sum pauper nihil habeo et nihil dabo

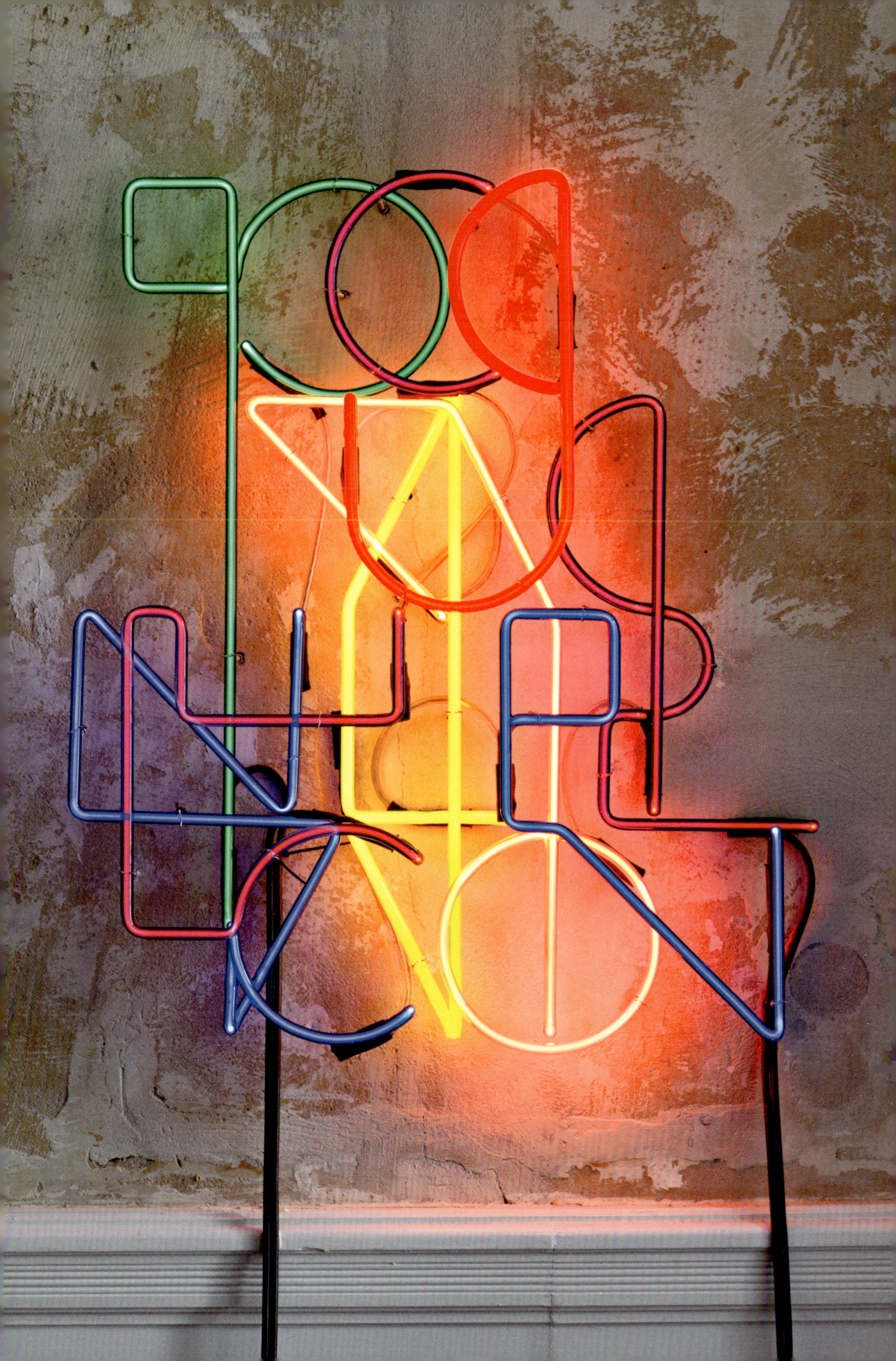

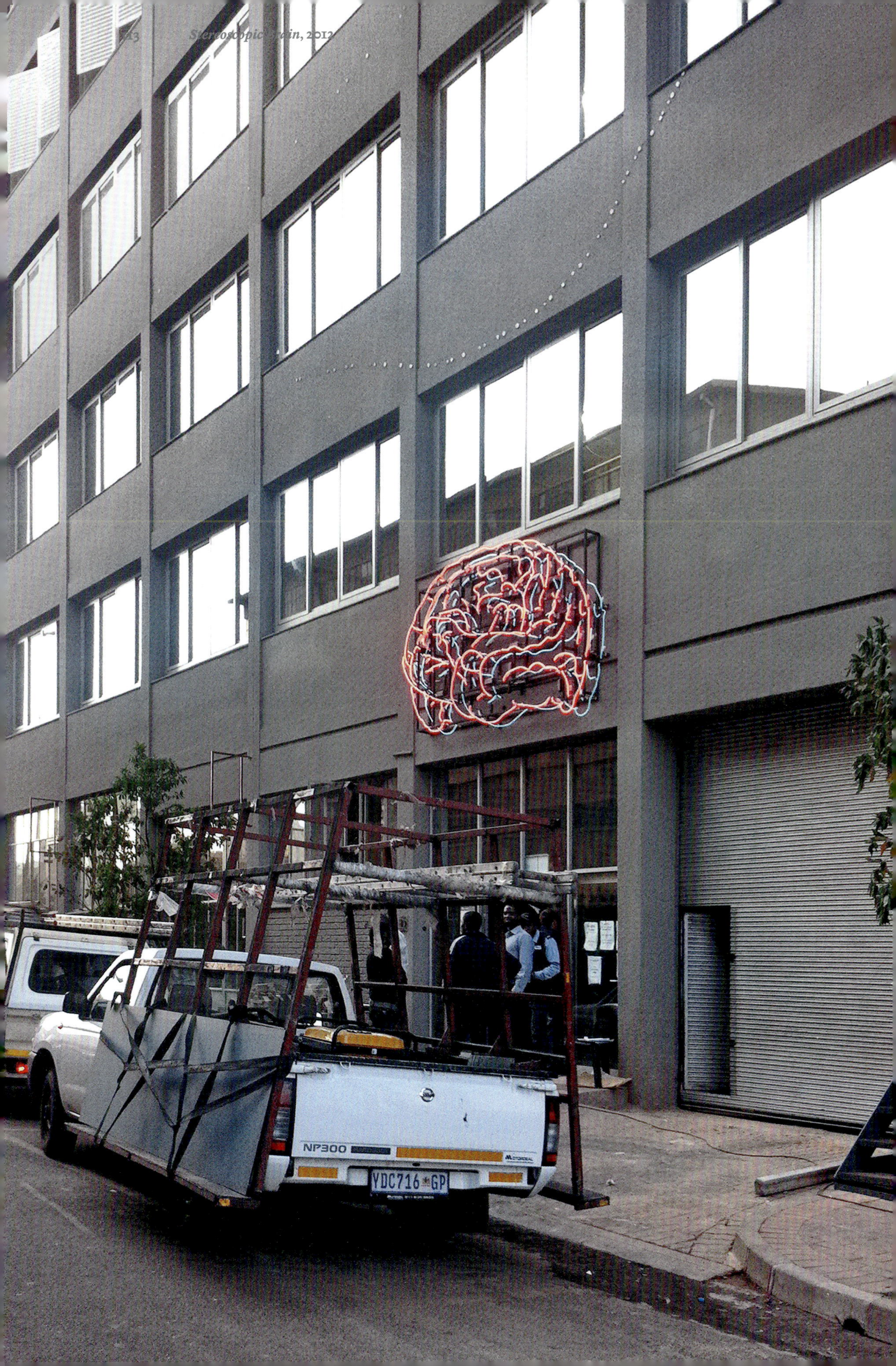

Stereoscopic Brain, 2012

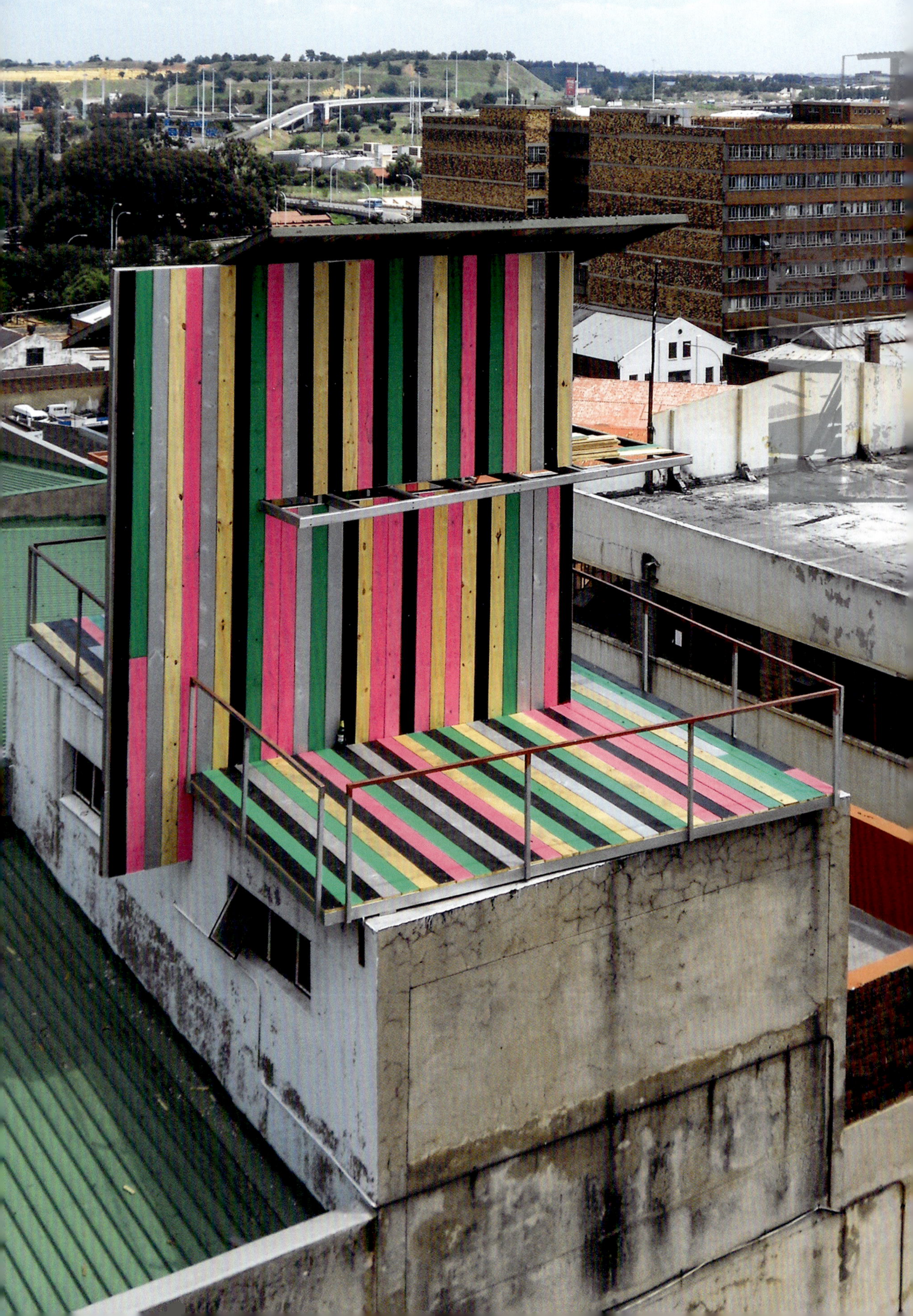

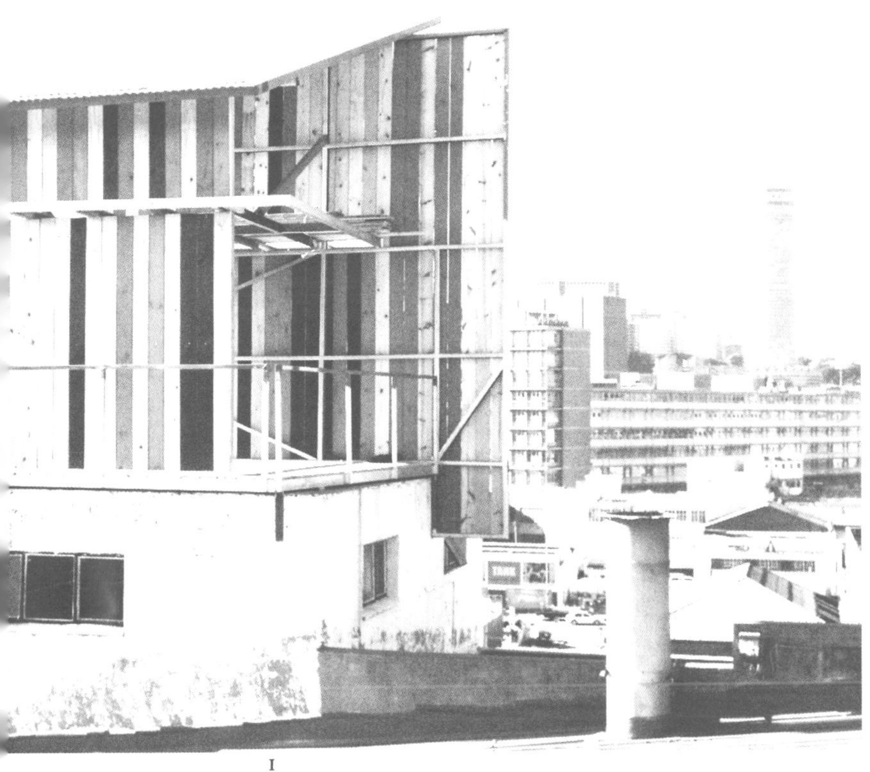

I

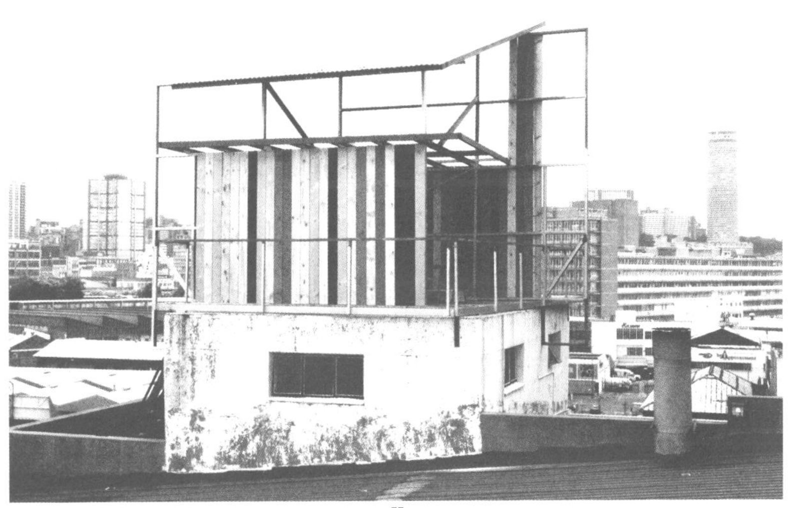

II

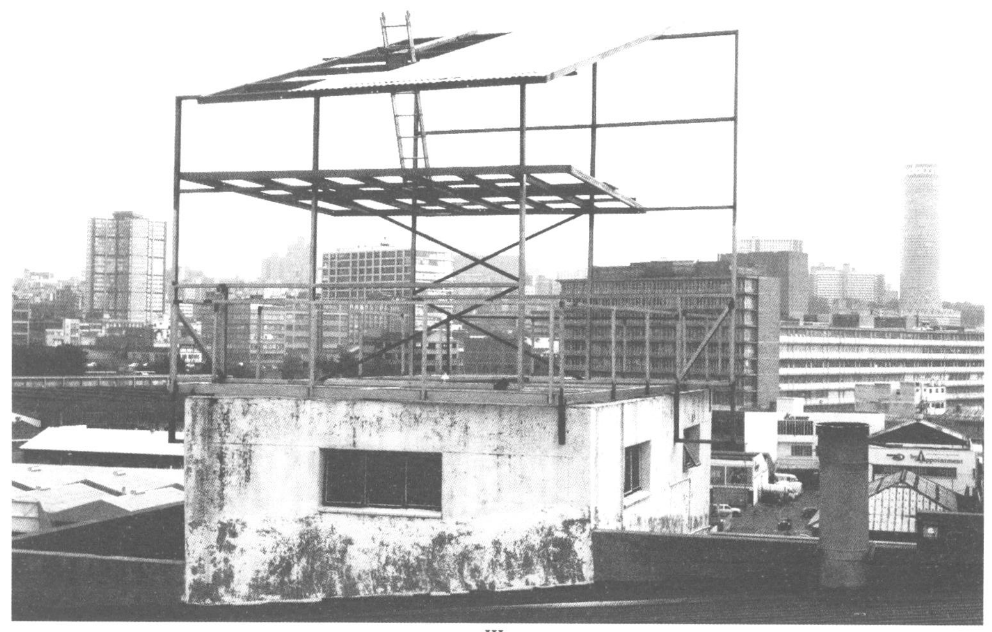

III

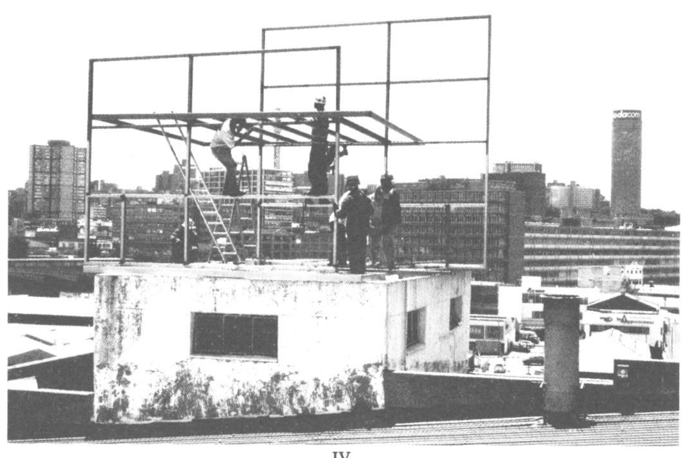

IV

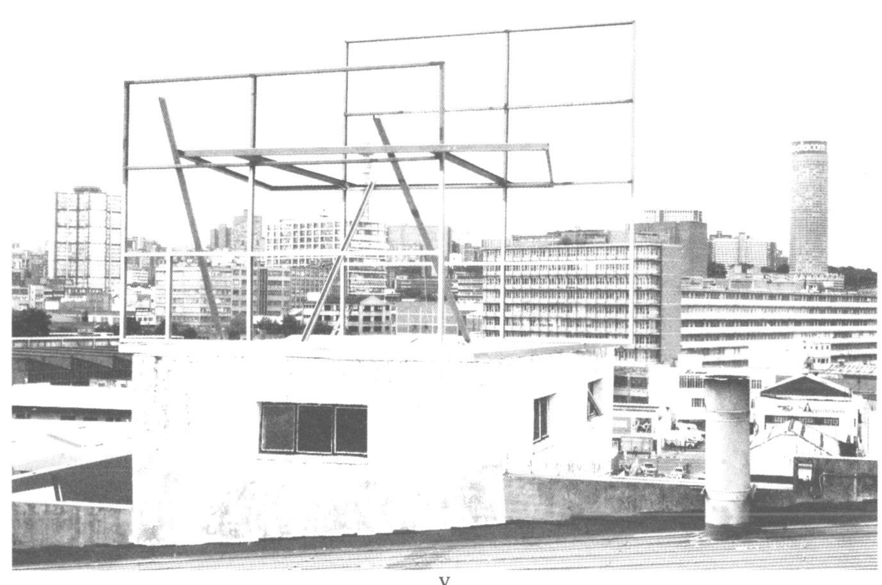
V

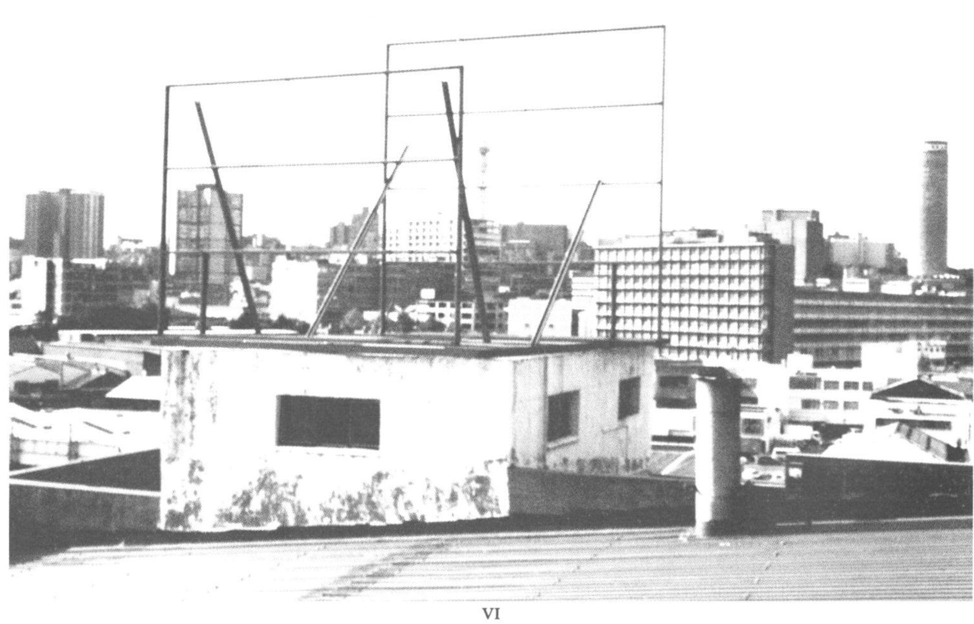
VI

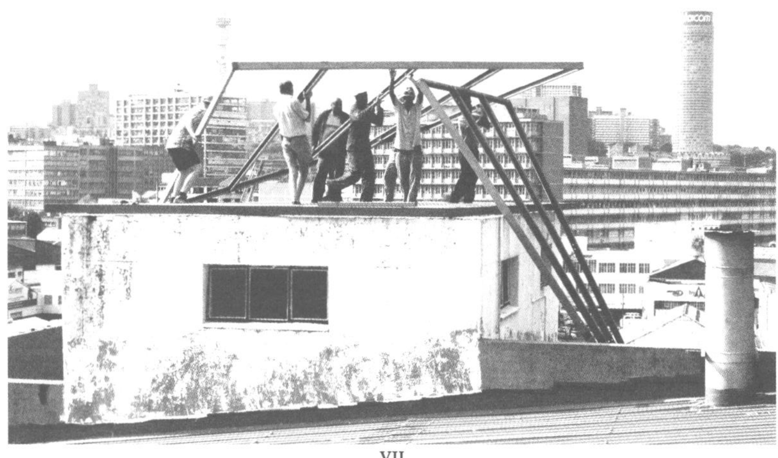

VII

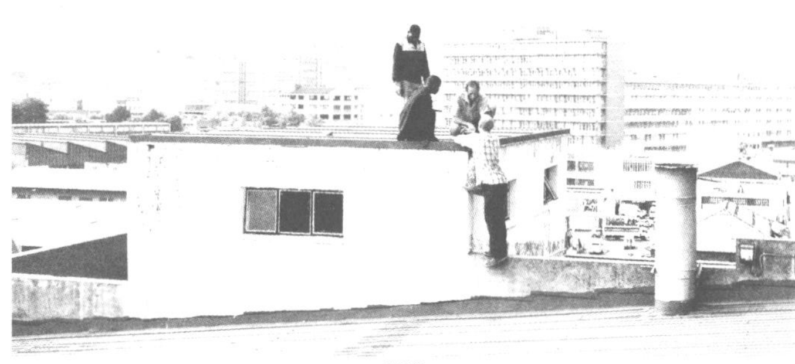

VIII

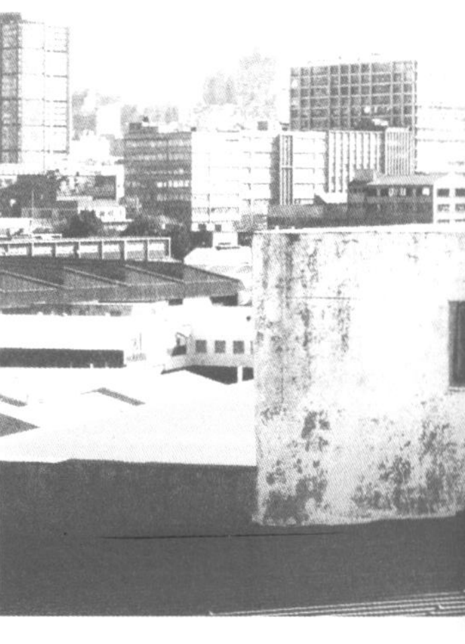

Pineal Horseshoe, 2012

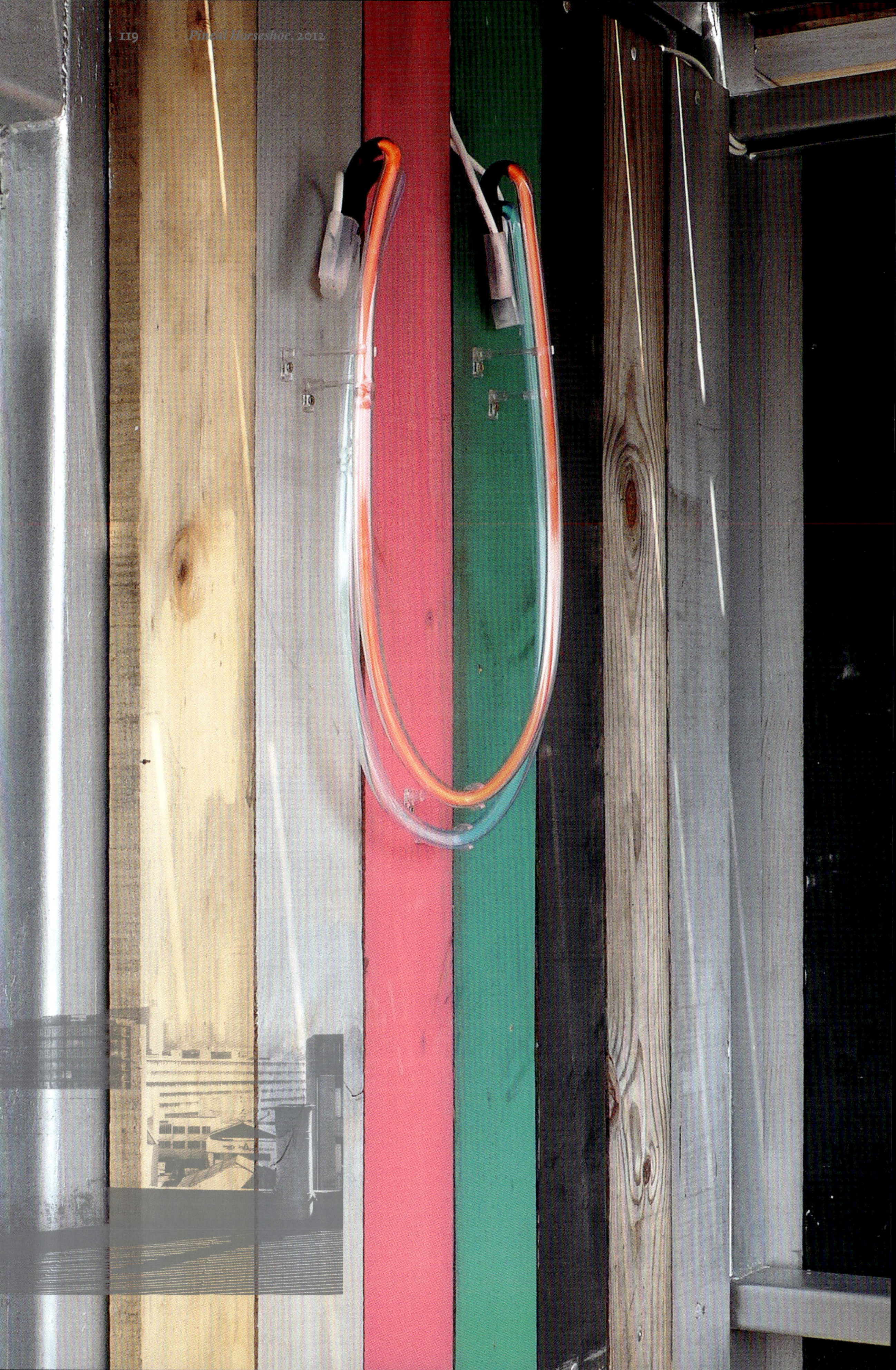

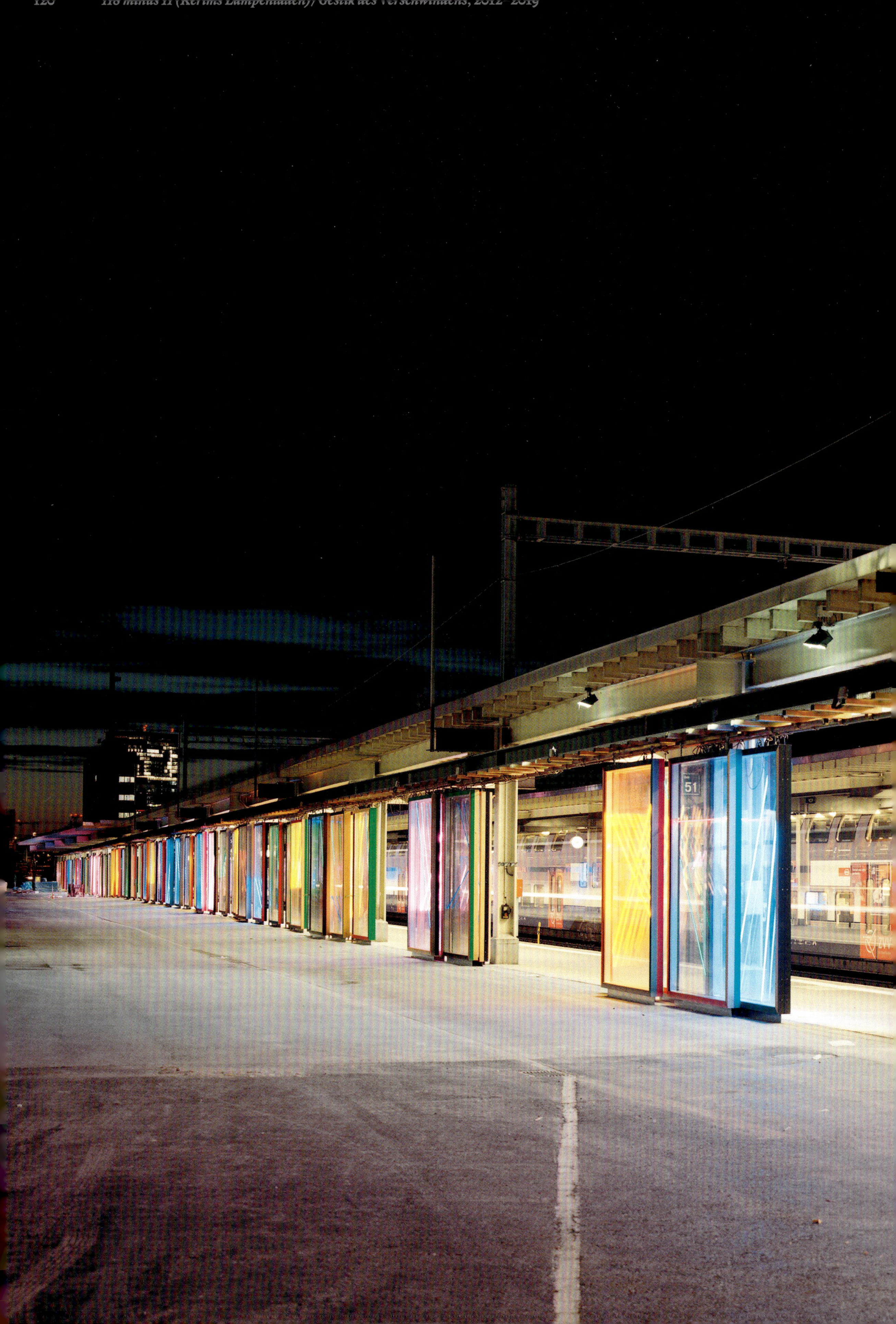
51

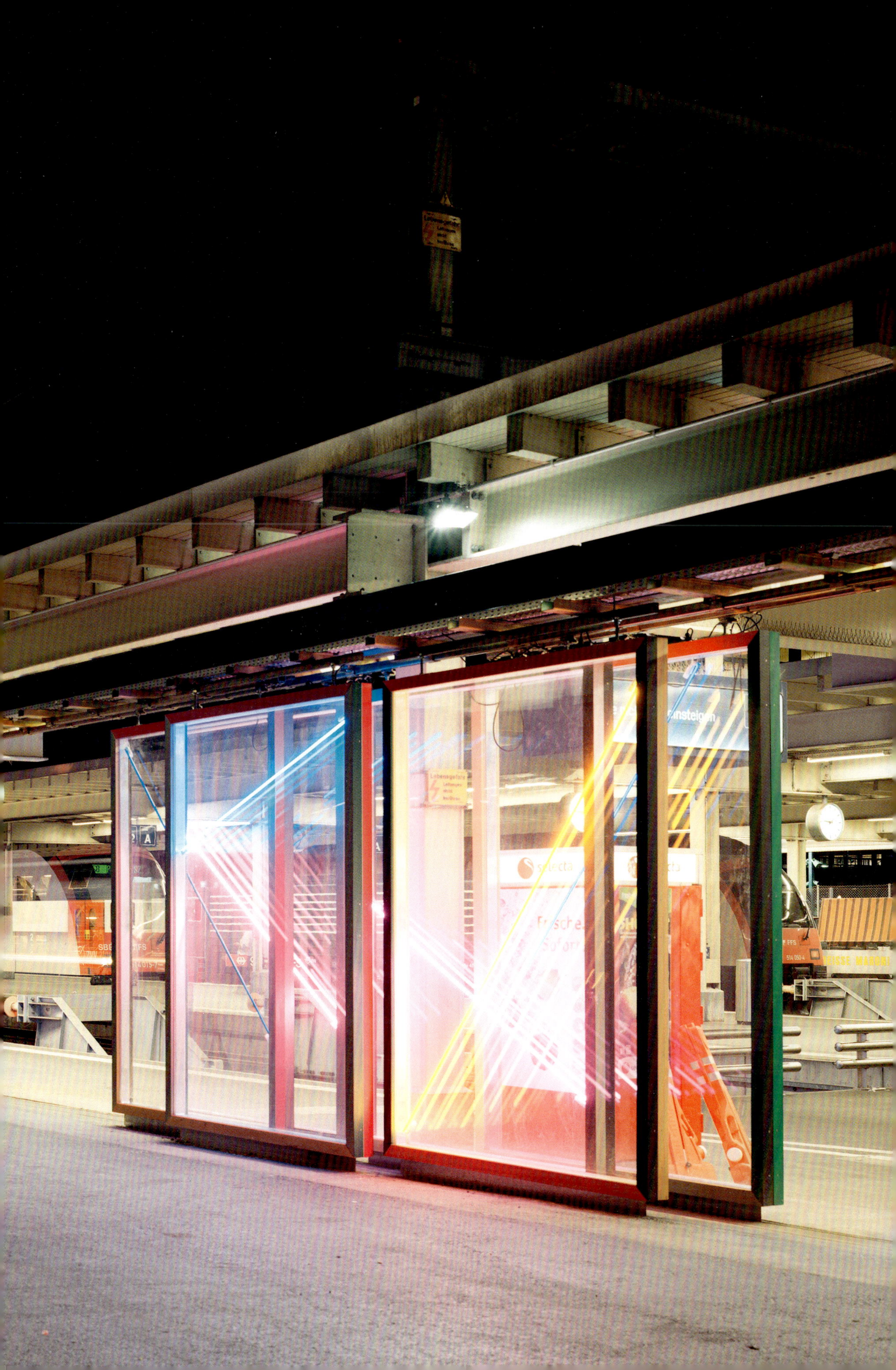
selecta

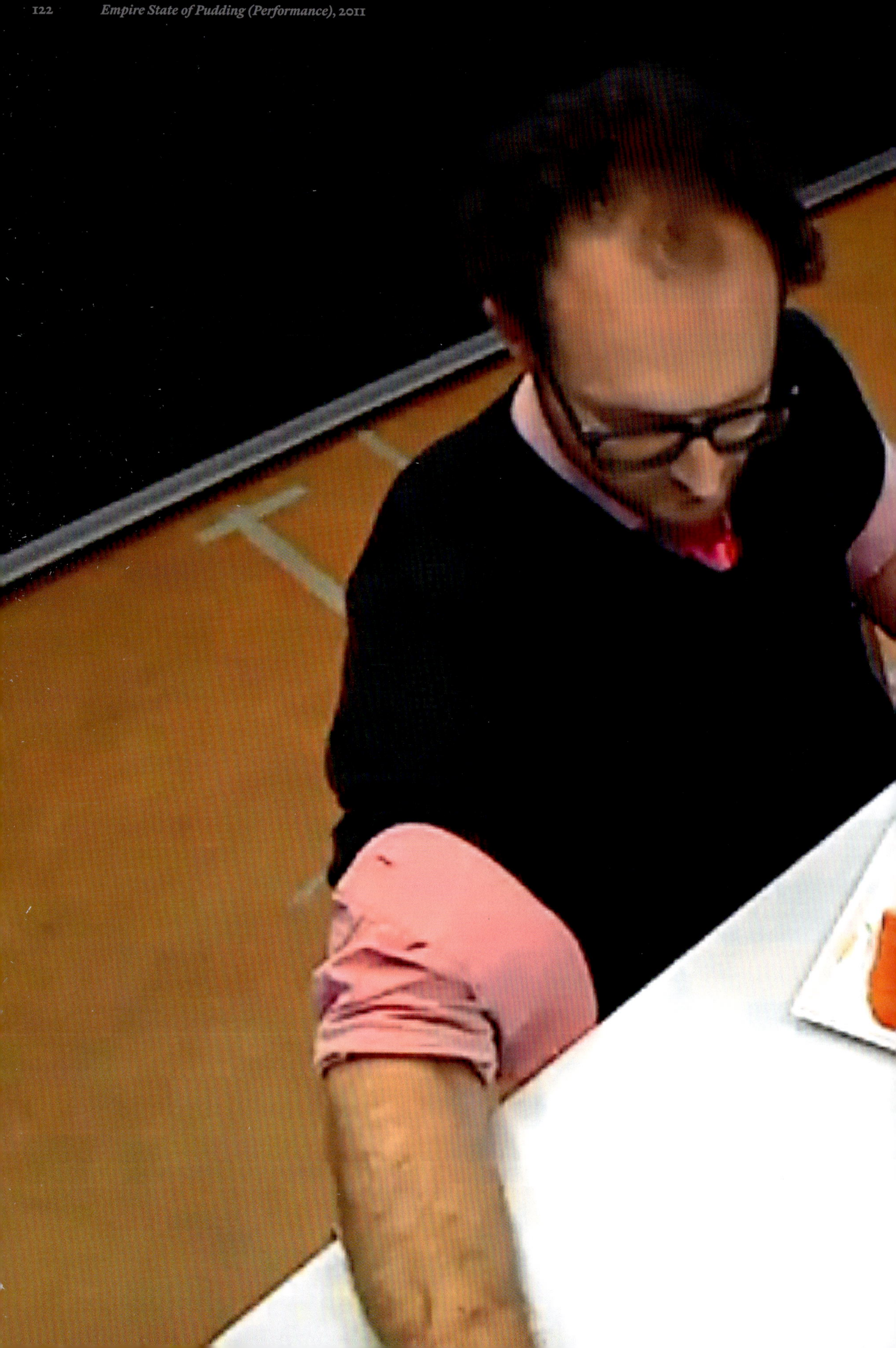

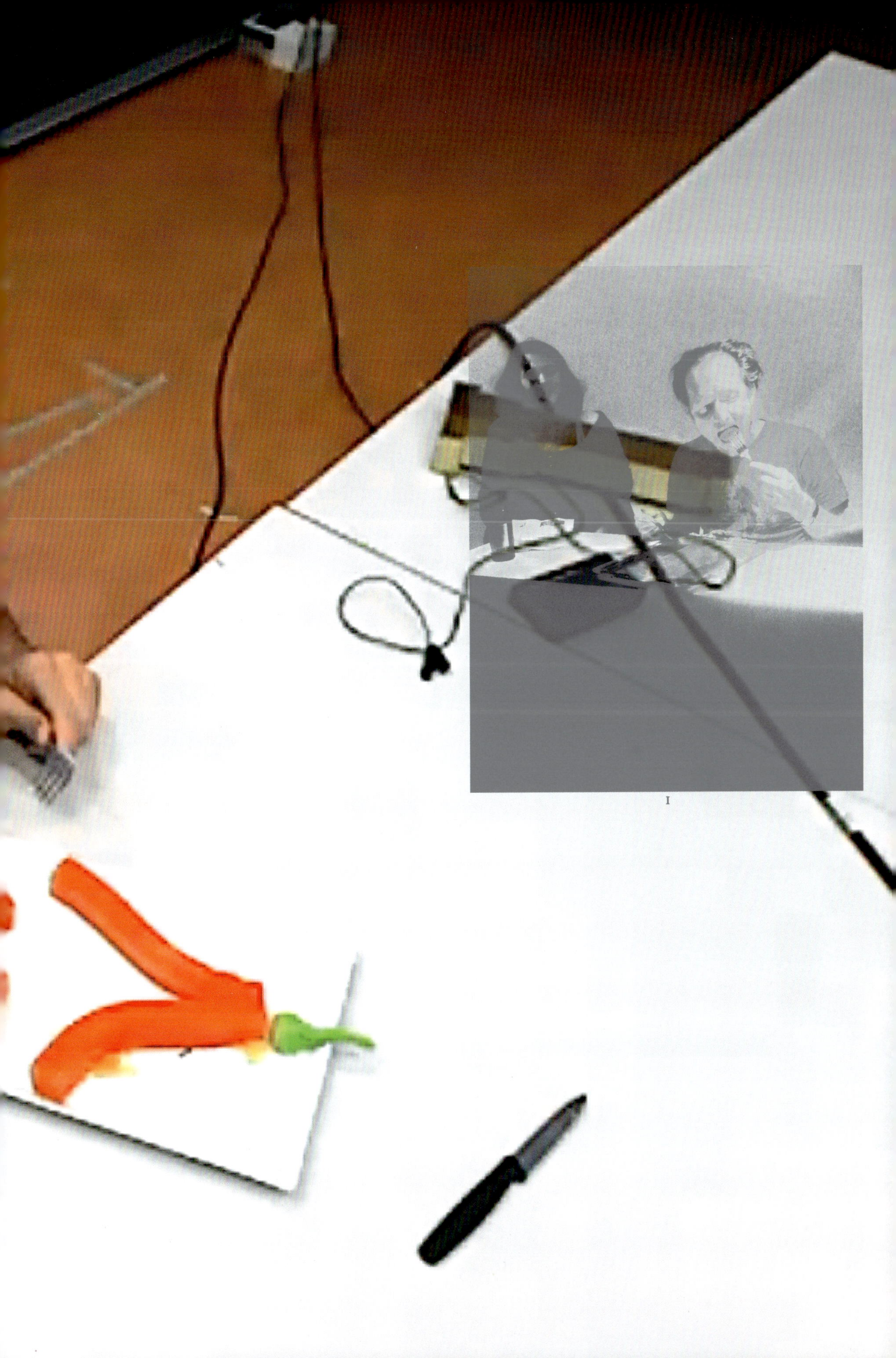

1

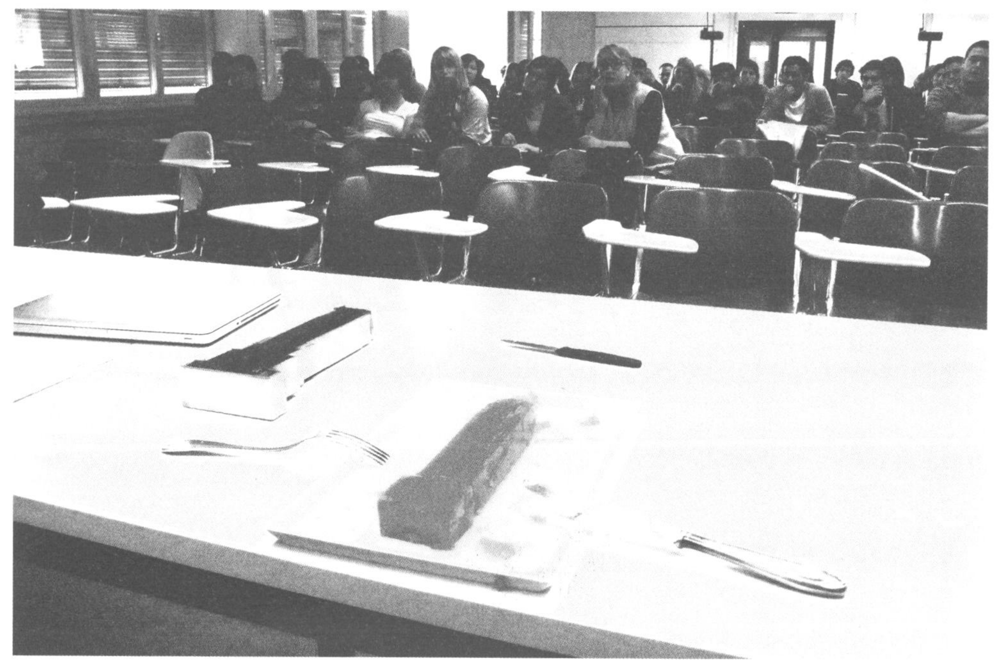

II

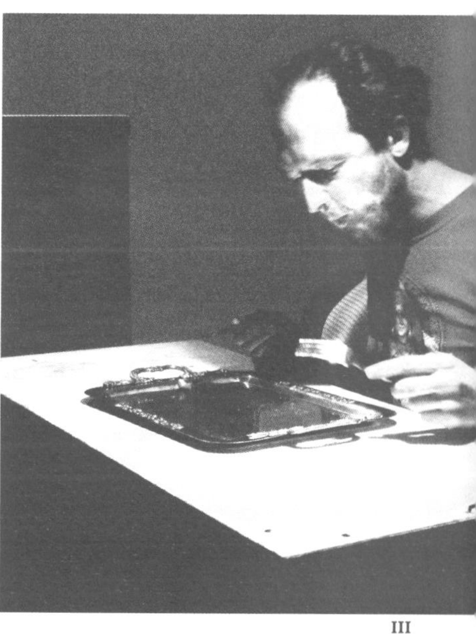

III

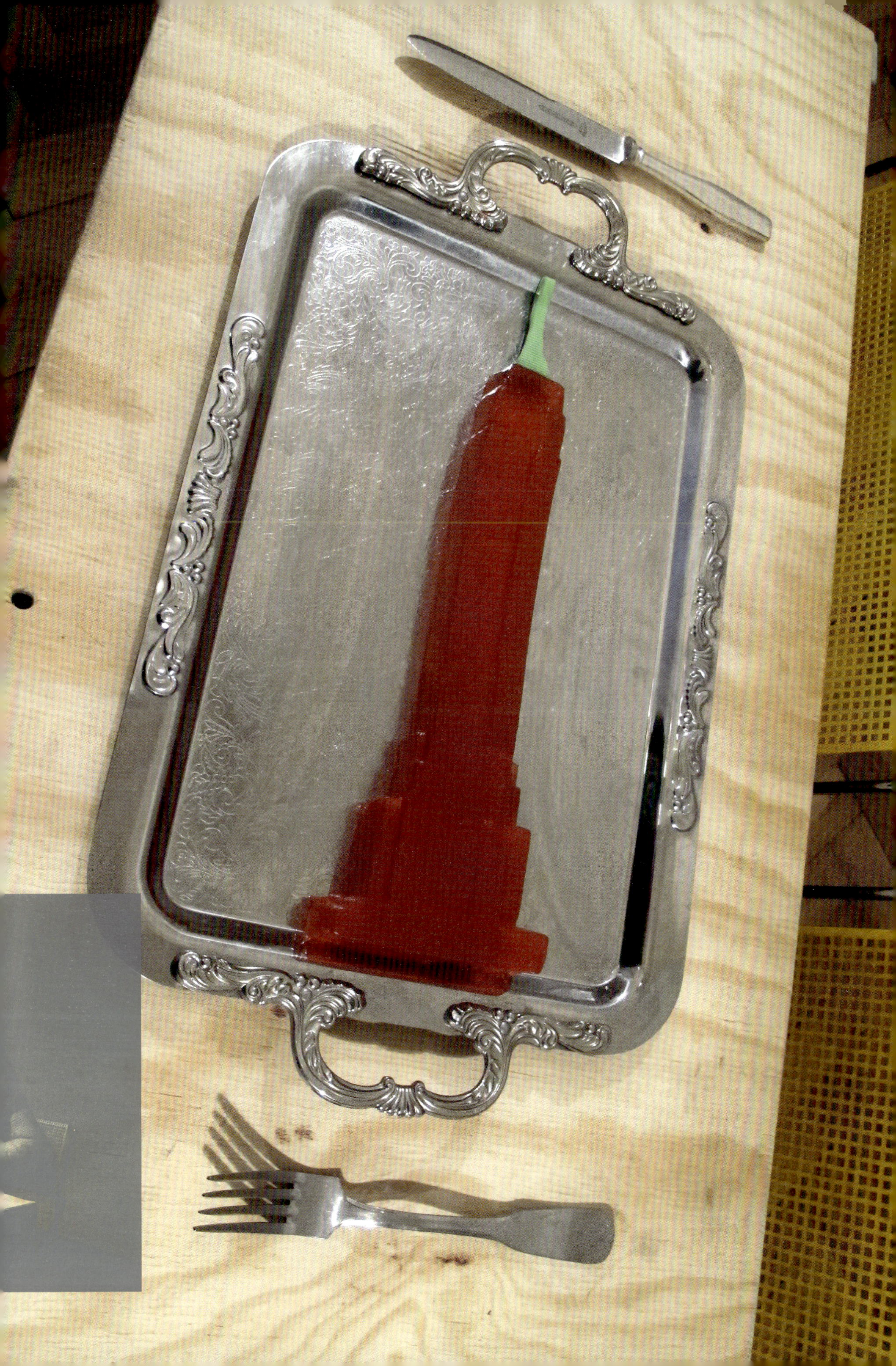

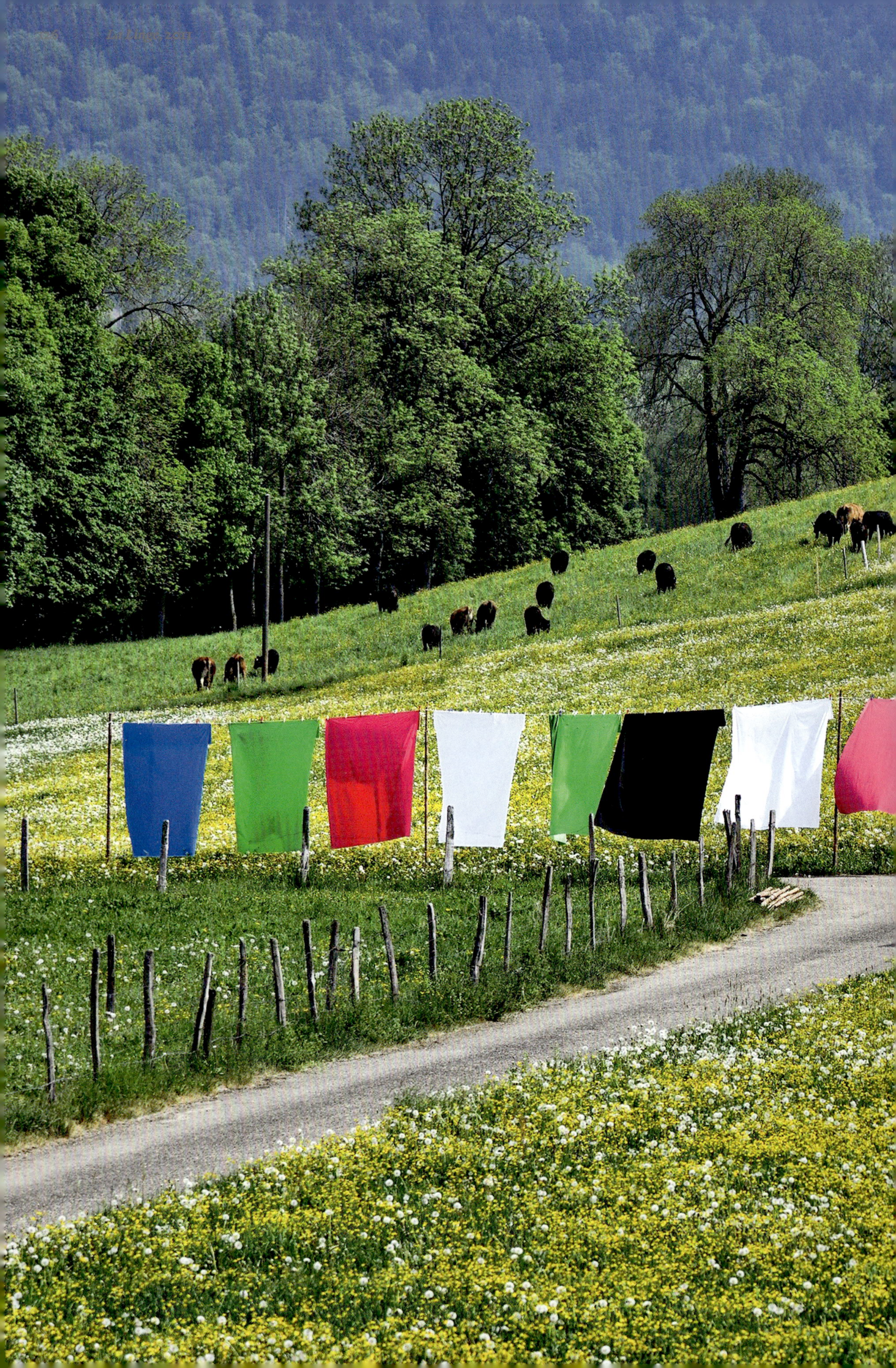

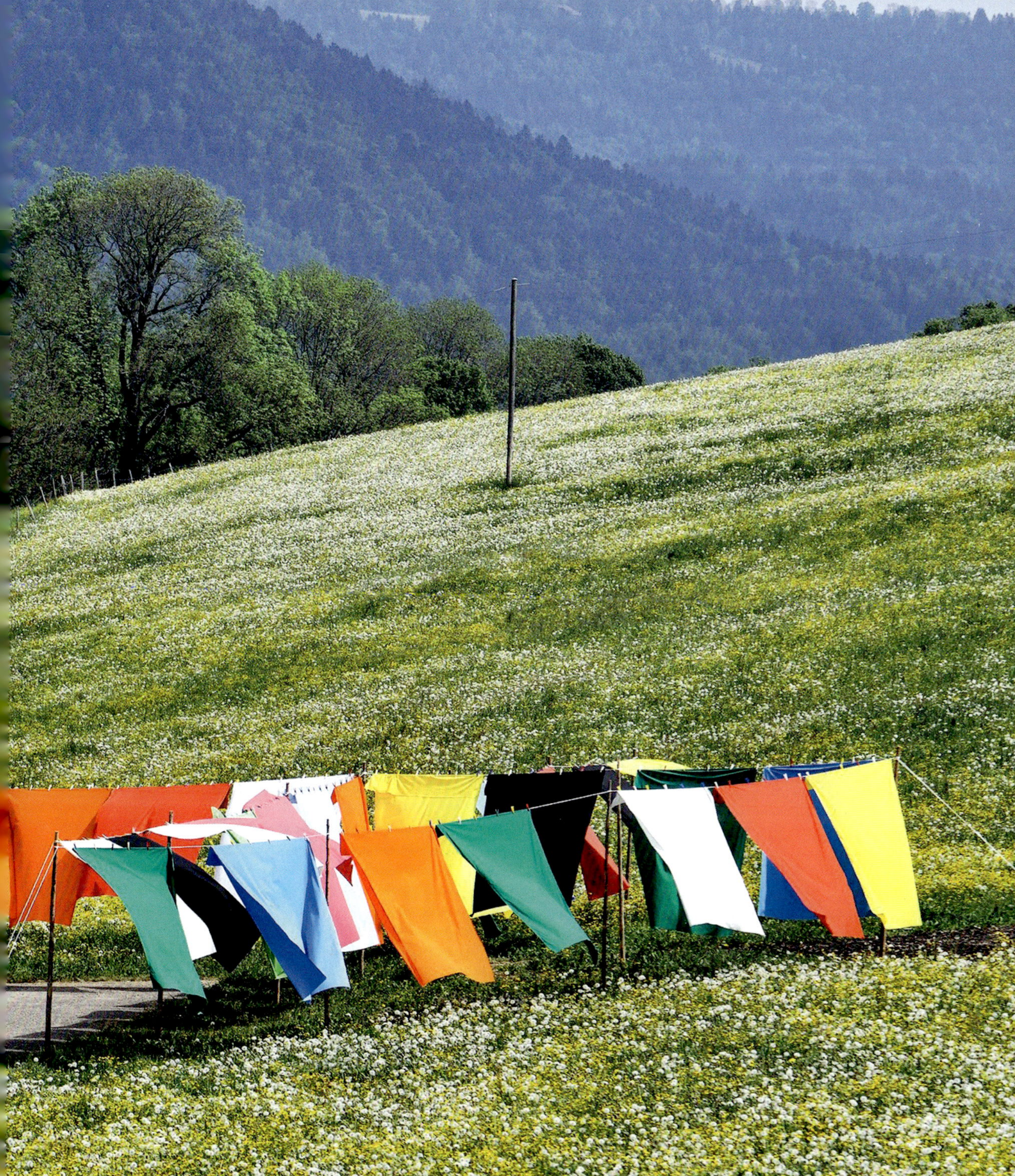

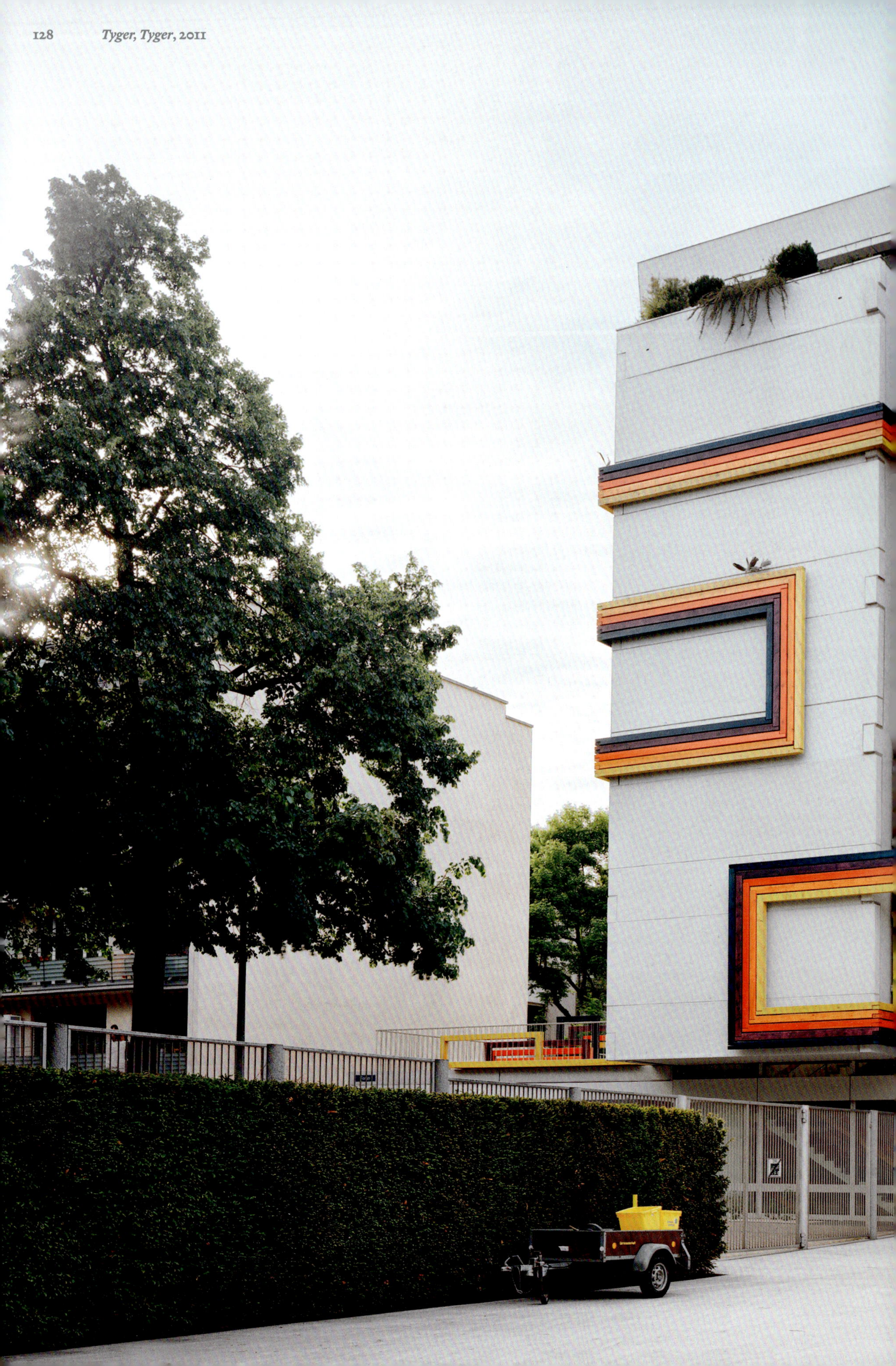

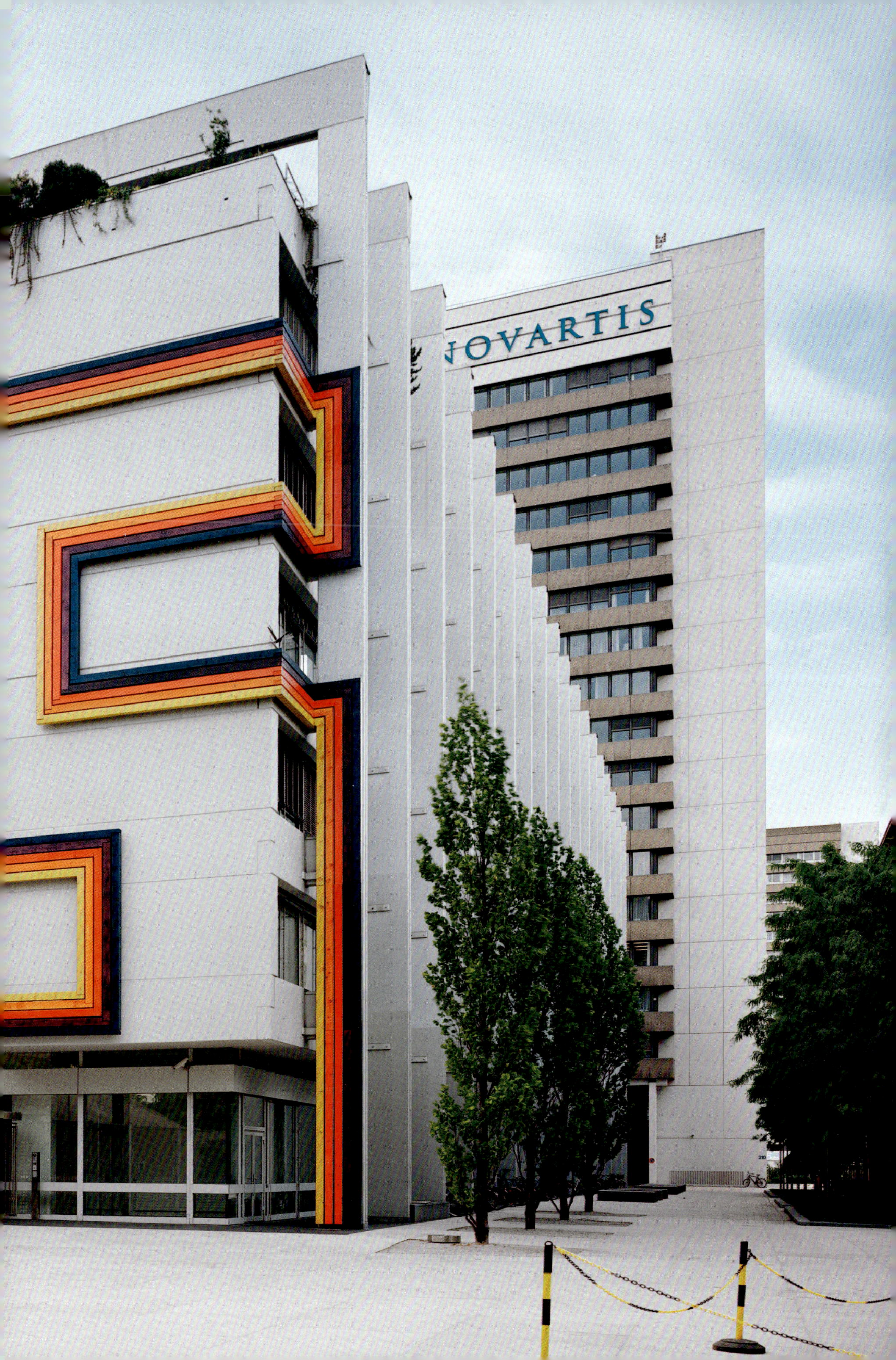
NOVARTIS

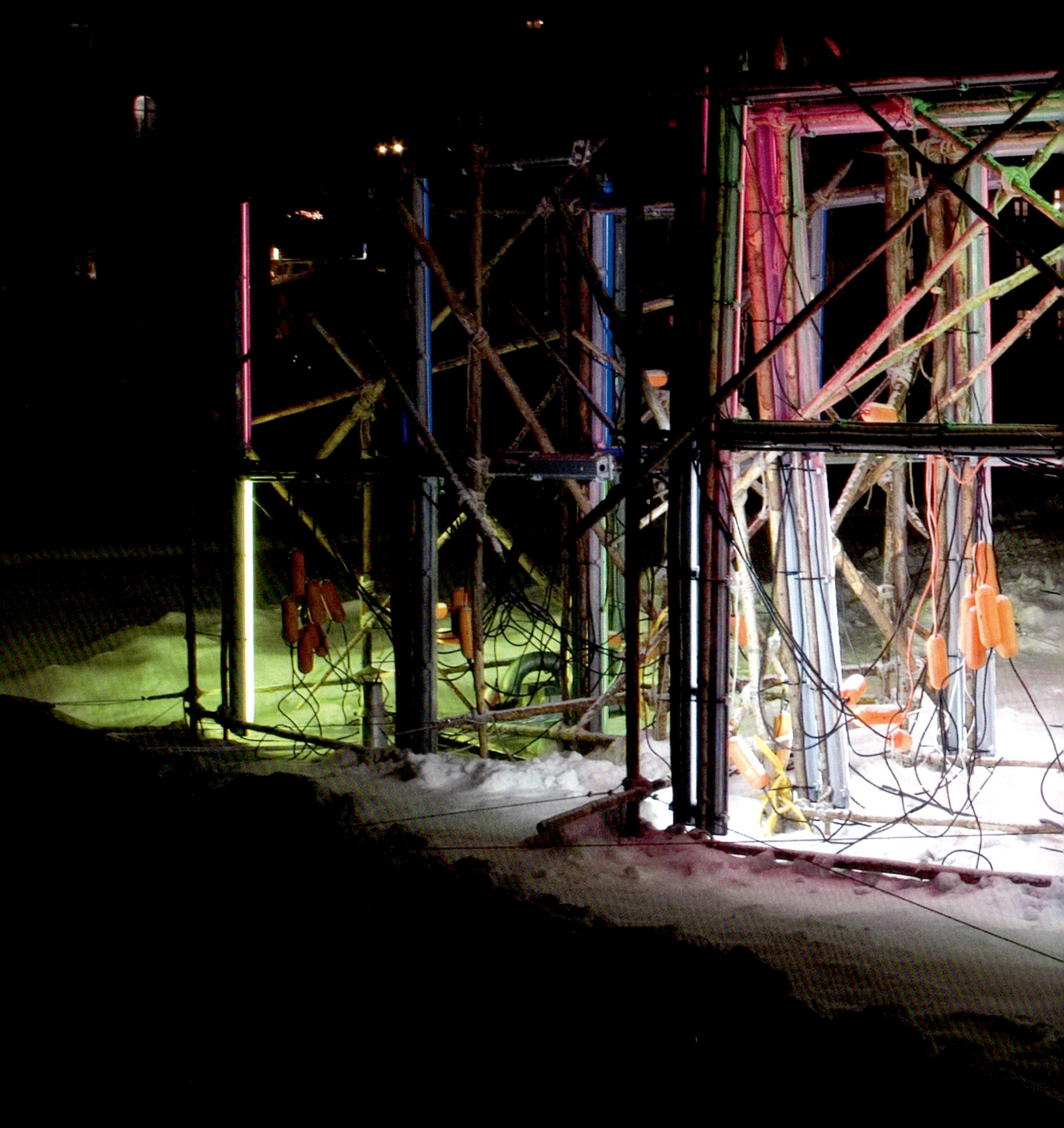

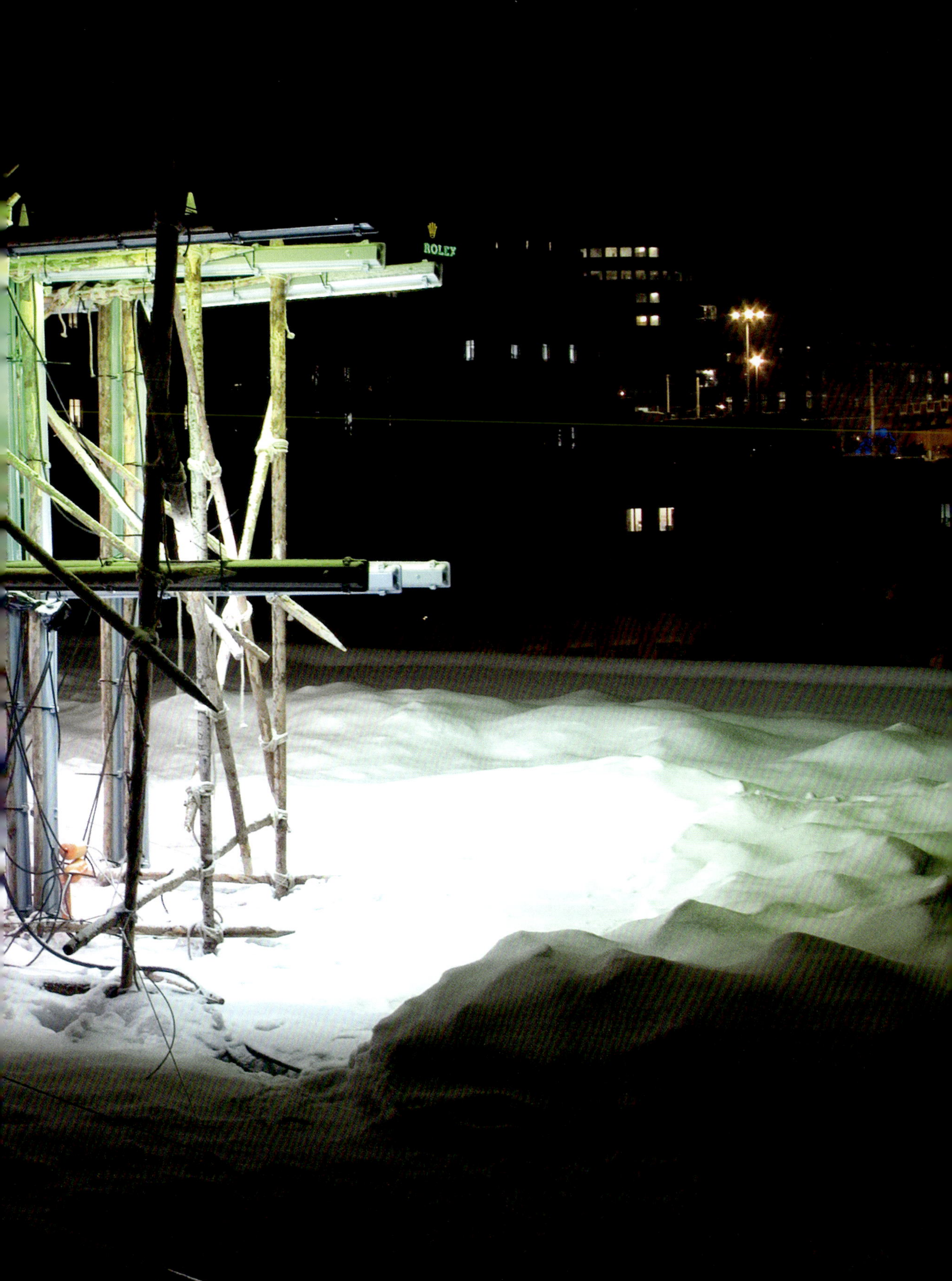
ROLEX

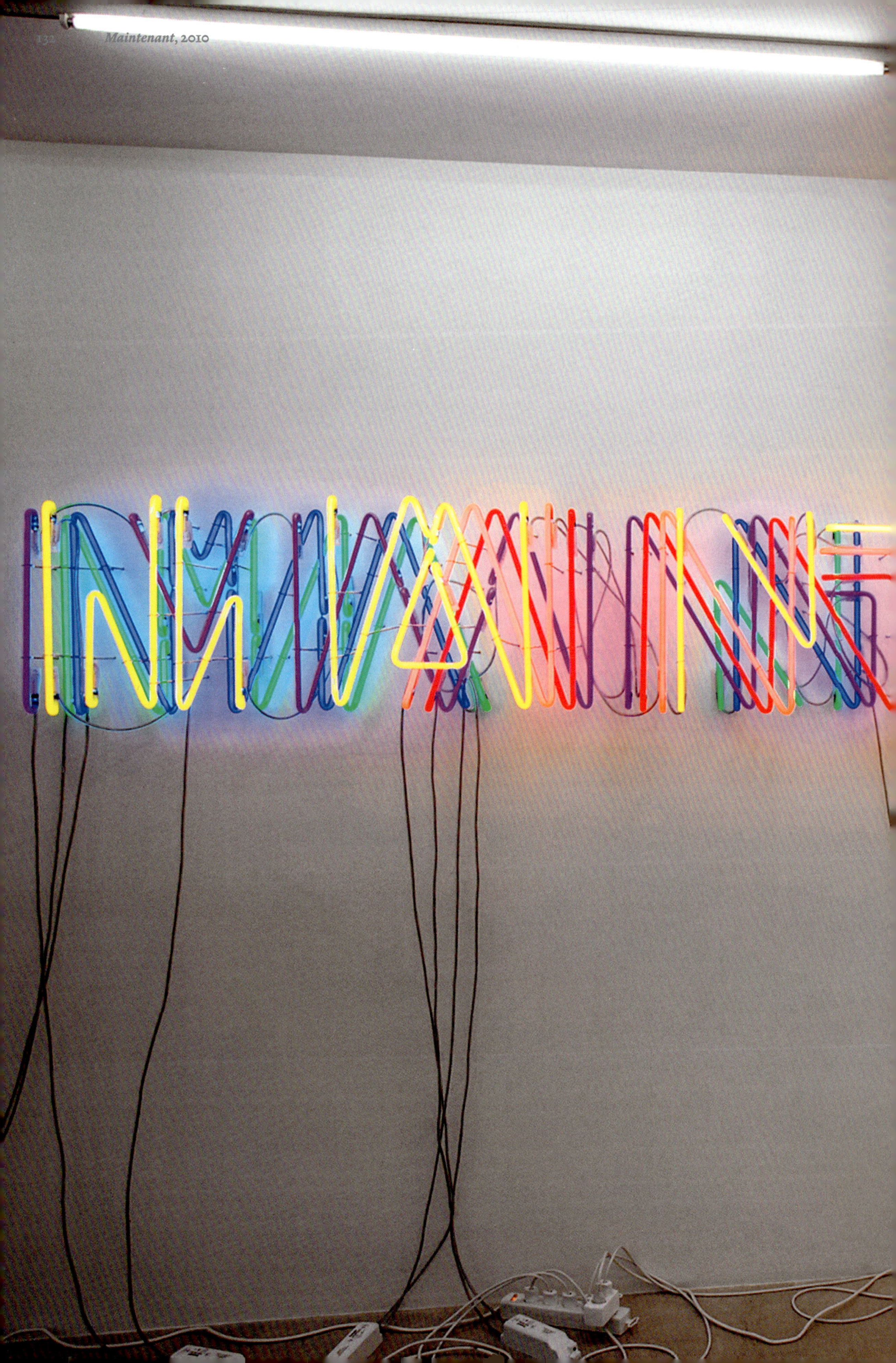

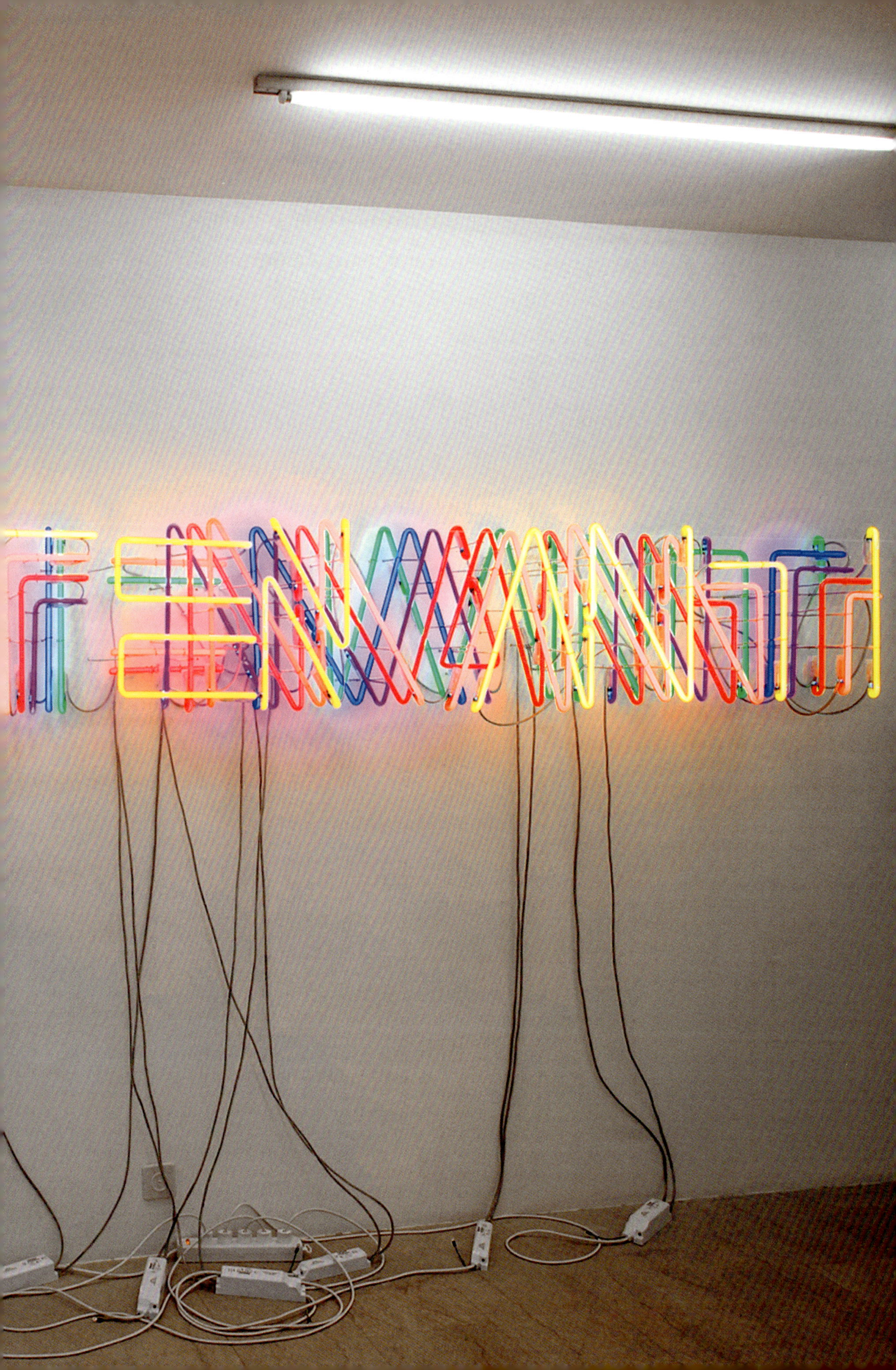

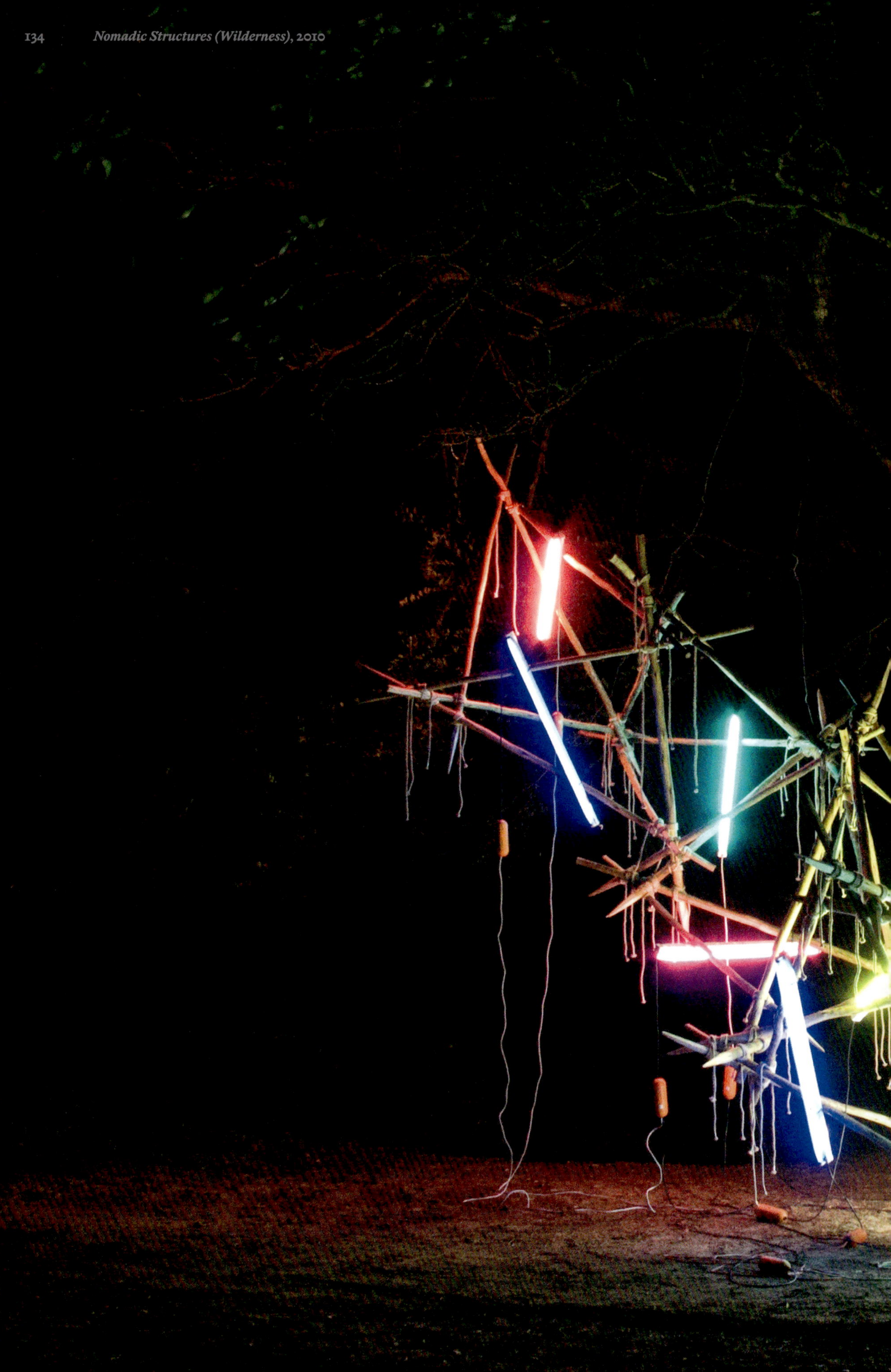

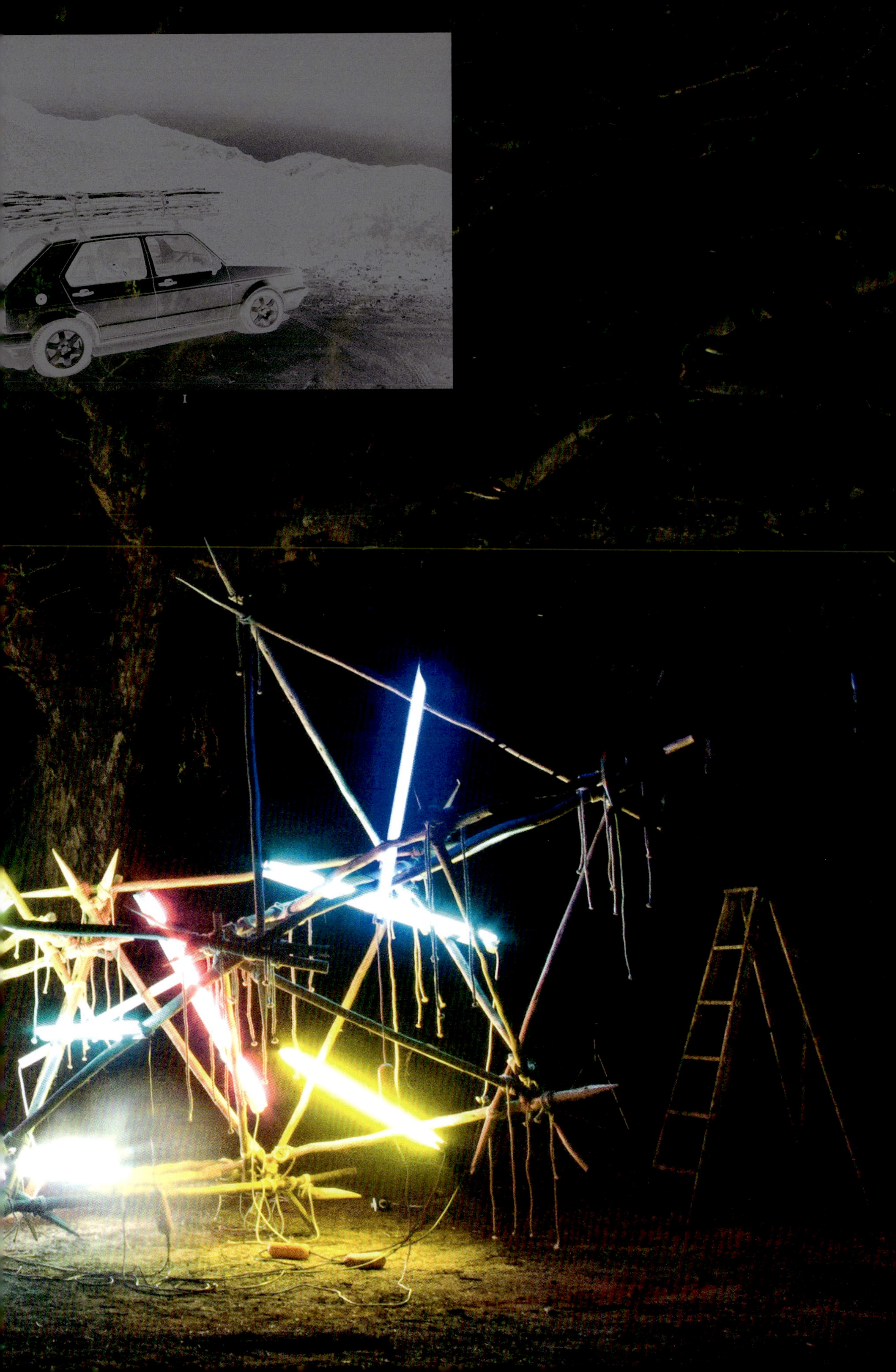

I

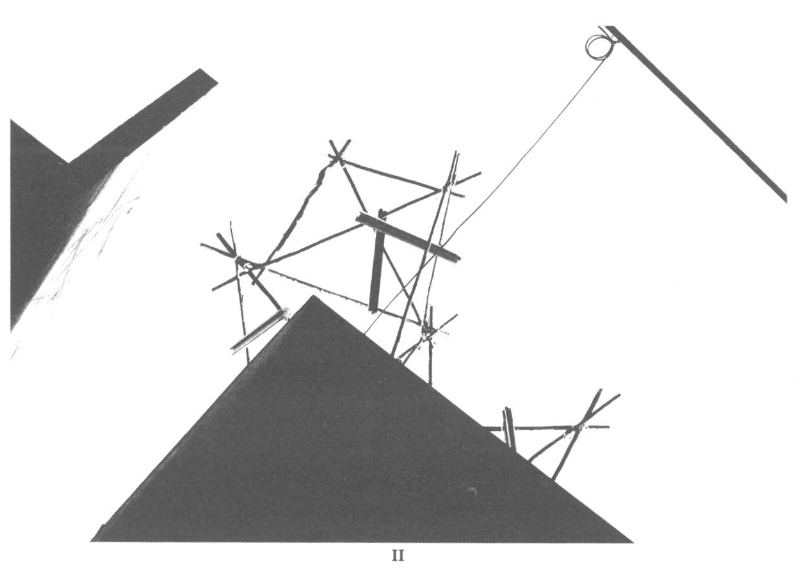

II

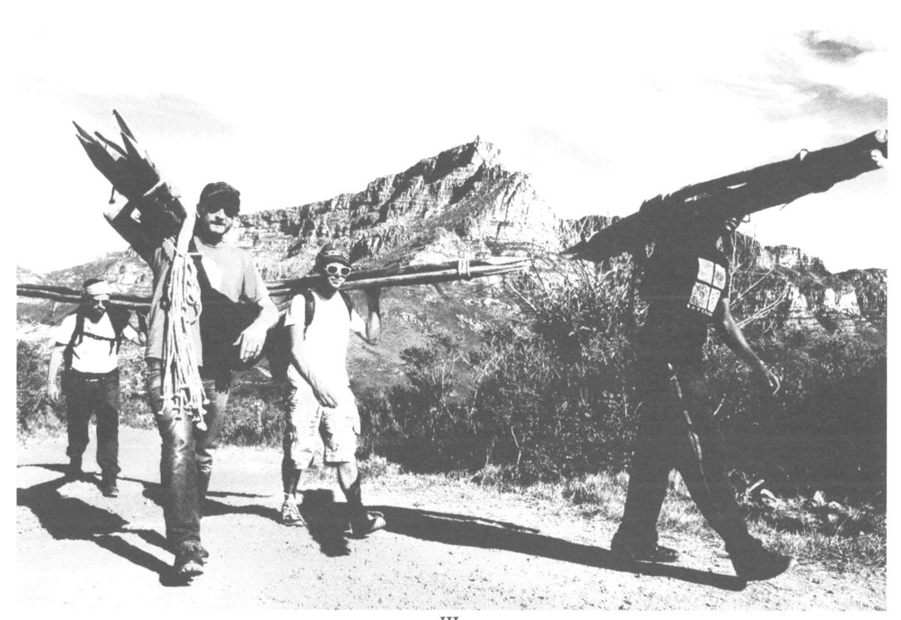

III

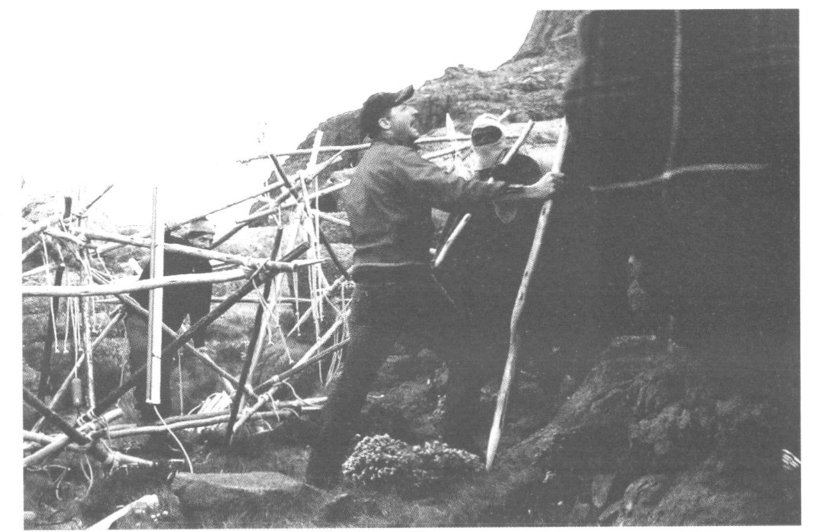

IV

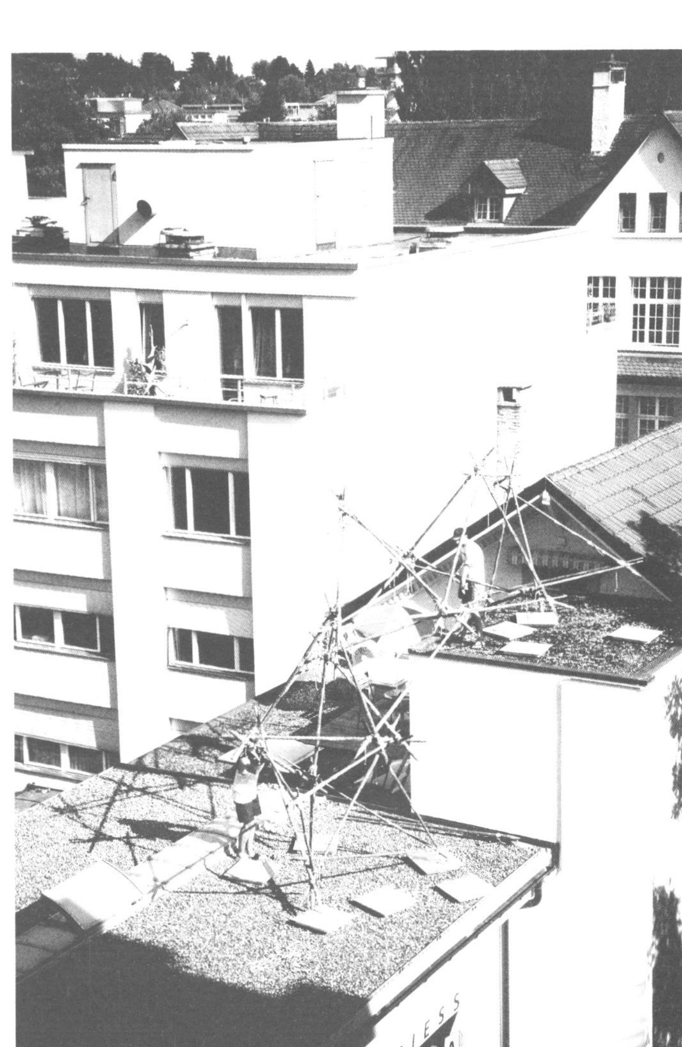

V

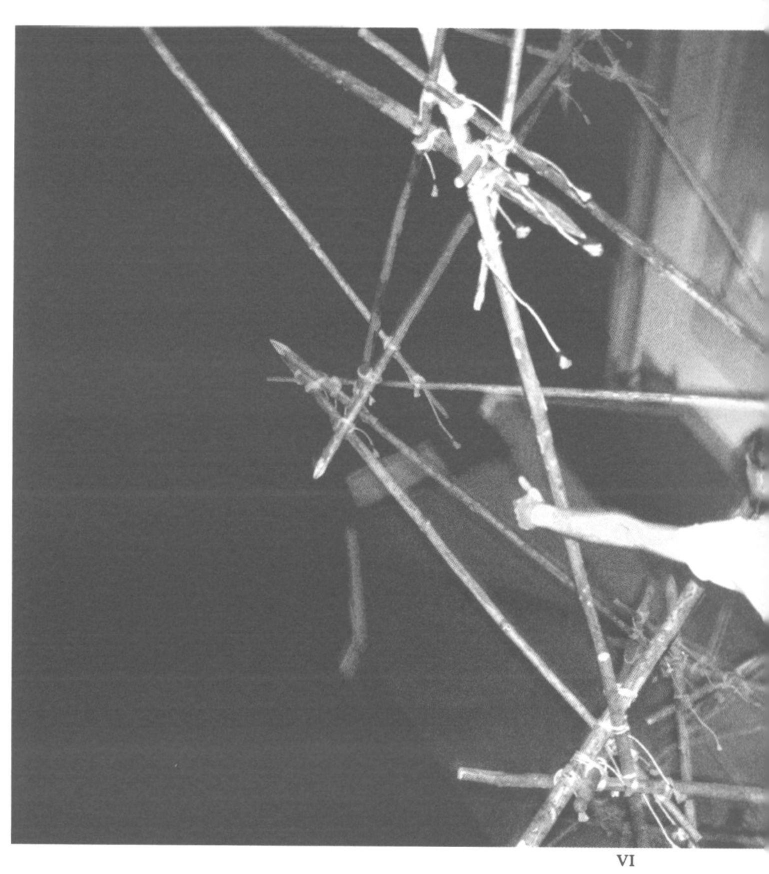

VI

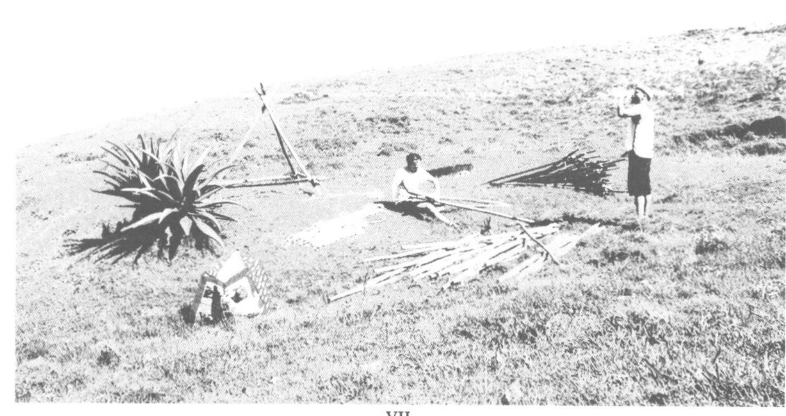

VII

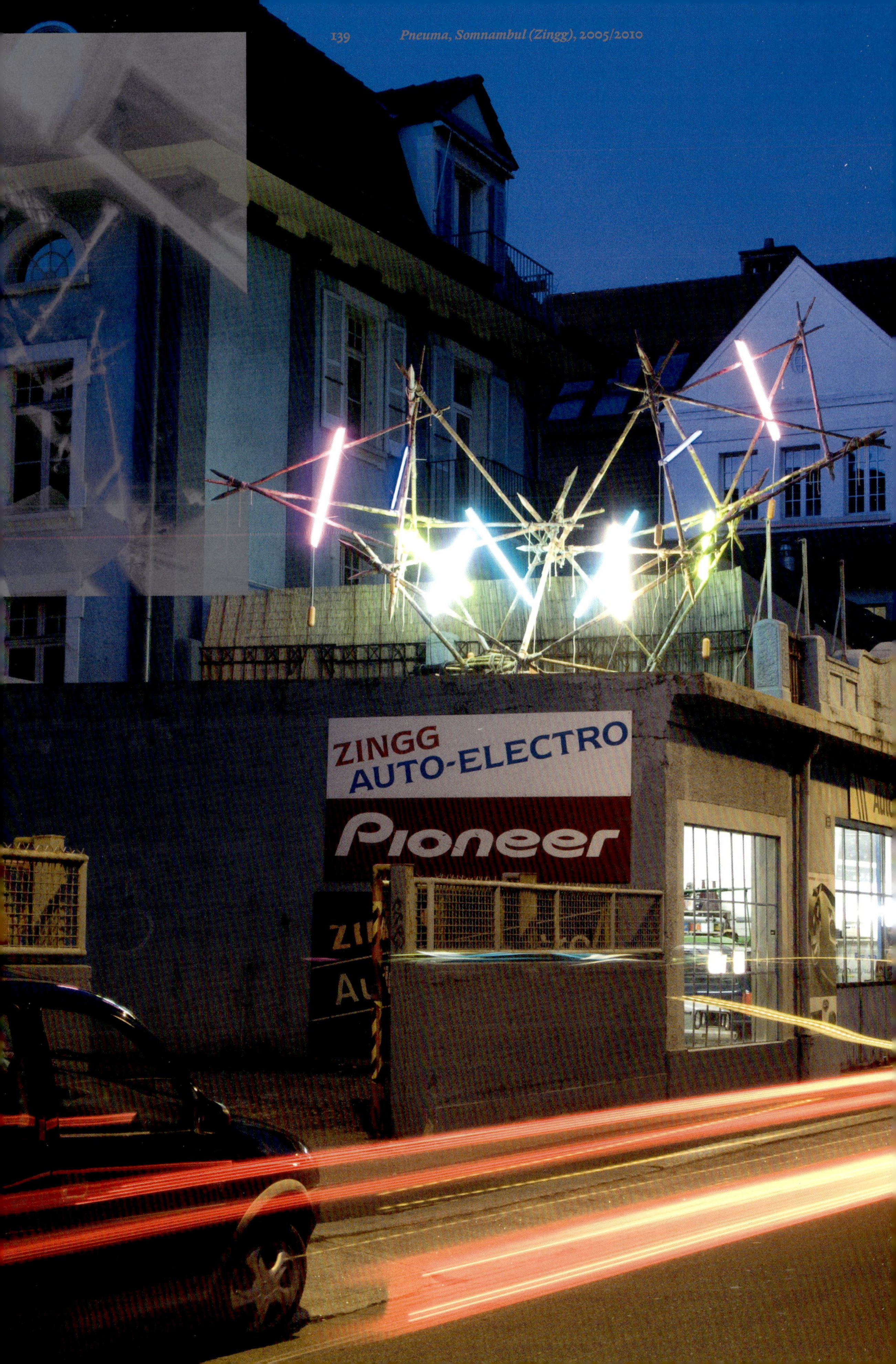
ZINGG
AUTO-ELECTRO
Pioneer

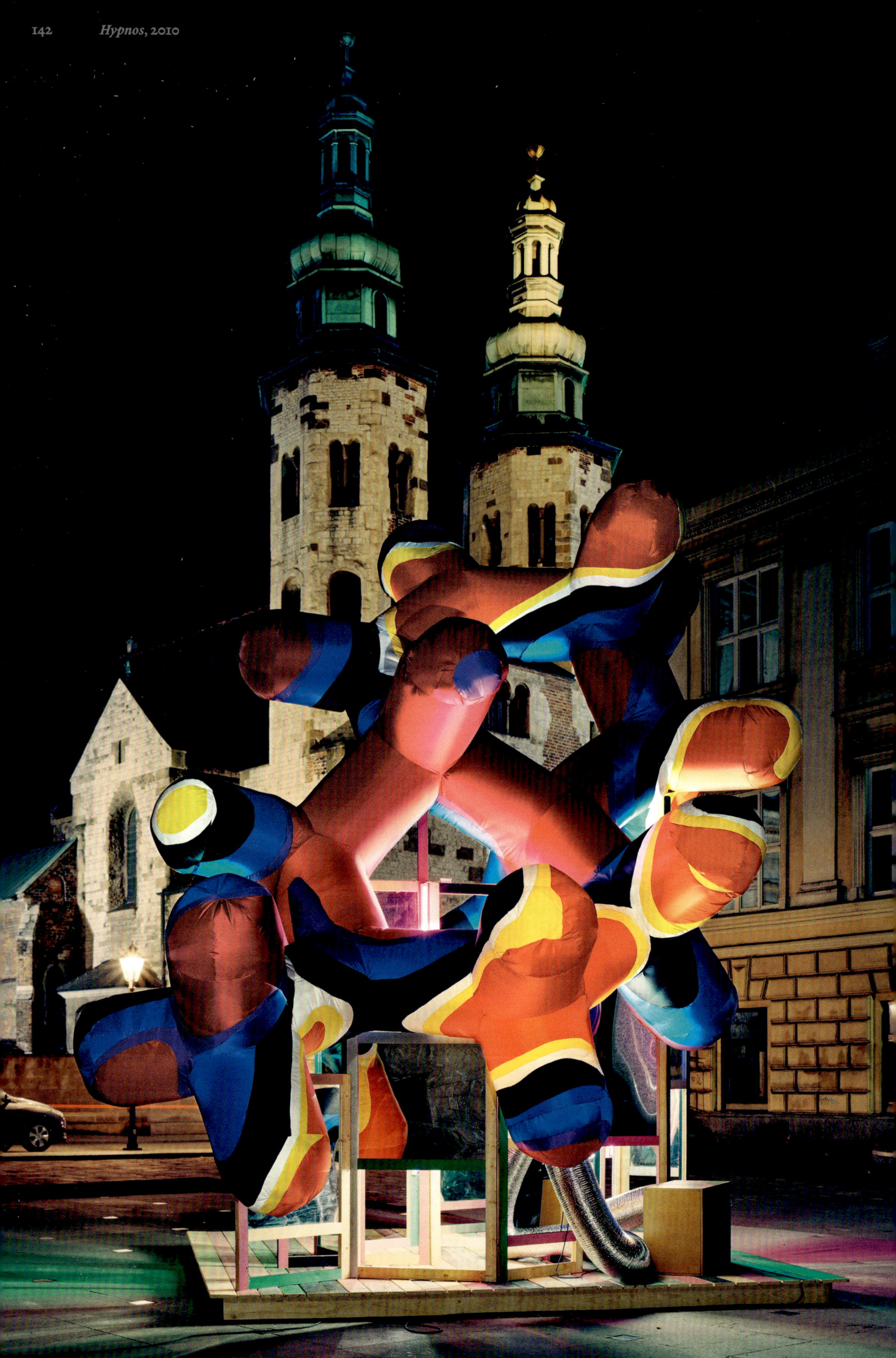

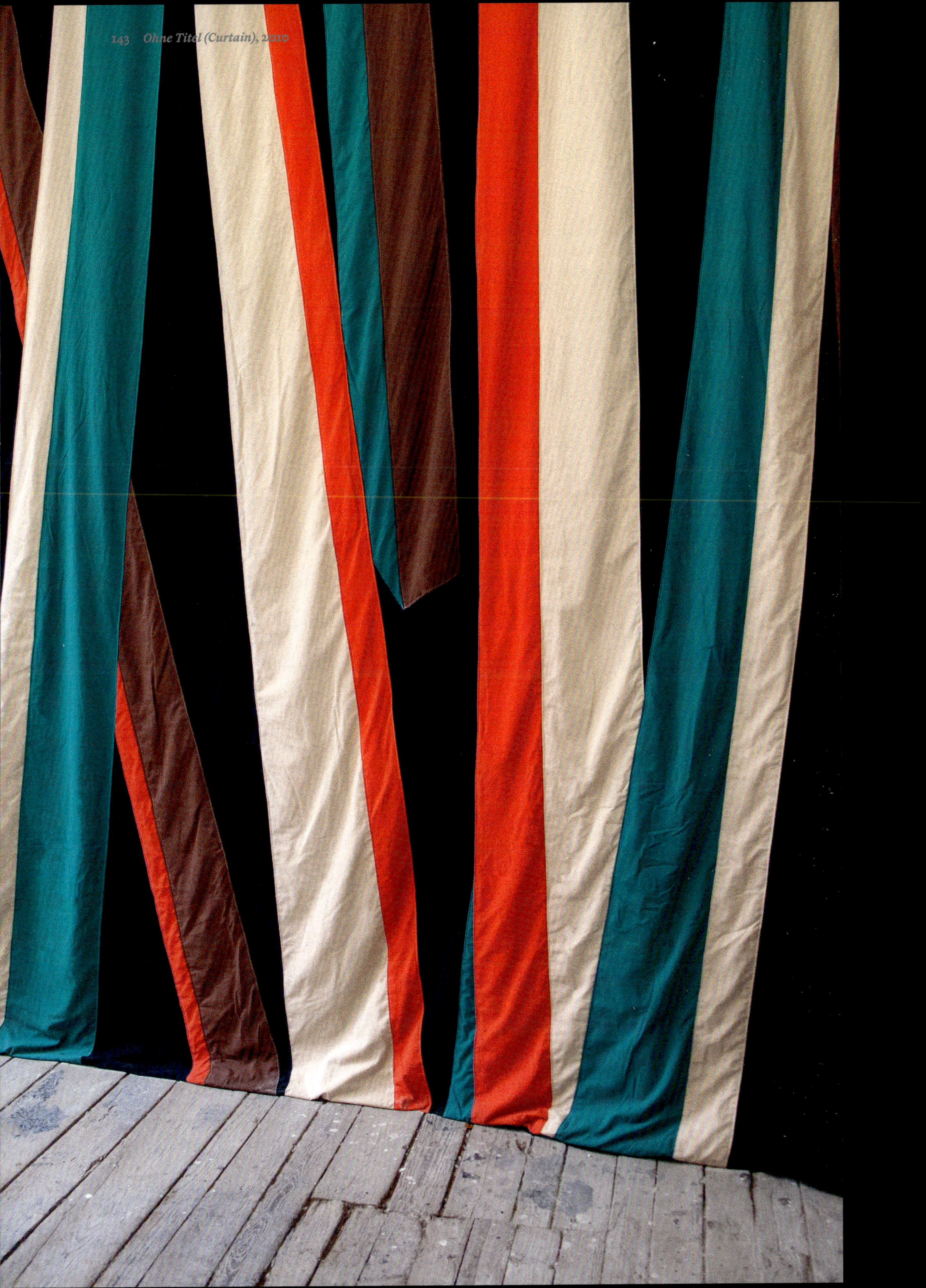

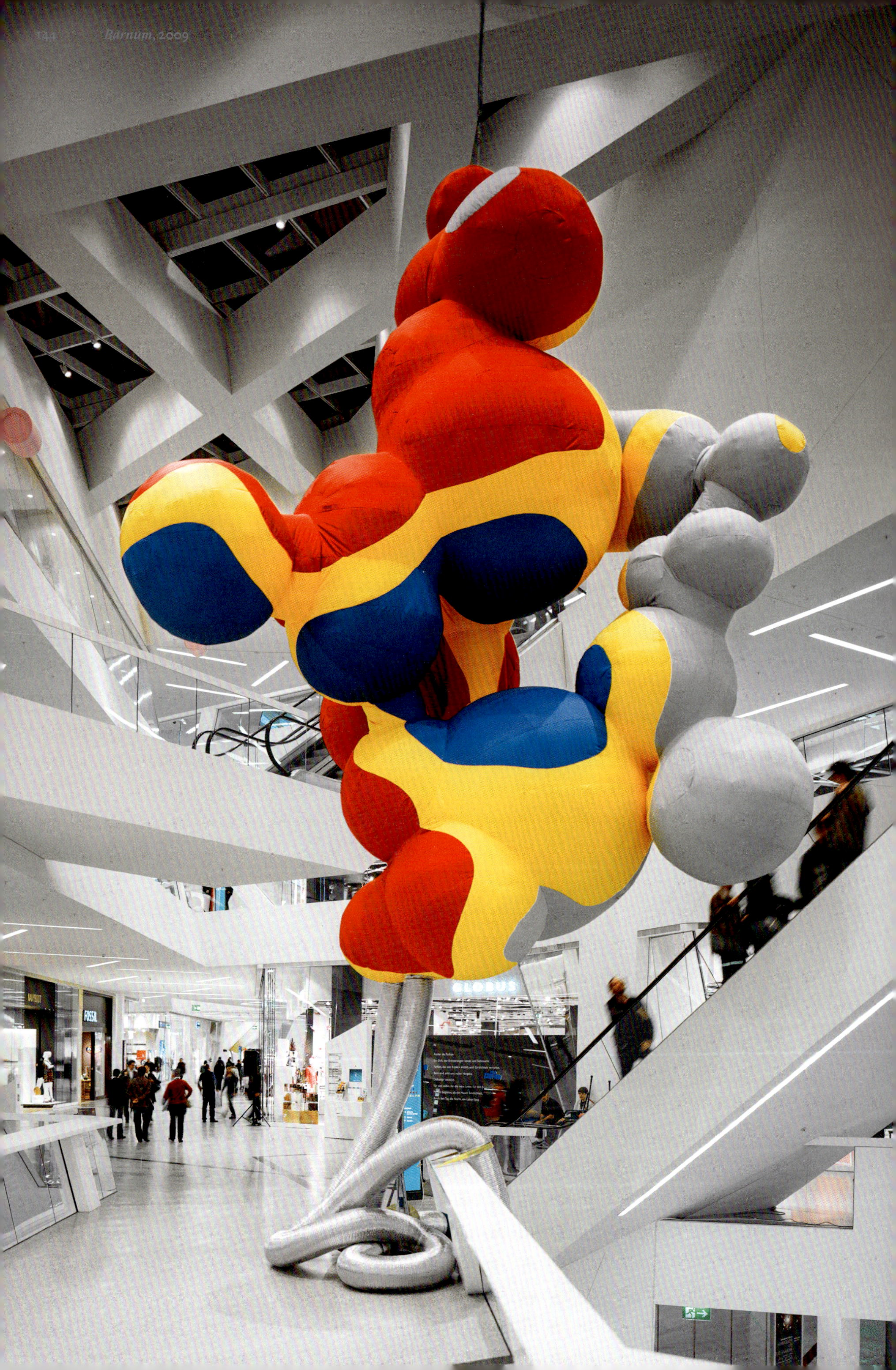

Barnum, 2009

Gulliver, 2009

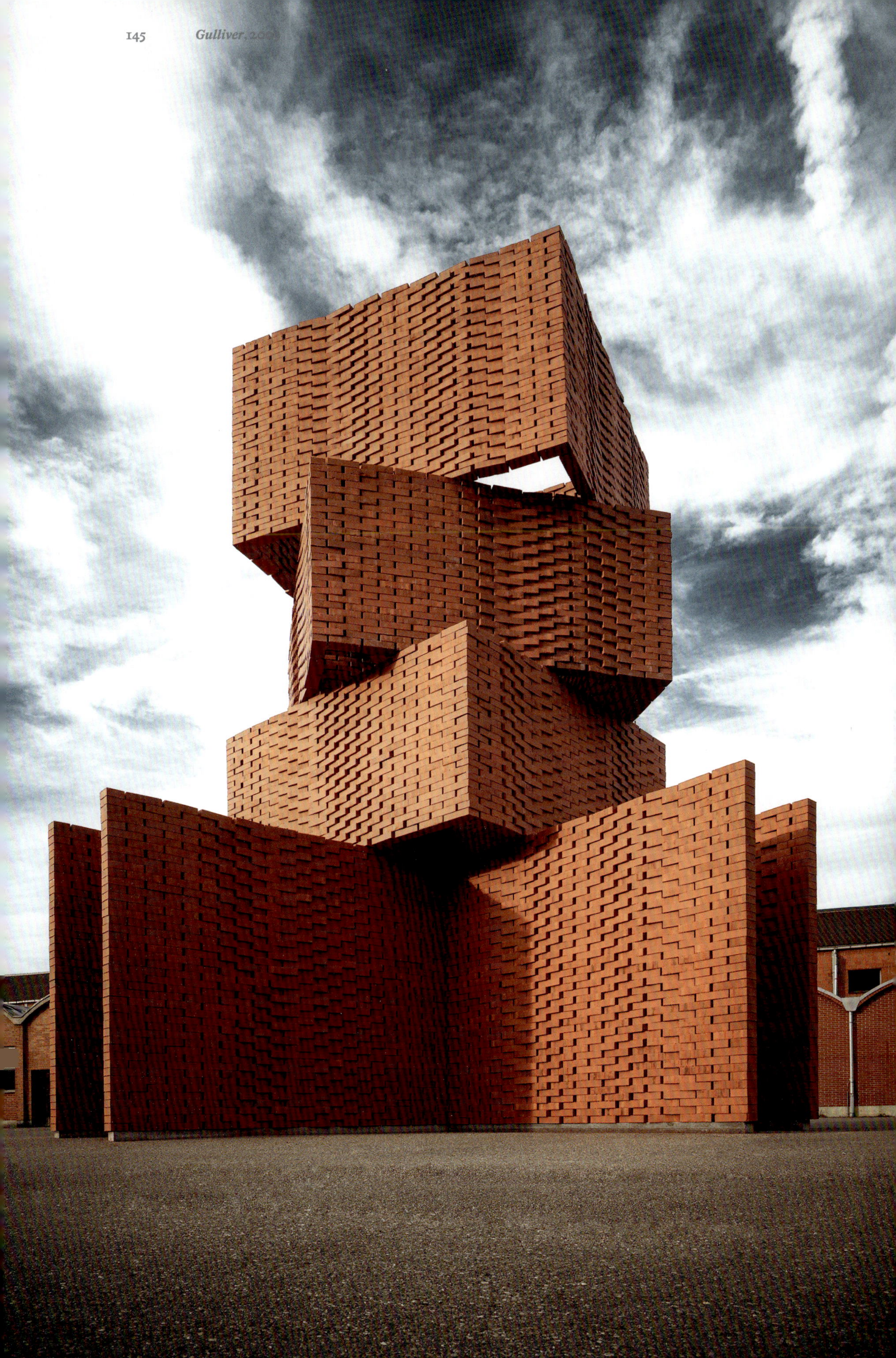

Artúr (Pochutla), 2009

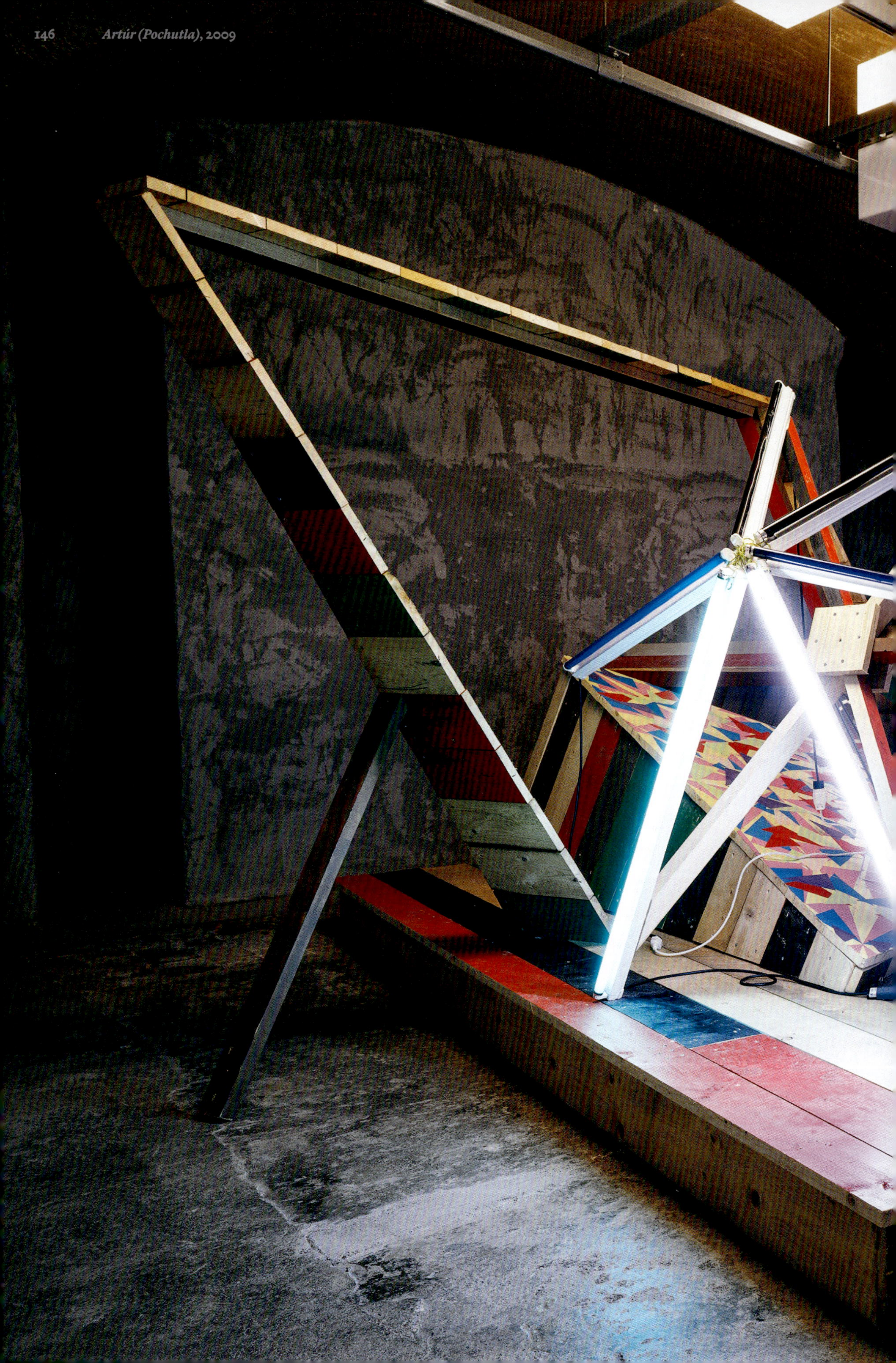

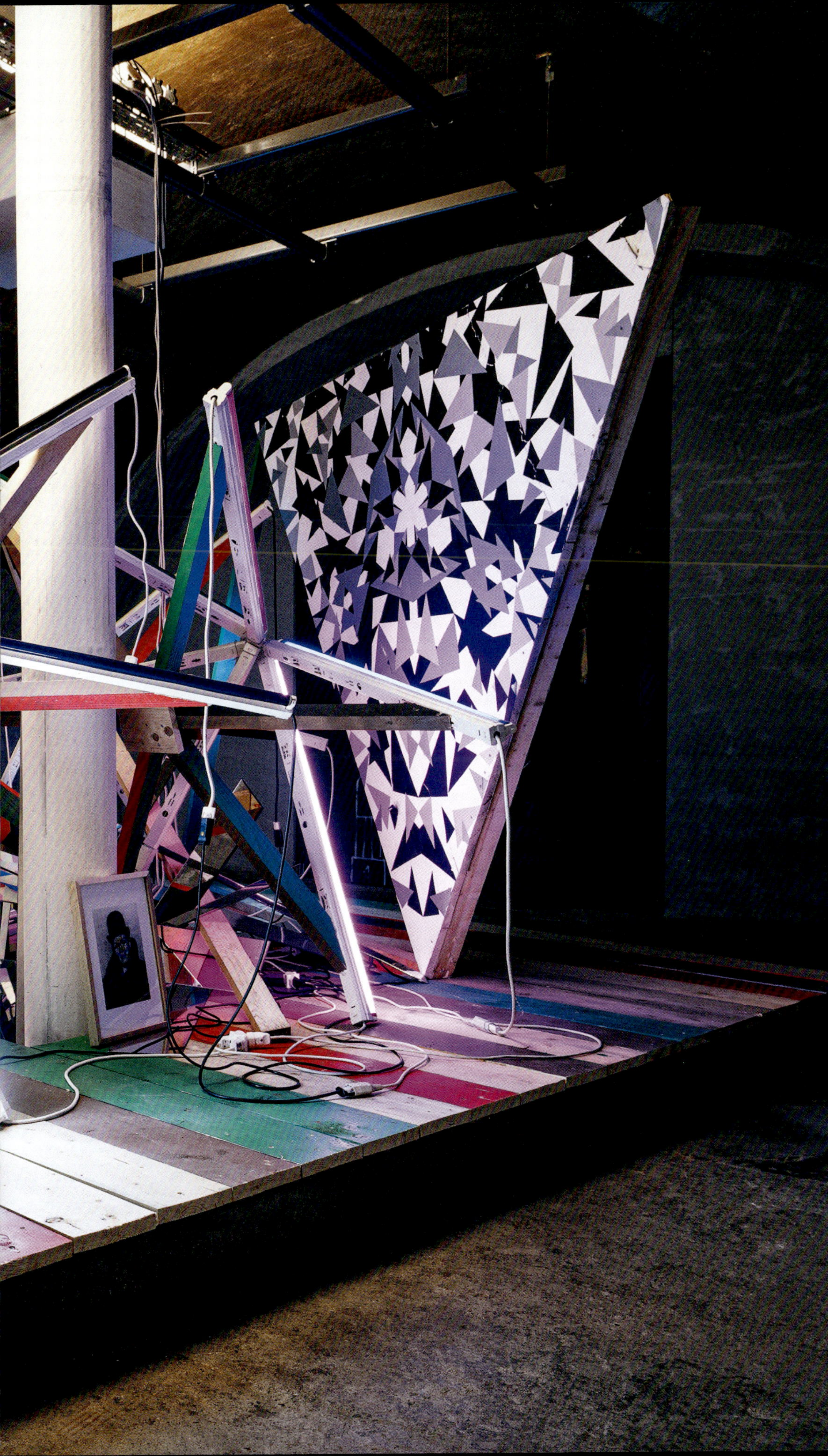

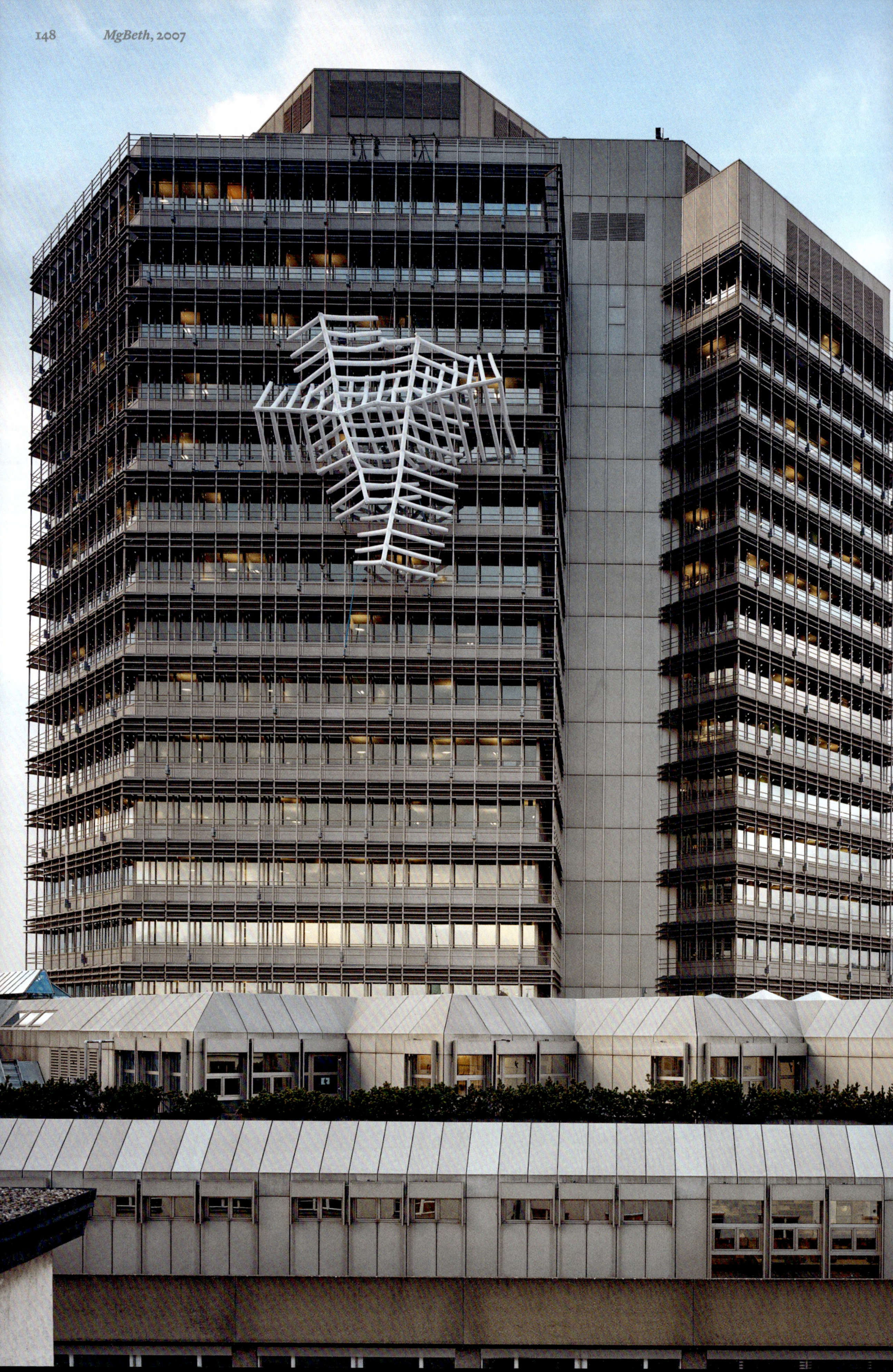

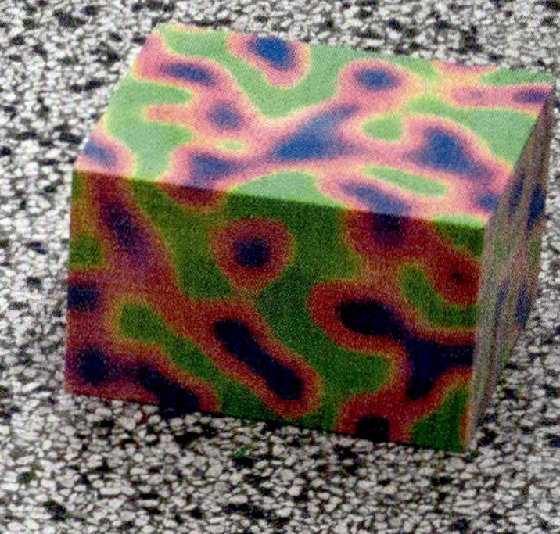

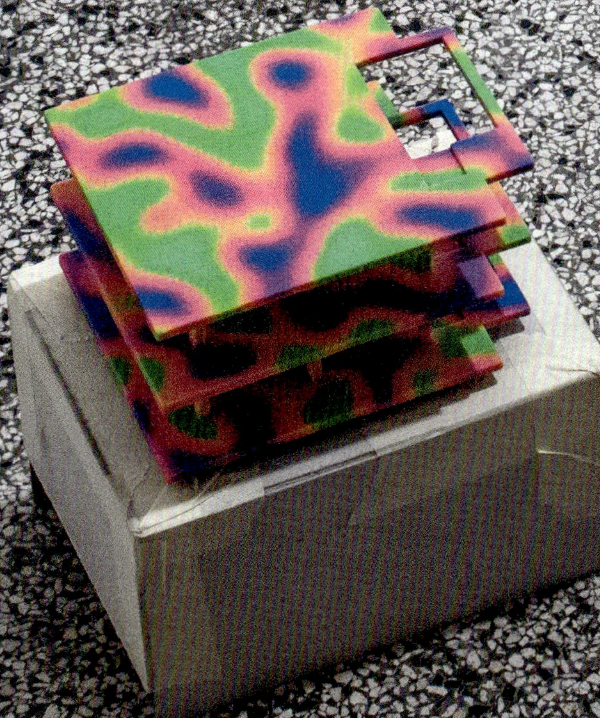

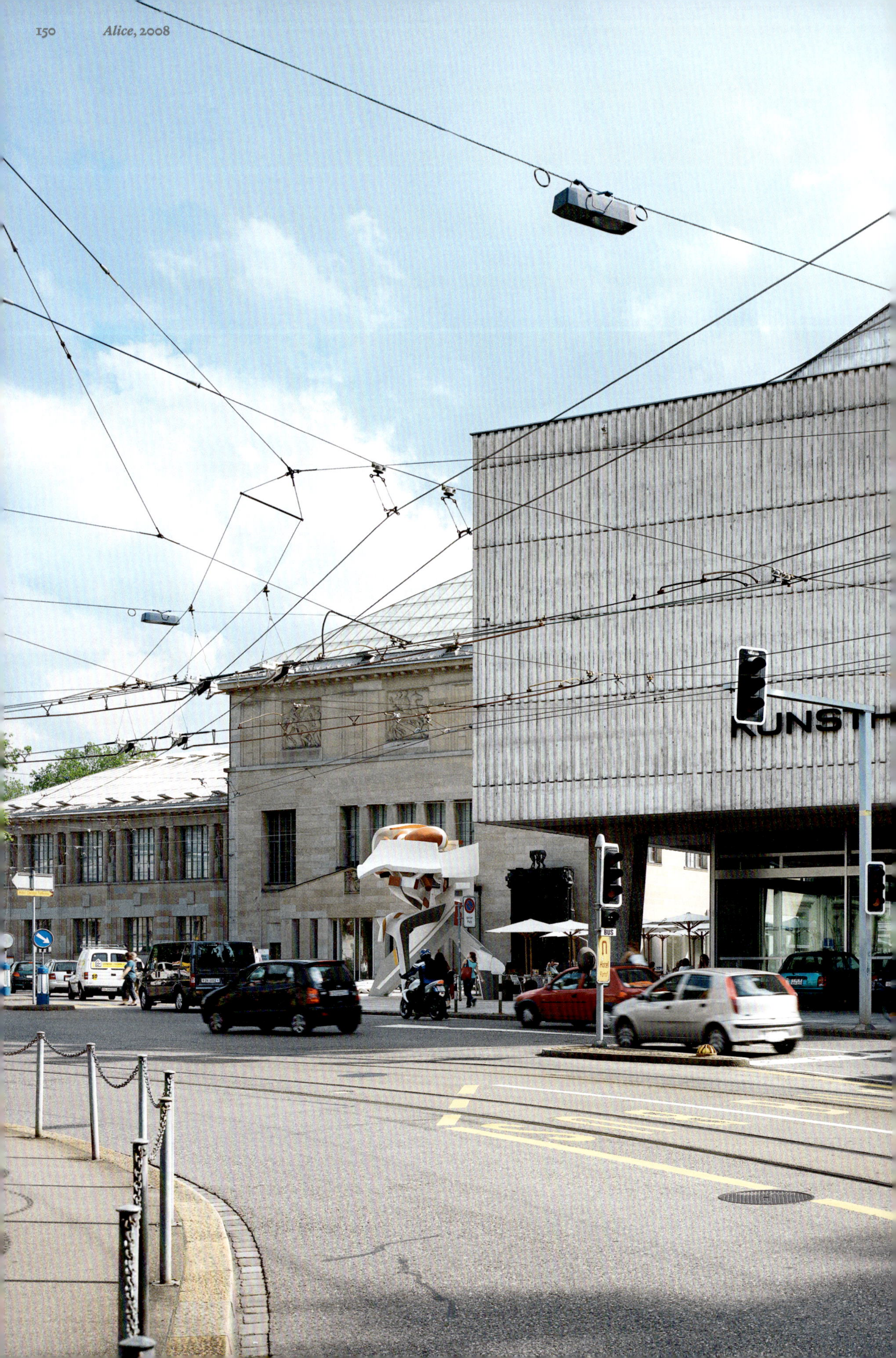
KUNST

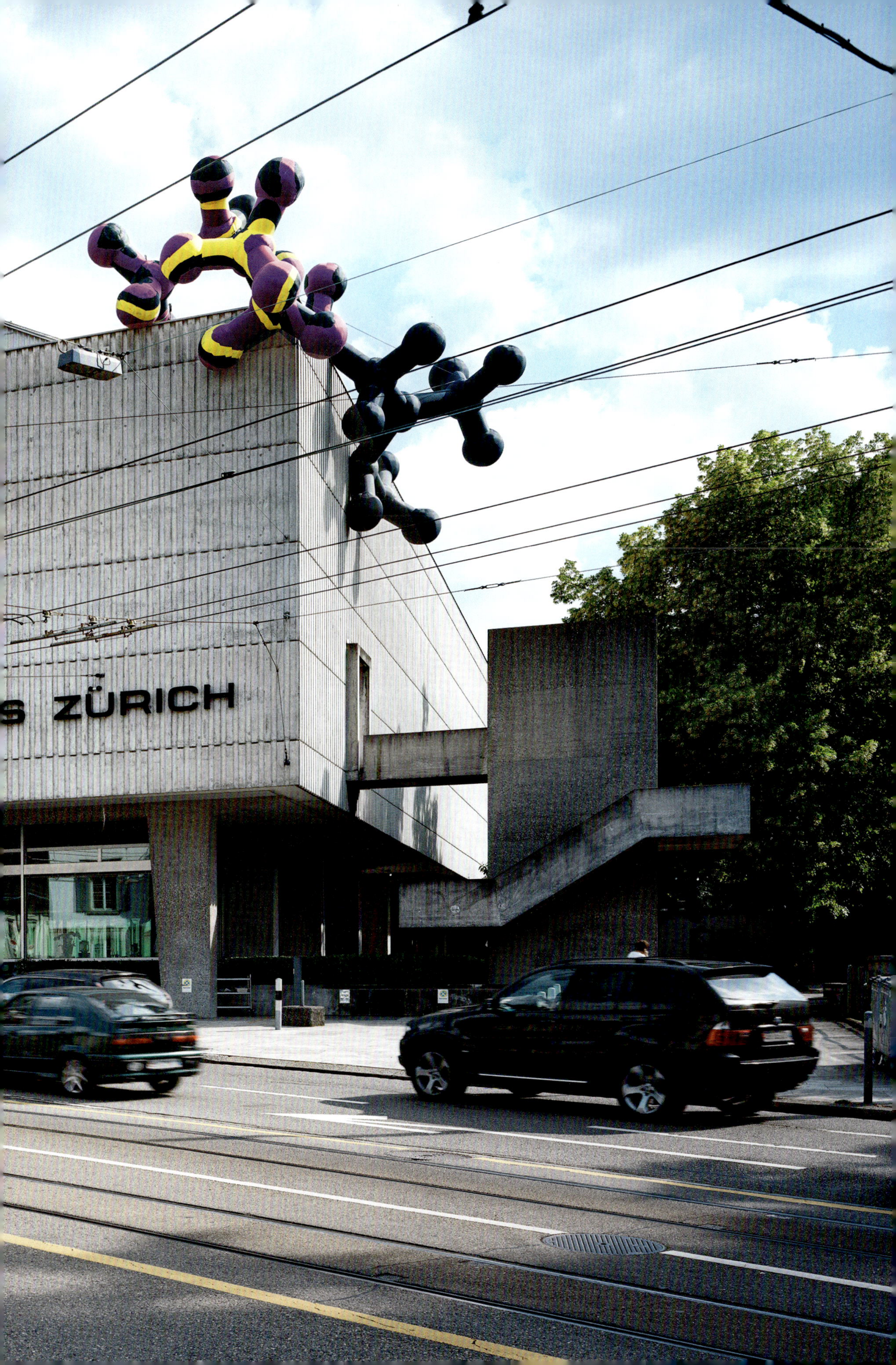
S ZÜRICH

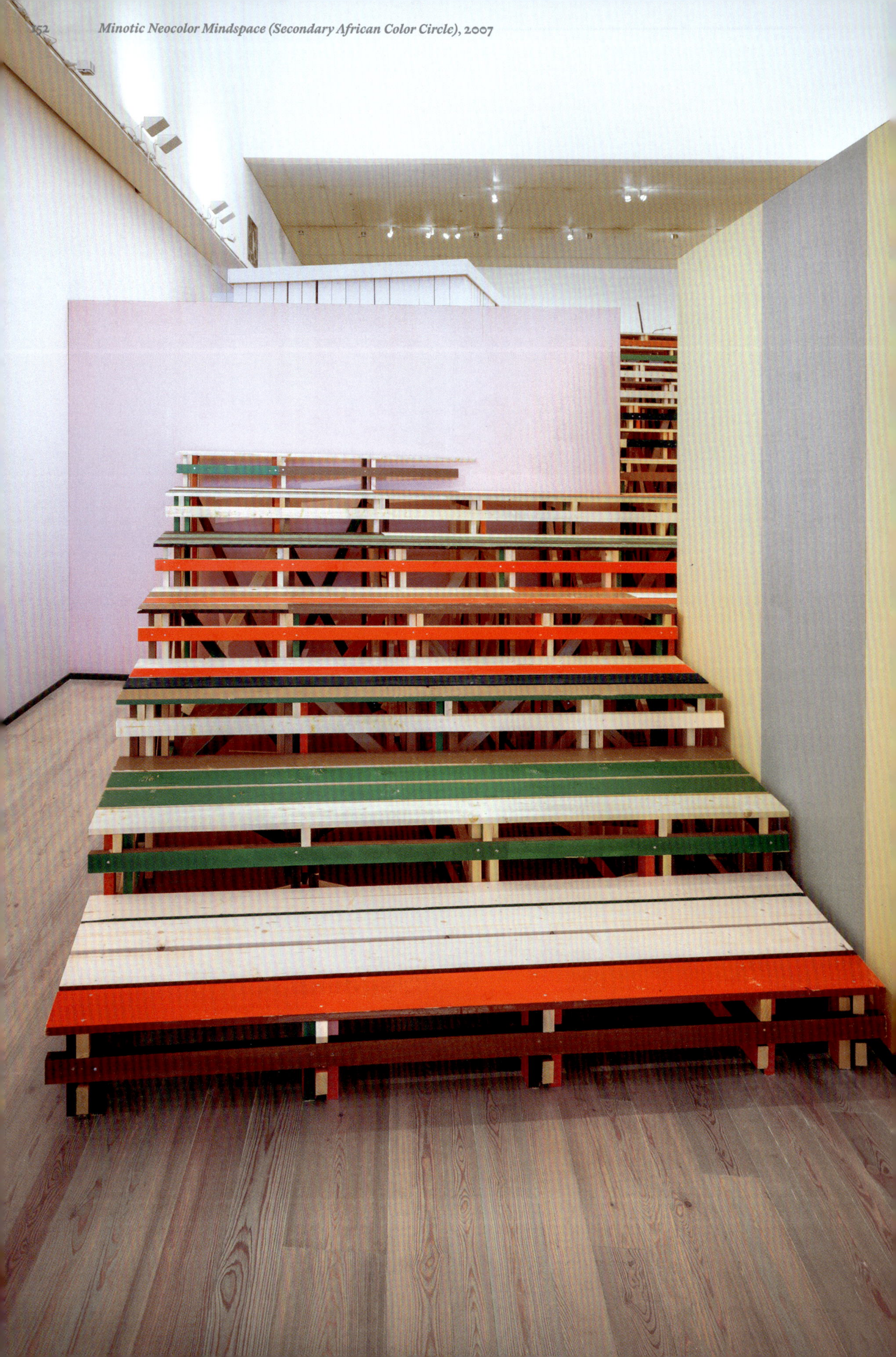

Minotic Neocolor Mindspace (Secondary African Color Circle), 2007

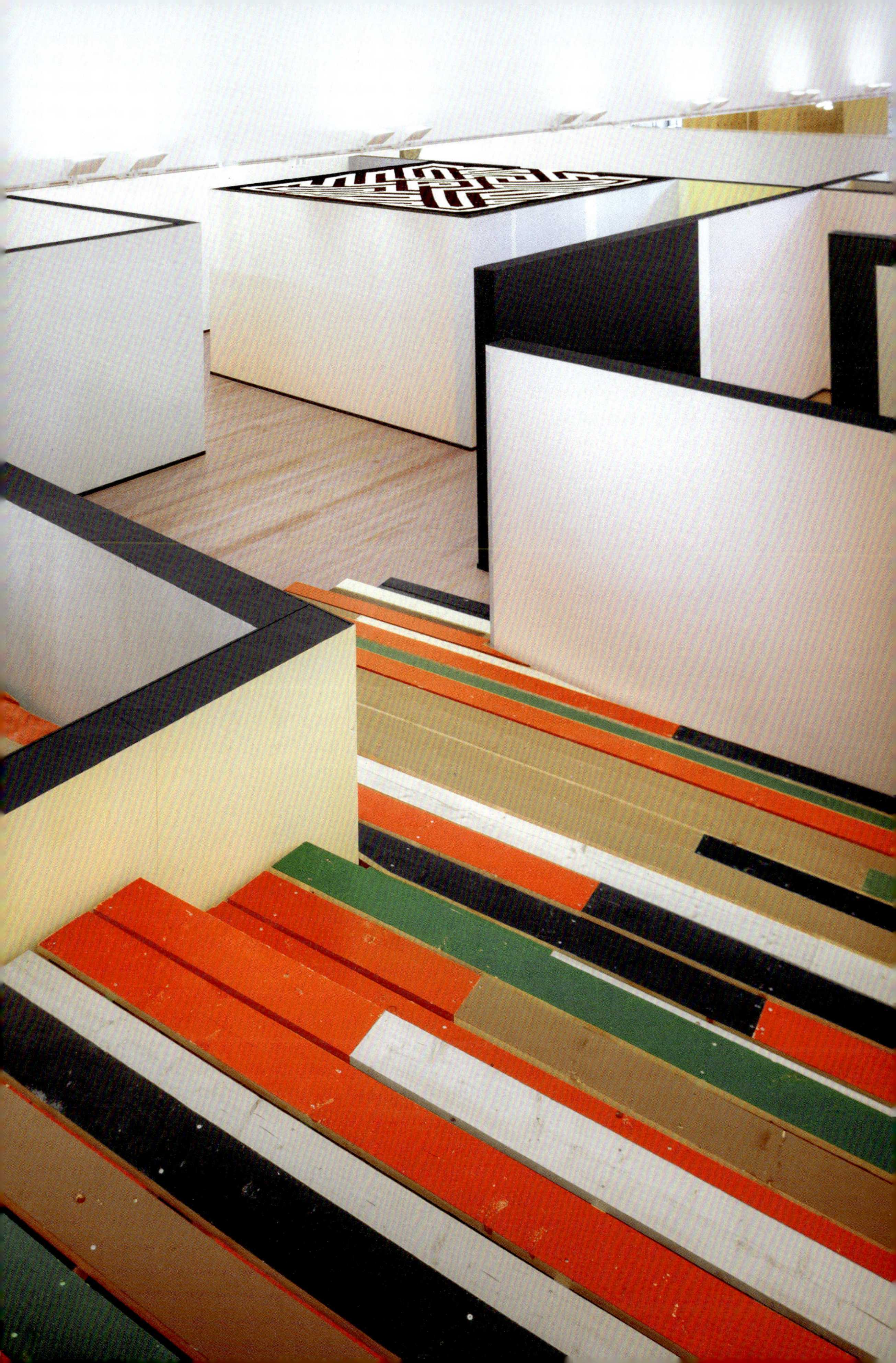

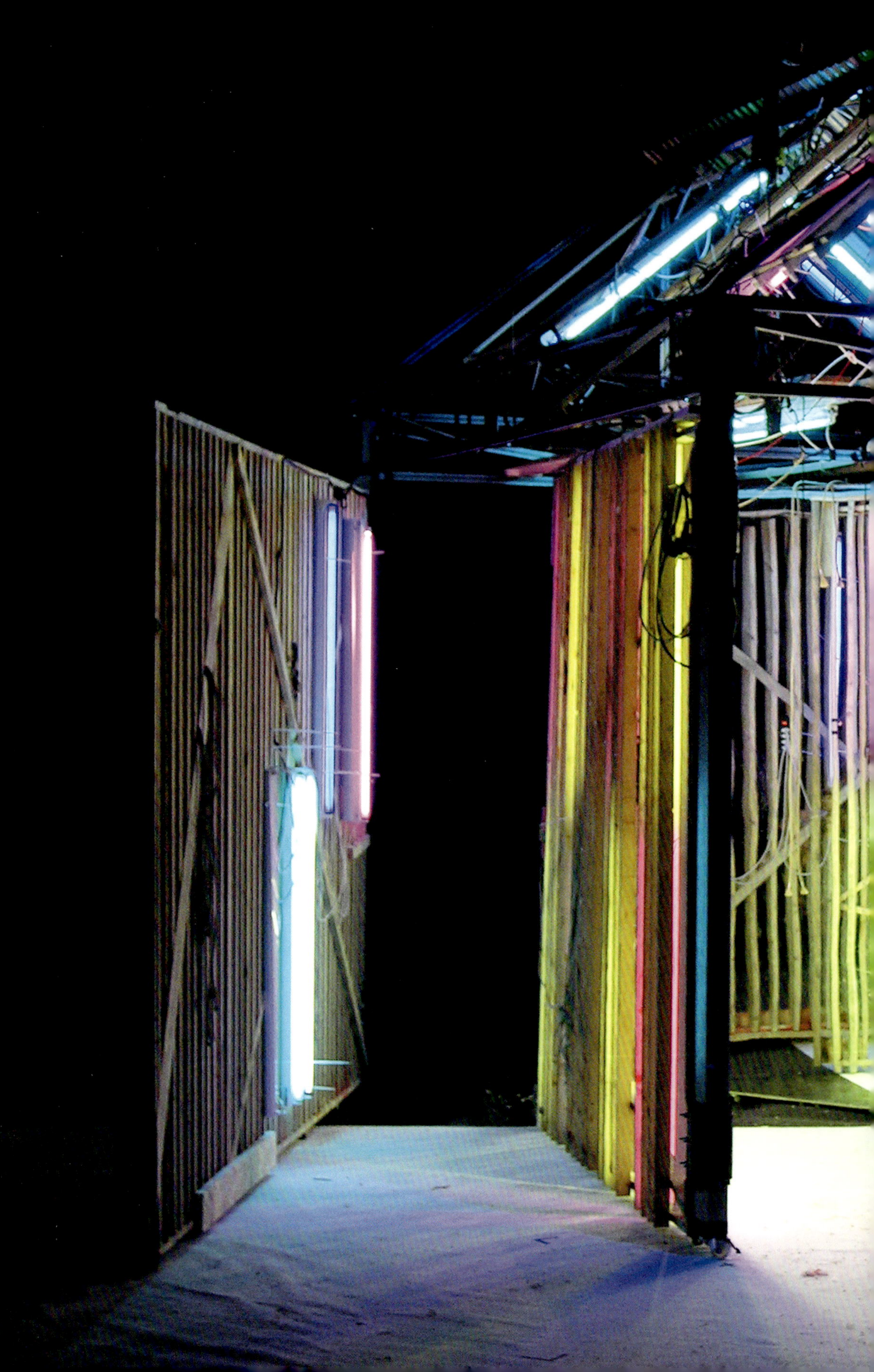

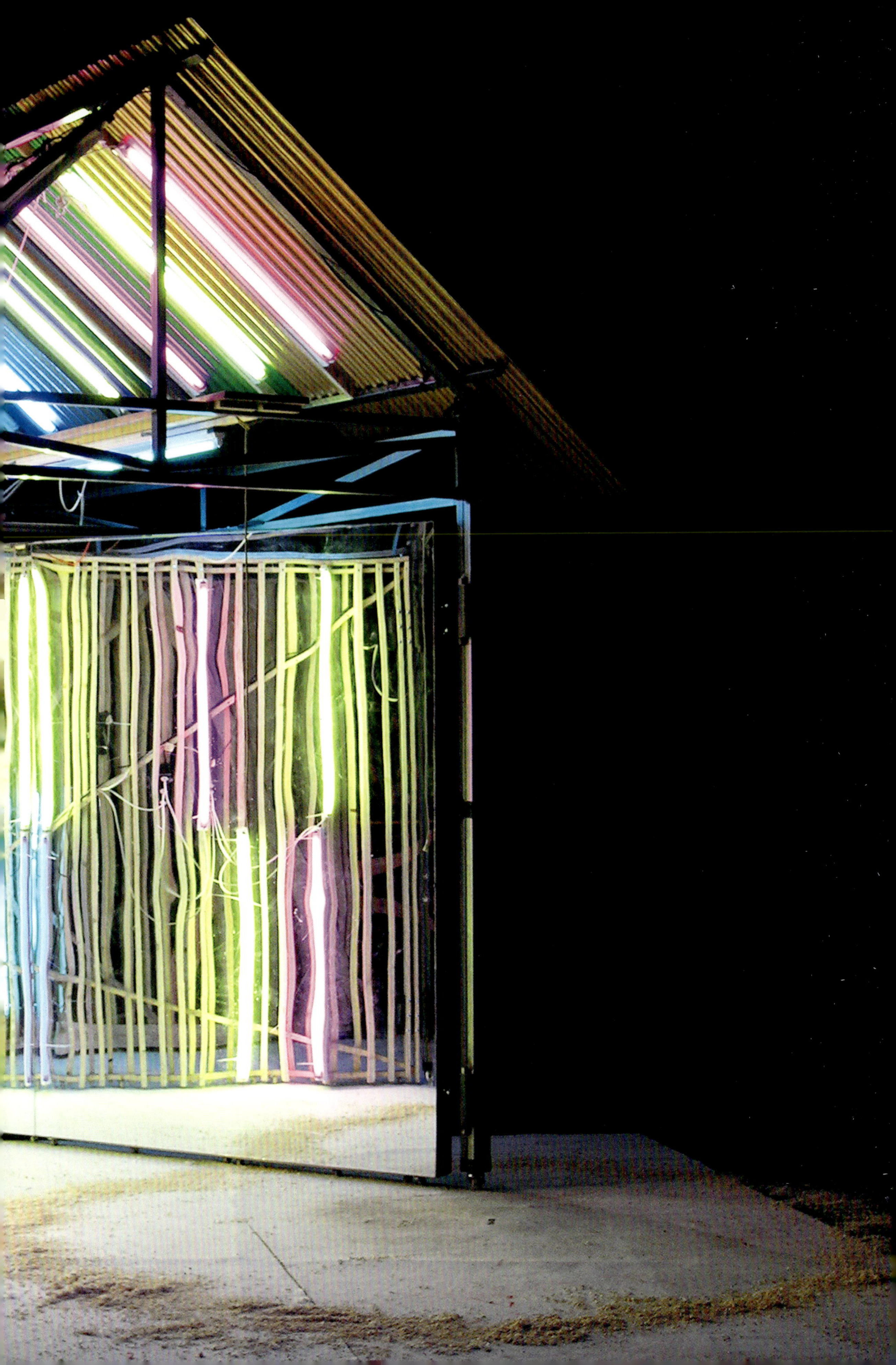

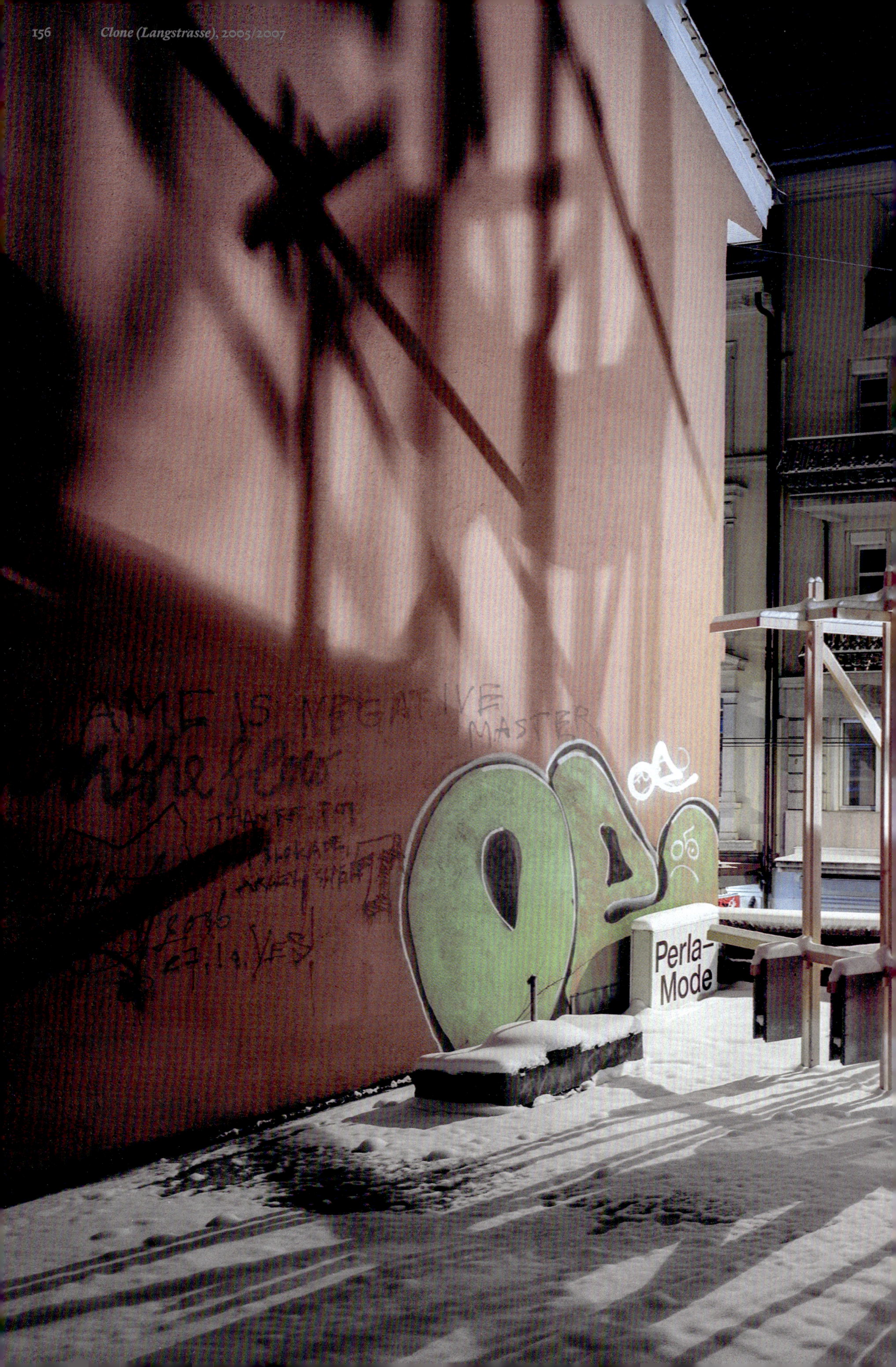
Perla-
Mode

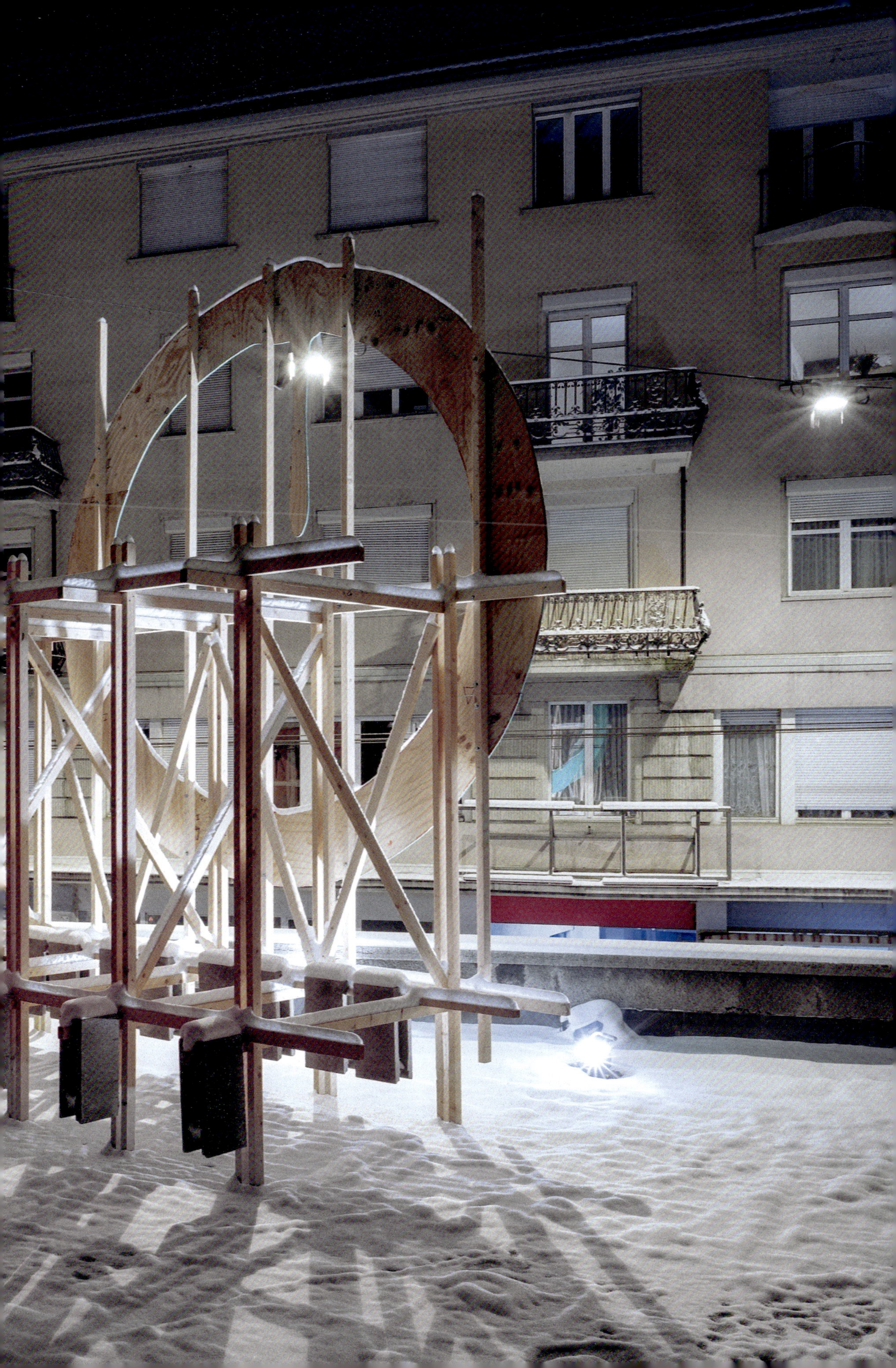

48 *Jean Arp*, 1998
Embossed aquatint on Zerkall 250g;
Sheet: 38×27.3 cm (Image: 29.1×20.9 cm);
Edition of 17

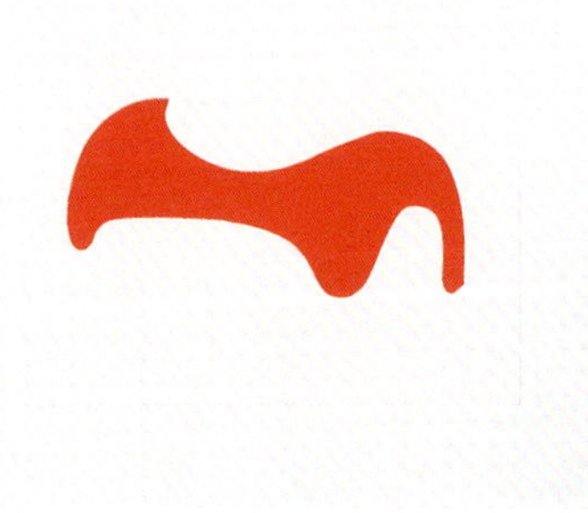

49 *Jean Arp*, 1998
Embossed aquatint on Zerkall 250g;
Sheet: 38×27.3 cm (Image: 29.1×20.9 cm);
Edition of 17

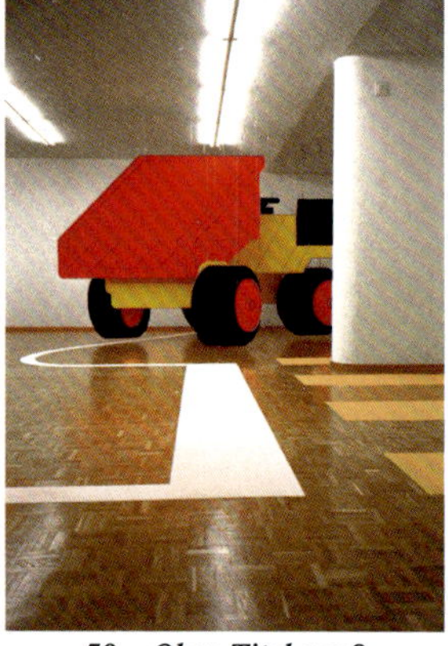

50 *Ohne Titel*, 1998
Acrylic paint, hot-melt marking paint, medium-density fiberboard, screws, wire rope; Dimensions variable; Installation view Serge Ziegler Galerie, Zürich

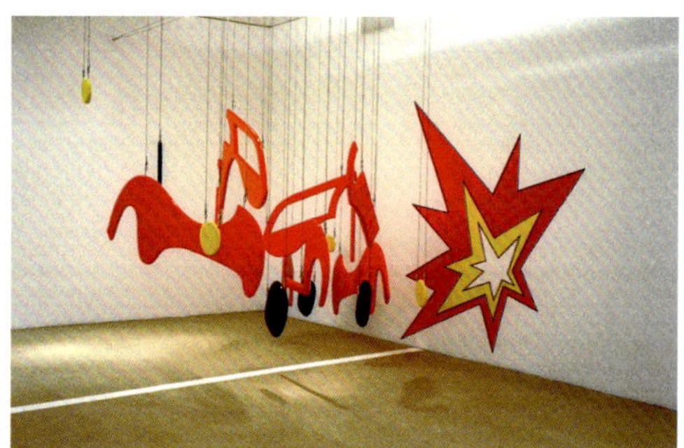

51 *Ohne Titel (Tex Avery)*, 1998
Acrylic paint, pavement marking tape, screws, silicone, two component lacquer, wire rope; Installation view *Freie Sicht aufs Mittelmeer*, Kunsthaus Zürich

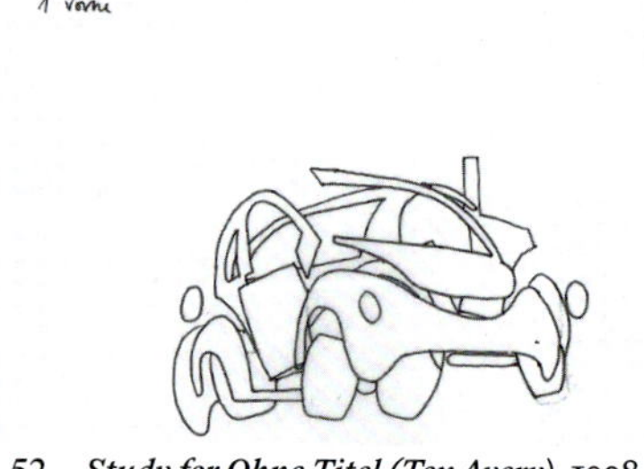

52 *Study for Ohne Titel (Tex Avery)*, 1998
Marker on tracing paper; 29.7×21 cm

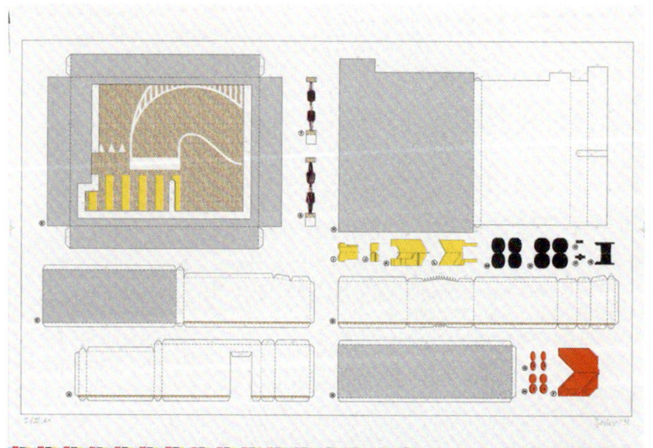

53 *Die Galerie*, 1998
CMYK offset print on coated offset paper; Sheet: 50×69.8 cm (Image: 41×65.8 cm); Edition of 38

Quality Gravure Printing
The Graphic Work of Kerim Seiler
Paul Tanner

Usually, artists do not turn to printmaking during their time at an academy or art school, but only after some artistic activity. They only seize this opportunity when they feel the need to rethink what they have created so far, or in order to realize individual works once again in another medium. Not so Kerim Seiler. He was still enrolled at the Hochschule für bildende Künste Hamburg at the age of almost twenty-four when he started his first portfolio, *Jean Arp*, in 1998. Nevertheless, his graphic work is not very extensive. Counted by title, it comprises a good dozen portfolios and sheets. Yet, it reflects his artistic work in a surprisingly multifaceted way.

COINCIDENCES

On his way to his gallery's owner, Pablo Stähli in Zürich, with whom he had been associated for some time, André Thomkins discovered in 1976 that Peter Kneubühler had recently set up a printing studio in the same building. Kneubühler was already and remained probably the most important and experienced copperplate printer in Switzerland until the late 1990s. Thomkins, one of the most important Swiss artists of the second half of the 20th century, seized the opportunity and without hesitation began to work in Peter Kneubühler's studio. With him he now became acquainted with all the finesses of copperplate printing and mastered them with virtuosity: etching, aquatint, vernis mou and more.

Anyone who now thinks that Kerim Seiler would follow in Thomkins' footsteps a good twenty years later and turn to the most diverse printmaking techniques is mistaken. For him, Thomkins, who produced a decidedly delicate work that sometimes almost tended to implode, belonged to the previous generation. For his part, Seiler stood out from the beginning with large, almost explosive works. He was later to benefit decisively from the technical know-how of the Atelier Kneubühler. But that's another story.

Peter Stiefel, a Zürich painter, drafts-man, and object artist, married Susanne G. Seiler in 1978. She brought the four-year-old Kerim into the marriage. In the 1970s he began to print on a small etching press in his Ticino studio. In 1980, he contacted Peter Kneubühler, hoping to realize his print products in better quality. He also wanted to venture into larger formats. Kneubühler recognized that Stiefel was talented in printing technology and enabled him to realize his own plans in his studio. Instead of printing just for himself, Stiefel became Kneubühler's assistant. Thus he chanced upon the best printing tools and techniques and was actively involved when Markus Raetz, Eric Fischl, James Turrell, Leiko Ikemura, John Baldessari, Martin Disler, Urs Lüthi, Klaudia Schifferle, Mario Merz, and many other artists came and went to Kneubühler and produced their best prints there. Later, Peter Stiefel set up his own small, well-functioning studio for copperplate and woodcut in Kilchberg near Zürich, where he also printed for other artists, such as the Grisons artist Matias Spescha.

THE FIRST PRINTMAKING ATTEMPT: A DIRECT HIT

The *Jean Arp* portfolio (1998, fig. 48–49) has a special history: At the beginning of 1998, Kerim Seiler showed an installation in Serge Ziegler's Zürich gallery, consisting of MDF panels hanging from the ceiling, cut to different sizes and colored with acrylic, which, due to their staggering and special arrangement, created the image of a dump truck from a certain point of view (fig. 50; p. 15, fig. 6). In the same year he further developed this type of (immovable) mobile. A VW Beetle in the version of the *New Beetle* was shown exploding. The individual wooden panels now showed much more complex shapes, which Seiler had prepared by drawings (fig. 52). He had further developed the *Shaped canvases* with the help of the computer. They were the templates for the panel cut-outs realized with a milling plotter. This exploding car, *Ohne Titel (Tex Avery)* (fig. 51; p. 15, fig. 5), was shown in the summer of 1998 in the exhibition *Freie Sicht aufs Mittelmeer: Junge Schweizer Kunst mit Gästen und Gastmahl* at the Kunsthaus Zürich, curated by Bice Curiger. The Zürich collector Ruedi Bechtler acquired it. Today, the work is on permanent loan from the Walter A. Bechtler Stiftung and is in the Kunsthaus depot, as is just about all the young art acquired for the Kunsthaus in 1998 from the aforementioned exhibition.

The plate forms developed for the *New Beetle* were exceptional and showed similarities to the formal language of Jean Arp. However, the title of the above-mentioned portfolio can at best be understood as a winking homage. In a reduced form, the cut copperplates were the templates for the graphics, printed as aquatint in red, yellow, and black (fig. 48–49). The printing was very demanding, explained Peter Stiefel, who died in the summer of 2019. He had had to use all his printing skills for this. It had been crucial that the edges of the cut-out copperplates were cleaned very carefully so that the edges of the printed forms would not become blurred. With the first larger edition, Seiler took a decisive step with the help of Stiefel. Here, it became clear that the more and more conceptually working artist began to develop the important intuition to find the best in their field in order to entice them to his work.

For the sake of correctness, we mention here that the portfolio *Jean Arp* was preceded by the offset print *Die Galerie* (fig. 53). This was a model sheet for cutting out, published in 1998 in the Serge Ziegler Edition Zürich.

THE GRAVURE PRINTING TECHNIQUES PROVE THEMSELVES

After six years, in 2004, the artist ventured into a new, now large-format graphic series, again printed as colored aquatint by Peter Stiefel. It was published as an edition by the Susanna Kulli Gallery Zürich. The sheets with the titles *Blase*, *Draco*, *Raster*, *Spritzer*, and *Streifen* are each printed in a different color, in a pale ecru, in dark blue, beige-gray, red, and yellow (fig. 54). As much as the colors vary, so too differ the graphics in their forms: each sheet is a clear individual statement. They are all forms that one can derive from Seiler's installations of those years. The splashes of paint (*Spritzer*) are an element he used in 2001 in his temporary modification of the Theater an der Winkelwiese in Zürich. The sheet with the grid (*Raster*) clearly shows a wooden construction as it was realized by Seiler at that time. He processed the five motifs on the computer and transferred them to copperplates that were cut with a laser device. The sheet *Spritzer* was selected in 2005 as a model for the poster of the exhibition *Schweizer Druckgraphik 1980–2005. Die Graphische Sammlung der ETH zu Gast im Helmhaus Zürich.* In the same year, the artist recieved the Förderpreis der Stiftung für die Graphische Kunst in Switzerland, which is part of the Graphische Sammlung der ETH.

Two years later, in 2006, a whole series of blind embossings was created, a total of 16 motifs (fig. 55). Kerim Seiler worked on drawn brushstrokes on the computer for these motifs. The contours of these enlarged brushstrokes were again cut out of printing plates by laser (fig. 56). The thin plates prepared in this way were placed individually on the press and a moistened hand-made paper was positioned over them. A felt mat attached to the press was then placed on top and the whole thing was rotated through the press. It was important to the artist that only unique pieces were obtained, only one blind embossing per plate. The uniqueness of the brushstroke should thus also be expressed in print or embossing. In 1965, when the American artist Roy Lichtenstein transformed his famous *Brushstroke* into a coarsely screened reproduction and painted it magnified as a picture, he undermined with one stroke every expressive gesture that had been so important to Abstract Expressionism (fig. 57). Kerim Seiler repeated this act with his blind embossing in a highly original way—albeit by other means.

In 2007 the very complex graphic *Kalinka* was created (fig. 58). The gallery owner Susanna Kulli also acted as publisher for it. The work, consisting of four sheets, was printed in Peter Stiefel's studio. Forms, as known from Rorschach tests, were cut out of the plates with a laser. Then the plates, which had an aquatint grain, were rolled in with iridescent colors. The blank spaces in the plates then created the raised white blind embossing, surrounded by the iridescent colors. Kerim Seiler thus embarked on his very own technical path in copperplate printing. Such complex graphic prints are otherwise only known from American artists such as Frank Stella. Seiler left nothing to chance: he even specified the type of framing. The sheets were mounted as a floating block of four in a flat box-like frame.

IN SEARCH OF NEW PRINTING TECHNIQUES

In 2008, the Cabaret Voltaire in Zürich published a small computer print: *Cravan (Klein)* (fig. 59; Cover; p. 97, fig. 47). As the title suggests, a photograph of the poet, amateur boxer and artist Arthur Cravan served as the model. From 1913, Cravan appeared, among other things, as a *conférencier* in Paris and with his chaotic soirées is therefore considered a forerunner of the Dada movement. On the print, the avant-garde artist's face is covered by prismatic splinters of color, as seen through a kaleidoscope, a toy popular with children. The C-print, created in Berlin, was also mounted on aluminum.

What appeared on Cravan's face in small format took on poster size in a five-part series. It is entitled *Space, Color, Structure* and was started at the end of 2008 and completed in 2009 (fig. 60). These are inkjet prints, also known as *Micro Piezo Prints*, created in the FBM Studio of Franziska and Bruno Mancia-Bodmer in Zürich. They were also mounted on aluminum and delivered framed only. Some of the colorful motifs are directly inspired by the aesthetics of Pop Art images of the 1960s and early 1970s, while others echo Seiler's own installations. With the resounding titles *Dillinger Space, Barnum, Minotic Neocolor Mindspace, Entrée,* and *Prisma*, the sheets are without doubt loud, colorful, and matte, and, as already mentioned, mounted on aluminum, they appear weighty in their frames. In contrast to the classical intaglio printing techniques Seiler had worked with before, these works now have a certain flat smoothness. In fact, at first you might think you are looking at offset prints and not original graphics. It is therefore not surprising that Seiler turned to classical printing techniques again in 2010. Now it was a woodcut right away: *Labyrinth*, again printed by Atelier Peter Stiefel (fig. 61).

THE CLASSICAL PRINTING TECHNIQUES REVIVED

In the same year, a four-part series with the sheets *LSD, Raum, Rosette,* and *Neon* was created (fig. 62–63). These are multi-colored woodcuts, whereby here, as in the preceding xylography, the woodblocks or plates were processed with the milling plotter. Since the prints were again created in collaboration with Peter Stiefel and heavy Rives handmade paper was used for this purpose, the colors do not only lie on the surface as in inkjet prints, but also combine with the paper, so to speak. The moistened handmade paper absorbs the colors in a completely different way than a coated offset paper.

The first sheet shows the image of the chemical formula for LSD, mirrored so that the motif looks like a geometric Rorschach test in the mirroring and doubling. The fact that the different colors were not printed congruently results in a flickering effect. One could also say that the drug starts to take effect and things are only perceived in a blurred way. The second sheet repeats a neon work by the artist. All in all, the sheets reflect colors and forms as we know them from Pop Art.

In 2011 the four-color silkscreen *A View from Spaceship Earth* was created, printed by Arni Siebdruck in Basel (fig. 64). The famous peace sign used here was designed in 1958 by the British artist Gerald Holtom for the world's first Easter march from London to the nuclear weapons research center in Aldermaston. According to Holtom, the symbol represents a combination of two characters from the maritime alphabet (semaphore), which is designed with flag movements. *N* for *nuclear*—the flags point diagonally down to the left and right—and *D* for *disarmament*. The flags of this letter point vertically up and down. The surrounding circle symbolizes the entire earth. Printing the peace sign in blue over a supernova therefore makes double sense.

The *Polar Bear and Neon Lights* series from 2014, consisting of nine prints, is the most extensive of Seiler's graphic series to date (fig. 65–67). The series reproduces various neon works in simple symbolic form, and the little bear in white on a black background is a small reminder of the sculpture the artist executed in white marble (p. 61). He began to print the series himself in the studio of Peter Stiefel. The drypoint worked plates had to be provided separately for all colors. The printing of the motifs with up to six plates in an edition of eight was correspondingly complex.

In the same year, the Galerie Grieder Contemporary in Küsnacht published a sheet in unlimited edition: *Relay (Situationist Space Program)* (p. 17, fig. 14; p. 72, 100, 114–118), a xerox on corresponding paper (fig. 68). The sheet is somewhat reminiscent of Seiler's first edition, the handicraft sheet *Die Galerie.*

NEW PRINTER, OLD TECHNOLOGY

Verkehrte Welt is the name of an edition from 2015, a multicolor heliogravure (fig. 69). It was printed by Willi Jesse. Willi Jesse runs a renowned art print and etching workshop in Berlin. The sheet shows a reversed map

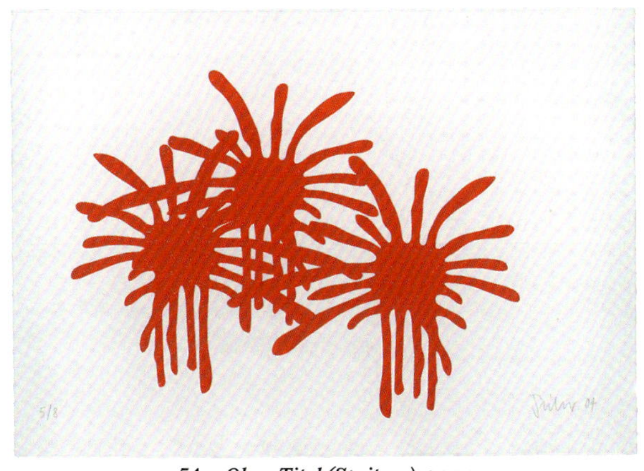

54 *Ohne Titel (Spritzer)*, 2004
Embossed aquatint on Zerkall 250g; Sheet: 76×107 cm
(Image: 59.6×77 cm); Edition of 8

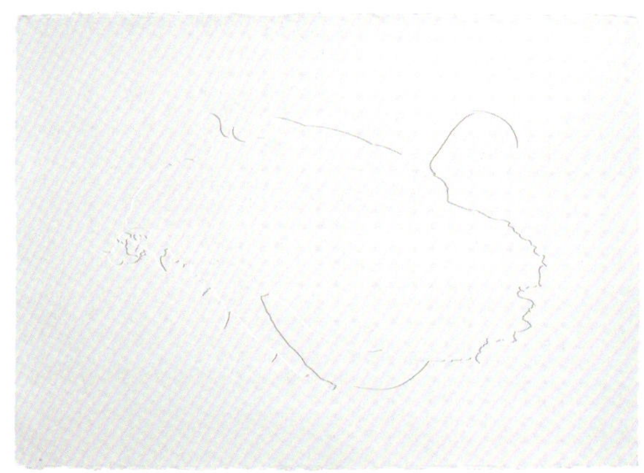

55 *Trace 12*, 2006
Blind embossing on Bütten 600g;
Sheet: 78×107 cm (Image: 48.8×77 cm); Unique

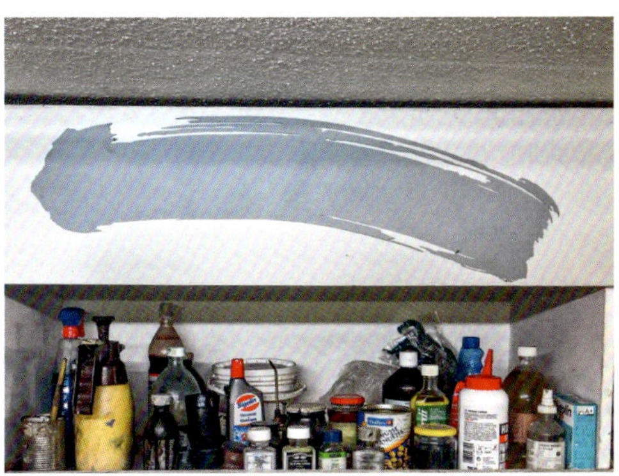

56 Printing plate for blind embossing *Trace 04*, 2006

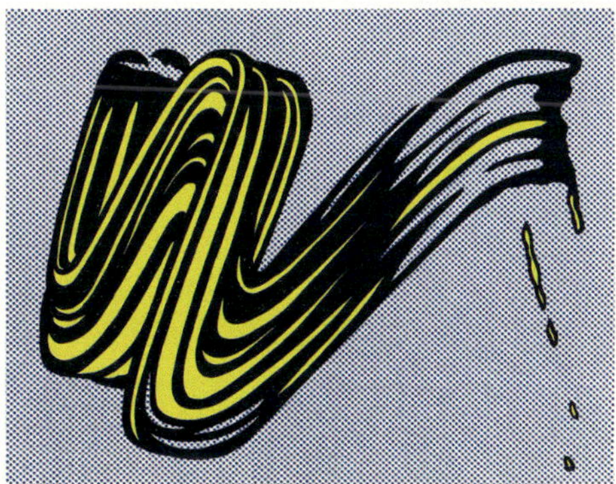

57 Roy Lichtenstein: *Brushstroke*, 1965
Screenprint on paper; 58.4×73.6 cm; Edition of 280

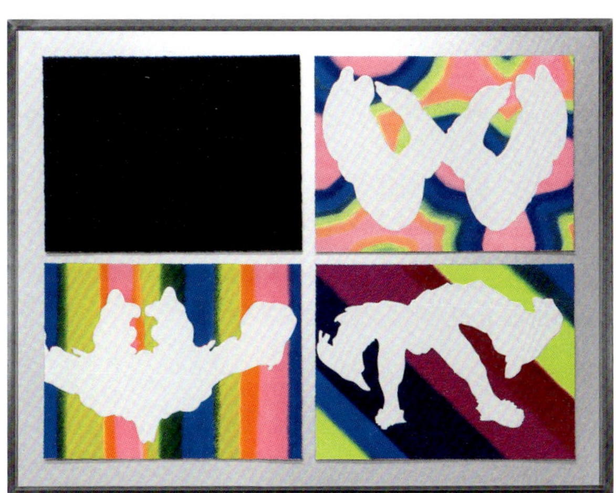

58 *Kalinka*, 2007
Four multicolored aquatints with raised embossing
on Alt Bern 250g in aluminum frame; Frame: 53,7×67,7 cm
(Sheets: each 21×28 cm); Edition of 15

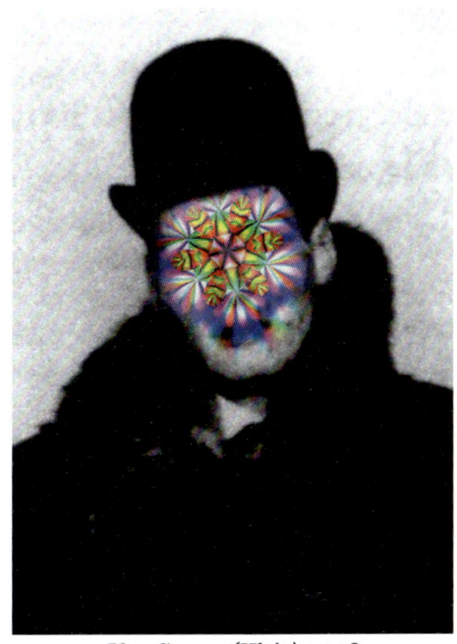

59 *Cravan (Klein)*, 2008
C-print on archive photo paper; 25×20 cm;
Edition of 5

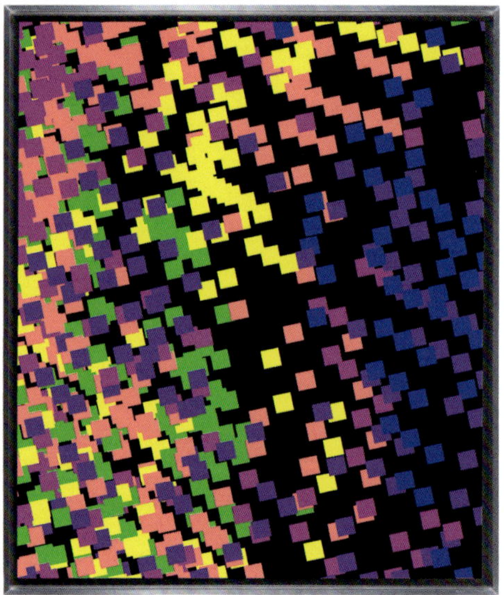

60 *Space, Color, Structure (Dillinger)*, 2008/09
Micro piezo print on paper in aluminum frame;
Frame: 120×100 cm (Sheet: 120×100 cm); Edition of 3

61 *Labyrinth*, 2010
Woodcut on Rives 300g; Sheet: 76.5×76.5 cm
(Image: 70×70 cm); Edition of 16

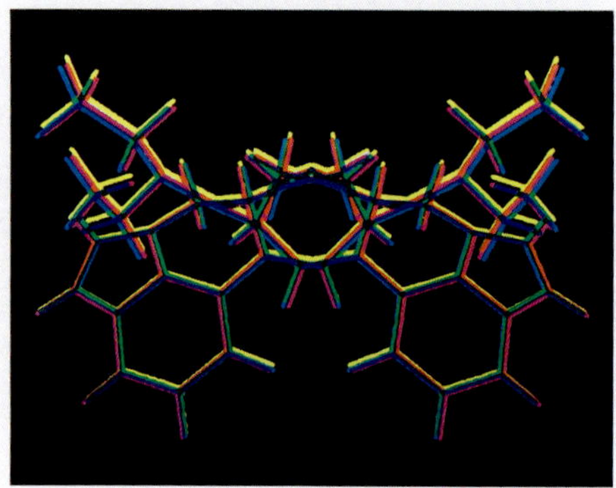

62 *Ohne Titel (LSD)*, 2010
Multi-color woodcut on Rives 300g; Sheet: 80×100 cm
(Image: 76×96 cm); Edition of 8

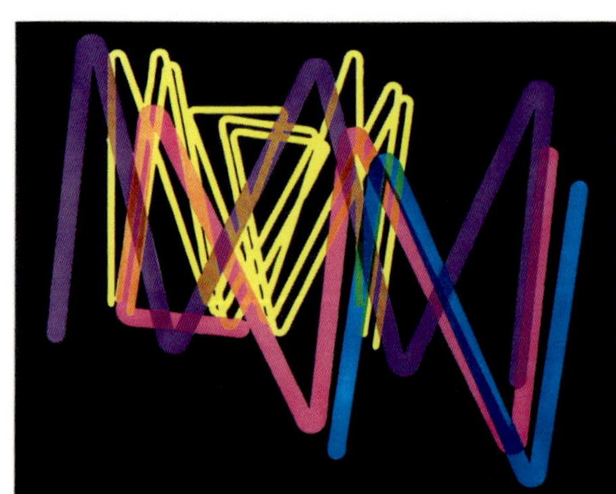

63 *Ohne Titel (Neon)*, 2010
Multi-color woodcut on Rives 300g; Sheet: 80×100 cm
(Image: 76×96 cm); Edition of 8

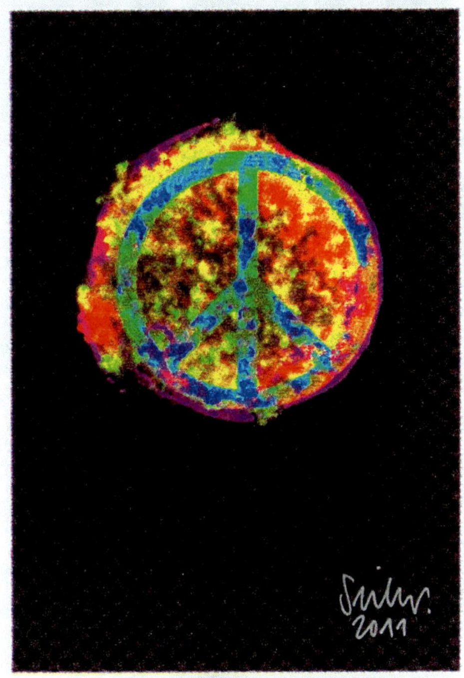

64 *A View from Spaceship Earth*, 2011
Screenprint on Munken; Sheet: 31×21 cm
(Image: 29.2×19.5 cm); Edition of 80

65 *Polar Bear and Neon Lights (Maintenant)*, 2014
Multi-color drypoint on paper in colored white frame;
Sheet: 104.5×24 cm (Image: 94.5×14 cm); Edition of 8

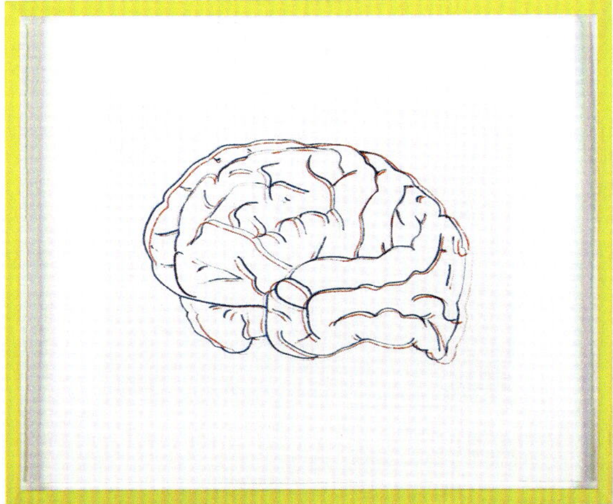

66 *Polar Bear and Neon Lights (Stereoscopic Brain)*, 2014
Multi-color drypoint on paper in colored yellow frame;
Sheet: 39×32 cm (Image: 29×22 cm); Edition of 8

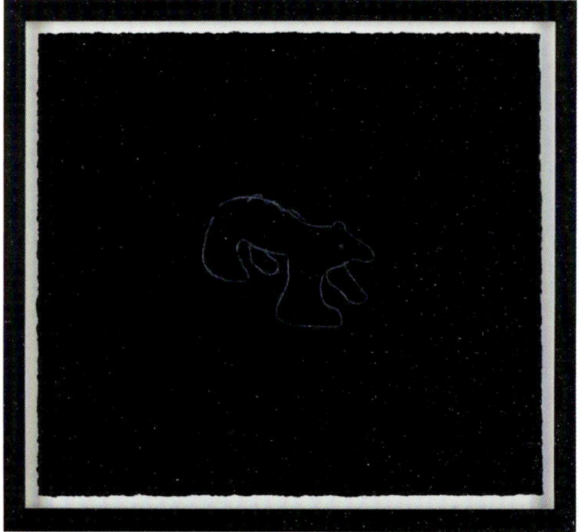

67 *Polar Bear and Neon Lights (Polar Bear)*, 2014
Multi-color drypoint on paper in colored black frame;
Sheet: 24×22 cm (Image: 14×12 cm); Edition of 8

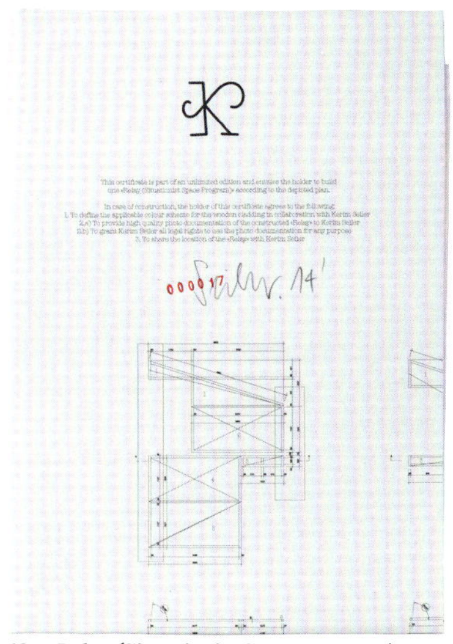

68 *Relay (Situationist Space Program)*, 2014
Xerox on paper; Sheet: 84.1×119.8 cm
(Image: 75.7×110.9 cm); Edition ∞

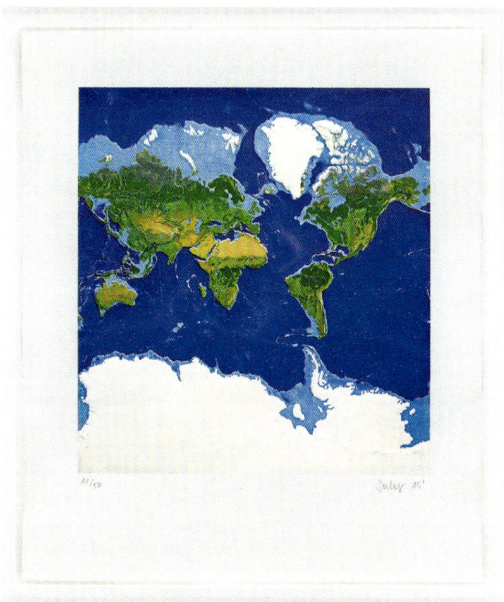

69 *Verkehrte Welt*, 2015
Multi-color photogravure; Sheet: 70×58 cm
(Image: 49×44 cm); Edition 50

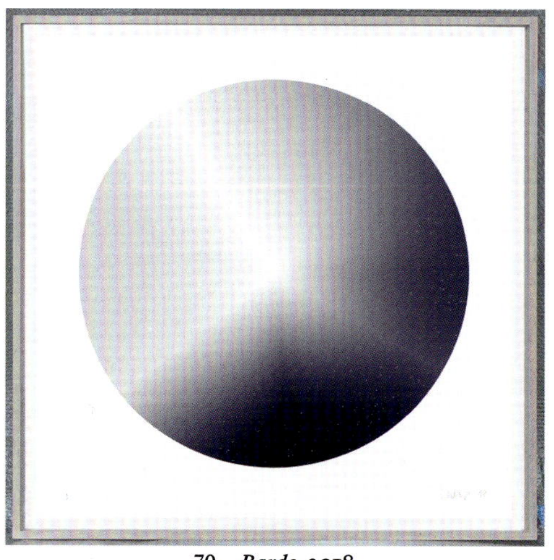

70 *Bardo*, 2018
Inkjet on paper; Sheet: 112×112 cm
(Image: 94×94 cm); Edition of 8

of the world in the Mercator projection. The photogravure was published in an edition of 50 copies by the SOS-Edition. This supports the SOS Children's Villages worldwide.

In 2018 a print was produced with titled *Bardo* (fig. 70). According to the teachings of Tibetan Buddhism, this refers to an intermediate state of consciousness. It is about states of consciousness as they can be experienced in this world and the hereafter. The motif looks like a shiny, hunchbacked round shield whose surface shimmers to light or dark. The work was originally also intended to be printed as heliogravure, but the fine black and white gradient on the round shield could not be satisfactorily realized in this way. Thus, the FBM Studio in Zürich initially produced a digital print in an edition of eight copies. It is not impossible that Kerim Seiler will find another possibility to realize the motif in a refined copperplate print. One way or another, Kerim Seiler is fascinated by copperplate printing. The fact that the artist and printer Peter Stiefel became his father was not something Seiler had chosen. However, he found himself immersed in the atmosphere of a printer's workshop early on. But there were also bad surprises: as a small boy he once tasted a tube of yellow paint, believing it to be mayonnaise. Since then, Kerim Seiler has always treated printing inks with the greatest respect. For his further development as an artist, the encounter with Stiefel was a great opportunity. Seiler might come up with yet another crazy idea, but the experienced master printer always found a perfect technical solution.

Seiler's graphic work, although not so extensive, is characterized by an astonishing variety. Even though he selects and uses the various techniques very precisely, he has by no means become a graphic tinkerer. The conceptual aspect of his artistic work always takes precedence. His graphics could be called classical in that—as with the great masters of the trade—they always reflect his artistic work and transpose it once again, transporting one medium into another.

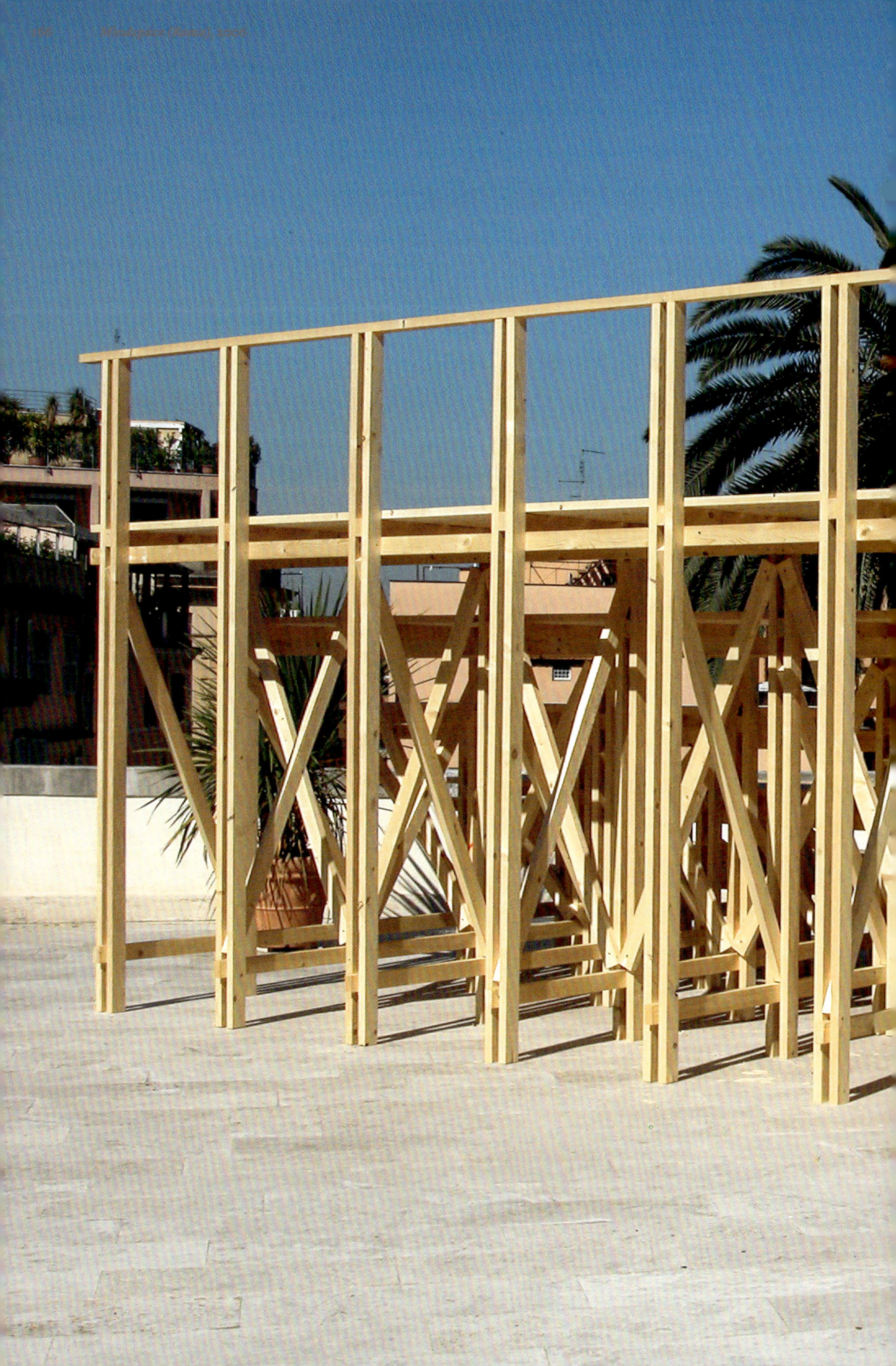

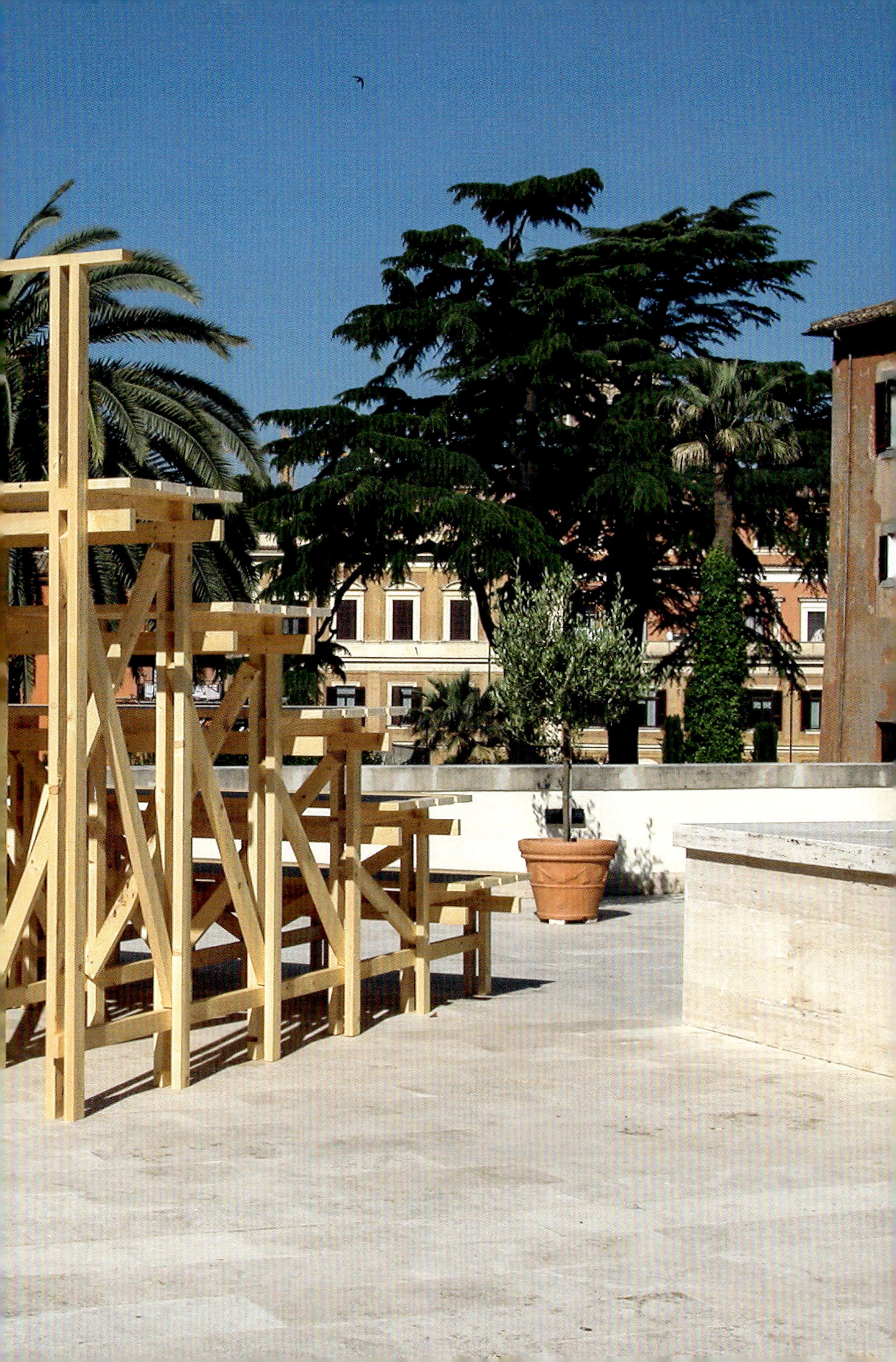

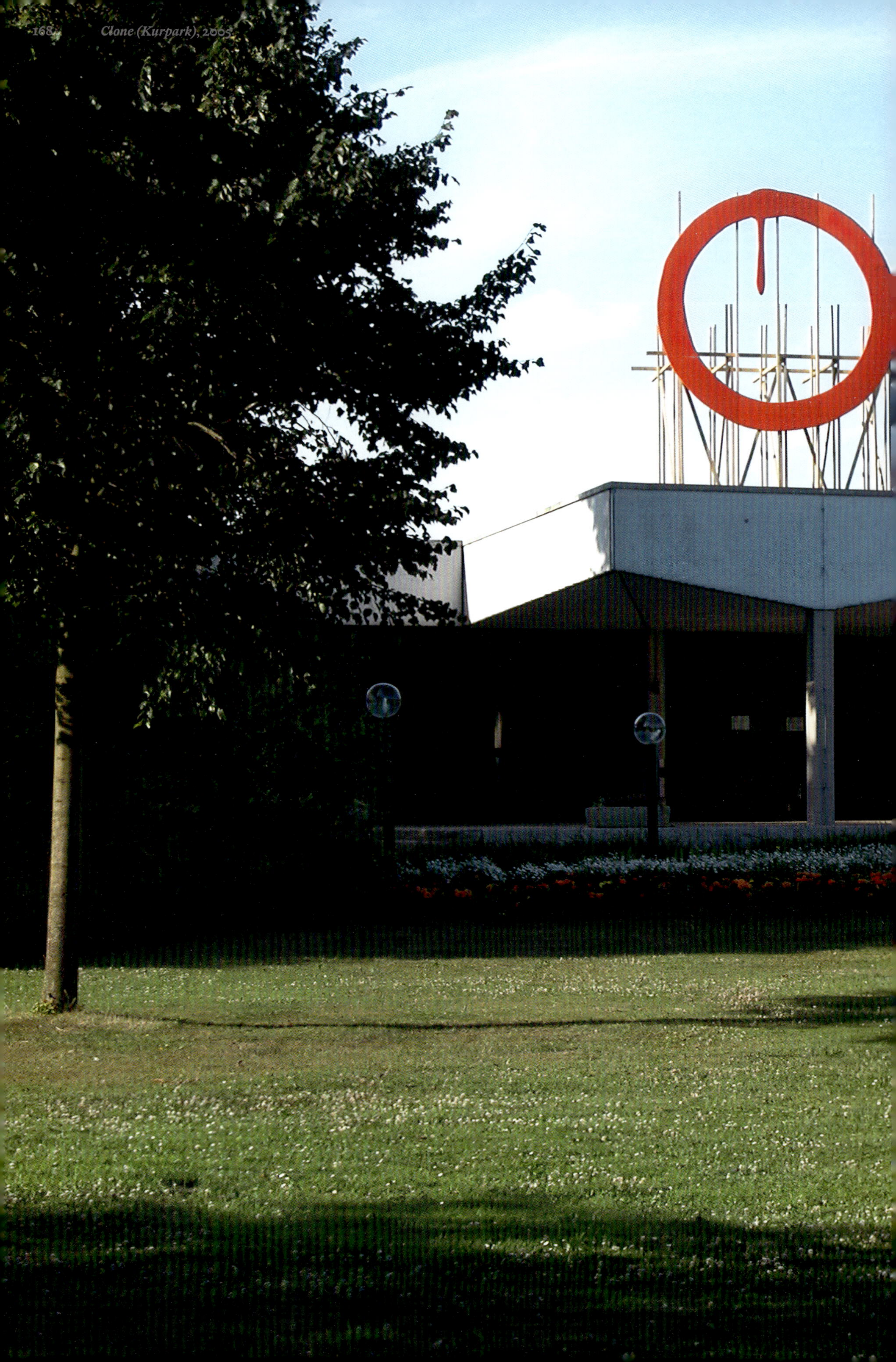

Clone (Kurpark), 2003

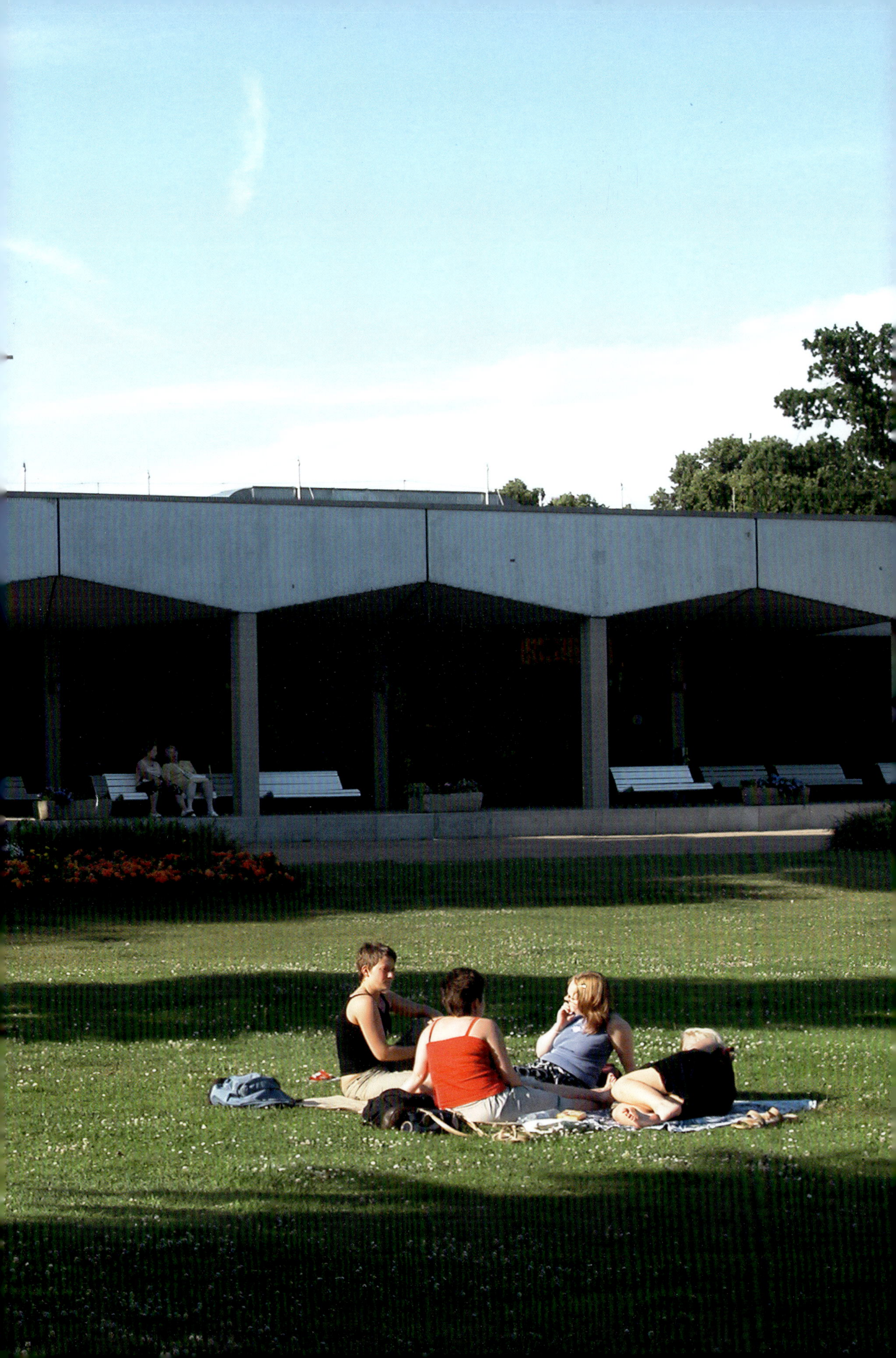

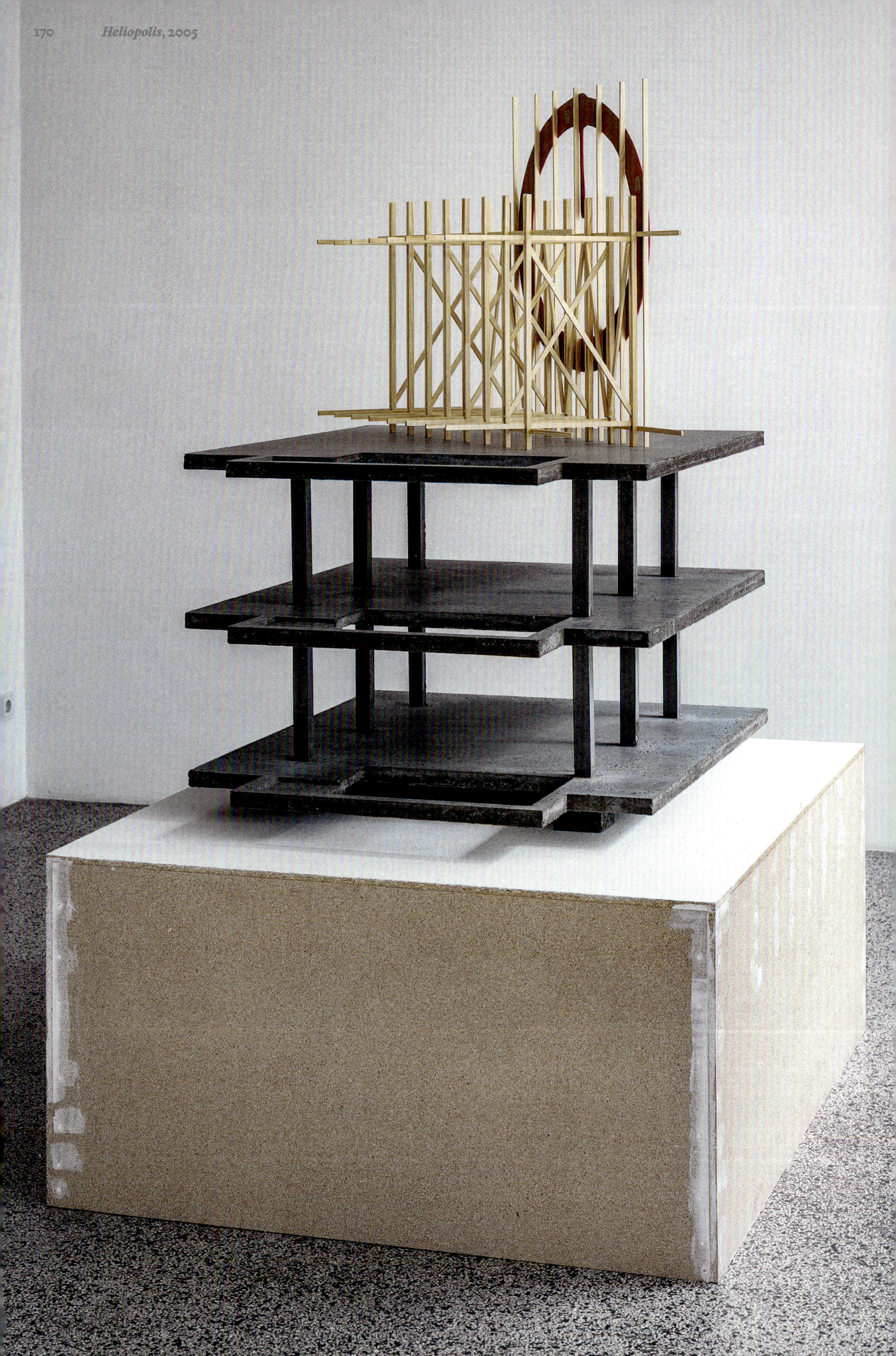

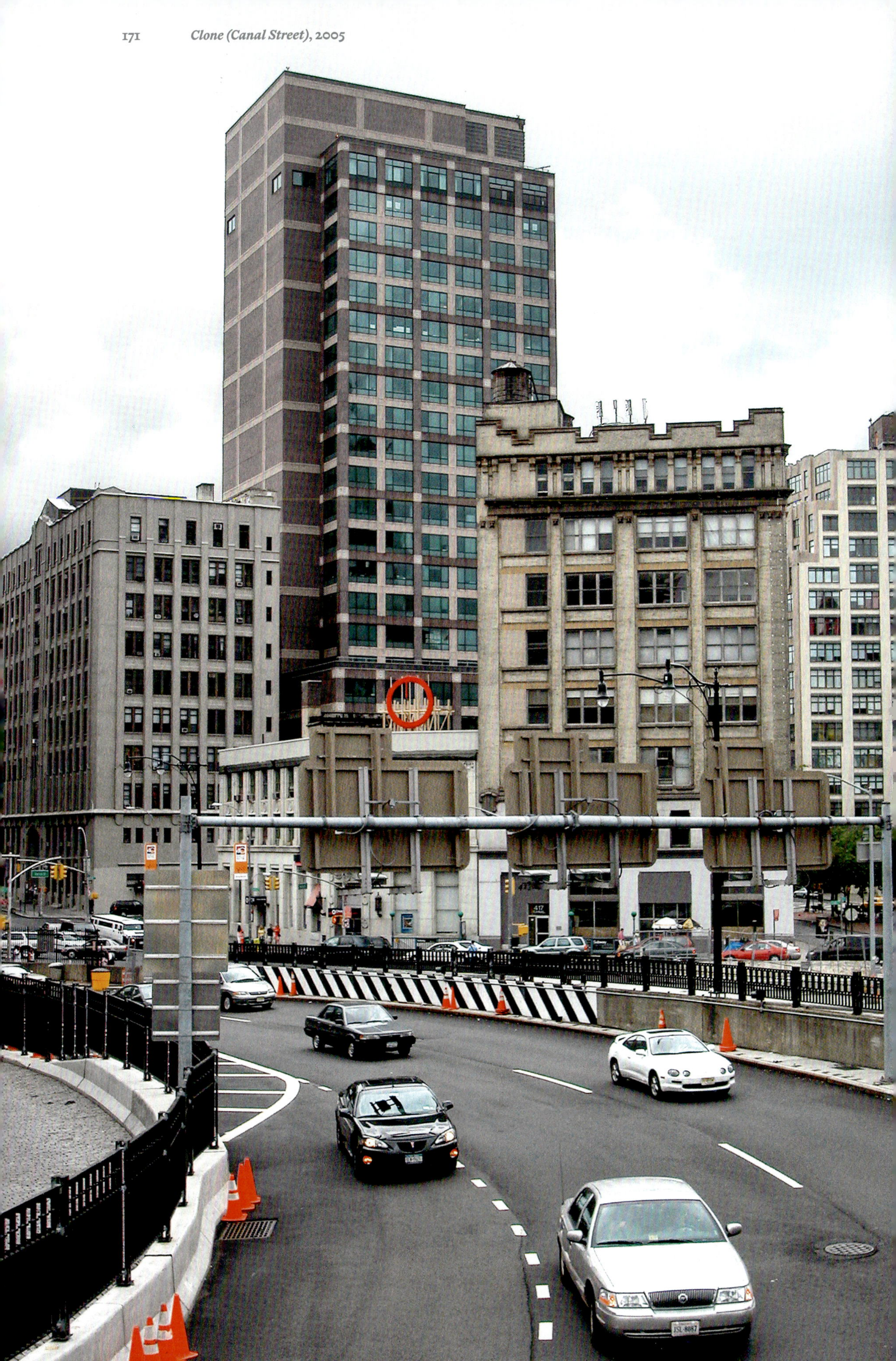

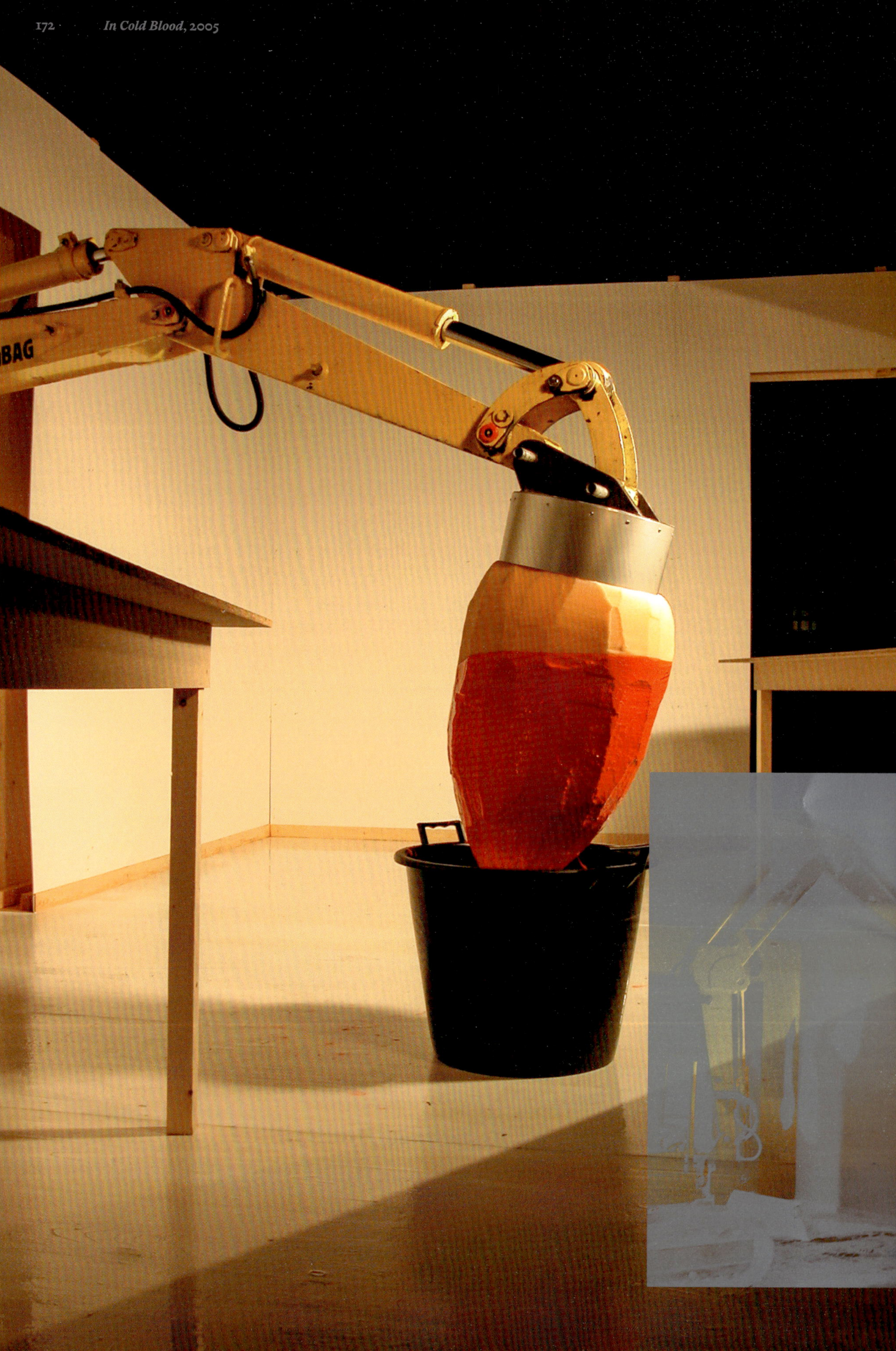
BAG

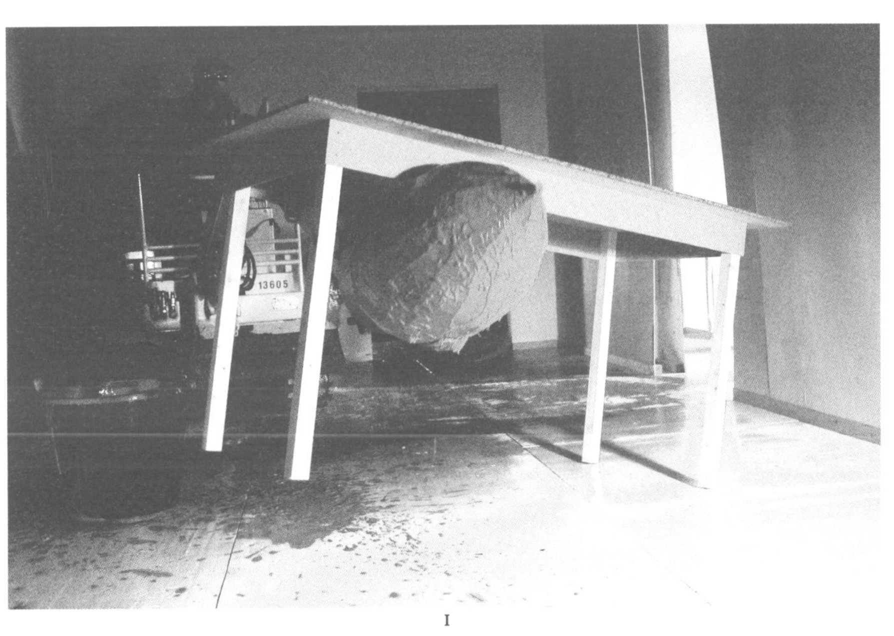

I

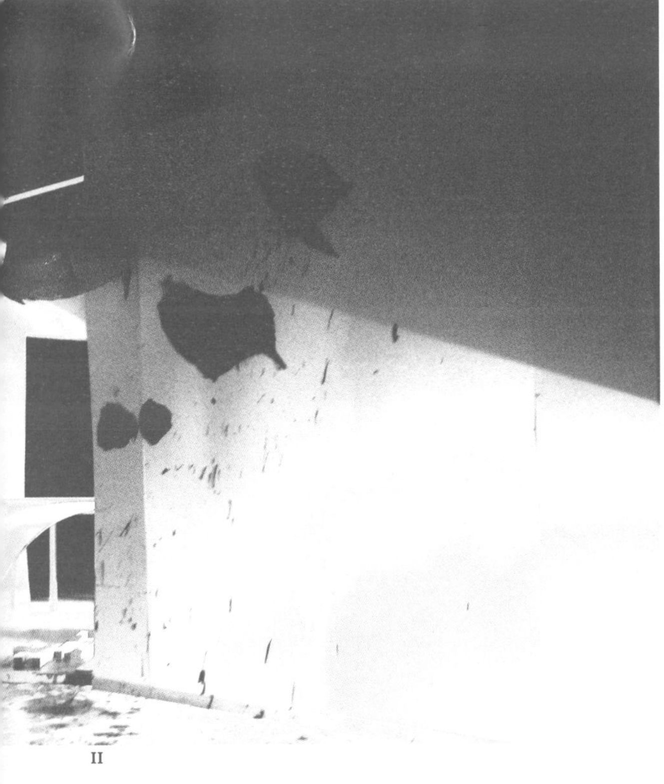

II

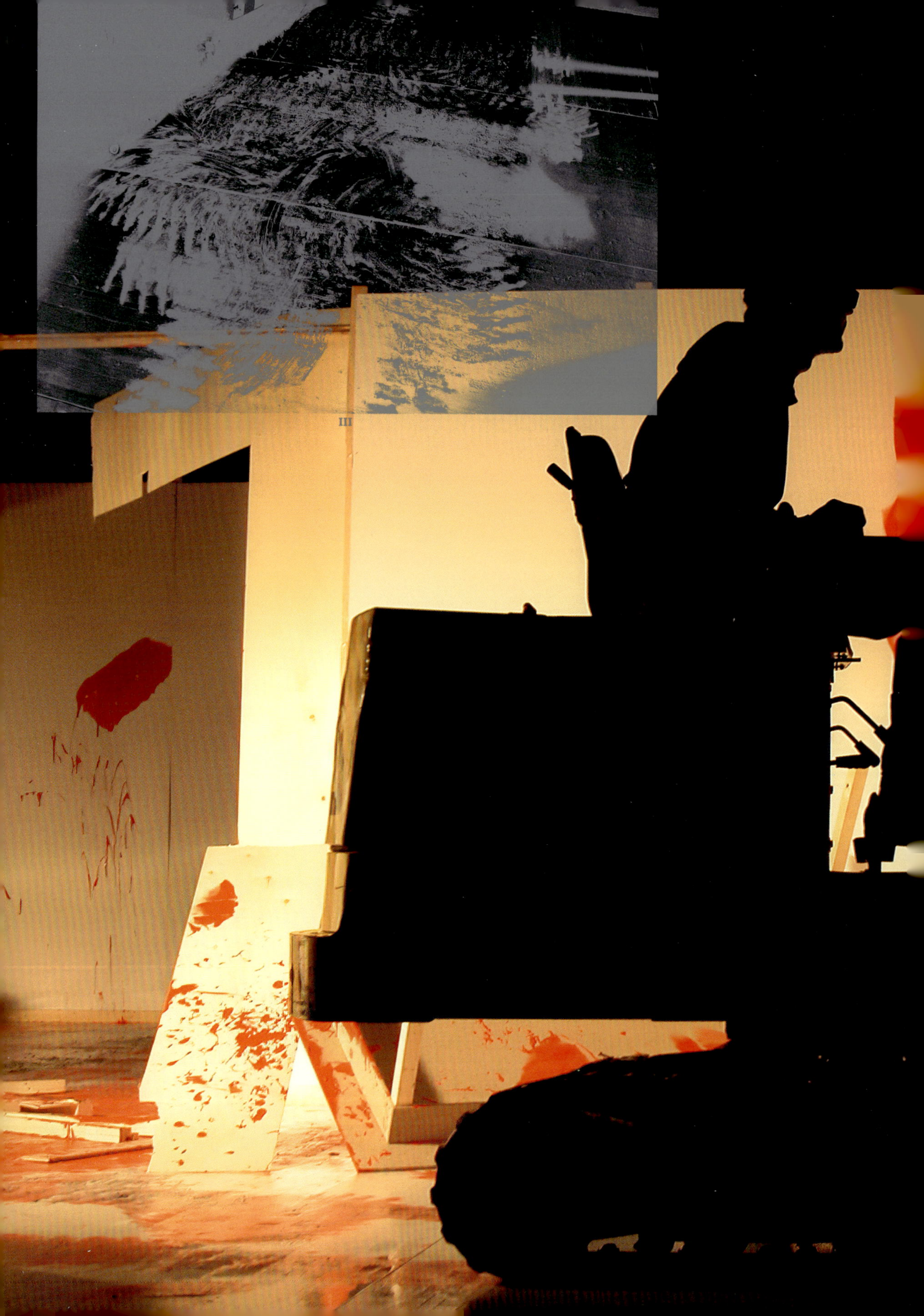

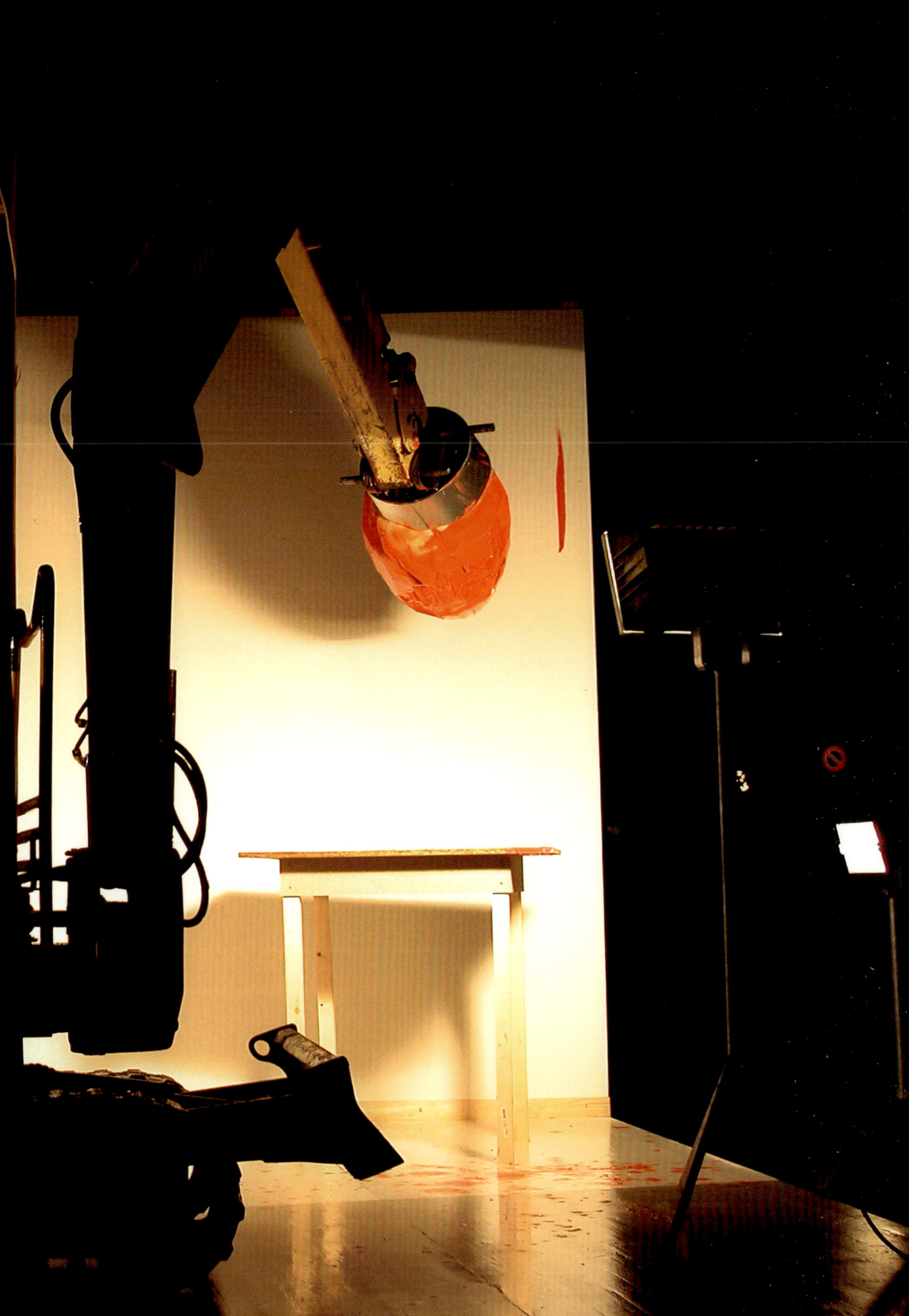

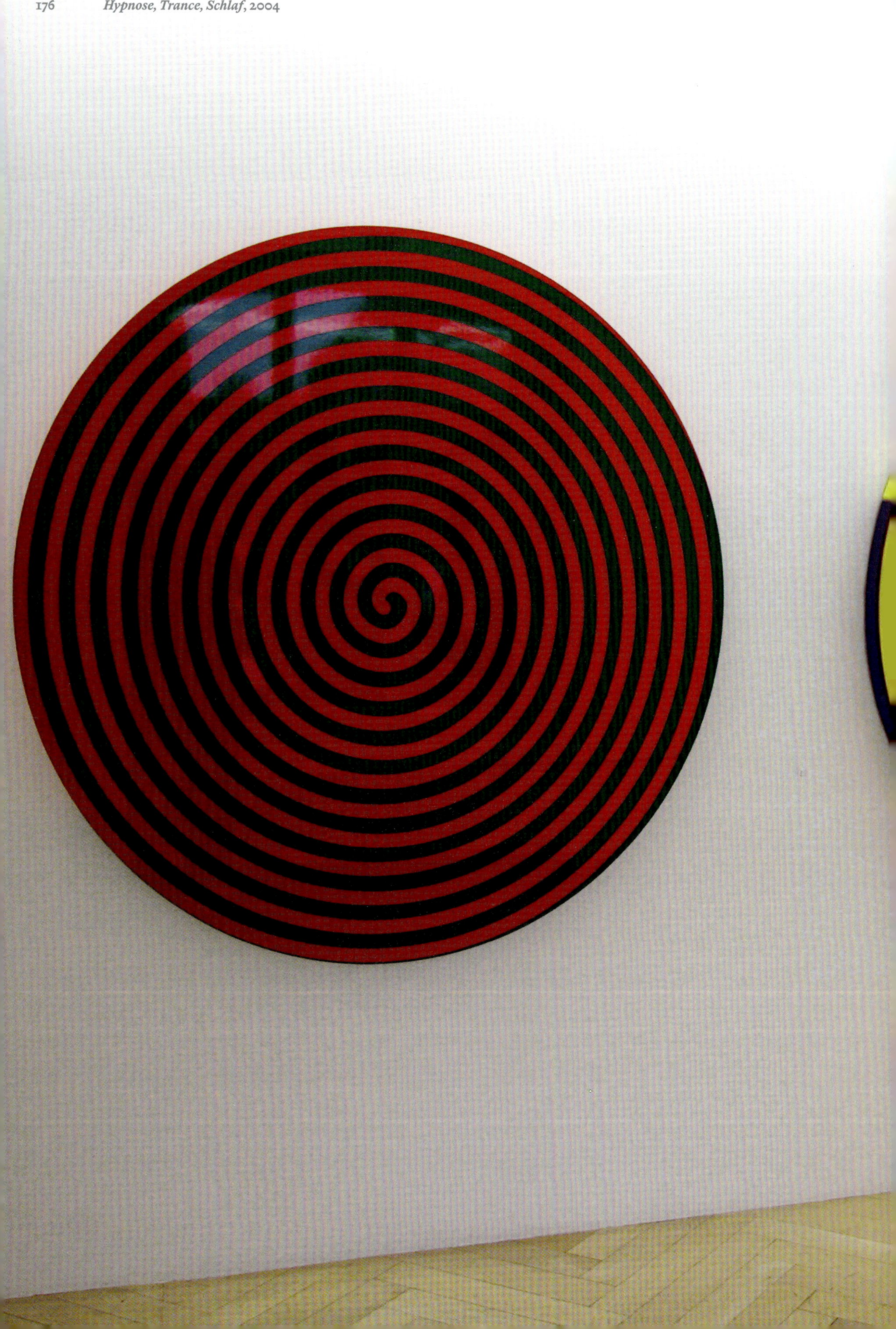

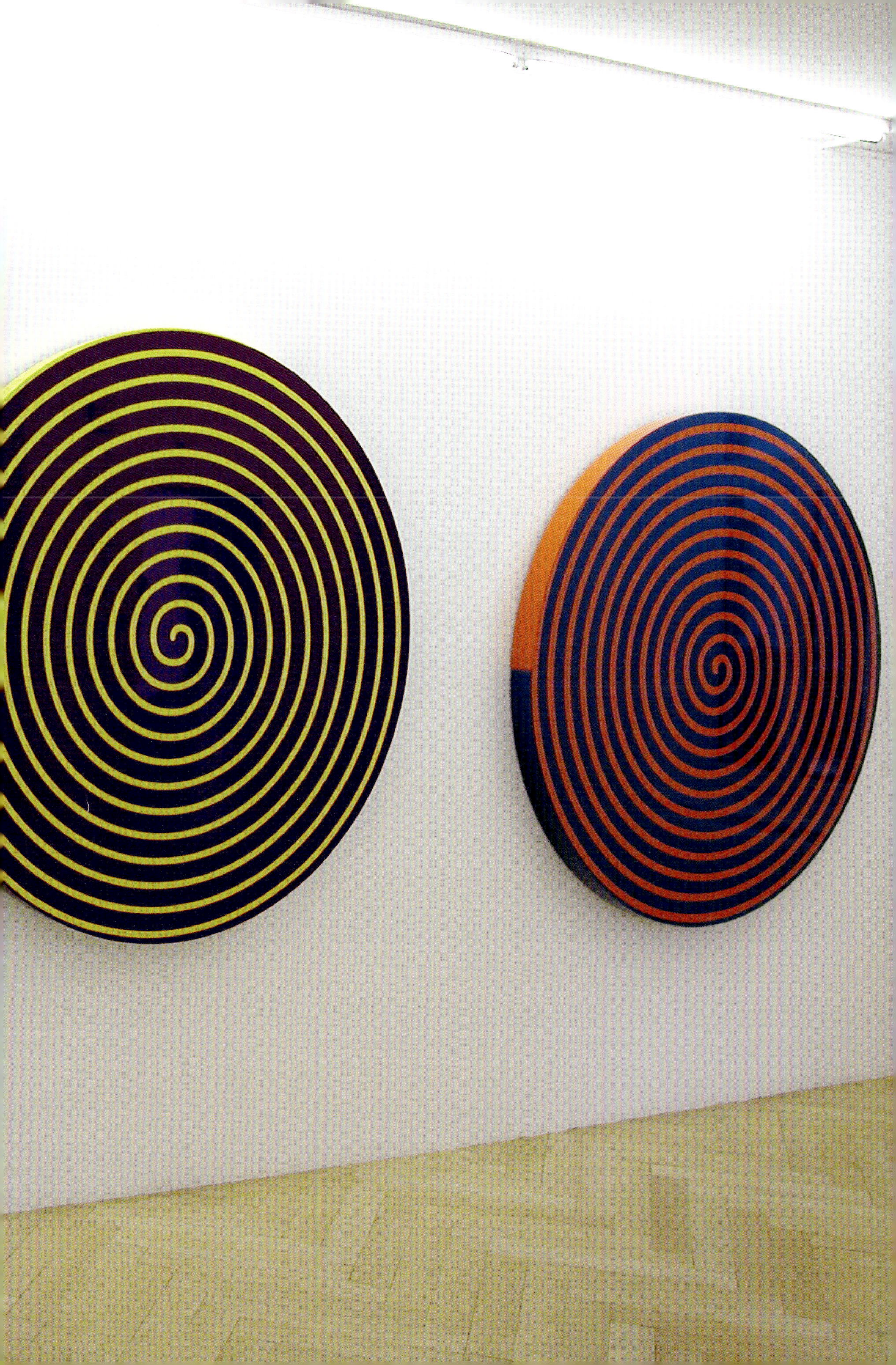

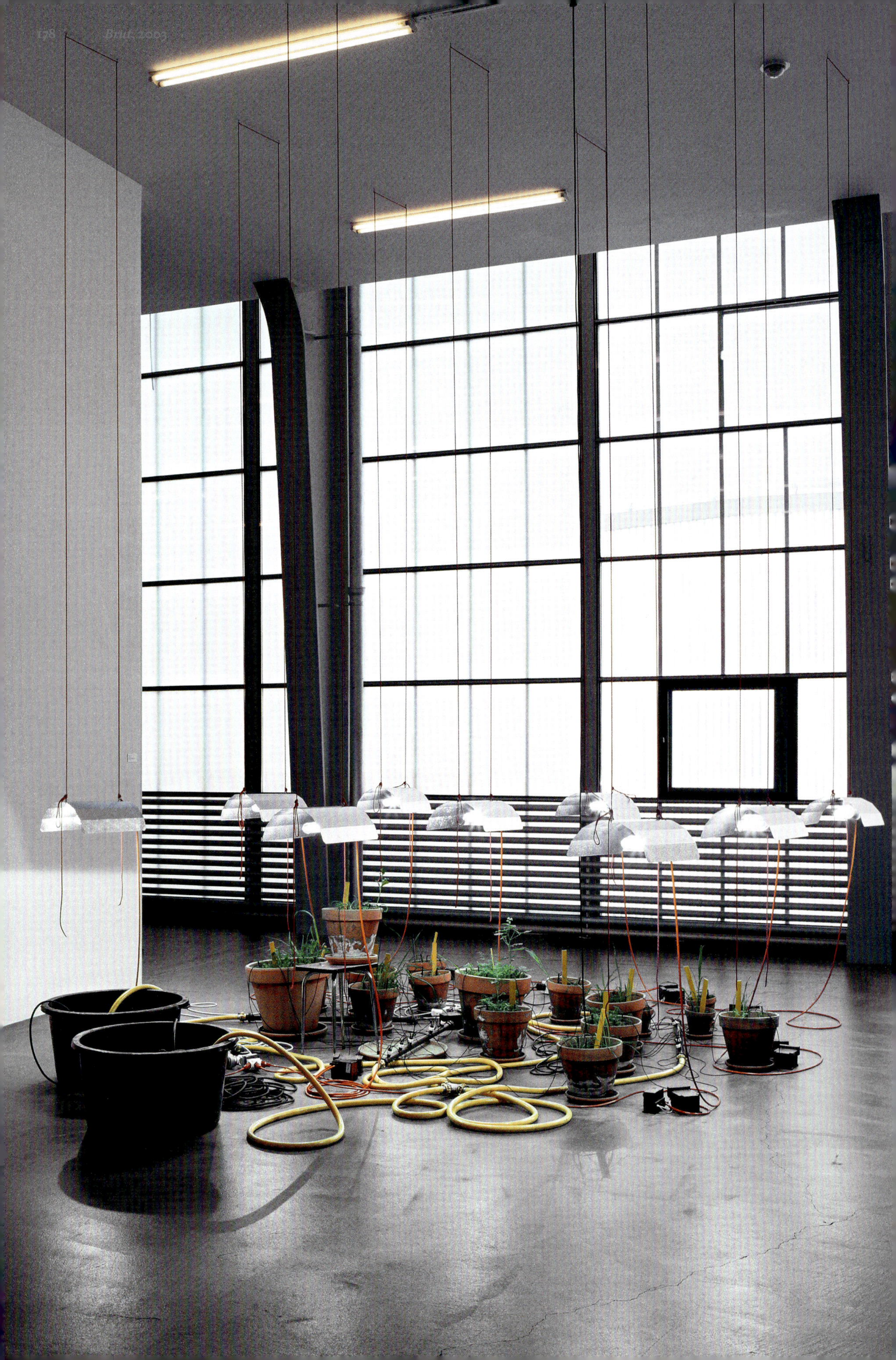

Aus der Hundeperspektive, 20

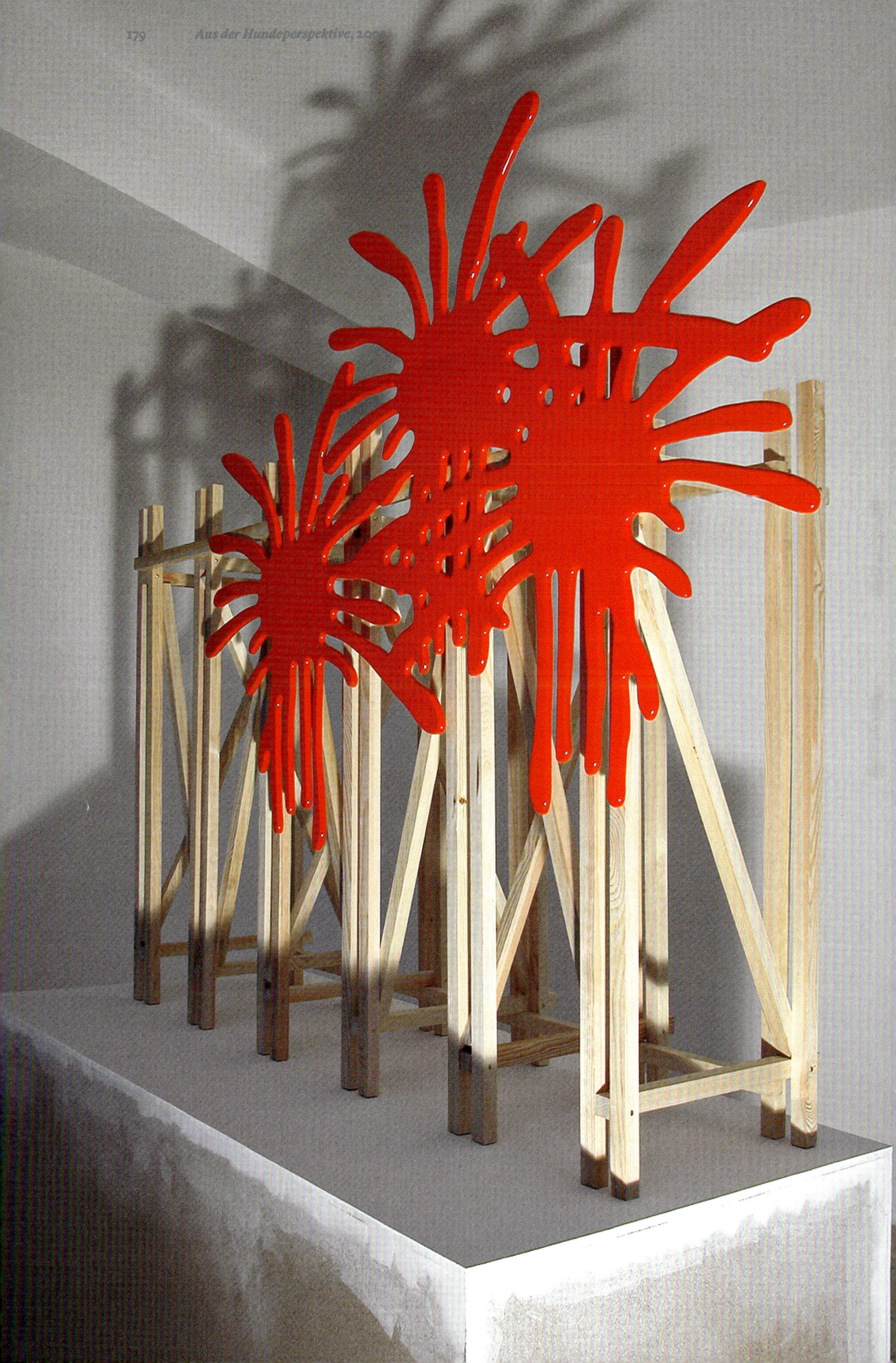

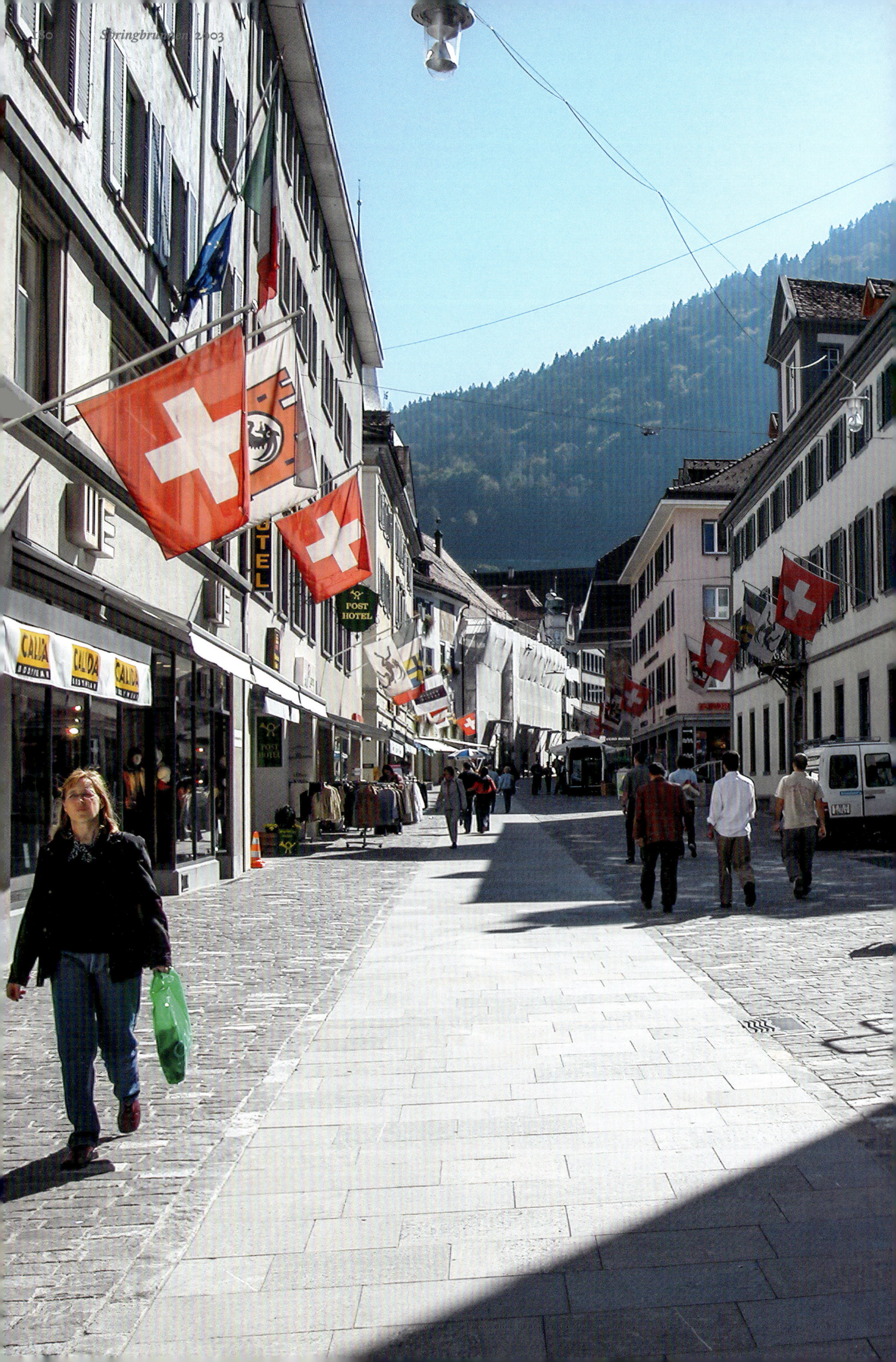
CALIDA
CALIDA
CALIDA
POST HOTEL
POST HOTEL

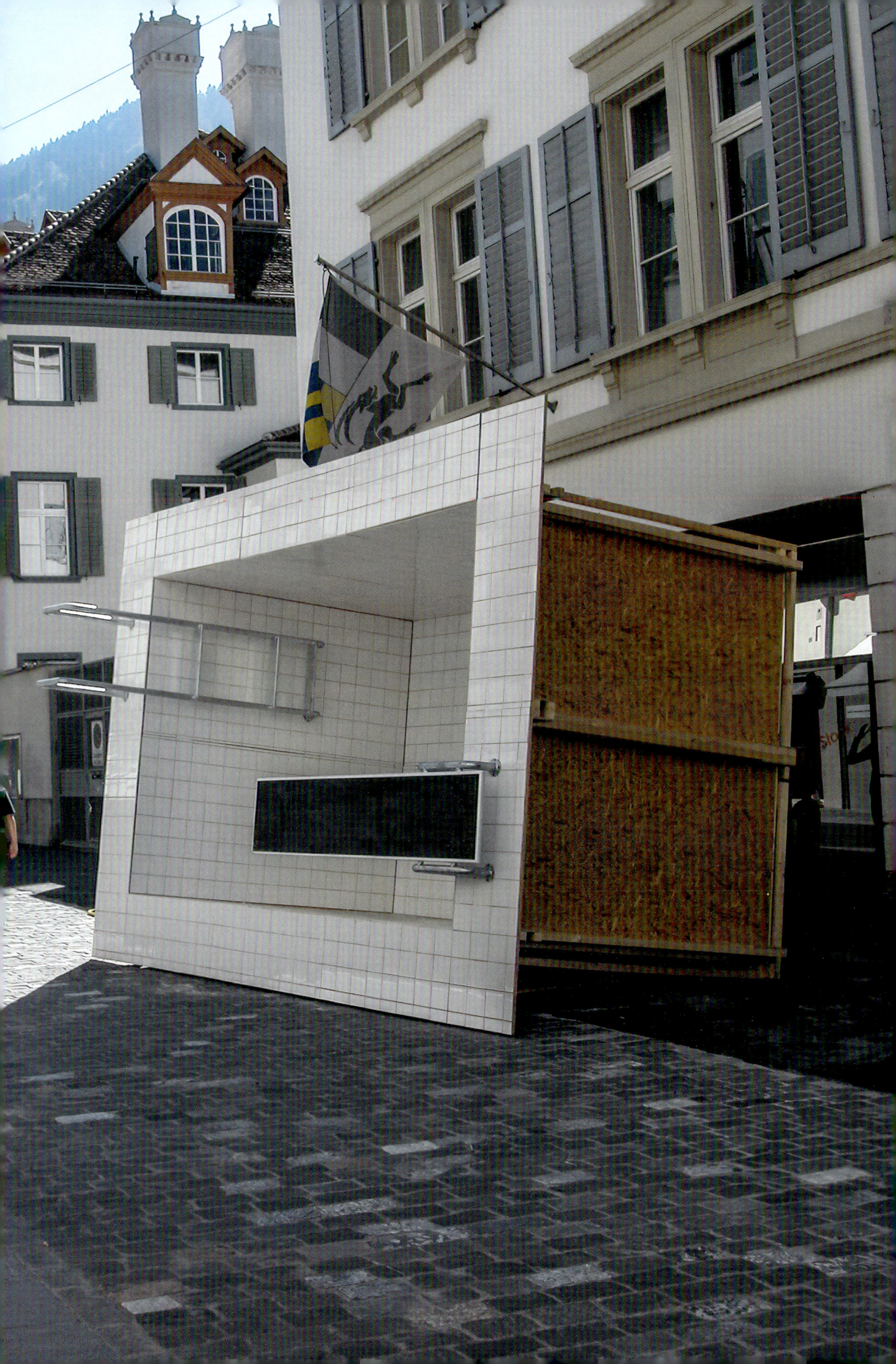

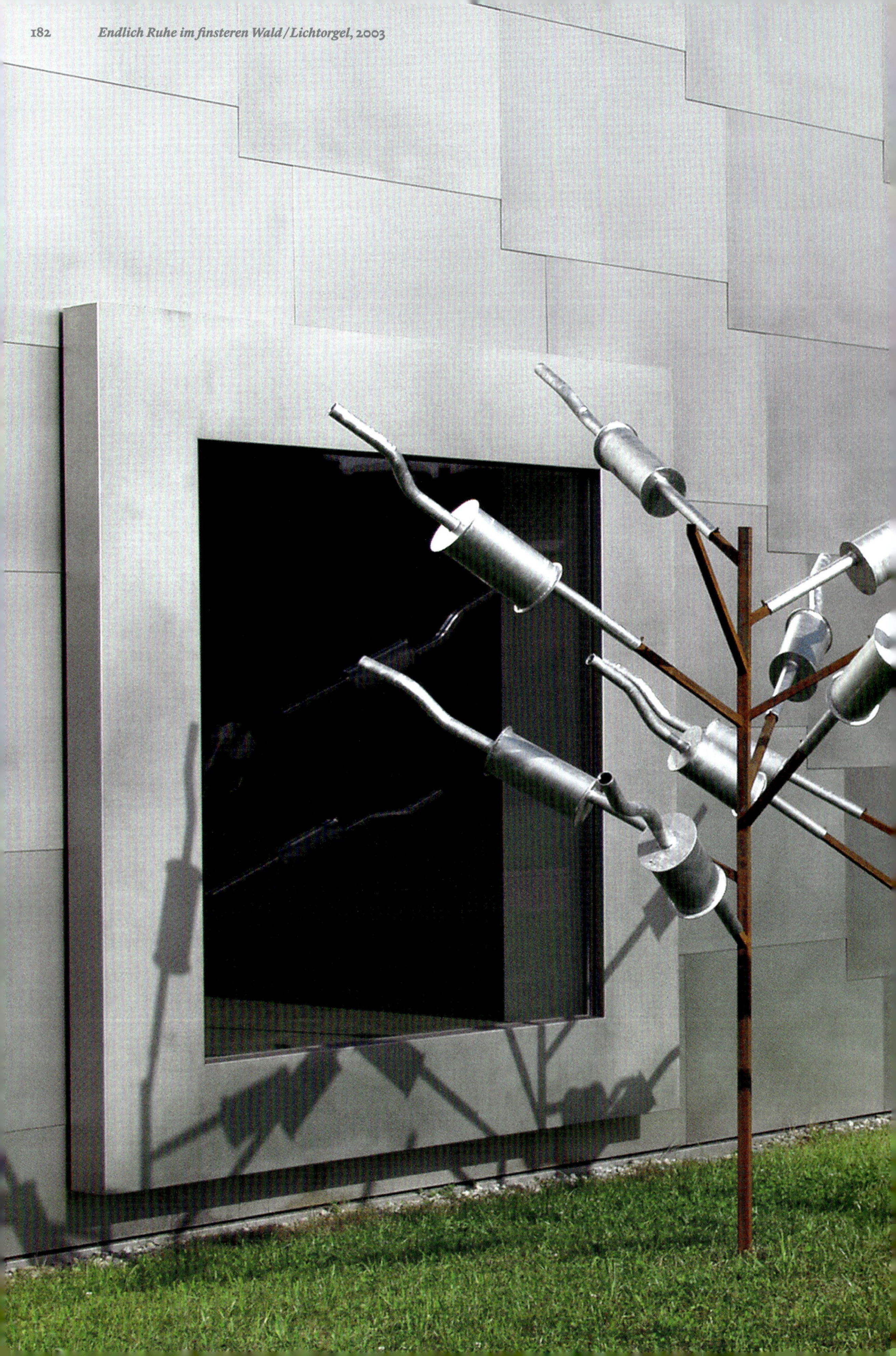

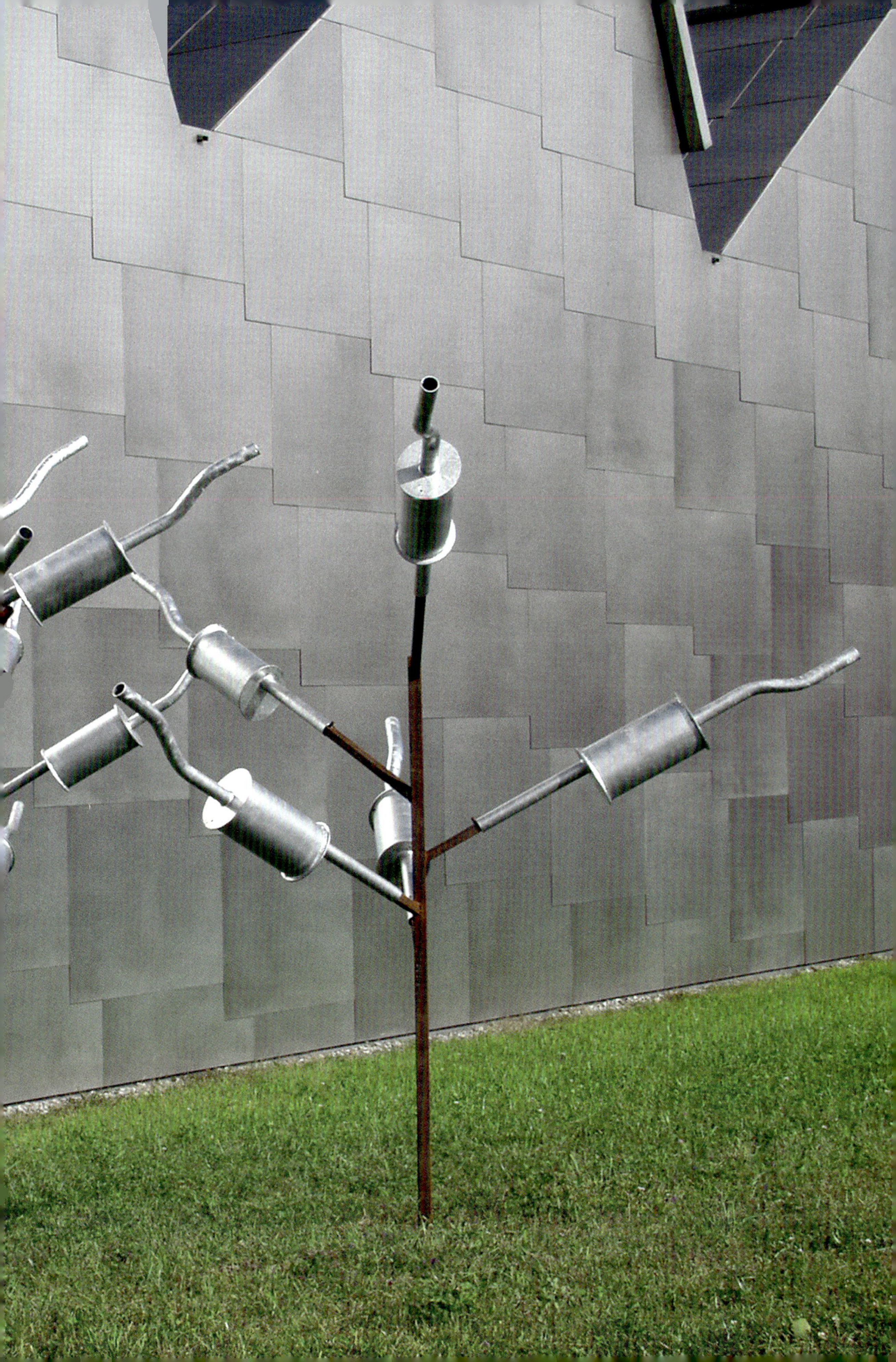

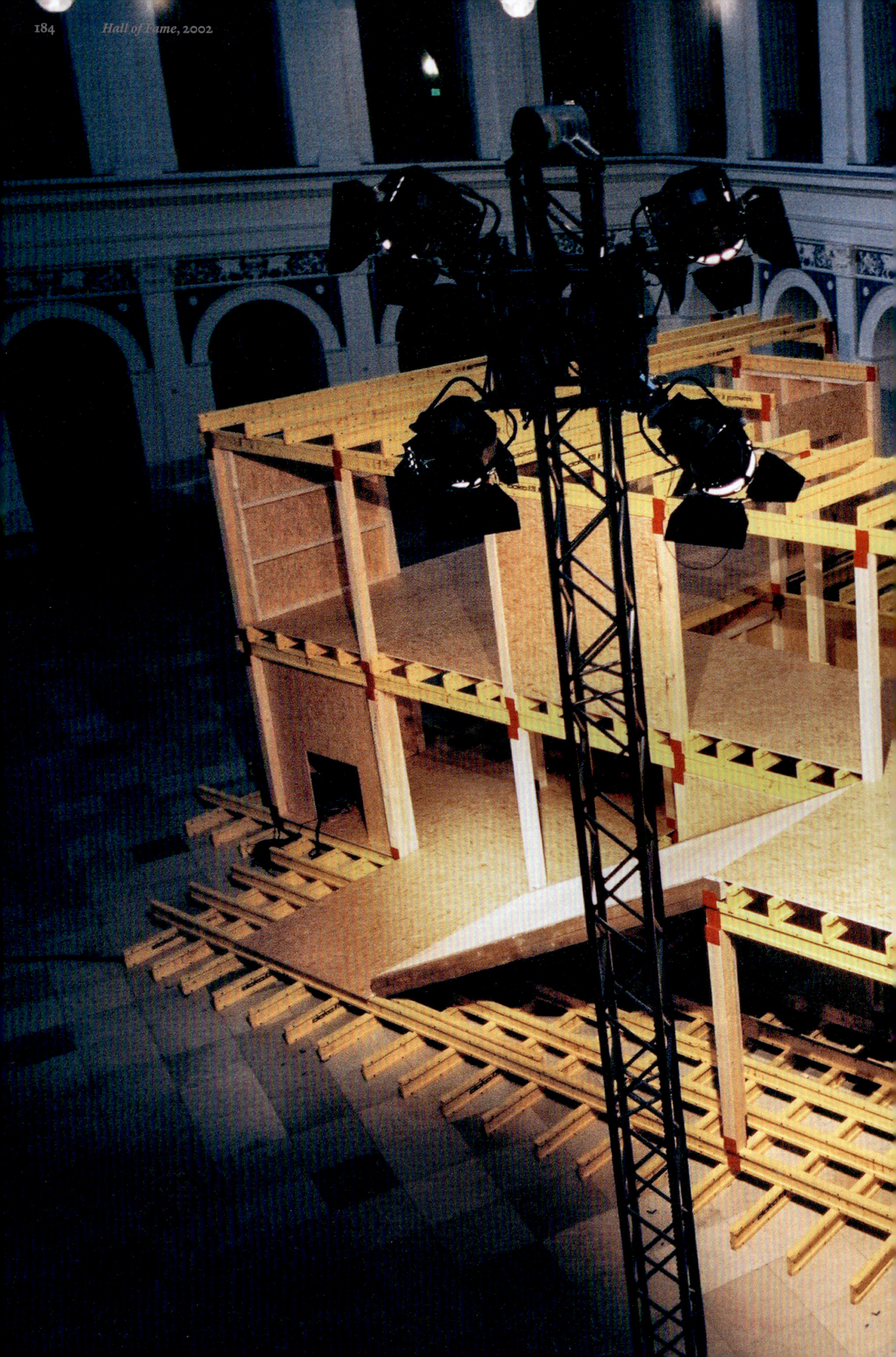

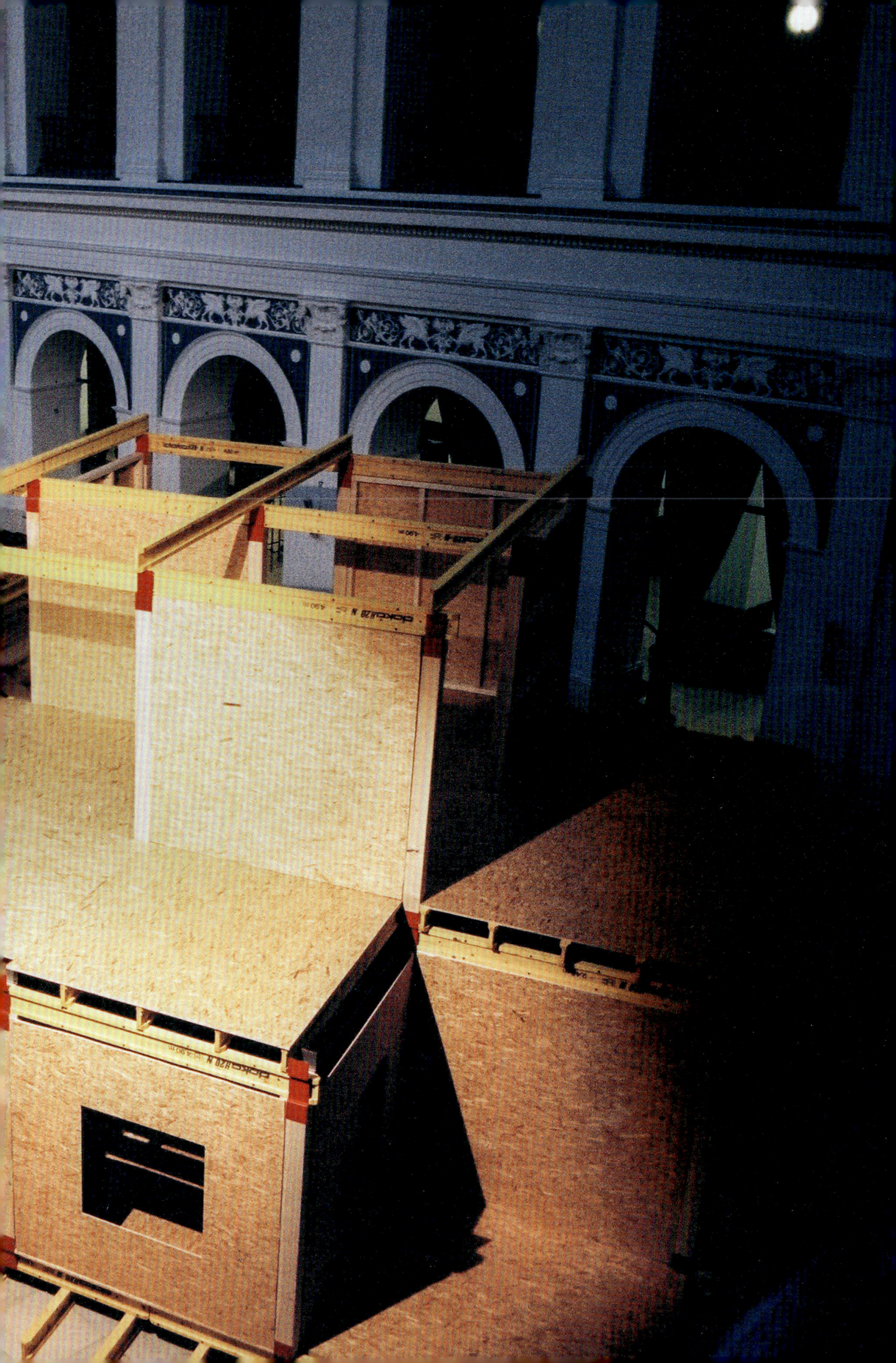

Lattenwald (Raster), 2002

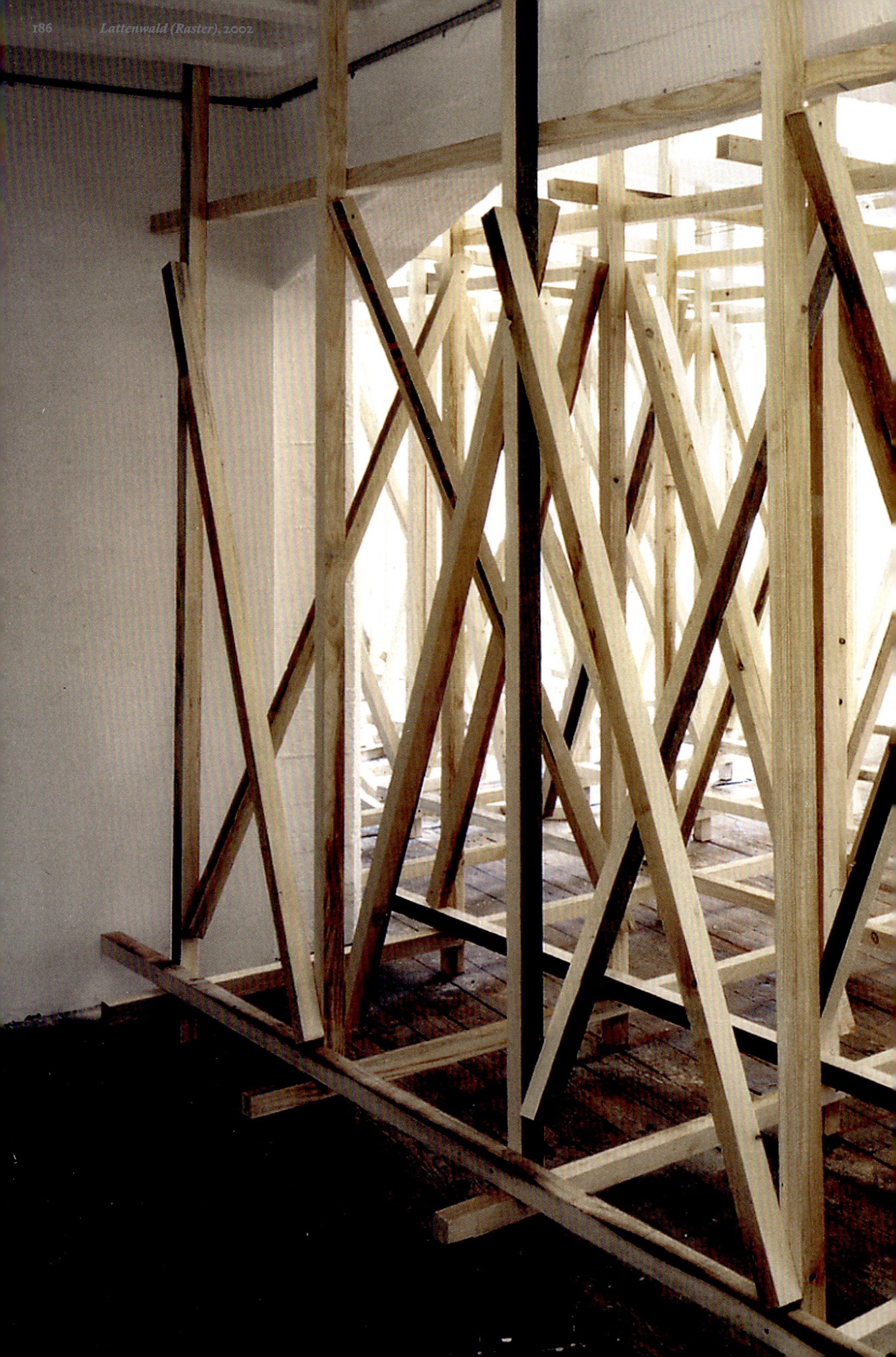

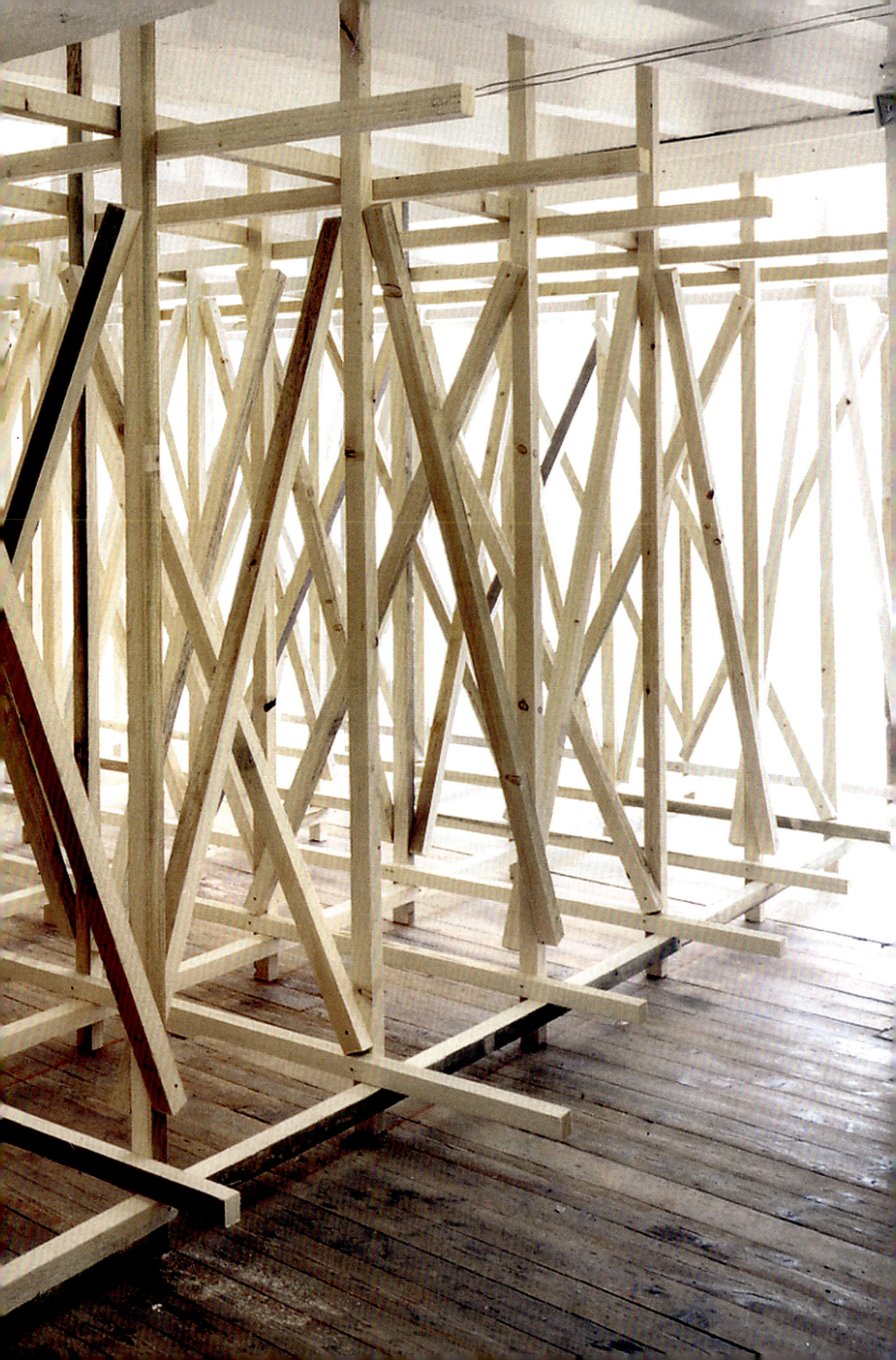

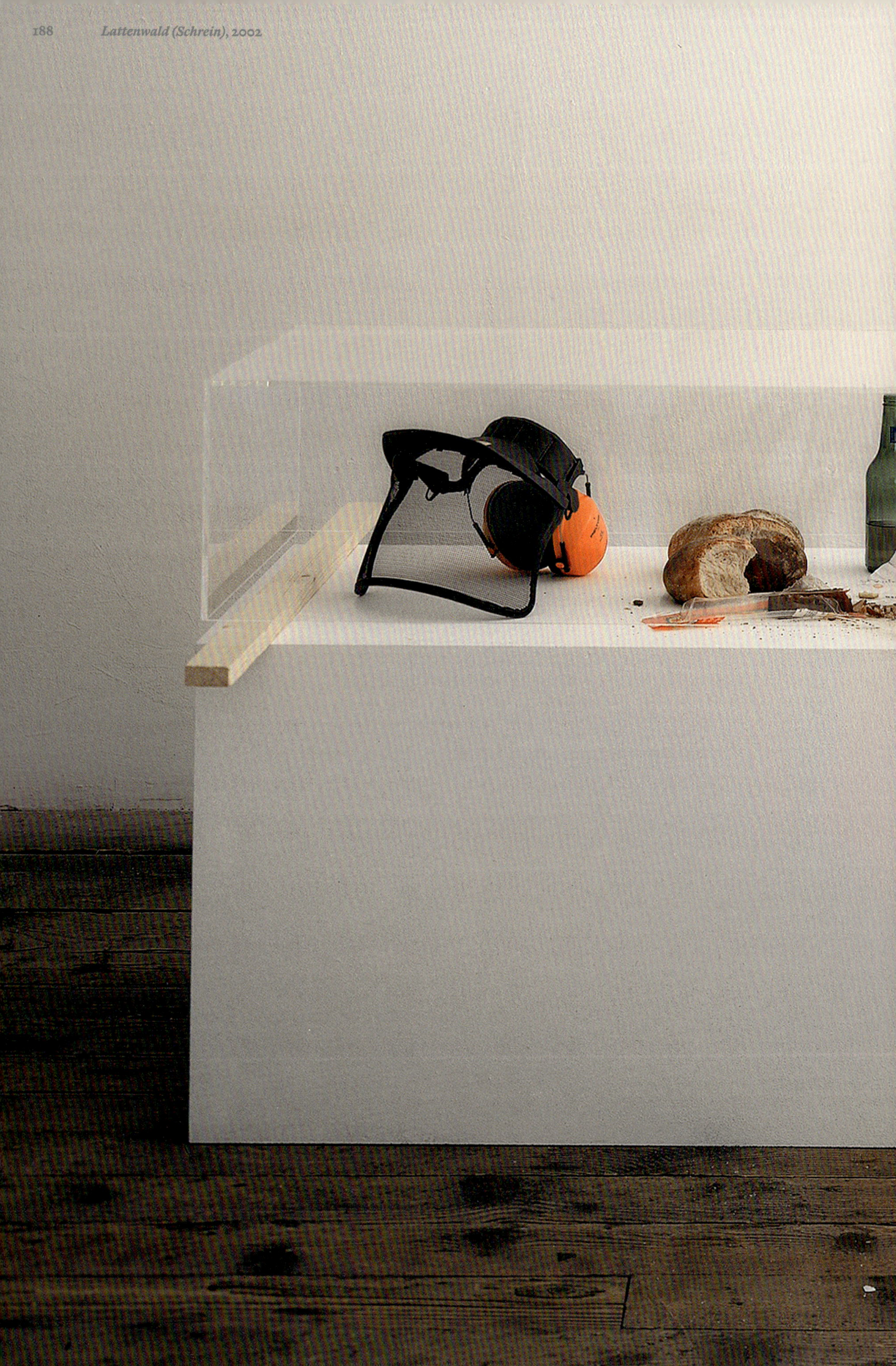

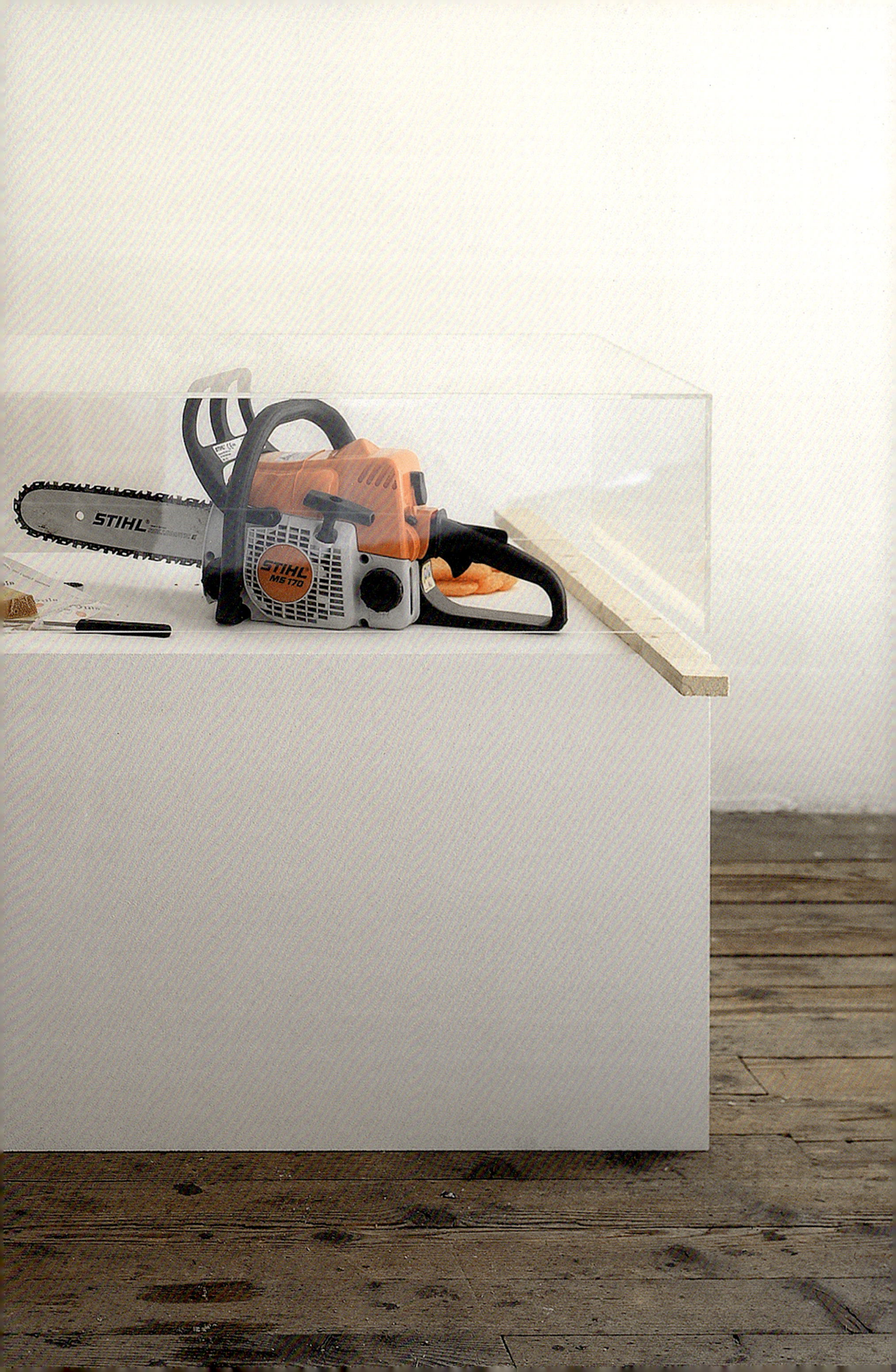
STIHL
STIHL
MS 170

Arthurs Träne (bei Mexiko im Licht der kleinen Bärin Ursuta Ursa Minor, bringt Arthurs Träne Arthurs Ruderboot zum Überlaufen), 2002

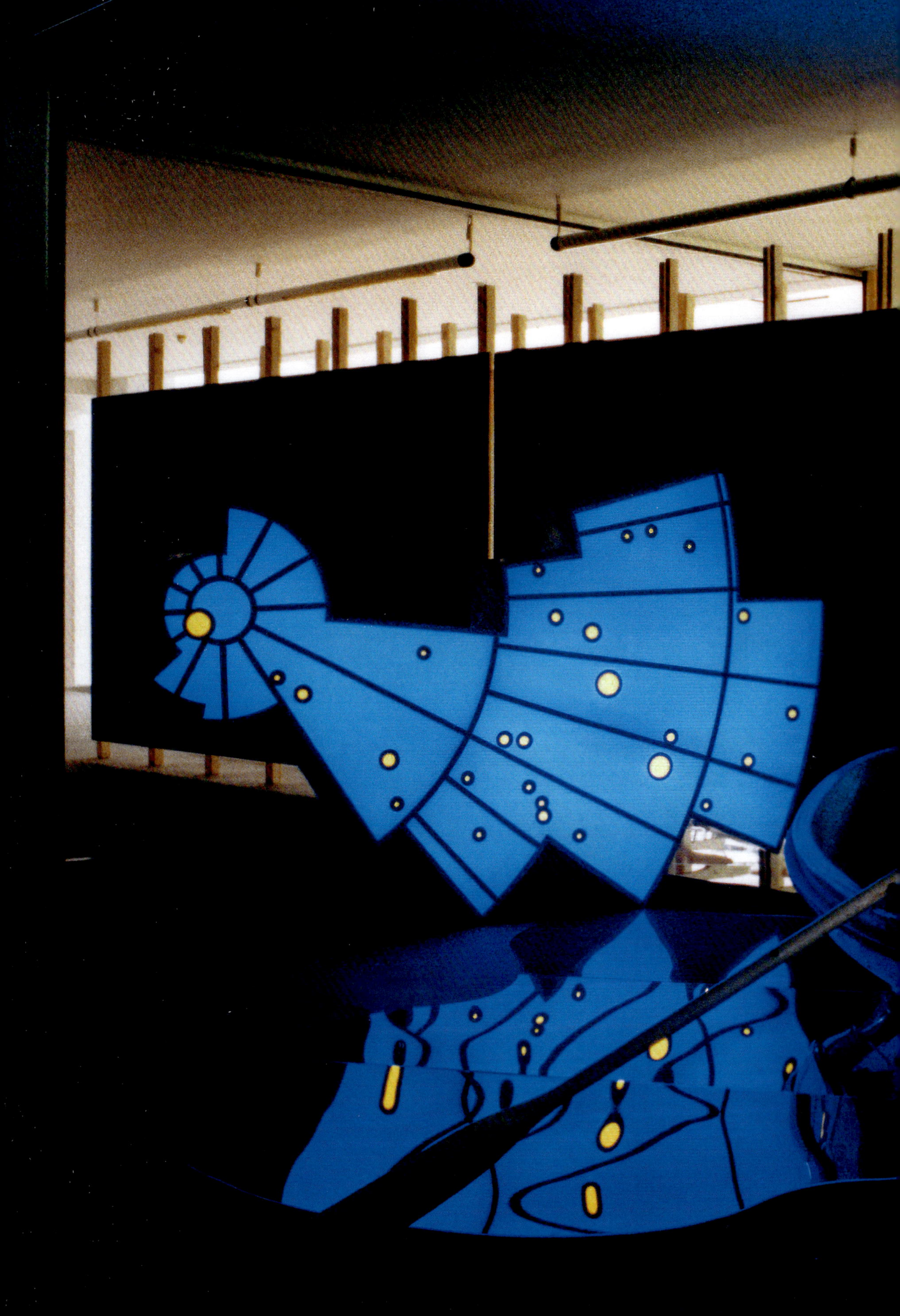

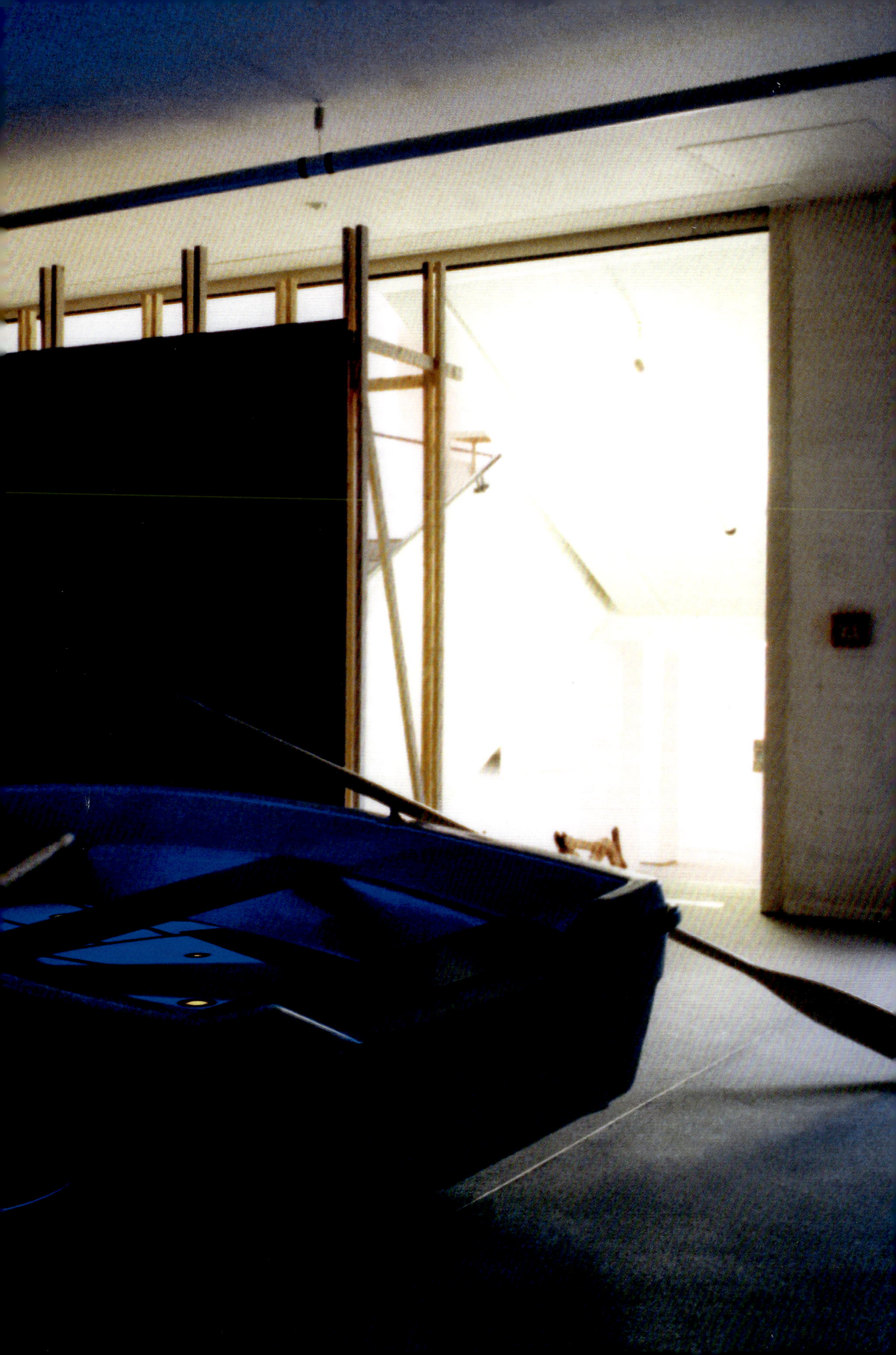

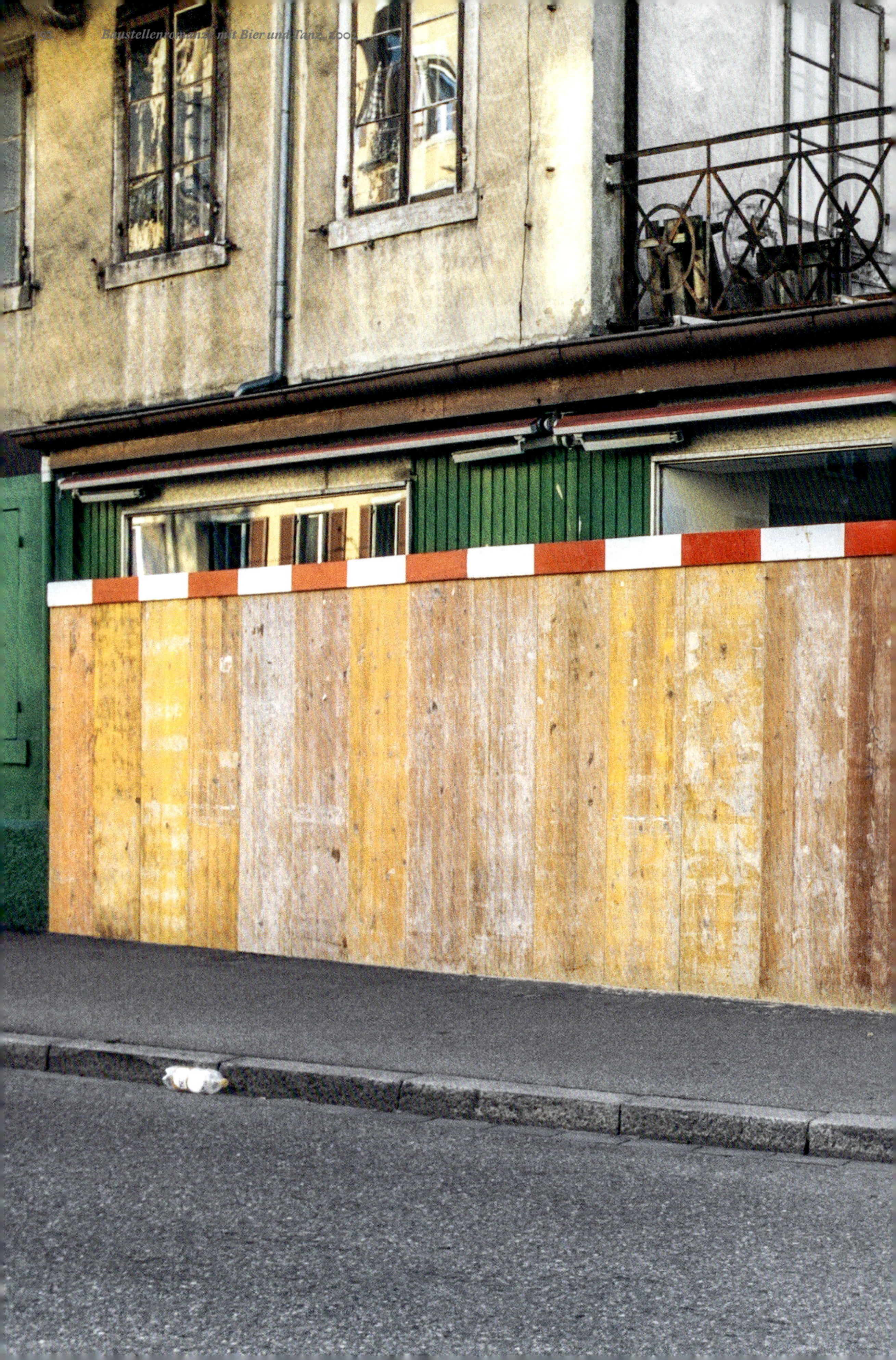

Baustellenromanze mit Bier und Tanz, 2001

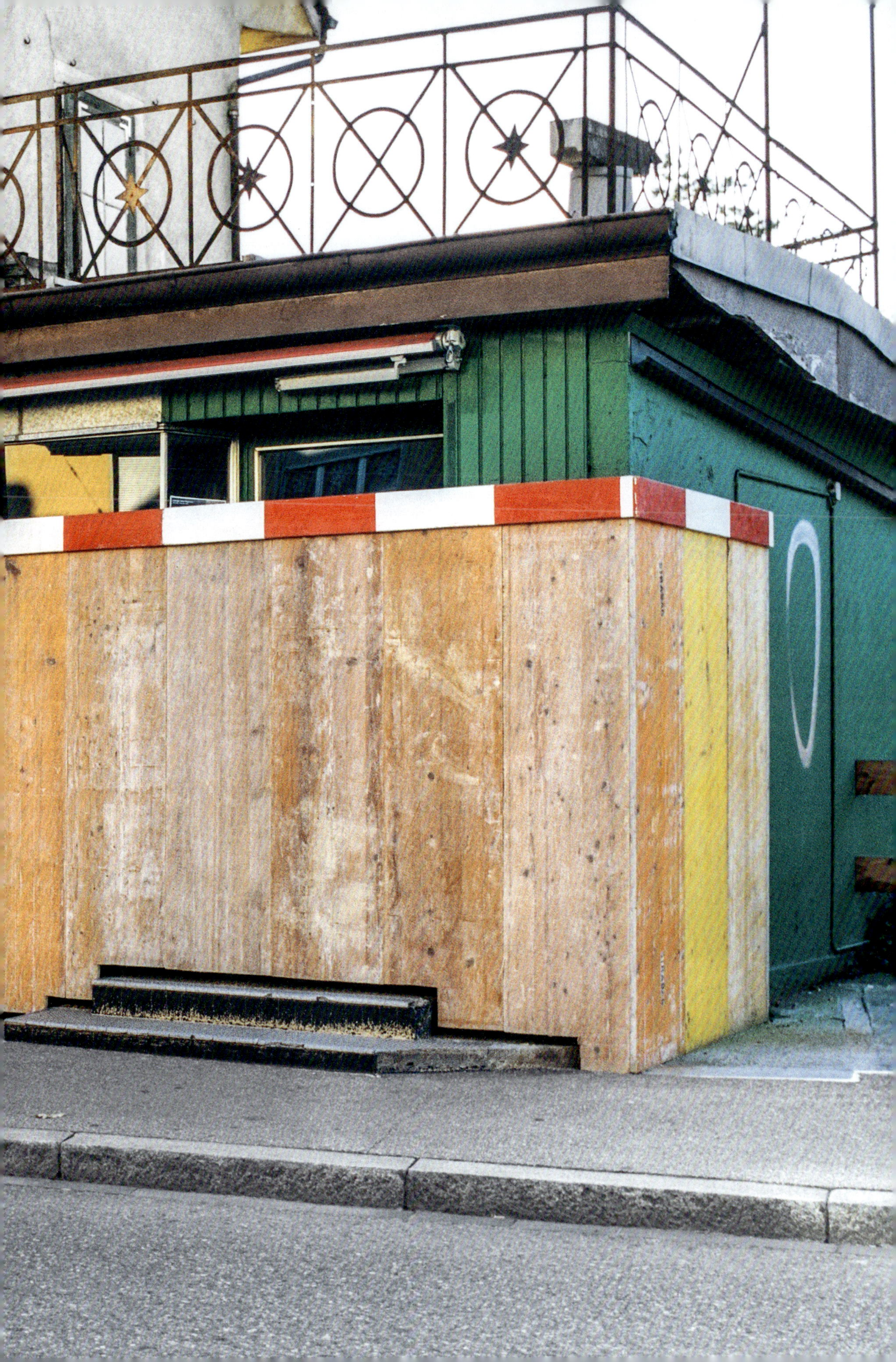

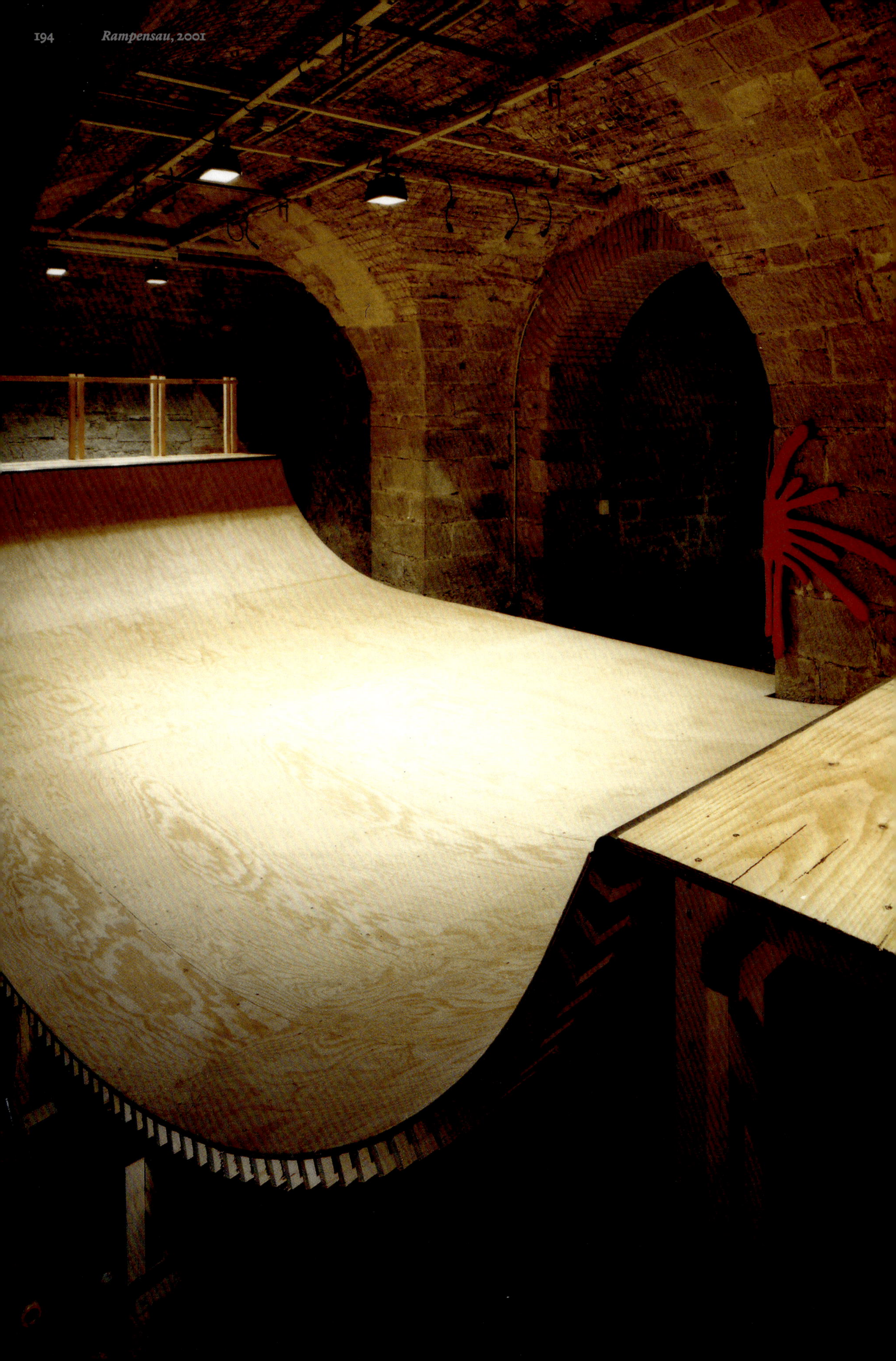

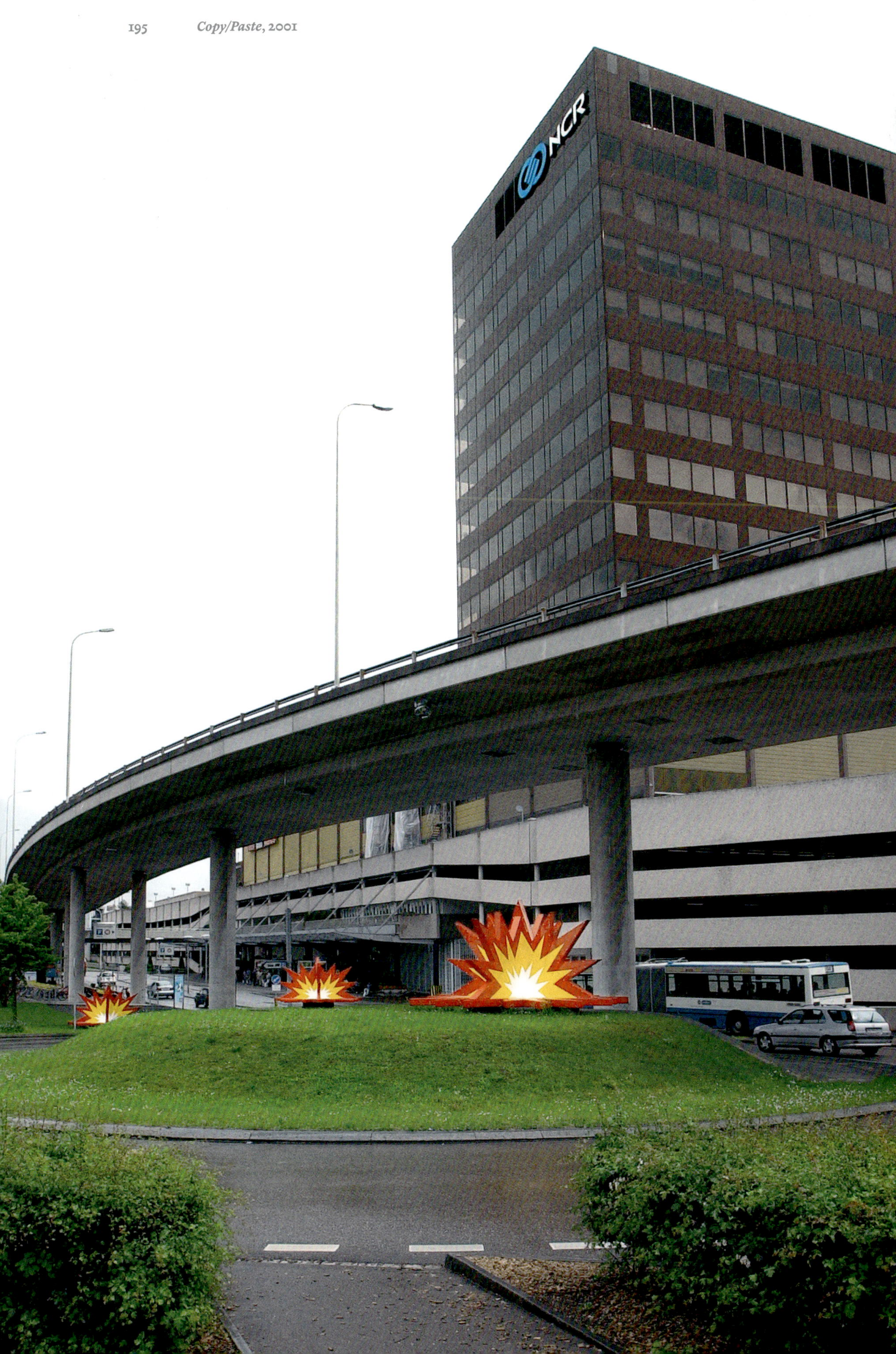
NCR

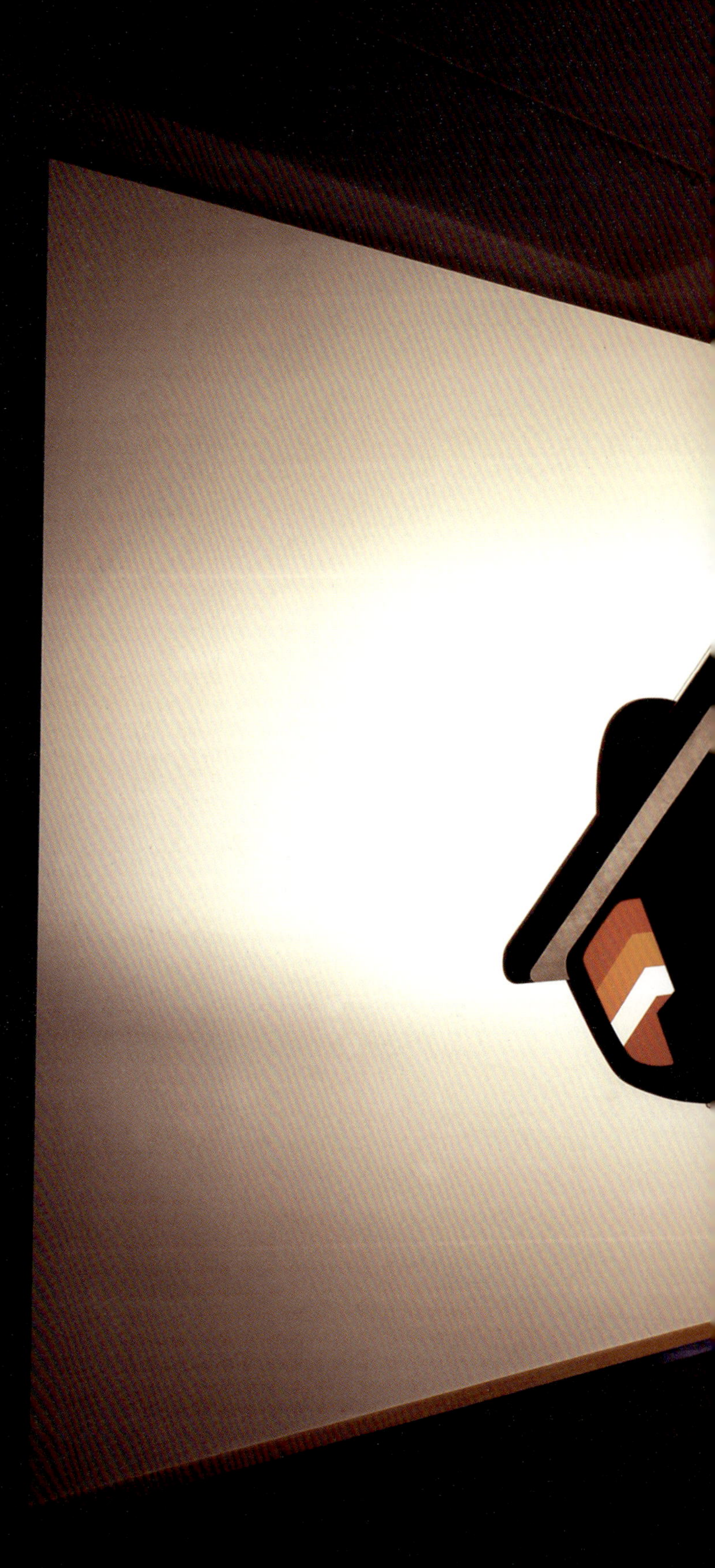

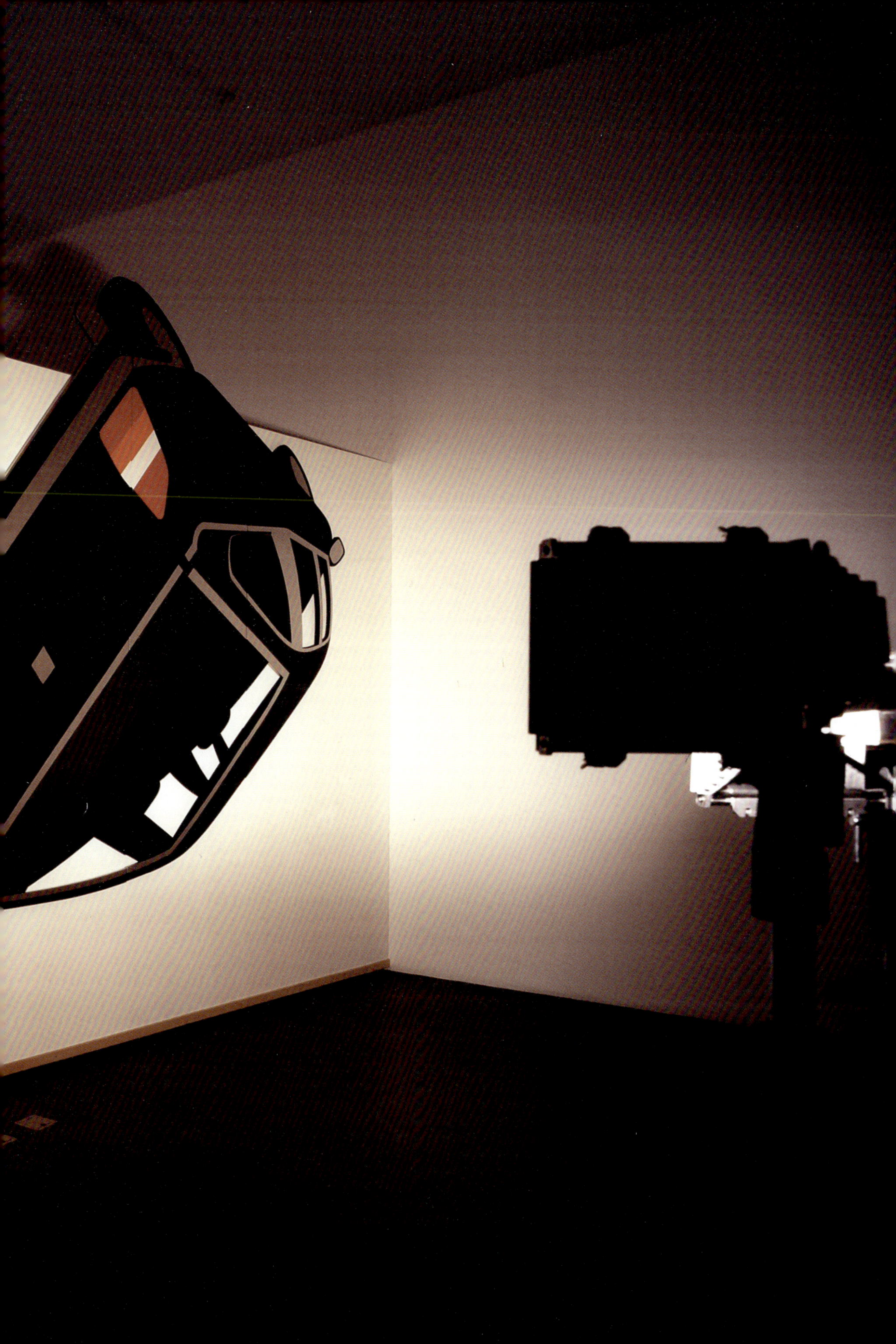

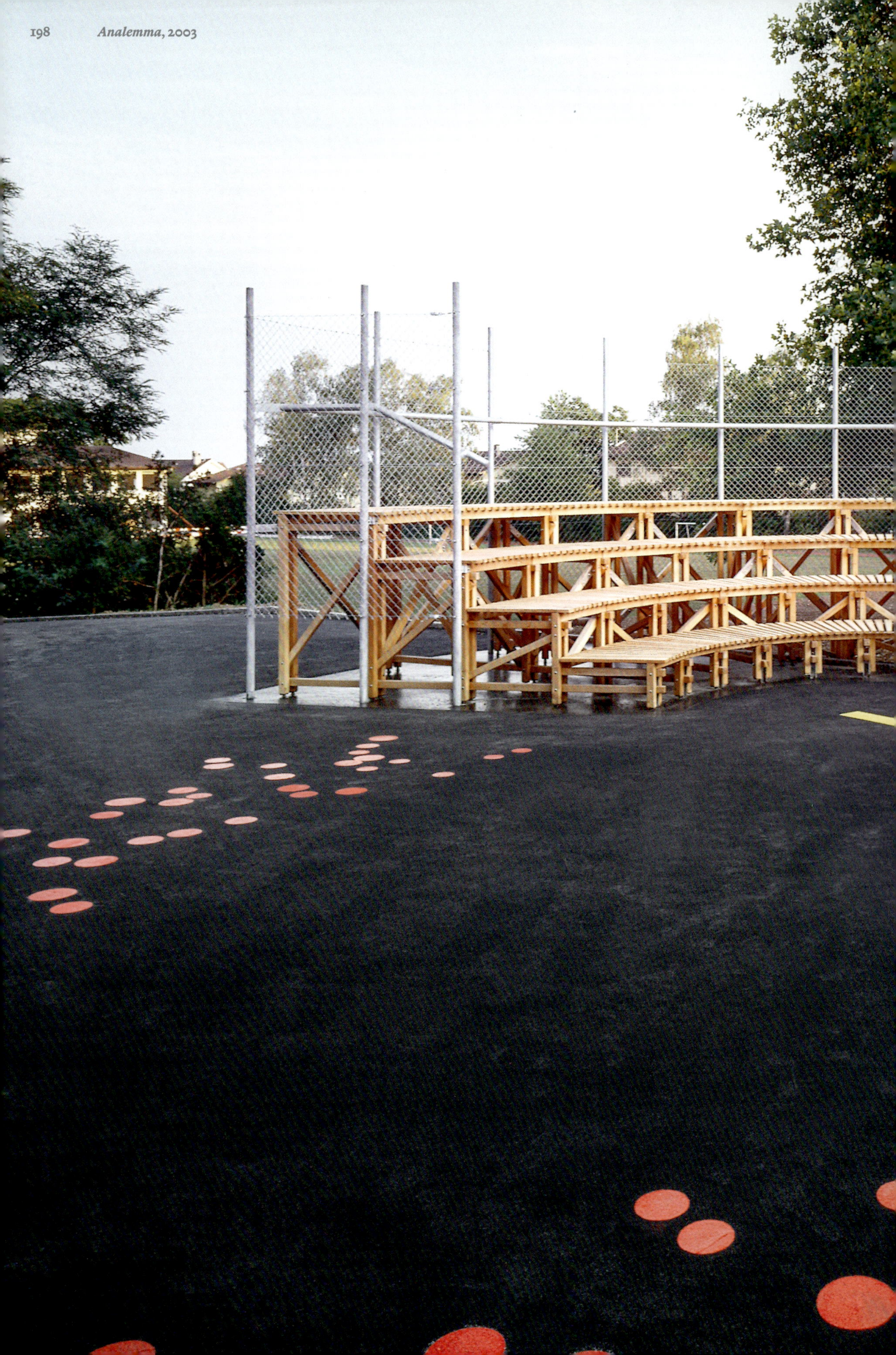

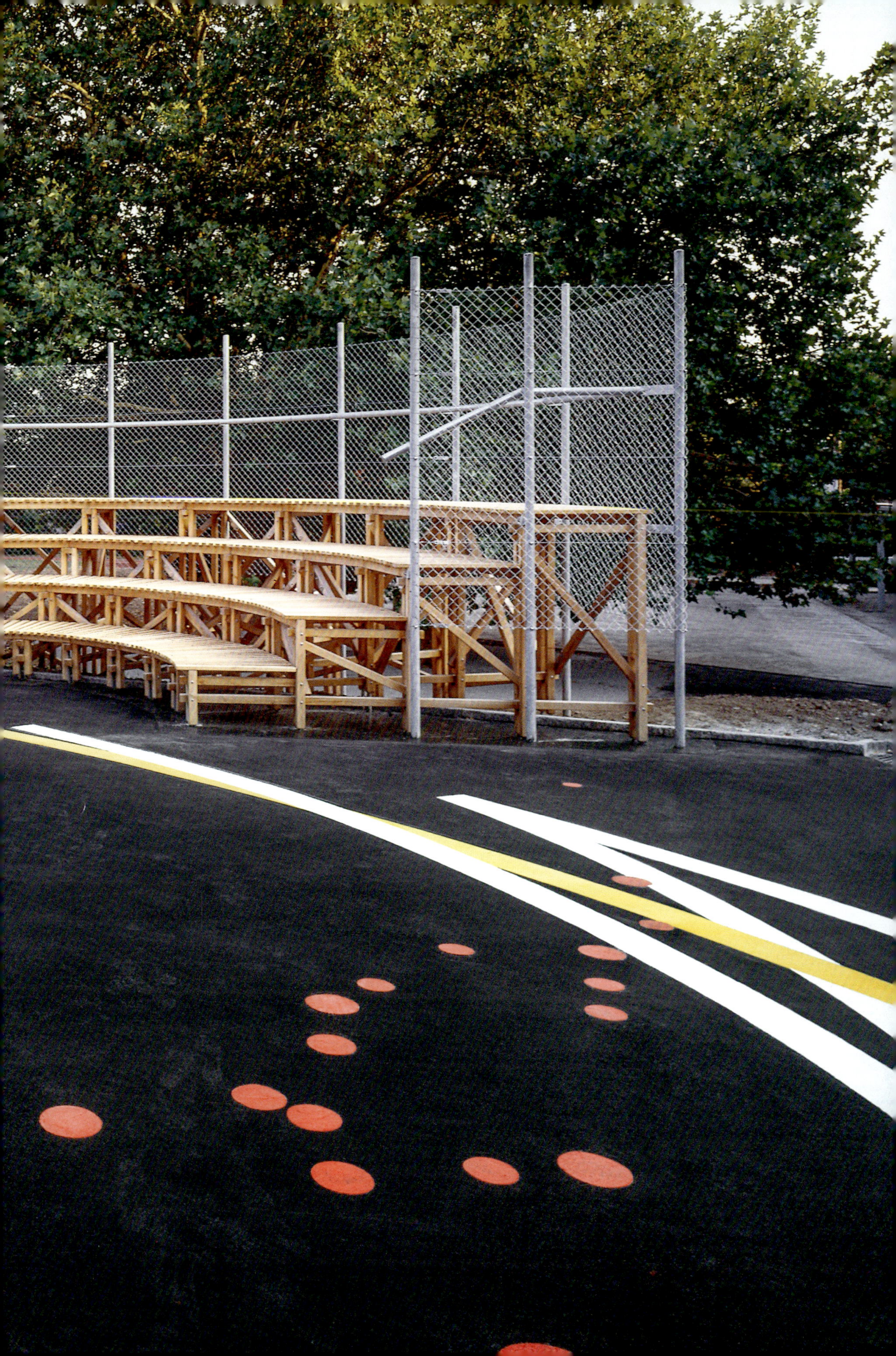

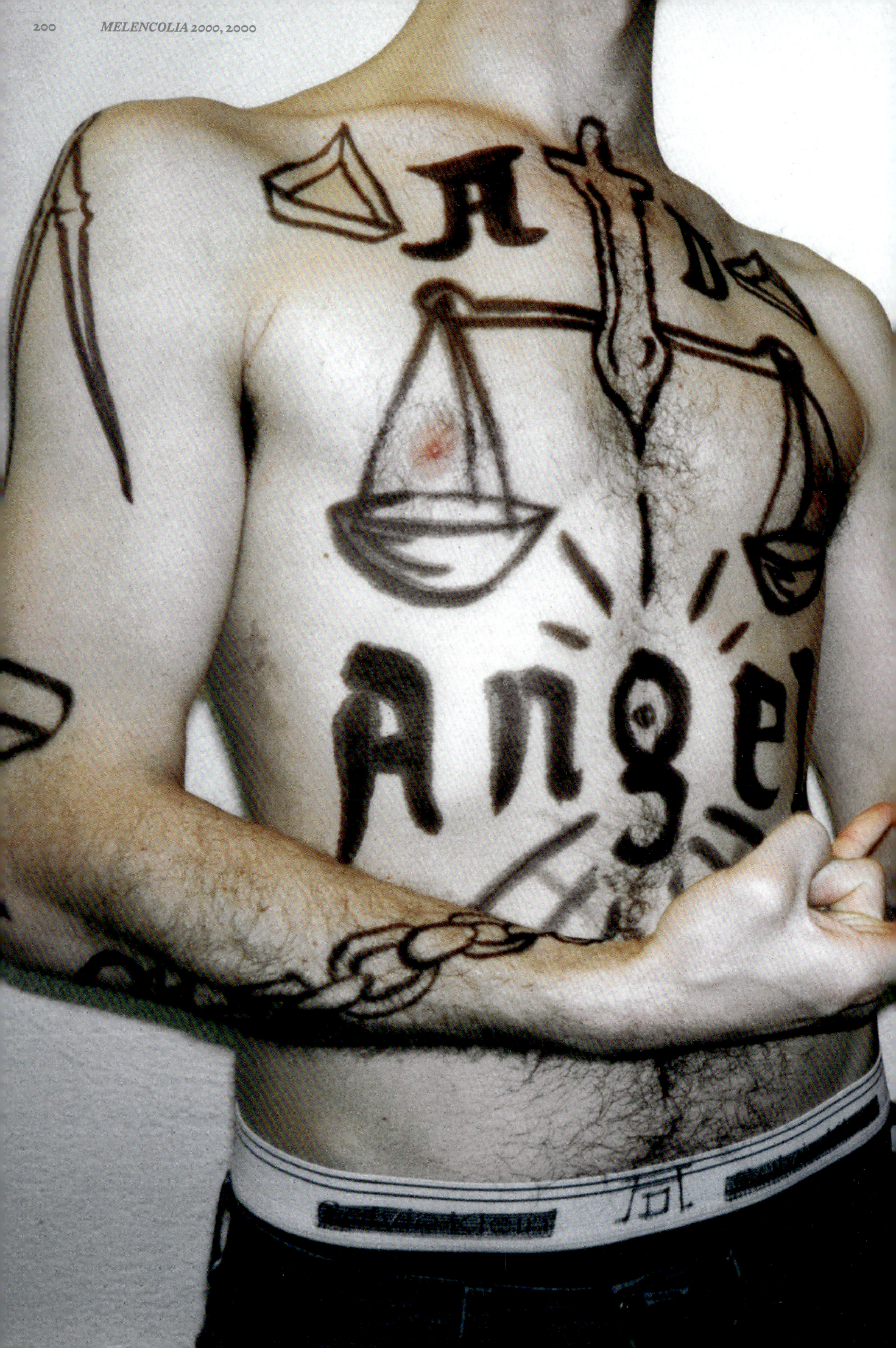
Angel

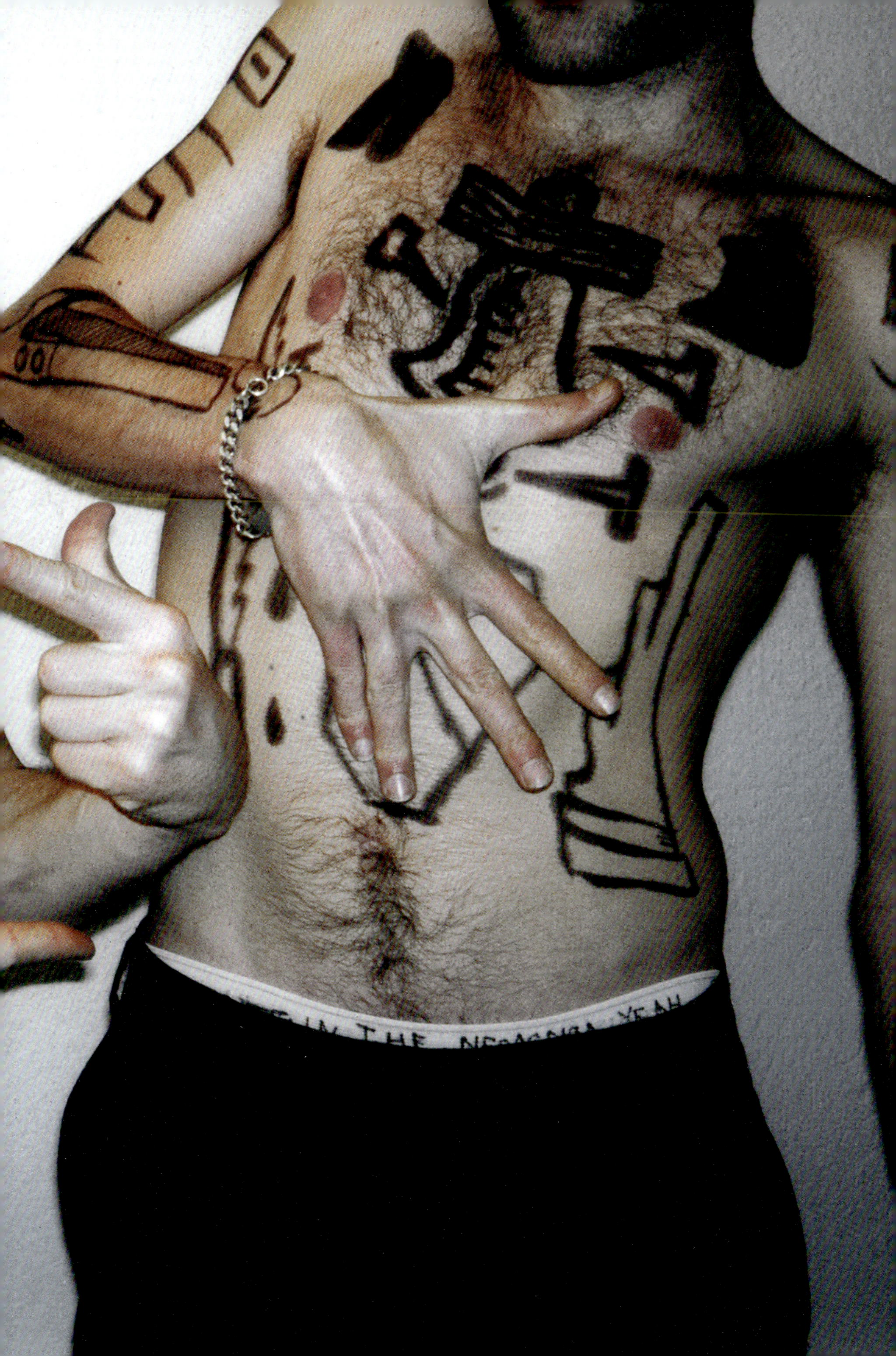
IN THE
YEAH

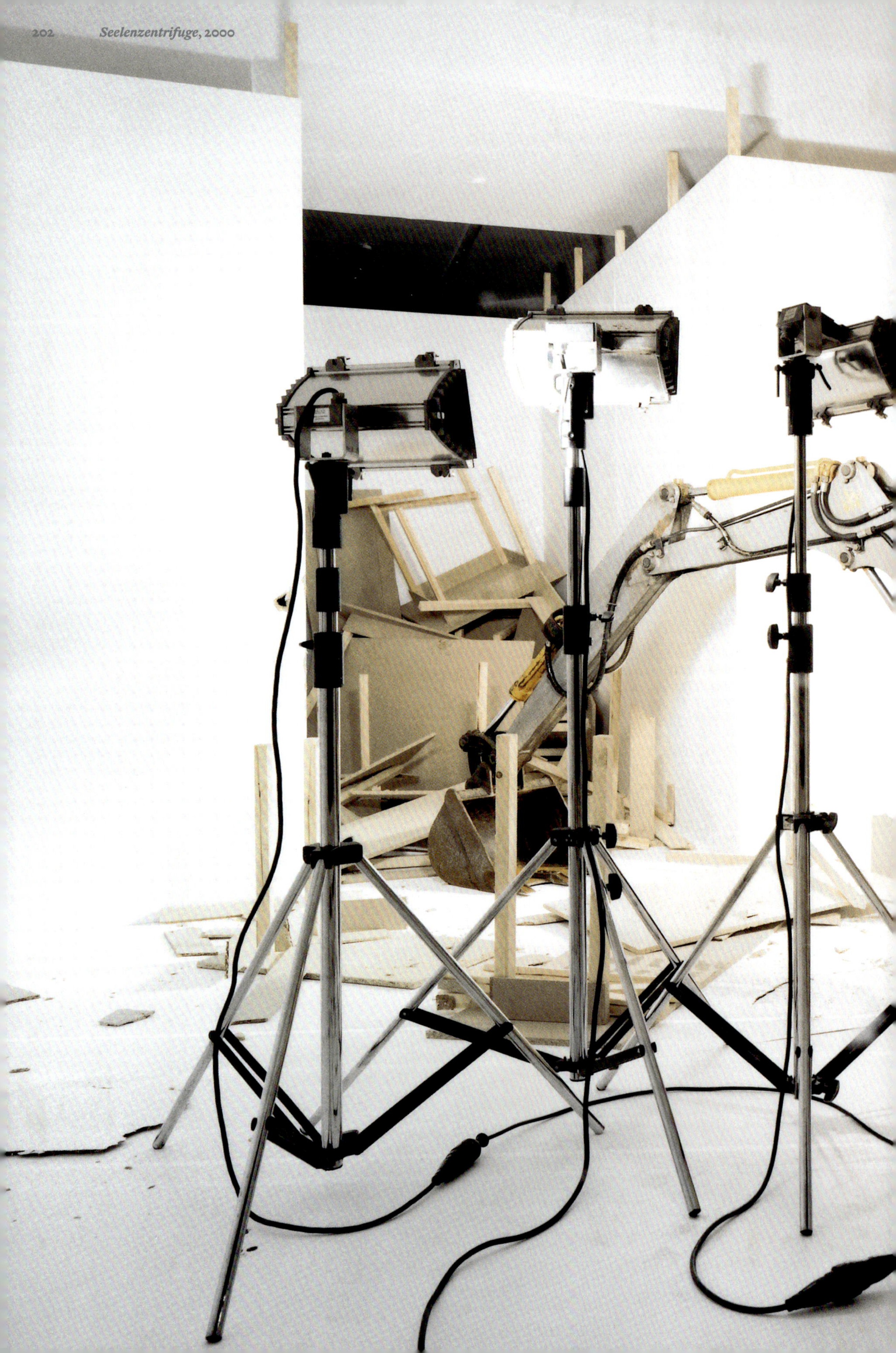

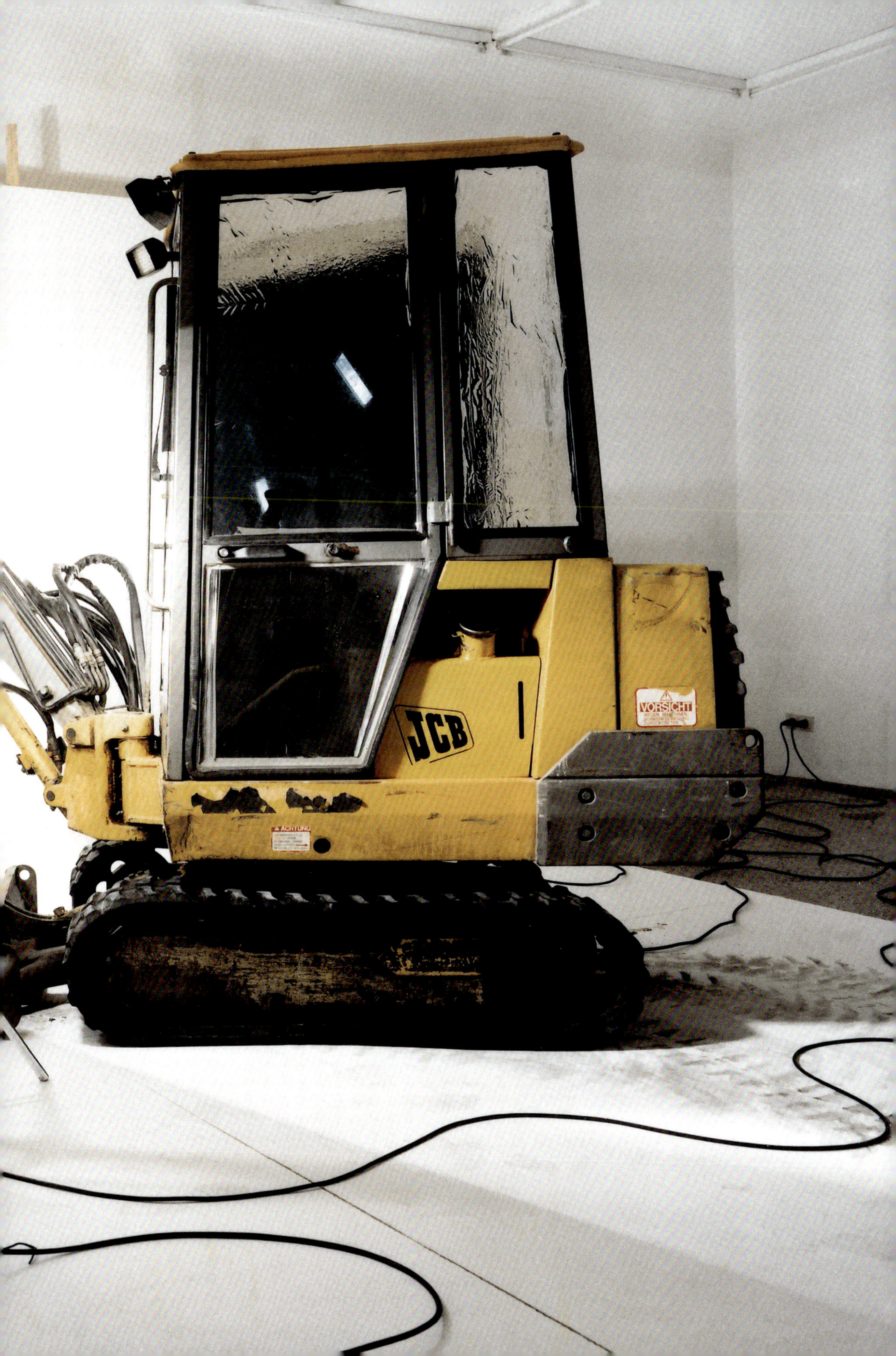
VORSICHT
JCB
ACHTUNG

Cover *Cravan*, 2008
Digital collage; Dimensions variable

p. 1 *Copy/Paste*, 2001/2022
Two component lacquer, rivets, steel; Dimensions variable; Installation view *Kulturweg Limmat*, Ennetbaden; Gift of the artist; With generous support of the Migros Museum für Gegenwartskunst, Zürich

2 *Come together (Situationist Space Program)*, 2021
Acrylic laquer, concrete masonry units, color gel, corrugated polyester sheets, fluorescent lamps, fire-resistant fabric, galvanized steel, gravel, metallic paint, plywood, pulleys, rivets, rope, scaffolding, screws, stainless steel, steel, string lights, timers, winches, wood, wooden poles; ø 100 m; Installation view *Rotonda by La Mobiliare*, Locarno Film Festival; The Mobilière Cooperative's art collection

4 *Puls (work@mobi, BG35)*, 2016–2021
Acrylic paint, aluminum, colored float glass, carpet, curtain, fabric, felt, furniture, iron, neon tubing, wood, stainless steel, screws, thread, wire, white paint; All over; Outside view Bundesgasse, Bern; With Ueli Berger's *Chribel*, 1986, Steel, 16x4x3 m, © Verein U+S Berger, Wabern; The Mobilière Cooperative's art collection; Photo: Caspar Martig, Bern

6 *Spaceknot (Leuenhof)*, 2021
Fire-resistant string, neon tubing; 4×24.4×5.8 m; Installation view auditorium Leuenhof, Zürich; Collection Pictet; Photo: Ariel Huber, Lausanne

8 *Farbsockel*, 2021
Color glaze, galvanized steel, screws, wood; 40×419×419 cm; Installation view Bülach; Collection City of Bülach; Photo: Ariel Huber, Lausanne

12 fig. 1 *What If (Situationist Space Program)*, 2016
Acrylic lacquer, colored float-glass, neon tubing, corrugated polyester sheets, fabric, galvanized steel, perspex, pillows, rivets, screws, silicone, thread, wood; 8.5×19×19 m; Production still *Gottardo 2016*, Pollegio; The Mobilière Cooperative's art collection; Photo: Tobias Madörin

fig. 2 *Lolek und Bolek*, 2012
Acrylic lacquer, screws, wood; 75×175×82 cm; Installation view *Freak Magnet*, Galerie Melike Bilir, Hamburg

fig. 3 *Copy/Paste*, 2001
Calcareous grassland, green Andeer granite, two component lacquer, rivets, steel; Dimensions variable; Installation view Glattzentrum, Wallisellen; Sammlung Migros Museum für Gegenwartskunst, Zürich; Photo: Mancia/Bodmer, FBM Studio, Zürich

fig. 4 *KEIN TITEL IV (Walze)*, 1997
Acrylic paint, pavatex; 99×195 cm; Installation view Goethestrasse 20, Zürich; Private Collection, Switzerland

15 fig. 5 *Ohne Titel (Tex Avery)*, 1998
Acrylic paint, medium-density fiberboard, pavement marking tape, screws, silicone, two component lacquer, wire rope; Dimensions variable; Installation view *Freie Sicht aufs Mittelmeer*, Schirn Kunsthalle Frankfurt; Kunsthaus Zürich, long-term loan of the Walter A. Bechtler Stiftung; Photo: Mancia/Bodmer, FBM Studio, Zürich

fig. 6 *Ohne Titel*, 1998
Acrylic paint, hot-melt marking paint, medium-density fiberboard, screws, wire rope; Dimensions variable; Installation view *Ohne Titel*, Serge Ziegler Galerie, Zürich; Collection of Serge, Renée & Maurice Ziegler, Zürich; Photo: Mancia/Bodmer, FBM Studio, Zürich

fig. 7 *Manöver I für Barbara*, 1998
Hot-melt marking paint; c. 25×25 m; Installation view Art and Appenzell, Appenzell

fig. 8 Carnival group *Funkebaabe* quoting *Manöver I für Barbara* on their costumes; Photo: Marie-Louise Dörig

16 fig. 9 *Ohne Titel (Sprechblasenfahne)*, 2002
Fabric, galvanized steel; 2×2×1.5 m; Installation view *Baustellenromanze mit Bier und Tanz*, message salon, Zürich; Photo: Esther Eppstein, Zürich

fig. 10 *Wolke, Sprechblase*, 1999
Cotton cord, medium-density fiberboard, screws, two component lacquer, white paint, wood; Dimensions variable; Installation view *Swiss Art Awards*, Basel; Collection F. & B. Mancia, Zürich; Photo: Mancia/Bodmer, FBM Studio, Zürich

fig. 11 *Clone (Guguletu)*, 2005
Acrylic lacquer, concrete masonry unit, plywood, screws, wood; 5.5×6×3 m; Installation view *Clones International – Stop 1: Africa*, Ikhwezi Community Centre, Guguletu; Photo: Melanie Hofmann, Zürich

fig. 12 Study for *ego sum pauper*, 2012
Digital collage

fig. 13 Bruce Nauman: *The True Artist Helps the World by Revealing Mystic Truths (Window or Wall Sign)*, 1967
Glass, neon tubing; 150×140×5 cm; Edition of 3 + 1 AP; Kunstmuseum Basel; © Bruce Nauman / 2023, ProLitteris, Zürich, Kunstmuseum Basel; Photo: Martin P. Bühler

17 fig. 14 *Relay (St. Moritz)*, 2012/2013
Acrylic lacquer, neon tubing, corrugated polyester sheets, steel, perspex, rivets, screws, wood; 5.5×8.2×6.4 m; Unlimited edition; Installation view *St. Moritz Art Masters*; Photo: Tobias Madörin

fig. 15 *Analemma*, 2003
Chain-link fence, galvanized steel, hot-melt marking paint, screws, wood; 3.2×ø10.6 m; Installation view Schulhaus Lachenzelg/Imbisbühl, Zürich; Art and Architecture City of Zürich; Photo: Adrian Fritschi, Zürich

fig. 16 *Rampensau*, 2001
Medium-density fiberboard, plywood, screws, steel, two component lacquer; 260×412×484 cm; Installation view *Rampensau*, Theater an der Winkelwiese, Zürich; Private Collection, Switzerland; Photo: Unknown

fig. 17 *Mindspace (Neuenkirchen)*, 2008
Acrylic lacquer, neon tubing, screws, wood; 244×294×416 cm; Installation view with Oskar Minich, *Diskurs im Grünen*, Springhornhof, Neuenkirchen; Photo: Arvild Baud, Hamburg

18 fig. 18 *Mindspace (Siegen)*, 2010
Acrylic lacquer, neon tubing, screws, wood; 244×294×416 cm; Installation view *Blickwechsel*, Parkhaus Rathaus, Siegen

fig. 19 *Mindspace (Tarantula)*, 2013
Acrylic lacquer, screws, wood; 120×168×260 cm; Installation view Tarantula, Berlin

fig. 20 Bruce Nauman: *Indoor Outdoor Seating Arrangements*, 1999
Steel and wood seating bleaches; Dimensions variable; Installation view Nationalgalerie im Hamburger Bahnhof, Berlin, SMB; © Bruce Nauman / 2023, ProLitteris, Zürich, bpk / Nationalgalerie im Hamburger Bahnhof, SMB; Photo: Roman März

fig. 21 *Fusionsobjekt*, 2006/2007
Acrylic lacquer, galvanized steel, screws, wood; 111×400×324 cm; Installation view *Art en plain air*, Môtiers

20 fig. 22 *Lattenwald*, 2002
Beer, bread, chainsaw, cheese, forest helmet, white paint, particle board, perspex, screws, wood; Dimensions variable; Installation view *Handlungsräume*, Halle für Kunst, Lüneburg; Sammlung Migros Museum für Gegenwartskunst, Zürich; Photo: Hans-Jürgen Wege, Lüneburg

fig. 23 *Seelenzentrifuge*, 2000
Excavator, one-way mirror film, white paint, particle board, screws, spotlights, tripods; Dimensions variable; Installation view *Horten Out bei Bochynek*, Düsseldorf; Photo: Stefan Hostettler, Düsseldorf

fig. 24 *Wilibalds Traum / Wilibalds Morgen*, 2002
Excavator, one-way mirror film, hot-melt marking paint, particle board, screws, spotlights, tripods, white paint, wood; Dimensions variable; Installation view HFBK, Hamburg

fig. 25 *Petit Déjeuner / Frühstück*, 2000
Excavator, one-way mirror film, hot-melt marking paint, particle board, screws, spotlights, tripods, white paint, wood; Dimensions variable; Installation view *Petit Déjeuner / Frühstück*, message salon caravan & PAC, Fribourg

21 fig. 26 *Autoscooter*, 2003
Collaboration with David Renggli; Bumper cars, white paint, particle board, screws; Dimensions variable; Installation view Löwenbräu Areal; Photo: Mancia/Bodmer, FBM Studio, Zürich

fig. 27 *Space Is My Canvas (Performance)*, 2014
Amplifier, clothes line, clothespins, contact microphone, flat iron, ironing board, mixing console, sheets, sound system; Dimensions variable; Performance view *International Contemporary Art Festival*, Bomb Gallery, Mostar; Photo: Melanie Hübner, Berlin

fig. 28 Chico Aragão: *James Rosenquist Ironing His Trousers*, 1981
Black and white photograph; 43,2×30,5 cm; Edition of 250; © C. B. Aragão, 2023

23 fig. 29 *Andyandme (Honeymooners)*, 2005
Digital photography; Dimensions variable

fig. 30 *Daisyandme (Honeymooners)*, 2006
Digital photography; Dimensions variable

fig. 31 *Saving the Desert (Honeymooners)*, 2022
Digital photography; Dimensions variable

fig. 32 *Usthere (Honeymooners)*, 2006
Digital photography; Dimensions variable

24 fig. 33 Constant: *Hangende Sector (Hanging Sector)*, 1961
Aluminum, copper, iron, oil paint, steel; 76×130×99 cm; Collection Kunstmuseum Den Haag; © Constant/Fondation Constant, 2023, ProLitteris, Zürich; Photo: Tom Haartsen

fig. 34 *Minotic Neocolor Mindspace (Secondary African Color Circle)*, 2007
Acrylic lacquer, color filters, fabric, fluorescent lamps, white paint, timer, screws, wood; Dimensions variable; Installation view with Constant's *Hangende Sector (Hanging Sector)*, 1961 (Aluminum, copper, iron, oil paint, steel, 76×130×99 cm, Collection Kunstmuseum Den Haag); *Ode à l'Odéon (Tribute to the Odéon)*, 1969 (Aluminum paint, linen, oil paint, spray paint, 190.7×200.2cm, Collection Fondation Constant longterm loan to Collection Kunstmuseum Den Haag); *Klein Labyr (Small Labyr)*, 1959 (Crayon, metal, oil paint, plexiglass, wood, 70×35×56 cm, Collection Kunstmuseum Den Haag); *Spatiovore [V] (Space Eater [V])*, 1960 (Ink, metal, paint, plexiglass, wood, 64×105×155.1 cm, Collection Kunstmuseum Den Haag); *The International Situationist: 1957–1972. In girum imus nocte et consumimur igni*, Museum Tinguely, Basel; © Constant/Fondation Constant, Kerim Seiler, 2023, Pro Litteris, Zürich, Museum Tinguely, Basel; Photo: Christian Baur

fig. 35 Constant: *Gele sector (Yellow Sector)*, 1958
Blotting paper, copper, ink, iron, lead, metal, oil paint, plexiglass, wood; 21×87.3×77.5 cm; Collection Kunstmuseum Den Haag, NL; © Constant/Fondation Constant, 2023, ProLitteris, Zürich; Photo: Tom Haartsen

fig. 36 *Birdhouse I*, 2014
Acrylic lacquer, perspex, rivets, steel, wood; 400×143×139 cm; Photo: Done Studio – Ulf Saupe, Berlin

27 fig. 37 *Iris*, 2014
Aluminum blinds, two component lacquer; 36×85×20 m Installation view Wiesenstrasse, Schlieren; Photo: Tobias Madörin

fig. 38 *118 minus 11 (Kerims Lampenladen) / Gestik des Verschwindens*, 2012–2019
Acrylic lacquer, aluminum, neon tubing, galvanized steel, perspex, screws, silicone, wood; Dimensions variable; Installation view Europaallee / Zürich Hauptbahnhof; Photo: Tobias Madörin

fig. 39 *Carwash (New Babylon) / NEW/NOW*, 2013–2016
Collaboration with Benjamin Dillenburger and Steffen Lemmerzahl; Rendering

28 fig. 40 *Pneuma, somnambul*, 2005
Beanpoles, color filters, electrical wiring, fluorescent lamps, power generator, ropes, timer; Dimensions variable; Installation view *För Hitz ond Brand*, Fünfeckpalast, Trogen

fig. 41 *Nomadic Structures*, 2010
Collaboration with Gregor Metzger; Beanpoles, color filters, electrical wiring, fluorescent lamps, power generator, ropes, timer; Dimensions variable; Performance still Lion's Head, Cape Town

fig. 42 See p. 28, fig. 41; Installation view Qaukeni Great Place, Mpondoland

29 fig. 43 *Minotic Neocolor Mindspace (Secondary African Color Circle)*, 2007
Acrylic lacquer, color filters, fabric, fluorescent lamps, white paint, timer, screws, wood; Dimensions variable; Installation view *The International Situationist: 1957–1972. In girum imus nocte et consumimur igni*, Museum Tinguely, Basel; Photo: Adrian Fritschi, Zürich

fig. 44 *Flag of Mars*, 2018
Canvas, oil paint; 226×339 cm; Photo: Done Studio – Ulf Saupe, Berlin

fig. 45 R. Buckminster Fuller holding a *Tensegrity sphere*, 1979; Courtesy The Estate of R. Buckminster Fuller; © The Estate of R. Bukminster Fuller

31 *Tender is the Night (Locarno)*, 2019/2021
Acrylic lacquer, aluminum, neon tubing, galvanized steel, perspex, screws, silicone, wood; Dimensions variable; Installation view *Rotonda by La Mobiliare*, Locarno Film Festival; Photo: Ariel Huber, Lausanne

32 *Flag*, 2019
Aluminium, code, hardware, LED panels, screws, wood 78.6×117 cm; Edition of 3; Exhibition view *Make Zürich Small Again*, Kupper Modern, Zürich; Photo: Mancia/ Bodmer, FBM Studio, Zürich

34 *Spaceknot (Pfefferberg)*, 2019
Neon tubing, wire; 3.7×12.5×9.5 m; Installation view Kink Bar and Restaurant, Berlin; Photo: Tobias Madörin

36 *Spaceknot (Bundesgasse)*, 2019
Neon tubing, wire; 3.4×14.2×11.6 m; Installation view foyer Bundesgasse 35, Bern; The Mobilière Cooperative's art collection; Photo: Tobias Madörin

38 *CMYK*, 2018
Alucore, two component lacquer; 148×422 cm; Installation view *Afraid of Red, Yellow and Blue*, Grieder Contemporary, Küsnacht; Private Collection, Switzerland; Photo: Done Studio – Ulf Saupe, Berlin

40 See p. 29, fig. 44
Installation view *Afraid of Red, Yellow and Blue*, Grieder Contemporary, Küsnacht; Photo: Done Studio – Ulf Saupe, Berlin

42 *Frühling (Spring)*, 2015/2018
Acrylic laquer, screws, wood; 80×260×75 cm; Installation view *Afraid of Red, Yellow and Blue*, Grieder Contemporary, Küsnacht; Photo: Done Studio – Ulf Saupe, Berlin

44 *Puls (work@mobi, Nyon)*, 2016–2018
Acrylic paint, aluminum, colored float glass, carpet, curtain, fabric, felt, furniture, iron, neon tubing, wood, stainless steel, screws, thread, wire, white paint; All over; Installation view Chemin de la Redoute, Nyon; The Mobilière Cooperative's art collection; Photo: Tobias Madörin

46 See p. 12, fig. 1; Installation view Locarno Garden la Mobiliare, Locarno Film Festival; The Mobilière Cooperative's art collection; Photo: Tobias Madörin

48 *NEW/NOW (Medium)*, 2018
Galvanized steel, neon tubing; 187.5×520.5×87 cm; Installation view Locarno Garden la Mobiliare, Locarno Film Festival; The Mobilière Cooperative's art collection Photo: Tobias Madörin

50 *Power (Chäshalde)*, 2018
Collaboration with Tobias Madörin; Analog photography Edition of 5; Private Collection, Switzerland

52 *NEW/NOW (Glattalstrasse)*, 2017/2018
Collaboration with Tobias Madörin; Analog photography Edition of 5; Private Collection, Switzerland

54 *NE TRAVAILLEZ JAMAIS (Hürstholz)*, 2018
Collaboration with Tobias Madörin; Analog photography Edition of 5; Private Collection, Switzerland

56 *IOU (Thurgauerstrasse)*, 2014/2018
Collaboration with Tobias Madörin; Analog photography Edition of 5; Private Collection, Switzerland

57 *Halo (Ettenfeldstrasse)*, 2018
Collaboration with Tobias Madörin; Analog photography; with Hans Josephsohn's *Ohne Titel*, 1962, Brass, 212×72×49 cm; © Josephsohn Estate and Kesselhaus Josephsohn St.Gallen; Edition of 5; Private Collection, Switzerland

58 *Bar*, 2018
Acrylic lacquer, chain-link fence, neon tubing, fabric, galvanized steel, perspex, rivets, screws, silicone, thread, wood; Dimensions variable; Installation view *Spazio Cinema*, Locarno Film Festival; The Mobilière Cooperative's art collection; Photo: Tobias Madörin

61 *Ours d'àpres Regine Gallard (Paradeplatz)*, 2014/2018
Carrara marble; 105×204×75 cm; Installation view Gasträume, Zürich

62 *Ceci n'est pas un onion*, 2017–2019
Galvanized steel pipes, screws, spotlights, varnish, wood; 20×659×239 cm; Performance stage for *Fun & Fury!*, Cabaret Voltaire, Zürich; With Adrian Notz's frescoes *Firmament Dada on the ceiling and Dada Portraits (left to right: Paris, Cologne, Hannover, Berlin, New York)*, both made by Andy Ineichen, 2013; Photo: Nicolas Duc, Zürich

64 *Labyrinth (Mos_Espa)*, 2012/2017
Xerox on paper; Dimensions variable; Installation view Mos_Espa, Motel Campo, Carouge; Photo: Dylan Perrenoud, Genève

65 *Cabaret Voltaire*, 2016
Acrylic laquer, foamcore, plaster, white paint, wood 162.5×31.2×70.7 cm; Installation view Cabaret Voltaire, Zürich; Collection of the artist

66 See p. 12, fig. 1; Installation view *Gottardo 2016*, Pollegio; The Mobilière Cooperative's art collection; Photo: Tobias Madörin

68 *Tschutschu (Situationist Space Program)*, 2016
Acrylic lacquer, corrugated polyester sheets, galvanized steel, rivets, screws, silicone, string lights, thread, wood; 8.5×19×19 m; Installation view *Gottardo 2016*, Rynächt; The Mobilière Cooperative's art collection; Photo: Tobias Madörin

70 *Labil, Stabil, Indifferent*, 2016
Steel, neon tubing; 165×680 cm; Installation view Trottenhaus, Bebra; Collection Annabelle & Steffen Lemmerzahl, Switzerland

72 *Relay (Oschwand)*, 2012/2016
Acrylic lacquer, neon tubing, corrugated polyester sheets,steel, perspex, rivets, screws, wood; 5.5×8.2×6.4 m; Unlimited edition; Installation view Cuno Amiet's garden, Oschwand

74 See p. 21, fig. 27; Performance view *S.O.S. DADA – The World Is A Mess,* Salon Suisse, Palazzo Trevisan degli Ulivi, 56th Venice Biennale; Photo: Claire Dugan, Berlin

I See p. 21, fig. 27; Performance view *Bomb Gallery*, Art Radionica Lazareti, Dubrovnik

75 II See p. 21, fig. 27; Performance view Kunstraum Walcheturm, Zürich; Photo: Lorenzo Pusterla, Zürich

76 III See p. 21, fig. 27; Performance view Kunstraum Walcheturm, Zürich

IV See p. 21, fig. 27; Performance view *S.O.S. DADA – The World Is A Mess, Salon Suisse,* Palazzo Trevisan degli Ulivi, 56th Venice Biennale; Photo: Claire Dugan, Berlin

77 V See p. 21, fig. 27

VI See p. 21, fig. 27; Performance view Bomb Gallery, Art Radionica Lazareti, Dubrovnik

78 VII See p. 21, fig. 27; Performance view *Solutions from Zürich*, Divo Institute, Prague; Photo: Joaquin Luzoro, Berlin

VIII See p. 21, fig. 27; Performance view Grieder Contemporary, ABC Berlin; Photo: Done Studio – Ulf Saupe, Berlin

79 See p. 21, fig. 27; Performance view Bomb Gallery, Art Radionica Lazareti, Dubrovnik

IX See p. 21, fig. 27; Performance view Die Zweite Heimat, Hamburg; Photo: Juri Steiner, Lausanne

80 *gelf, rôt unde blâ*, 2015
Color glaze, primer, screws, wood; 240×240×15 cm; Installation view *Signalwege*, Lusamgärtchen, Würzburg

82 *New Babylon*, 2015/2016
Acrylic lacquer, concrete, perspex, rivets, screws, steel, wood; 659×210×215 cm; Installation view Kunsthalle Mannheim; Photo: Stefanie Patruno

83 *Space Is My Canvas (Vinyl Edition)*, 2015
Direct-to-disc recording on transparent vinyl-dubplate; ⌀ 12 inches; Edition of 12

84 *Llloblyekk && Bboolyekk*, 2015
Acrylic laquer, bleach, dye, fabric, pillows, screws, wood Dimensions variable; Installation view, Lobby, Bundesgasse 35, Bern; With Balthasar Burkhard's *Esel*, 1996, Photograph on Baryte paper, 90×98 cm, © Vida Burkhard / Courtesy Fotostiftung Schweiz); The Mobilière Cooperative's art collection; Photo: Stefan Altenburger Photography, Zürich

86 *Birdhouse II*, 2014
Acrylic lacquer, rivets, steel, wood; 7×1.3×2 m; Installation view *Émergences*, Bex & Arts

87 *Körper & Geist*, 2015
Neon tubing; 6.3×22.5 m; Installation *Signalwege*, Kilianshaus, Würzburg

88 See p. 27, fig. 37

90 fig. 46 *NE TRAVAILLEZ JAMAIS (Rue de Seine)*, 2019
Analog photography; Edition of 5

97 fig. 47 See Cover; Installation view *Rewriting Words: Dada Moscow*, Special Project for the Fourth Moscow Biennale of Contemporary Art

98 *Mindspace (Berlin)*, 2014
Acrylic lacquer, screws, rebar, wood; 240×4.1×3.2 m; Installation view Little Wood, Berlin; Photo: Done Studio – Ulf Saupe, Berlin

100 See p. 17, fig. 14

102 *Working Space*, 2013
Neon tubing; 278×460×25 cm; Private Collection, Switzerland

104 *A Postcard to A. Loos*, 2013
acrylic laquer, clamp, cotton cord, hemp cordage, linen thread, new wool, pulleys, screws, wood; Dimensions variable; Installation view *Im Würgegriff der Kunst*, Swiss Architecture Museum, Basel

106 *Carwash (New Babylon)*, 2013
Collaboration with Benjamin Dillenburger and Steffen Lemmerzahl; Rendering / digital collage

107 *Lightsaber (Gold)*, 2012
Beanpole, neon tubing, screws; ca. 225×⌀7.5 cm; Edition 3; Installation view *Floccinaucinihilipilification*, Grieder Contemporary, Berlin

108 *Constructivist Tower*, 2012
Aluminium, neon tubing, screws, wire rope; 488×244×244 cm; Installation view *Omnitlotl*, Kunstraum Walcheturm, Zürich

110 *ego sum pauper*, 2012
Neon tubing, steel; 244×223×5 cm; Edition of 3; Installation view *Omnitlotl*, Kunstraum Walcheturm, Zürich; Kunsthaus Zürich, donation of the Dr. Georg and Josi Guggenheim-Foundation, 2012

111 *Floccinaucinihilipilification*, 2012
Neon tubing; 63×51 cm; Private Collection, Switzerland

113 *Stereoscopic Brain*, 2012
Neon tubing, steel; 210×290×25 cm; Installation view *The Main Change Building*, Johannesburg; Private Collection, South Africa

114 *Relay (Situationist Space Program)*, 2012
Acrylic lacquer, corrugated iron, corrugated polyester sheet, furniture, garage door, glass, insulation, neon tubing, plumbing, screws, sink, shower, steel, toilet, rivets, wood; 5.5×8.2×6.4 m; Unlimited edition; Installation view Maboneng Precinct, Johannesburg

115–118 I-IX See p. 114

119 *Pineal Horseshoe*, 2012
Neon tubing; 60×45×8 cm; Edition of 3; Installation view *Relay (Situationist Space Program)*, Maboneng Precinct, Johannesburg

120 See p. 27, fig. 38

122 *Empire State of Pudding (Performance)*, 2011
Collaboration with Nele Dechmann; Marzipan, pudding, wooden mold; Performance view, Institute of Architecture, EPFL Lausanne

123 I See p. 122; Performance view *Architektur im Würgegriff der Kunst*, Kunstverein Zürich

124 II See p. 122; Performance view Institute of Architecture, EPFL Lausanne

III See p. 122; Performance view *Architektur im Würgegriff der Kunst*, Kunstverein Zürich

125 See p. 122; Performance view *Architektur im Würgegriff der Kunst*, Kunstverein Zürich

126 *La Linge*, 2011
Beanpoles, clothes line, clothespins, sheets; Dimensions variable; Installation view *Art en plain air*, Môtiers; Photo: Alain Germond, Neuchâtel

128 *Tyger Tyger*, 2011
Color glaze, primer, screws, stainless steel, wood; 14.7×19.3×9.9 m; Installation view Novartis Campus, Basel; Novartis Art Collection; Photo: Tobias Madörin

130 *Playtime*, 2010/2011
Beanpoles, color filters, electrical wiring, fluorescent lamps, power generator, ropes, controler; Dimensions variable; Installation view *Les Urbaines*, Lausanne

132 *Maintenant*, 2010
Neon tubing; 40×440×25 cm; Edition of 3; Installation view *Maintenant*, Grieder Contemporary, Küsnacht; Photo: Axel Linge, Zürich

134 See p. 28, fig. 41
Installation view Wilderness

135 I See p. 28, fig. 41; Performance still Die Hel

136 II *Spume*, 2007
Beanpoles, color filters, electrical wiring, fluorescent lamps, power generator, ropes, timer; Dimensions variable; Installation view *Spume/ Holotypes*, Daniel Hug Gallery, Los Angeles

III See p. 28, fig. 41; Performance still Lion's Head, Cape Town; Photo: Bettina Malcomess, Johannesburg

137 IV See p. 28, fig. 41; Performance still Masubasuba Pass; Photo: Gregor Metzger, Zürich

V See p. 28, fig. 40; Installation view U-Topics, Biel/ Bienne; Photo: Guy Perrenoud, Biel/Bienne

138 VI See p. 28, fig. 40; Installation view *Oliver Ross und Kerim Seiler stellen aus*, message salon, Zürich

VII See p. 28, fig. 41; Performance still Mpande

139 See p. 28, fig. 40; Installation view *U-Topics*, Biel/Bienne

140 *Effetto Barnum (Situationist Space Program)*, 2009
Collaboration with CAAD, ETH Zürich; Acrylic lacquer, fire-resistant fabric, fan, flexible duct, fluorescent lamps, mirror, screws, wood; 8.4×10×10 m; Installation view *Babel – Edition 2009*, Piazza della Foca, Bellinzona; Photo: Anna Leader

142 *Hypnos*, 2010
Collaboration with CAAD, ETH Zürich; Acrylic lacquer, fire-resistant fabric, fan, flexible duct, mirror, screws, wood; 8×6×6 m; Installation view *ArtBoom Festival*, Kraków; Photo: Tobias Madörin

143 *Ohne Titel (Curtain)*, 2010
Curtain rail, fabric, gliders, thread; 476×714 cm; Installation view *The Anteroom*, Andreiana Mihail Gallery, Bucharest

144 *Barnum*, 2009
Collaboration with CAAD, ETH Zürich; Fabric, fan, flexible duct; 8.6×5.7×6.2 m; Installation view Westside, Bern; Photo: Tobias Madörin

145 *Gulliver*, 2009
Adhesive, brick, reinforced concrete; 6.9×7×7 m; Installation view Pfungen; Collection Keller Systems, Pfungen; Photo: Valentin Jeck, Stäfa

146 *Artúr (Pochutla)*, 2009
Collaboration with Adrian Notz and Caroline Pachoud Acrylic lacquer, color filters, fabric, fan, flexible duct, fluorescent lamps, mirror, screws, timer, wood; 2.4×6×4.5 cm; Installation view *Cravan*, Cabaret Voltaire, Zürich; Photo: Adrian Fritschi, Zürich

148 *MgBeth*, 2007
Collaboration with CAAD, ETH Zürich; Fabric, fans, fire-resistant string, flexible duct; 3.2×14.8×13.7 m; Installation view Migros Building, Zürich; Photo: Tobias Madörin

149 *Farbklotz/Dom-Ino*, 2007
pigments, plaster, sugar water, wax; 6.6×6.3×8.4 cm; 12.3×8.7×10.8 cm; Installation view *Irisinns Souvenir*, Ruzicska///Weiss, Düsseldorf

150 *Alice*, 2008
Collaboration with CAAD, ETH Zürich; Fabric, fan, flexible duct; 8×12×6 m; Installation view *Shifting Identities*, Kunsthaus Zürich; Photo: Tobias Madörin

152 See p. 29, fig. 43

154 *Shrine*, 2007
Collaboration with Gregor Metzger; Color gel, chalkboard paint, corrugated polyester sheet, electrical wiring, fluorescent lamps, mirror, screws, wood; 5.8×9.2×5,2 m; Installation view *P.U.S.H.*, Theaterhaus Gessnerallee, Zürich; Photo: Tobias Madörin

156 *Clone (Langstrasse)*, 2005/2006
Acrylic lacquer, concrete masonry unit, plywood, screws, wood; 5.5×6×3 m; Installation view *Clones International – Stop 2: Europe*, message salon, Zürich; Photo: Tobias Madörin

158 fig. 48 *Jean Arp*, 1998
Embossed aquatint on Zerkall 250g; 17 motives with coversheet in slipcase; Sheet: 38×27.3 cm (Image: 29.1×20.9 cm); Edition 10/17 (II AP + I PP); Printer: Atelier Peter Stiefel, Kilchberg; Publisher: Serge Ziegler Edition, Zürich; Collection Graphische Sammlung ETH Zürich

fig. 49 See p. 158, fig. 48

fig. 50 See p. 15, fig. 6

fig. 51 See p. 15, fig. 5

fig. 52 Study for *Ohne Titel (Tex Avery)*, 1998
Marker on tracing paper; 29.7×21 cm

fig. 53 *Die Galerie*, 1998
CMYK offset print on coated offset paper; Sheet: 50×69.8 cm (Image: 41×65.8 cm); Edition I/III AP (38); Printer: OK Druck, Zürich; Publisher: Serge Ziegler Edition, Zürich; Collection Graphische Sammlung ETH Zürich

161 fig. 54 *Ohne Titel (Spritzer)*, 2004
Embossed aquatint on Zerkall 250g; Sheet: 76×107 cm (Image: 59.6×77 cm); Edition 5/8 (II HC + I AP); Printer: Atelier Peter Stiefel, Kilchberg; Publisher: Galerie Susanna Kulli, Zürich; Collection Graphische Sammlung ETH Zürich

fig. 55 *Trace 12*, 2006
Blind embossing on Bütten 600g; Sheet: 78×107 cm (Image: 48.8×77 cm); Edition 1/1 (I AP); Printer: Atelier Peter Stiefel, Kilchberg; Publisher: Galerie Susanna Kulli, Zürich

fig. 56 Printing plate for blind embossing *Trace 04*, 2006

fig. 57 Roy Lichtenstein: *Brushstroke*, 1965
Screenprint on paper; Sheet: 58.4×73.6 cm; Edition of 280; Printer: Chiron Press, New York; Publisher: Leo Castelli, New York; © Estate of Roy Lichtenstein / 2023, ProLitteris, Zürich

fig. 58 *Kalinka*, 2007
Four multicolored aquatints with raised embossing on Alt Bern 250g in aluminum frame; Frame: 53,7×67,7 cm (Sheets: each 21×28 cm); Edition 6/15 (II AP + 1 HC + I PP); Printer: Atelier Peter Stiefel, Kilchberg; Publisher: Grieder Contemporary, Küsnacht; Collection Graphische Sammlung ETH Zürich

fig. 59 *Cravan (Klein)*, 2008
C-print on archive photo paper; 25×20 cm; Edition 5 / 2 AP; Printer: Pixel Grain, Berlin; Publisher: Cabaret Voltaire, Zürich

162 fig. 60 *Space, Color, Structure (Dillinger)*, 2008/09
Micro piezo print on paper in aluminum frame; Frame: 120×100 cm (Sheet 120×100 cm); Edition 1/3 / (I AP); Printer: Mancia/Bodmer, FBM Studio, Zürich; Publisher: La Rada, Locarno; Collection Graphische Sammlung ETH Zürich

fig. 61 *Labyrinth*, 2010
Woodcut on Rives 300g; Sheet: 76.5×76.5 cm (Image: 70×70 cm); Edition 3/16 (II AP + I PP); Printer: Atelier Peter Stiefel, Kilchberg; Publisher: Grieder Contemporary, Küsnacht; Collection Graphische Sammlung ETH Zürich

fig. 62 *Ohne Titel (LSD)*, 2010
Multi-color woodcut on Rives 300g; Sheet: 80×100 cm (Image: 76×96 cm); Edition 3/8 (I HC); Printer: Atelier Peter Stiefel, Kilchberg; Publisher: Grieder Contemporary, Küsnacht; Collection Graphische Sammlung ETH Zürich

fig. 63 *Ohne Titel (Neon)*, 2010
Multi-color woodcut on Rives 300g; Sheet: 80×100 cm (Image: 76×96 cm); Edition 3/8 (I HC); Printer: Atelier Peter Stiefel, Kilchberg; Publisher: Grieder Contemporary, Küsnacht; Collection Graphische Sammlung ETH Zürich

163 fig. 64 *A View from Spaceship Earth*, 2011
Screenprint on Munken; Sheet: 31×21 cm (Image: 29.2×19.5 cm); Edition 80 + 20 / 10 AP; Printer: Arni Siebdruck, Allschwil; Publisher: Reto Thürig, Artcollector Magazine, Basel

fig. 65 *Polar Bear and Neon Lights (Maintenant)*, 2014
Multi-color drypoint on paper; Sheet: 104.5×24 cm (Image: 94.5×14 cm); Edition 1/8 (II AP + II HC + I PP); Printer: Atelier Peter Stiefel, Kilchberg; Publisher: Grieder Contemporary, Küsnacht; Collection Graphische Sammlung ETH Zürich; Photo: Done Studio – Ulf Saupe, Berlin

fig. 66 *Polar Bear and Neon Lights (Stereoscopic Brain)*, 2014
Multi-color drypoint on paper; Sheet: 39×32 cm (Image: 29×22 cm); Edition 1/8 (II AP + II HC + I PP); Printer: Atelier Peter Stiefel, Kilchberg; Publisher: Grieder Contemporary, Küsnacht; Collection Graphische Sammlung ETH Zürich; Photo: Done Studio – Ulf Saupe, Berlin

164 fig. 67 *Polar Bear and Neon Lights (Polar Bear)*, 2014
Multi-color drypoint on paper; Sheet: 24×22 cm (Image: 14×12 cm); Edition 1/8 (II AP + II HC + I PP); Printer: Atelier Peter Stiefel, Kilchberg; Publisher: Grieder Contemporary, Küsnacht; Collection Graphische Sammlung ETH Zürich; Photo: Done Studio – Ulf Saupe, Berlin

fig. 68 *Relay (Situationist Space Program)*, 2014
Xerox on paper; Sheet: 84.1×119.8 cm (Image: 75.7×110.9 cm); Edition 17/∞; Printer: Alpha Copy, Berlin; Publisher: Grieder Contemporary, Küsnacht; Private Collection

fig. 69 *Verkehrte Welt*, 2015
Multi-color photogravure; Sheet: 70×58 cm (Image: 49×44 cm); Edition 11/50 (III AP / I PP); Printer: Druckerei Willi Jesse, Berlin; Publisher: SOS-Kinderdörfer Weltweit, Berlin; Collection Hohenlohe, Berlin

fig. 70 *Bardo*, 2018
Inkjet on paper; Sheet: 112×112 cm (Image: 94×94 cm); Edition 1/8 (I AP + II HC); Printer: Mancia/Bodmer, FBM Studio, Zürich; Publisher: Grieder Contemporary, Küsnacht; Private Collection

166 *Mindspace (Roma)*, 2006
Screws, wood; 240×332×422 cm; Installation view *Visioni del Paradiso*, Istituto Svizzero di Roma

168 *Clone (Kurpark)*, 2005
Acrylic lacquer, concrete masonry unit, plywood, screws, wood; 5.5×6×3 m; Installation view *Clones International – Stop 2: Europe*, Kurpark, Lüneburg

170 *Heliopolis*, 2005
Acrylic laquer, adhesive, particle board, reinforced concrete, white paint, wood; 174×87×108 cm; Installation view *Heliopolis*, Ruzicska///Weiss, Düsseldorf; Photo: Stefan Hostettler, Düsseldorf

171 *Clone (Canal Street)*, 2005
Acrylic lacquer, concrete masonry unit, plywood, screws, wood; 5.5×6×3 m; Installation view *Clones International – Stop 3: America*, Canal Street, New York

172 *In Cold Blood*, 2005
Acrylic laquer, buckets, excavator, foam rubber, galvanized steel, iron, particle board, plywood, rivets, screws, skirting, spotlights, stage decks, stainless steel, white paint; 3.4×8×8 m; Performance view *Unruhe Bitte*, Gessnerallee, Zürich; Photo: David Renggli, Zürich

173–174 I-III See p. 172

176 *Hypnose, Trance, Schlaf*, 2004
Alucore, planetary gearing, two component lacquer 150×550×15 cm; Edition of 3; Installation view *Planetengetriebe*, Gallerie Susanna Kulli, Zürich

178 *Brut*, 2003
Audiotracks, grow lights, irrigation system, portable audio players, terracotta pots, seeds, string; Dimensions variable; Installation view *Durchzug/Draft*, Kunsthalle Zürich; Photo: Alexander Troehler, Zürich

179 *Aus der Hundeperspektive*, 2003
Medium-density fiberboard, particle board, screws, spotlight, two component lacquer, white paint, wood Dimensions variable; Installation view *Episode*, Center, Berlin; Collection Matthias Dietz, Berlin

180 *Springbrunnen*, 2003
Acrylic lacquer, galvanized steel, hot-melt marking paint, particle board, screws, tiles, water nozzle, wood 3×5×3 m; Installation view *Transit*, Chur

182 *Endlich Ruhe im finsteren Wald / Lichtorgel*, 2003
Iron, galvanized steel, rusted steel; Dimensions variable Installation view *Unter 30*, Kunstmuseum Appenzell Collection Heinrich Gebert Kulturstiftung, Appenzell Photo: Kunstmuseum Appenzell

184 *Hall of Fame*, 2002
Collaboration with Tjorg Douglas Beer; Doka beams, hardboard, steel, two component lacquer, screws; 8×9.5×20.7 m; Installation view *artgenda – 4. Biennale für junge Kunst im baltischen Raum*, Handelskammer, Hamburg; Photo: Carmen Romatowski, Hamburg

186–188 See p. 20, fig. 22; Installation view *Lattenwald*, Stiftung Binz 39, Zürich; Sammlung Migros Museum für Gegenwartskunst, Zürich; Photo: Michela Montalbetti

190 *Arthurs Träne (bei Mexiko im Licht der kleinen Bärin Ursuta Ursa Minor, bringt Arthurs Träne Arthurs Ruderboot zum Überlaufen)*, 2002
Acrylic paint, adhesive film, fluorescent lamp, galvanized steel, particle board, perspex, rowboat, screws, wood; Dimensions variable; Installation view *Bonjour, mon amour / Layercake*, Lehmbruck-Museum, Duisburg

192 *Baustellenromanze mit Bier und Tanz*, 2002
Construction barriers, formwork panel, screws Dimensions variable; Installation view *Baustellenromanze mit Bier und Tanz*, message salon, Zürich

194 See p. 17, fig. 16

195 *Copy/Paste*, 2001
Calcareous grassland, green Andeer granite, two component lacquer, rivets, steel; Dimensions variable; Installation view Glattzentrum, Wallisellen; Sammlung Migros Museum für Gegenwartskunst, Zürich; Photo: Mancia/Bodmer, FBM Studio, Zürich

196 *Horizont*, 2001
Acrylic lacquer, hot-melt marking paint, medium-density fiberboard, screws, spotlights, tripods, wood; Dimensions variable; Installation view *Pflumm Seiler Stucky*, Kunsthalle Zürich; Photo: Alexander Troehler, Zürich

198 See p. 17, fig. 15

200 *MELENCOLIA 2000*, 2000
1 of 3×3 or 4×4 C-prints, 10×15 cm; Edition of 3

202 See p. 20, fig. 23

216 *Ohne Titel (Teermaschine)*, 2000
Acrylic paint, medium-density fiberboard; 125.6×114.1 cm; Private Collection; Photo: Katharina Lütscher, Zürich

218 *Kompromiss nach Eiland*, 1999
Collaboration with Nic Hess; grow lights, screws, sod, soil, watering can, wood; Dimensions variable; Installation view *Projekt Durchbruch*, Kunsthalle St.Gallen; Kunstmuseum St.Gallen, acquired 2000

220 *Made in Egypt*, 1999
Acrylic paint, picture frames, particle board, perspex, photo print, screws, spotlights, white paint, wood; Dimensions variable; Installation view *Made in Egypt*, Cairo-Berlin Gallery, Cairo

221 *Komm Schatz, wir gehen weiter*, 1999
Acrylic paint, plywood, screws, spotlights; Dimensions variable; Installation view HFBK, Hamburg

222 See p. 15, fig. 7

223 See page See p. 15, fig. 5

224 *KEIN TITEL V (Billetautomat)*, 1997
Acrylic paint, pavatex; 231×121 cm; Installation view Goethestrasse 20, Zürich; Collection Serge Ziegler, Zürich

Back See p. 28, fig. 41
Installation view Maboneng Precinct, Johannesburg; Photo: Gregor Metzger, Zürich

I See p. 28, fig. 41; Performance still Nyanga Arts Development Center; Photo: Gregor Metzger, Zürich

II See p. 28, fig. 41; Performance still Masubasuba Pass; Photo: Gregor Metzger, Zürich

II See p. 28, fig. 41; Performance still Masubasuba Pass; Photo: Gregor Metzger, Zürich

*If not specified, Photo: Kerim Seiler

MONOGRAPHS

2019 *Space Is My Canvas*, Kerim Seiler (ed.), Rafael Horzon, Dorothea Strauss, About Books, Zürich, 2019

2012 *Kerim in the Sky with Seiler: LSD – Fluxus – Konkret*, Patrick Huber, Kerim Seiler (eds.), Bettina Malcomess, Adrain Notz, Nieves, Zürich, 2012; *OMNITLOTL*, Kerim Seiler (ed.), Adrian Notz, Edizioni Periferia, Luzern, 2012

2008 *Cravan*, Adrian Notz, Caroline Pachoud, Kerim Seiler (eds.), Cabaret Voltaire & Nieves, Zürich, 2008

1999 *Fön 37 – Nic Hess & Kerim Seiler*, Dorothea Strauss (ed.), Kunsthalle St.Gallen, 1999

TEXTS

2016 *message salon*, Esther Eppstein, Benjamin Sommerhalder (eds.), Nadine Olonetzki, Scheidegger & Spiess, Zürich, 2016

2005 *Bellevue Zürich*, Nicolas Baerlocher, Stefan Zweifel (eds.), Kerim Seiler, et al., Verlag Neue Zürcher Zeitung, Zürich, 2005, p. 91–92

OTHER

2022 *Der Leuenhof Zürich*, Peter Zimmermann, Tilla Theus, Rolf Schläpfer (eds.), Swiss Prime Anlagestiftung, Olten, 2022, p. 141, 144–145, 206; *Open House*, Simon Lamunière (ed.), Scheidegger & Spiess, Zürich, 2022, p. 130–133; *La mia commedia dell'arte*, Jacqueline Burckhardt, Edition Patrick Frey, Zürich, 2022, p. 59; *C is for Curator: Bice Curiger – Eine Arbeitsbiographie*, Dora Imhof (ed.), Verlag der Buchhandlung Walther König, Cologne, 2022, p. 243

2021 *Leuenhof: Architektur, Design, Kunst*, Loa Pictet (ed.), Pictet Group, Zürich, 2021, p. 21

2020 *Eigenbedarf*, Isabelle Meiffert (ed.), Distanz Verlag, Berlin, 2020, p. 4, 28, 77, 122

2019 *FBM – Before and After the Storm*, Vadim & Maria Zakharov (eds.), Freehome Artist to Artist, Berlin, 2019, p. 164, 185; *Paradise Lost*, Christoph Doswald (ed.), Biennale Kulturort Weiertal, 2019, p. 182–187; *Zürich Kreis 11*, green-design (ed.), Elektro Compagnoni, Zürich, 2019, p. 81–95

2017 *33 Jahre Galerie Susanna Kulli*, Max Wechsler, Peter Zimmermann (eds.), Edition Galerie Susanna Kulli, St. Gallen, 2017, p. 162–163, 169, 180, 358–360, 374–375, 383

2016 *Freude, Trauer, Angst, Hoffnung*, Freidhelm Hofmann (ed.), Echter Verlag, Würzburg, 2016, p. 56–57, 60; *Im Rausch: Zwischen Höhenflug und Absturz*, Markus Landert, Sabine Hoch (eds.), Verlag für moderne Kunst, Vienna, 2016, p. 8–9, 120–125; *[V+K=I] Die Mobiliar Methode*, Dorothea Strauss (ed.), die Mobiliar, Bern, 2016, p. 133–135; *Let's Play*, Christiane Nill, Lionel Henriod (eds.), Till Schaap Edition, Bern, 2016, p. 132–134; *SOS Edition Weltweit*, Kristin zu Hohenlohe, Sabine Conquest (eds.), SOS-Kinderdörfer Weltweit, Munich, 2016; *In die Breite: Kunst für das Auge der Öffentlichkeit: zur Geschichte der Kunstsammlung des Kantons Zürich – vom Nationalstaat bis zur Globalisierung*, Kathrin Frauenfelder, Dissertation, Kunsthistorisches Institut, Universität Zürich, 2016, p. 360–361

2015 *Signalwege: Eine Begegnung von Kunst und Wissenschaft*, Ulrike Lorenz, Anne Vieth (eds.), Würzburg, 2015, p. 20–27

2014 *Émergences: Bex & Arts 2014*, Jessica Schupbach, Noémie Enz (eds.), art&fiction publications, Lausanne, 2014, p. 112–113

2013 *Architektur im Würgegriff der Kunst*, Nele Dechmann, Nicola Ruffo (eds.), gta Verlag, Zürich, 2013, p. 77–87; *Mystic Chemist: The Life of Albert Hofmann and His Discovery of LSD*, Dieter Hagenbach, Lucius Werthmüller (eds.), Synergetic Press, Santa Fe, 2013, p. 239; *Im Bett mit Mark Divo*, edition clandestin, Biel/Bienne, 2013, p. 128, 135, 187, 301; *Gasträume*, Christoph Doswald (ed.), Arbeitsgruppe Kunst im öffentlichen Raum, Zürich, 2013, p. 56; *Kunst und Architektur im Dialog*, Roderick Hönig (ed.), Hochparterre, Zürich, 2013; *Im Würgegriff der Kunst*, Nele Dechmann, Nicola Ruffo (eds.), S AM Swiss Architecture Museum, Basel, 2013, p. 11–14; *Inside Smartgeometry: Expanding the Architectural Possibilities of Computational Design*, Brady Peters, Terri Peters (eds.), John Wiley & Sons, Sussex, 2013

2012 *friendsandloversinunderground.de*, Dirk Meinzer (ed.), et al., Textem Verlag, Hamburg, 2012; *THIS WORK IS DESTROYED WHEN YOU STOP LOOKING AT IT AND RESTORED WHEN YOU LOOK AT IT*, Karine Vonna (ed.), Pierre Tillet, Villa Du Parc, Annemasse, 2012, p. 8–11; *Arts Visuels et Architecture*, Marie Sacconi (ed.), Séction d'architecture (SAR), EPFL, Lausanne, 2012; *Shine On*, Livio Baumgartner, Nele Dechmann, Nicola Ruffo (eds.), Kunstverein, Zürich, 2012

2011 *Albert Hofmann und sein LSD*, Dieter Hagenbach, Lucius Werthmüller (eds.), AT Verlag, Aarau, 2011, p. 252; *Swiss Art Awards 2011*, Bundesamt für Kultur, Bern, 2011, p. 158–161; *Rewriting Worlds: DADA Moscow*, Adrian Notz (ed.), 4. Moscow Biennale of Contemporary Art, Moscow, 2011, p. 20; *Art en Plain Air*, Pierre-André Delachaux (ed.), Môtiers, 2011, p. 39, 166–167

2010 *Hugo Ball Almanach: Neue Folge 1*, Hugo-Ball-Gesellschaft (ed.), Edition Text & Kritik, Munich, 2010, p. 153–154; *ArtBoom Festival*, Małgorzata Gołębiewska (ed.), Kraków Festival Office, Kraków, 2010, p. 76–83; *Jenseits des Rasters – Architektur und Informationstechnologie / Beyond the Grid – Architecture and Information Technology*, Ludger Hovestadt (ed.), Birkhäuser, Basel, 2010, p. 99, 104, 111, 184–189; *Schritte ins Verborgene: Kunst und das Geheimnis*, Dorothee Messmer (ed.), Verlag für moderne Kunst, Nuremberg, 2010, p. 74–77; *Kult Zürich Aussersihl*, Verein Kult Zürich Aussersihl (ed.), Verlag Um Die Ecke, Zürich, 2010, p. 593; *Blickwechsel NRW*, Bernd Apke (ed.), Albrecht Thomas / Franz-Josef Weber, et al., Kerber Verlag, Leipzig, 2010, p. 166–169; *AZB for ever: Die Arbeitsgemeinschaft Zürcher Bildhauer als Organismus*, Helmhaus, Zürich (ed.), Jürg Altherr, Kathrin Frauenfelder, Simon Maurer, Scheidegger & Spiess, Zürich, 2010, 66–69, 149; *Amazing Life*, Fabryka Sztuki, Łódź, 2010, p. 51; *Unterdessen*, Annalies Walter (ed.), Museum Bärengasse, Zürich, 2010, p. 36–37; *R/O/B – David Renggli, Kerim Seiler*, Keller AG Ziegeleien (ed.), Pfungen, 2010; *Utopics: Systems and Landmarks*, Simon Lamunière (ed.), JRP|Editions, Geneva, 2010, p. 122–123

2009 *Memorizer: Der Sammler Andreas Züst*, Stephan Kunz (ed.), Scheidegger & Spiess, Zürich, 2009, p. 163, 347–348, 373, 386; *Verordnete Entgrenzung*, Andrea Glauser, transcript Verlag, Bielefeld, 2009, p. 164–171; *Tsnuk? Und das ist Kunst?*, Roland Scotti, Daniela Mittelholzer (eds.), Stiftung Liner, Appenzell, 2009; *blank projects*, blank projects (ed.), Cape Town, 2009; *Wir verbessern Ihre Arbeit*, Instituto Divorciado (ed.), Galerie Sandra Bürgel, Berlin, 2009; *Archive*, Robert Meles (ed.), Ada Bojana Symposium, Ada Bojana, 2009, p. 7–9, 27, 50, 52

2008 *L'Art Imprimé en Suisse / Die Schweizer Druckgrafik 2004–2007*, Stéphanie Guex (ed.), Benteli Verlag, Bern, 2008, p. 4, 8, 16–17, 37–38, 51, 123–124, 130; *Druckgrafik*,

Karin Althaus (ed.), Scheidegger & Spiess, Zürich, 2008, p. 99, 200; *Shifting Identities. (Swiss) Art Now*, Mirjam Varadinis (ed.), JRP|Editions, Geneva, 2008, p. 208–209; *Migros Museum für Gegenwartkunst*, Heike Munder (ed.), JRP|Editions, Geneva, 2008, p. 338; *Construction Site: Metamorphoses in the City*, Marie Antoinette Glaser (ed.), Lars Müller Publishers, Baden, 2008, p. 48–49; *Olga und Hermann Rorschach*, Iris Blum, Peter Witschi (eds.), Ursula Badrutt, Appenzeller Verlag, Herisau, 2008, p. 35–36; *agent-provocateur.ch: Was uns ärgert und was nicht*, Plinio Bachmann, Martin Heller (eds.), Scheidegger & Spiess, Zürich, 2008, p. 71, 161, 314; *Art/Unlimited*, Art|39|Basel|4–8|6|08, Messe Schweiz, Basel, 2008, p. 136–137

2007 *Ästehetik der Kritik oder Verdeckte Ermittlung*, Jörg Huber, Philipp Stoellger, Gesa Ziemer, Simon Zumsteg (eds.), Edition Voldermeer Zürich / Springer, Vienna / New York, 2007, p. 105–111; *Art en Plain Air*, Pierre-André Delachaux (ed.), Môtiers, 2007, p. 181–185; *För Hitz und Brand*, Ursula Badrutt, Matthias Kuhn, Vera Marke (eds.), Ausserrhodische Kulturstiftung, Herisau, 2007

2006 *20 Jahre Kunsthalle St.Gallen 1985–2005*, Gianni Jetzer (ed.), JRP|Editions, Geneva, 2006, p. 57, 78, 136; *Visioni del Paradiso. Un dialogo sull'arte tra Svizzera e Italia*, Domenico Lucchini, Karin Frei, Pietro Bellasi (eds.), Istituto Svizzero di Roma / Mondadori Electa, Milan, 2006, p. 124–127, 147

2005 *Art/36/Basel*, Hatje Cantz Verlag, Ostfildern, 2005, p. 281; *Schweizerische Druckgrafik 1980–2005*, Eva Korazija (ed.), Schwabe Verlag, Basel, 2005, p. 187–188; *Dadaize*, Werner Oechslin, Stefan Zweifel, et al., Cabaret Voltaire, Zürich, 2005

2004 *Kunstlicht Kongress*, Tjorg Douglas Beer (ed.), Revolver Publishing, Berlin, 2004; *Lasso #1*, Bettina Steinbrügge, Hilmar Schäfer (eds.), Katharina Dohm, Revolver Publishing, Berlin, 2004, p. 56, 59, 61

2003 *Durchzug/Draft – 20 Jahre Stiftung Binz 39*, Beatrix Ruf (ed.), Stiftung Binz 39 / Kunsthalle Zürich, 2003, p. 18, 40, 111, 156; *Hybrid Zones: Art and Architecture in Basel and Zürich*, Karin Frei Bernasconi, Sibylle Omlin (eds.), Birkhäuser Publishers, Basel, 2003, p. 72, 142–145, 152; *10e Biennale de l'Image en Mouvement*, Clare Manchester (ed.), JRP|Editions, Geneva, 2003, p. 110, 148; *Unter 30 – Junge Schweizer Kunst*, Christoph Doswald (ed.), Museum Liner, Appenzell, 2003, p. cover, 3–6, back cover; *Kunst für die Kunst*, Gianni Jetzer (ed.), Verein Kunsthalle St.Gallen, 2003, p. 32; *Swiss Art Awards*, Bundesamt für Kultur, Bern, 2003, p. 65, 138

2002 *Ausstellungsraum Taubenstrasse 13, Hamburg, St. Pauli 1999 bis 2002*, Tjorg Douglas Beer, Tatjana Sarah Greiner (eds.), Verlag der Fachbuchhandlung Sautter + Lackmann, Hamburg, 2002, p. 25–26, 161; *Swiss Art Awards*, Bundesamt für Kultur, Bern, 2002, p. 54–55, 138; *Wonder Red Now*, Bundesamt für Kultur, Bern, 2002, p. 74–75, 104

2001 *2000–2001*, Stiftung Binz 39, Zürich, 2001; *Let's be friends A-Z*, Rein Wolfs (ed.), Migros Museum für Gegenwartskunst, Zürich, 2001, p. 7, 60, 167; *Pflumm Seiler Stucki*, Bernhard Mendes Bürgi (ed.), Kunsthalle Zürich, 2001; *Wald / Explosionen*, Simon Maurer (ed.), Helmhaus, Zürich, 2001, p. 50, 60

2000 *Drawing by Numbers*, Bettina Burkhardt & Rolf Staub (eds.), Universität Bern, 2000; *Centre D'Art Contemporain Fri-Art 2000*, Michel Ritter (ed.), Fri-Art, Fribourg, 2000, p. 68

1999 *Nic Hess*, Collection Cahiers des Artistes Pro Helvetia, Lars Müller Publishers, Baden, 1999, p. 10, 12–14

1998 *Freie Sicht aufs Mittelmeer: Junge Schweizer Kunst mit Gästen und Gastmahl*, Bice Curiger (ed.), Scalo Verlag, Zürich, 1998, p. 240–241, 291, 313; *message salon*, Esther Eppstein (ed.), Andreas Züst Verlag c/o Scalo Verlag, Zürich, 1998, p. 34–35; *Wahlverwandtschaften*, Rudolf Koella, et al., IG Art & Appenzell, 1998, p. 74–79

EDUCATION

2007–11 Master of Advanced Sciences in Architecture, CAAD D-ARCH, ETH Zürich
1997–02 Freie Kunst, Prof. B. J. Blume, Hochschule für bildende Künste, Hamburg
1993–95 Média Mixtes, École Supérieure des Beaux-Arts, Geneva
1991/92 Vorkurs, Schule für Gestaltung, Zürich

SOLO EXHIBITIONS

2022 *Kerim Seiler*, Fabricca Culturale Giornico
2020 *Tender is the Night*, Turmplatz AZB, Schlieren
2019 *Kreis 11*, Stadtraum Kreis 11, Zürich
2018 *Afraid of Red, Yellow and Blue*, Grieder Contemporary, Küsnacht
2017 *Some New Works*, Art25, Berlin
2016 *Das Cabaret Voltaire als Skulptur*, Cabaret Voltaire, Zürich; *New Babylon*, Kunsthalle Mannheim; *Relay (Situationist Space Program)*, Atelier Cuno Amiet, Oschwand; *Relay (Situationist Space Program)*, Enea Baummuseum, Jona
2015 *Llloblyekk && Bboolyekk*, die Mobiliar, Bern; *Sommes Some Sum*, NR/Projects, Berlin; Éspace d'une Sculpture, Château de Nyon
2014 *Mindspace (Berlin)*, Little Wood, Berlin; *spouligenion*, Grieder Contemporary, Zürich; *Solutions from Zürich*, Salon Mark Divo, Prague
2013 *Collateral Neighbors*, Salon Neucologne, Berlin
2012 *Freak Magnet*, Galerie Melike Bilir, Hamburg; *Floccinaucinihilipilification*, Grieder Contemporary, Berlin; *Omnitlotl*, Kunstraum Walcheturm, Zürich
2011 *Relay (Situationist Space Program)*, Maboneng Precinct, Johannesburg; *Babel – Edition 2011*, Piazza della Foca, Bellinzona; *Mama Bar*, Dakini's Coffee & Bar, Zürich; *Architektur im Würgegriff der Kunst*, Wäscherei Kunstverein Zürich
2010 *Maintenant*, Grieder Contemporary, Küsnacht; *Nomadic Structures Digest*, blank projects, Cape Town; *Babel – Edition 2010*, Piazza della Foca, Bellinzona; *Molecolor*, Motel Campo, Genève; *The Anteroom*, Andreiana Mihail Gallery, Bucharest
2009 *Pneuma, somnambul*, Villa du Parc, Annemasse; *Effetto Barnum*, La Rada, Locarno; *Spiel des Lebens*, Neumarkt Theater, Zürich; *Babel – Edition 2009*, Piazza della Foca, Bellinzona; *Cravan*, Cabaret Voltaire, Zürich
2007 *MgBeth*, ETH & MGB, Zürich; *Irisinn's Souvenir*, Ruzicska///Weiss, Düsseldorf; *Tertascope*, ETH Zürich; *Spume/Holotypes*, Daniel Hug Gallery, Los Angeles
2006 *Kevin Seiler*, Galerie Susanna Kulli, Zürich; *Clones International – Stop 2: Europe*, message salon, Zürich; *Creature Comfort*, blank projects, Cape Town
2005 *In Cold Blood – After Truman Capote*, Theaterhaus Gessnerallee, Zürich; *Clones International – Stop 1: Africa*, public space, Cape Town; *Clones International – Stop 2:* Europe, public space, Lüneburg; *Clones International – Stop 3:* America, public space, New York City; *Heliopolis*, Ruzicska///Weiss, Düsseldorf
2004 *Planetengetriebe*, Galerie Susanna Kulli, Zürich; *Stroke*, Zimmer Frei, Lugano; *Im Lampenfieber*, Galerie Susanna Kulli, Zürich
2003 *Episode*, Center, Berlin; *Grosse Brut/Paravent*, Harburger Kunstverein, Hamburg;
2002 *Baustellenromanze mit Bier und Tanz*, message salon, Zürich; *Hall of Fame*, collab. Tjorg Douglas Beer, artGenda, Börse Hamburg; *Arthurs Träne*, Lehmbruckmuseum, Duisburg; *Lattenwald*, Stiftung Binz 39, Zürich
2001 *Rampensau*, Theater an der Winkelwiese, Zürich
2000 *Schlaf*, Ausstellungsraum Taubenstrasse, Hamburg; *Petit Déjeuner/Frühstück*, message salon caravan & PAC, Fribourg; *hypnose I, etc.*, Serge Ziegler Galerie, Zürich; *Seelenzentrifuge*, Horten out bei Bochynek, Düsseldorf
1999 *Made in Egypt*, Cairo-Berlin Gallery, Cairo; *Projekt Durchbruch*, collab. Nic Hess, Kunsthalle St.Gallen
1998 *Serge Ziegler Galerie*, Zürich
1997 *Kein Titel*, Akryl auf Pavatex, message salon, Zürich
1995 *Hustle*, Kurz Bar, Zürich
1994 *D-131174*, Studio Z&L, New York City

GROUP EXHIBITIONS

2022 *Open House*, Parc Genthod, Geneva; *Interactions 8*, Sexauer Showroom, Berlin; *Die unterbrochene Reise*, Birkewäldli, Unterägeri; *Summer Show*, Sexauer, Berlin
2021 *Common Ground*, Berliner Union Film Ateliers, Berlin
2020 *Manifest*, Uferhallen, Berlin; *Made in Zürich*, Grieder Contemporary, Küsnacht
2019 *Paradise Lost*, Biennale Kulturort Weiertal; *Make Zürich Small Again*, Kupper Modern, Zürich; *Eigenbedarf*, Uferhallen, Berlin
2018 *Zukunft*, Kunsthalle Schlieren; *All our Darlings*, Kunstmuseum Appenzell; *Play, Cat and Mouse – The Arcade Project*, Whiteleys Queensway, London
2017 *Ewige Gegenwart*, Helmhaus, Zürich; *Gasträume*, Paradeplatz, Zürich; *Mosespa*, Motel Campo, Geneva; *Center of the World*, Ebensperger, Salzburg
2016 *Works from the Collection*, Galerie Gebr. Lehmann, Berlin; *Im Rausch (Höhenflug und Absturz)*, Kunstmuseum Thurgau; *To go too far*, Petra Rinck Galerie, Düsseldorf
2015 *Bomb Gallery*, Art Radionca Lazareti, Dubrovnik; *S.O.S. DADA – The World is a Mess*, Salon Suisse, Palazzo Trevisan degli Ulivi, 56th Venice Biennale; *Signalwege – Eine Begegnung von Kunst und Wissenschaft im Rudolf-Virchow-Zentrum*, Würzburg; *Sculptumes et Costures*, Parc Mon Repos, Lausanne
2014 *Drive to Change*. 100plus, Zürich; *Bomb Gallery*, International Contemporary Art Festival, Mostar; *Echoing Bex & Arts*, Rolex Learning Center, EPFL Lausanne; *EMERGENCES*, Bex & Arts Triennale, Bex; *After & Before*, Bomb Gallery, Mostar
2013 *Im Würgegriff der Kunst*, Schweizerisches Architektur Museum, Basel; *St. Moritz Art-Masters 2013*; *Sezession*, SEZ, Berlin; *Tarantula*, Torstrasse 111, Berlin
2012 *Shine on you Crazy Diamond*, Ex-Ernst & Young, Zürich; *Palazzo Wyler*, Palazzo Wyler, Bern; *Kunst Zürich Aussersihl*, Helmhaus, Zürich; *Dancing Fundaments – The Aestethic of Inconvinience*, Irbis-12°, Samedan; *St. Moritz Art Masters 2012*
2011 *Kunstbegriffe*, Galerie Melike Bilir, Hamburg; *B12*, public space, Zürich; *Friends and Lovers in Underground*, Willy Brandt Strasse, Hamburg; *Kunst Zürich Aussersihl*, Malzfabrik, Berlin; *Swiss Art Awards*, Messe, Basel; *Wall Floor Piece*, von Bartha Garage, Basel; *Start Reloaded*, Grieder Contemporary, Zürich; *VideoEx*, Kunstraum Walcheturm, Zürich; *Art en plain air*, Môtiers; *Rewriting Worlds – DADA Moscow*, 4. Moscow Biennale of Contemporary Art, Moscow
2010 *AZB for ever*, Helmhaus, Zürich; *Schritte im Verborgenen*, Kartause Ittingen; *Blickwechsel*, public space, Siegen; *Under Pressure*, Fabrica Sztuki, Łódź; *Jahressausstellung D-ARCH*, ETH-Zürich; *Unterdessen*, Museum Bärengasse, Zürich; *Les Urbaines*, public space, Lausanne

2009 *U-Topics*, public space, Biel/Bienne; *Oliver Ross und Kerim Seiler stellen aus*, message salon, Zürich; *Wir verbessern Ihre Arbeit*, Instituto Divorciados @ Galerie Sandra Bürgel, Berlin; *Narcotica*, Galerie im Regierungsviertel @ Schalter, Basel; *Lichterlöschen*, WestSide, Bern; *Leftover*, Whitespace, Zürich; *Gruppenausstellung*, Kulturhaus Binz, Zürich; *Kult Zürich Aussersihl*, Galerie / Museum Baviera, Zürich; *Impression*, Stiftung Kunsthaus Grenchen

2008 *Sculpture Trail*, Grieder Contemporary, Küsnacht; *Shifting Identities*, Kunsthaus, Zürich; *Diskurs im Grünen*, Kunstverein Springhornhof, Neuenkirchen; *ArtUnlimited*, Art|39, Basel; *5th Dada Festival*, Kolín; *Werk- und Atelierstipendien Kanton Zürich*, F + F, Zürich; *Werk- und Atelierstipendien Stadt Zürich*, Helmhaus, Zürich; *Aeschlimann Corti Stipendium 2008*, Kunsthaus Pasquart, Biel/Bienne

2007 *Selected Works*, blank projects, Cape Town; *Odds and Ends*, Ruzicska///Weiss, Düsseldorf; *Triennale d'Estampes*, Musée des Beaux Arts, Le Locle; *The International Situationist: 1957–1972. In girum imus nocte et consumimur igni*, Museum Tinguely, Basel; *Kunst in Schlieren*; *Art en plain Air*, Môtiers; *För Hitz ond Brand*, Trogen; *Paper Tigers: Transgression / Excess*, Space Other, Boston; *Kunsteisbahn*, K3 Project Space, Zürich

2006 *Visioni del Paradiso*, Istituto Svizzero, Rome; *Contra Golpe*, Instituto Divorciados, Berlin; *Process*, National Gallery, Prague, *Schweizerische Druckgrafik 1980–2005*, Museum Kunst Palast, Düsseldorf

2005 *Re-Escape*, public space, Hamburg; *Celebration*, Halle für Kunst, Lüneburg; *Skulpturenschau in Zwischenräumen*, public space, Münsterlingen; *Schweizerische Druckgrafik 1980–2005*, Helmhaus, Zürich; *Rosa 9*, Kunstverein, Freiburg i. B.; *This is not an easy way down*, Bell-Roberts Gallery, Cape Town

2004 *Dadaize*, Cabaret Voltaire, Zürich; *L'occasion revée*, Triangle / Friche Belle de Mai, Marseille; *L'Air du Temps*, Migros Museum, Zürich; *Kunst für die Kunst*, Kunsthalle St.Gallen; *Atelier d'artisti*, Museo Elisarion, Minusio

2003 *Nos Rendezvous*, Galerie Michel Rein, Paris; *Unter 30 – Junge Schweizer Kunst*, Museum Liner, Appenzell; *Transit*, public space, Chur; *Feine Ware II*, Harburger Kunstverein, Hamburg; *Eidgenössische Stipendien / Kiefer Hablitzel Stiftung*, Messe Basel; *Durchzug / Draft*, Kunsthalle Zürich; *Handlungsräume*, Halle für Kunst, Lüneburg; *Aeschlimann Corti Stipendium*, Kunsthaus Langenthal

2002 *Reunited*, Ausstellungsraum 25, Zürich; *Eidgenössische Stipendien / Kiefer Hablitzel Stiftung*, Messe Basel; *Wilibalds Traum / Wilibalds Morgen*, Hochschule für bildende Künste, Hamburg

2001 *Wald & Explosionen*, collab. Nic Hess, Helmhaus, Zürich; *Aeschlimann Corti Stipendium*, Kunsthaus Langenthal; *Manshitsu*, Ausstellungsraum Taubenstrasse & Hinterconti, Hamburg; *Stipendiaten der Stiftung Binz39*, Zürich; *Pflumm Seiler Stucki*, Kunsthalle Zürich; *Werk- und Atelierstipedien der Stadt Zürich*, Helmhaus, Zürich

2000 *Friends*, Migros Museum für Gegenwartskunst, Zürich; *Dada Revivals*, Kunsthaus Zürich; *Stipendiaten der Stiftung Binz 39*, Zürich; *Werk- und Atelierstipendien der Stadt Zürich*, Helmhaus, Zürich

1999 *Eidgenössische Stipendien / Kiefer Hablitzel Stiftung*, Messe Basel; *Komm Schatz, wir gehen weiter…*, Hochschule für bildende Künste, Hamburg

1998 *Werk- und Atelierstipedien der Stadt Zürich*, Helmhaus, Zürich; *Freie Sicht aufs Mittelmeer: Junge Schweizer Kunst mit Gästen und Gastmahl*, Kunsthaus Zürich / Schirn Kunsthalle Frankfurt; *Wahlverwandtschaften*, IG Art & Appenzell; *Eidgenössische Stipendien / Kiefer Hablitzel Stiftung*, Messe Basel; *25 År*, Centro Adessa, Copenhagen; *Exposition privée*, Château de l'Aile, Vevey; *Dogdays are Over*, Centre Culturel Suisse, Paris; *von sfr. 2.- bis sfr. 1200.-*, Serge Ziegler Galerie, Zürich

1997 *Serge Ziegler Galerie*, Zürich; *Diskland / Snowscape*, collab. David Renggli, Shed im Eisenwerk, Frauenfeld

1995 *Assistent*, Stiftung Binz 39, Zürich

PROJECTS

2022 *Copy/Paste*, Kulturweg Limmat, Ennetbaden

2021 *Come together (Situationist Space Program) @* Rotonda by La Mobiliare, Film Festival Locarno; *Spaceknot (Leuenhof)*, The Pictet Group, Zürich; *Farbsockel*, Stadthalle, Bülach

2019 *NE TRAVAILLEZ JAMAIS*, Rue de Seine, Paris; *Spaceknot* (Pfefferberg), Kink, Berlin

2017–21 *work@Mobi*, die Mobiliar headquarters Bern, Nyon and Zürich

2017–18 *Ceci n'est pas un onion*, Fun & Fury!, Cabaret Voltaire, Zürich; *Situationist Space Program @* Spazio Cinema, Parco Bally and Castello Visconteo by la Mobiliare, Film Festival Locarno

2016 *Iris*, Färbi Areal, Schlieren; *What If?*, die Mobiliar / Gottardo 2016, Pollegio & Rynächt, 2016; *Raumknie*, Oh Panama, Berlin; *Stabil, Labil, Indifferent*, Trottenhaus, Bebra; *Spacknot*, Restaurant Spitz, Swiss National Museum, Zürich; *Space Is My Canvas (Performance)*, Die Zweite Heimat, Hamburg; *Spaceknee*, Oh Panama, Berlin

2015 *Space Is My Canvas (Performance)*, Kunstraum Walcheturm, Zürich

2014 *Space Is My Canvas (Performance)*, JAJAJA, Hamburg

2011 *Tyger Tyger*, Novartis Campus, Basel; Demeter, Katz Orange, Berlin

2010 *Nomadic Structures*, collab. Gregor Metzger, public space, South Africa

2009 *Gulliver*, Bahnhofplatz, Pfungen; Ada Bojana Symposium, Ada Bojana

2007 Scenography for *P.U.S.H.*, Gregor Metzger (dir.), Theaterhaus Gessnerallee, Zürich

2003 *An der grossen Frage wird nachwievor gearbeitet…*, collab. David Renggli, Schauspielhaus Zürich; *Autoscooter*, collab. David Renggli, *Lange Nacht der Zürcher Museen*

2002–05 *slauer baal*, collab. David Renggli, Löwenbräu, Zürich

2001 Scenography for *Brüderchen & Schwesterchen*, Barbara Weber (dir.), Staatstheater Schwerin

2000 Scenography for *Freundinnen*, Barbara Weber (dir.), various locations; *Installation*, Kunsthaus Pasquart, Biel/Bienne

1999 Scenography for *Gopf*, Blauer Saal, Zürich

1996–97 *SPACE*, collab. David Renggli, Dreieck, Zürich

1994 On tour with Béjart Ballet, Lausanne

1992 *Van Gogh TV – Piazza Virtuale*, Universcity-TV Zürich, Documenta IX, Kassel

Ohne Titel (Teermaschine), 2000

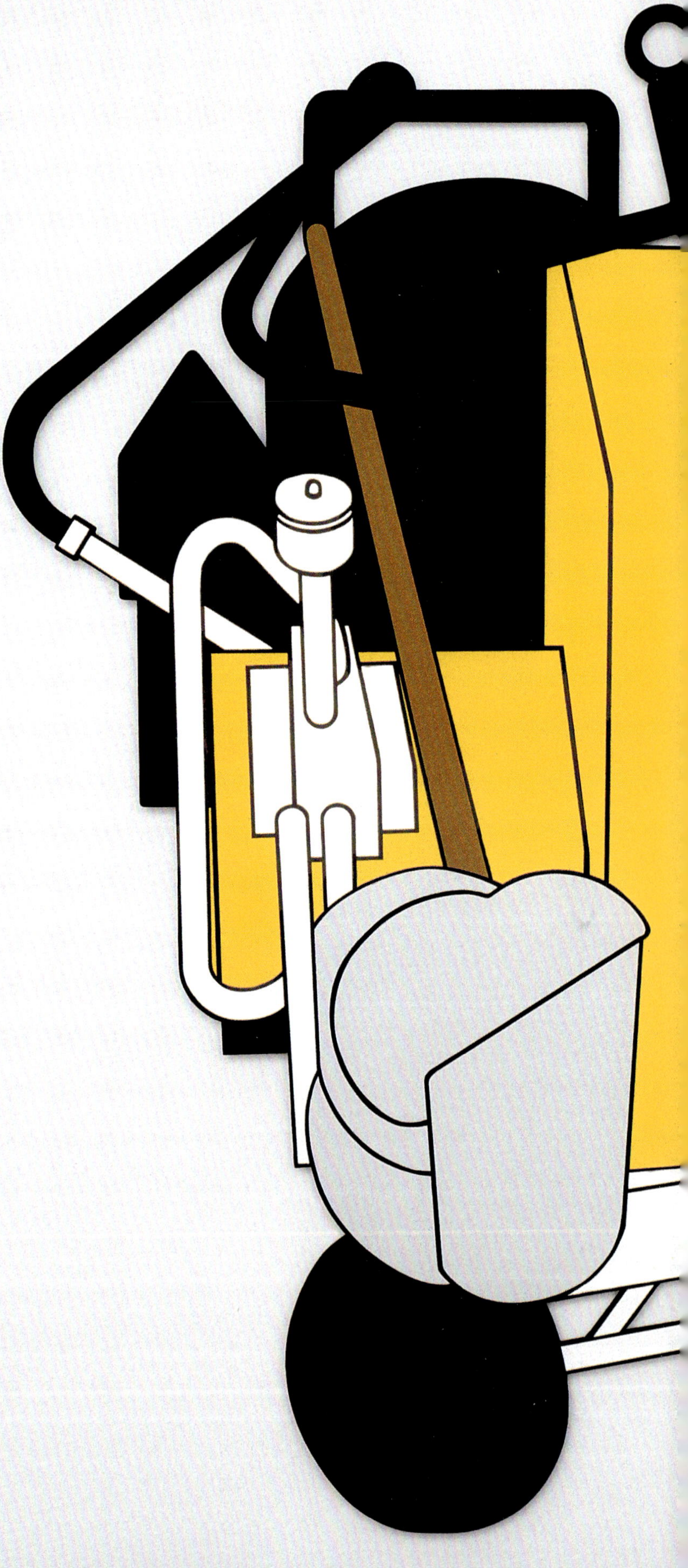

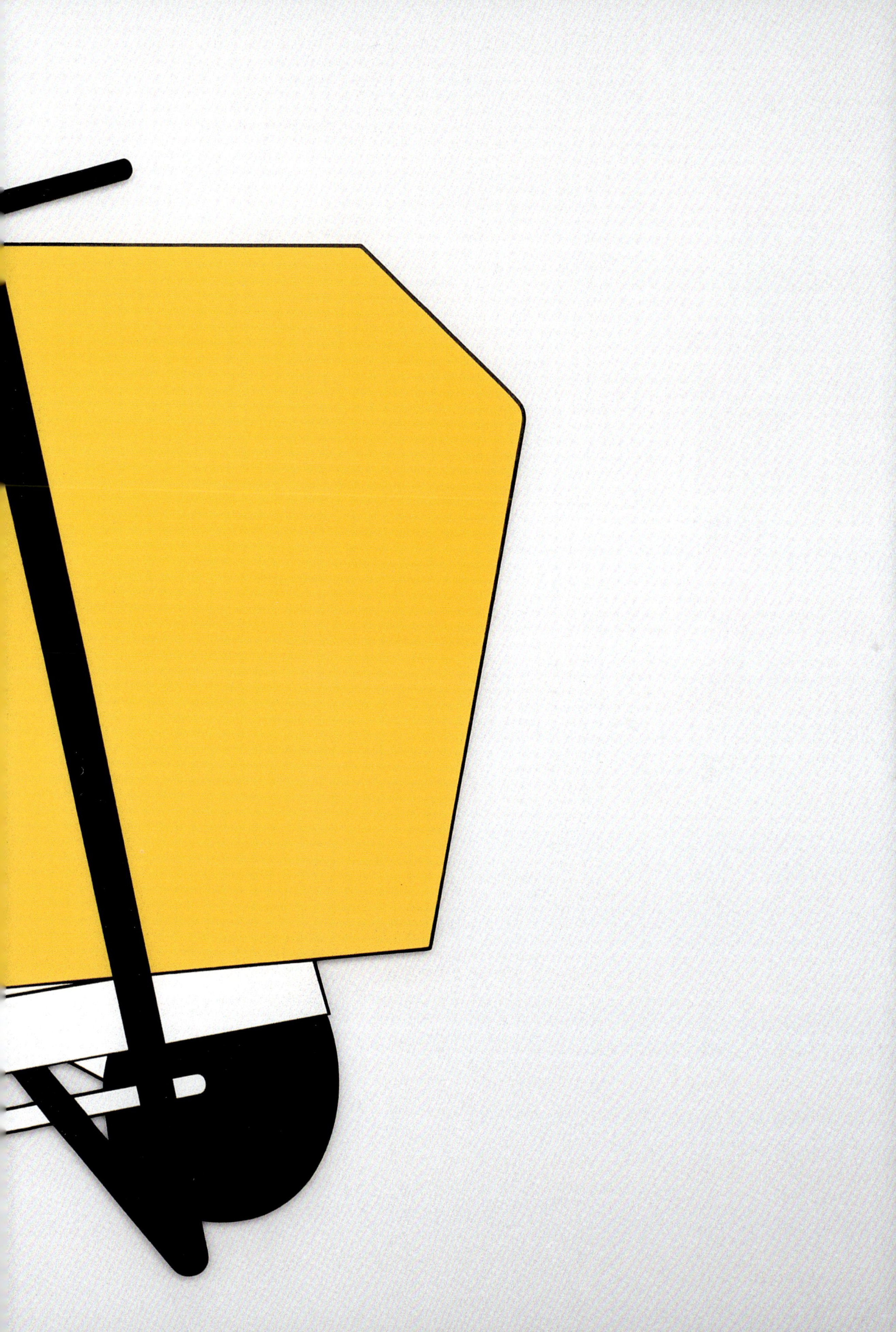

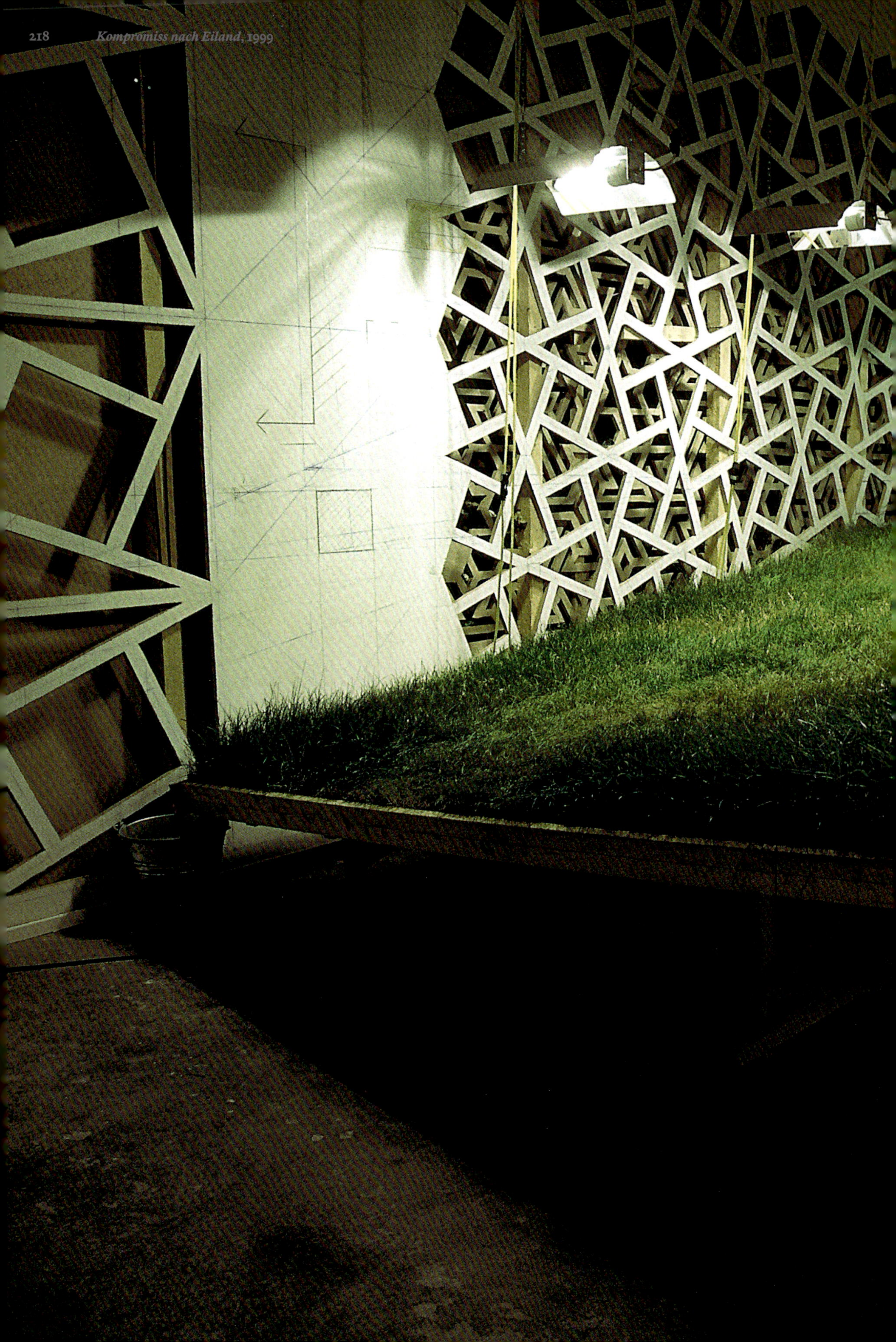

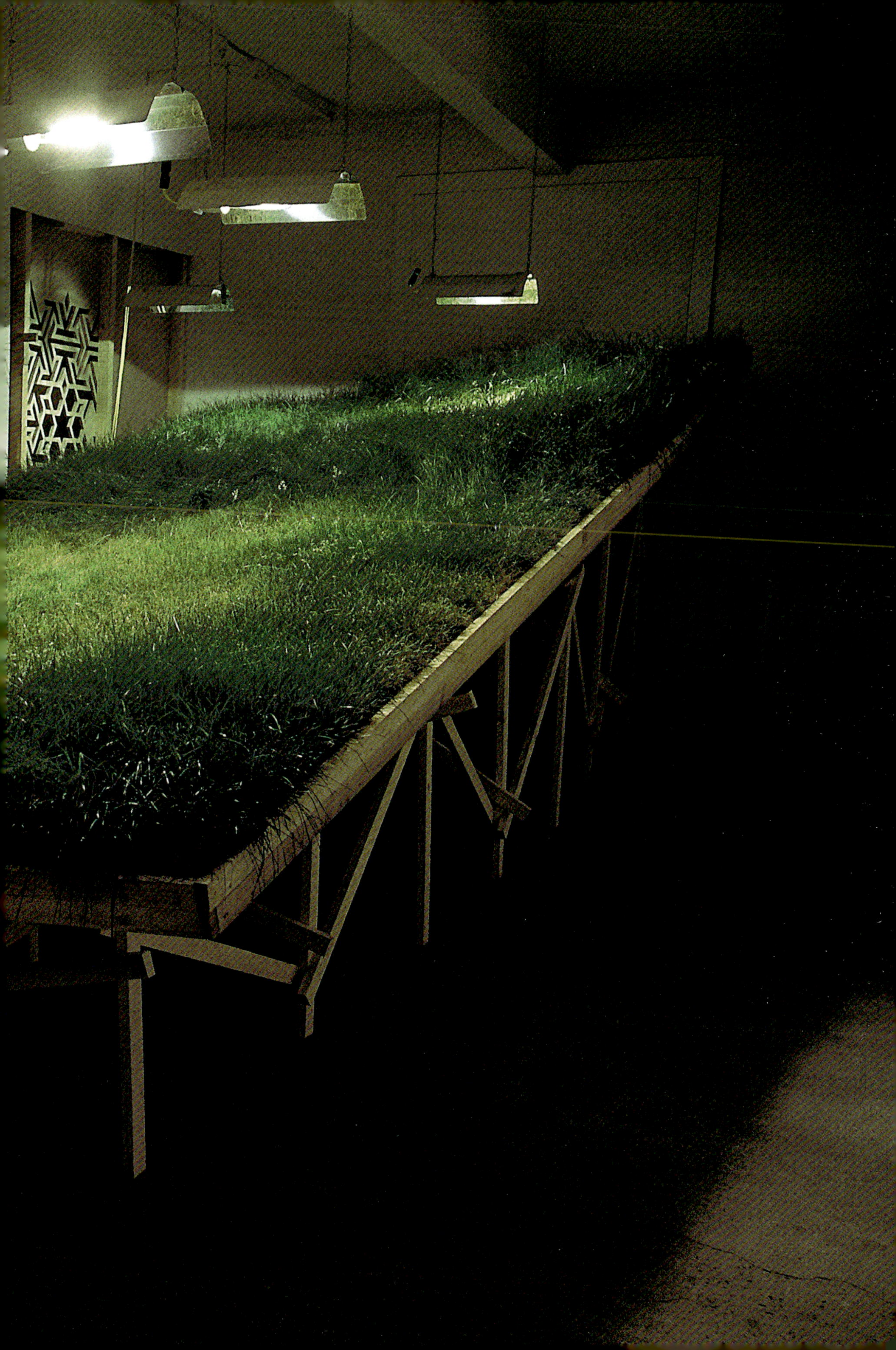

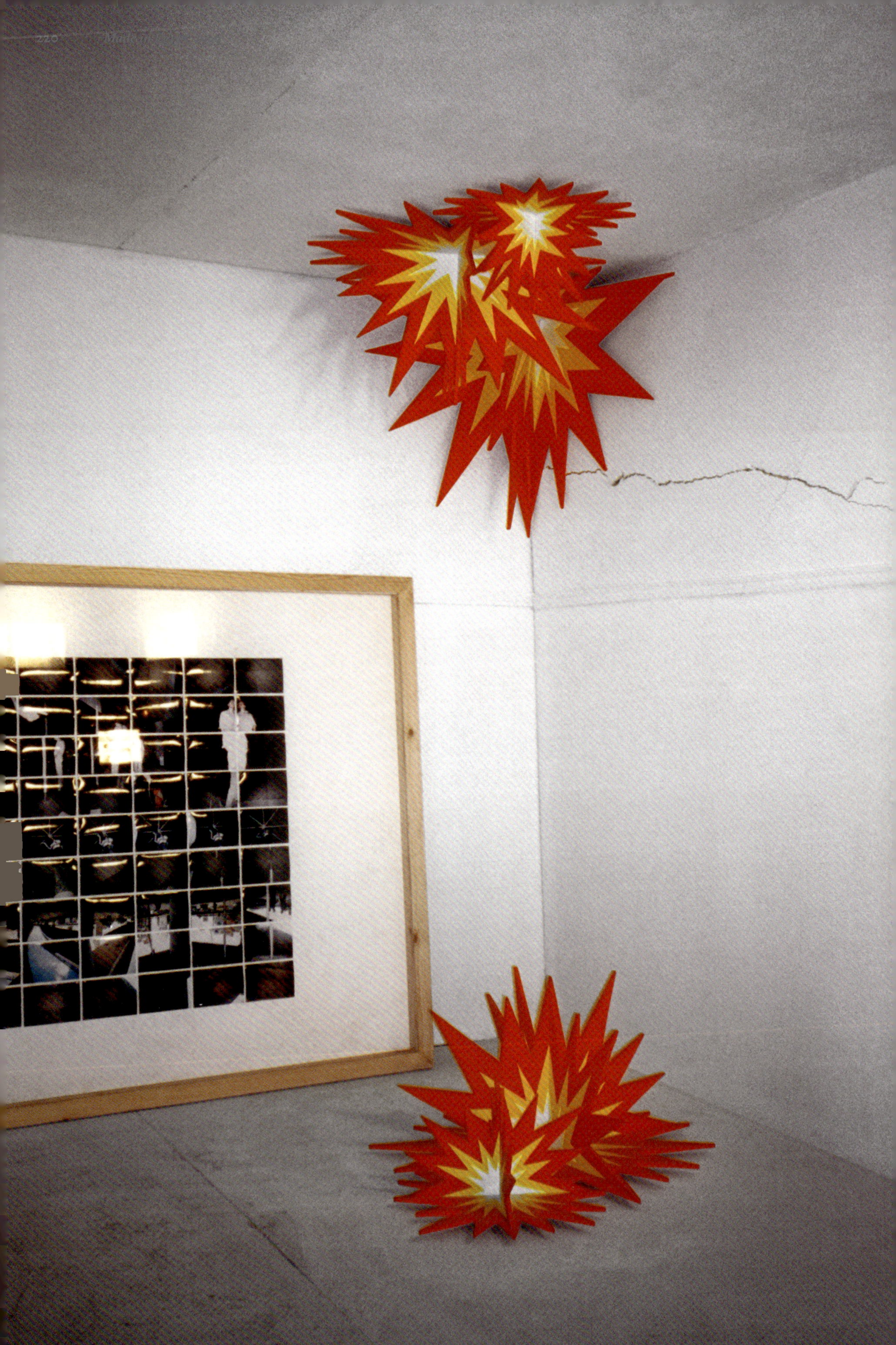

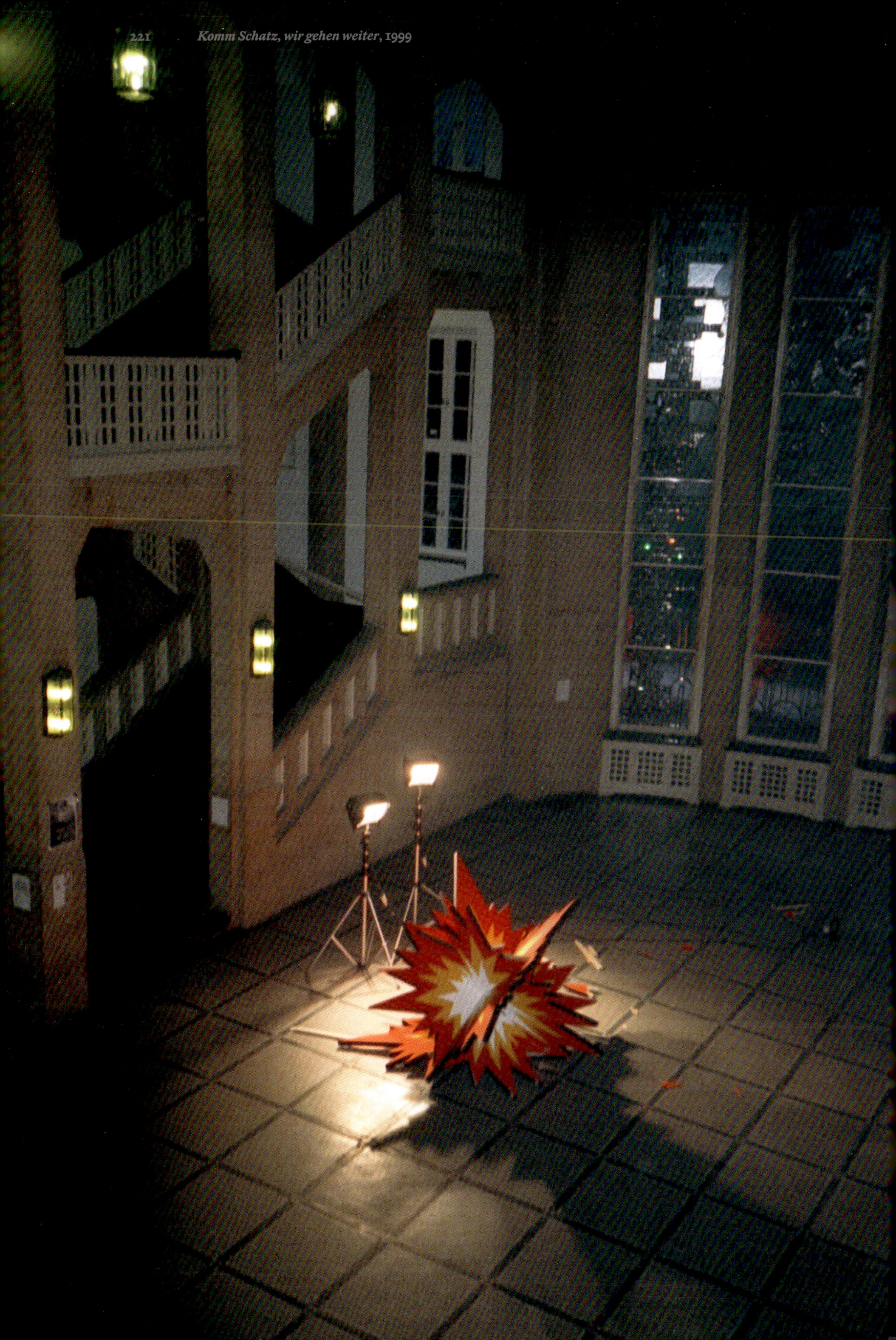

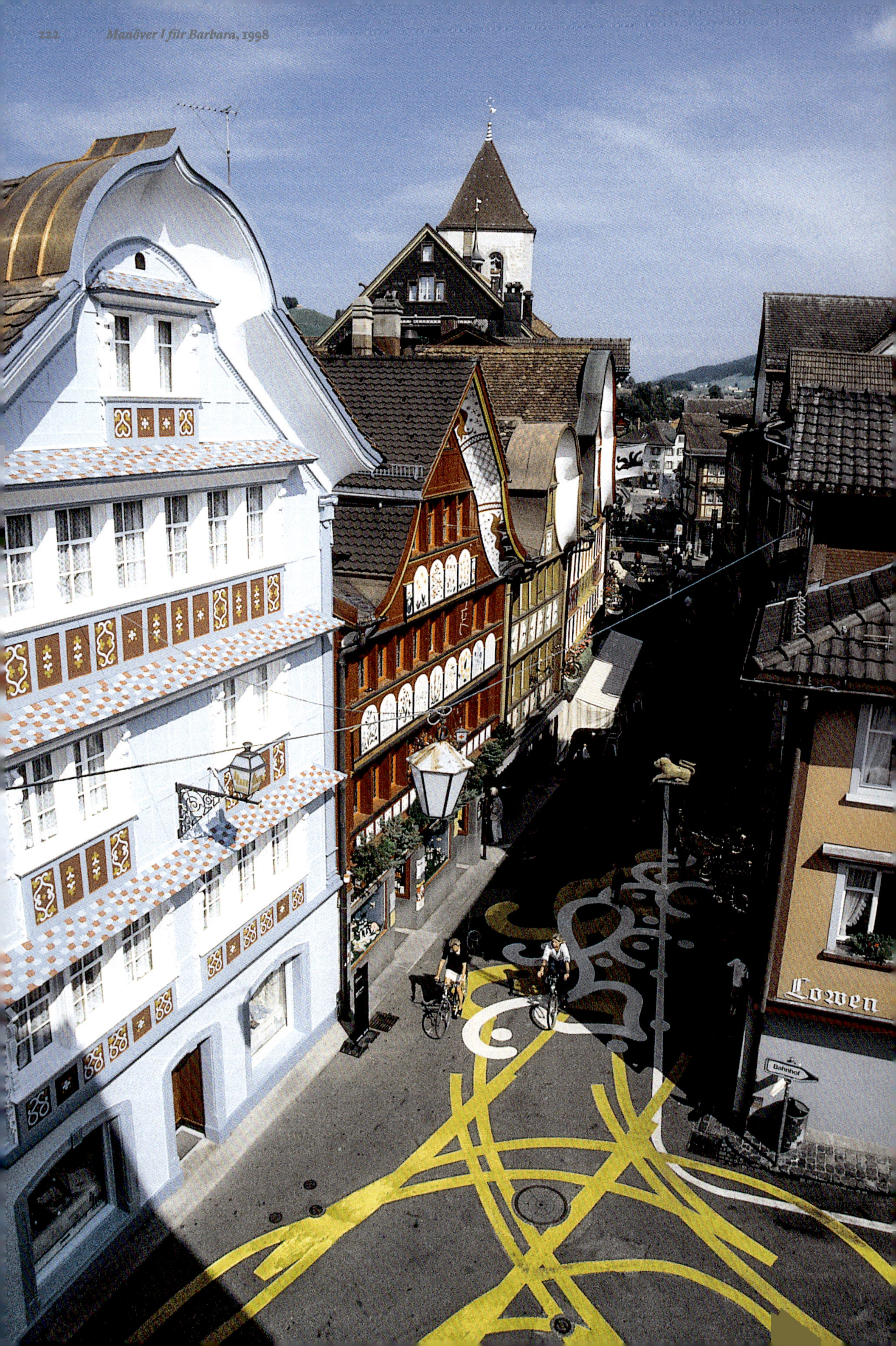
Lowen
Bahnhof

Ohne Titel (Tex Avery), 1998

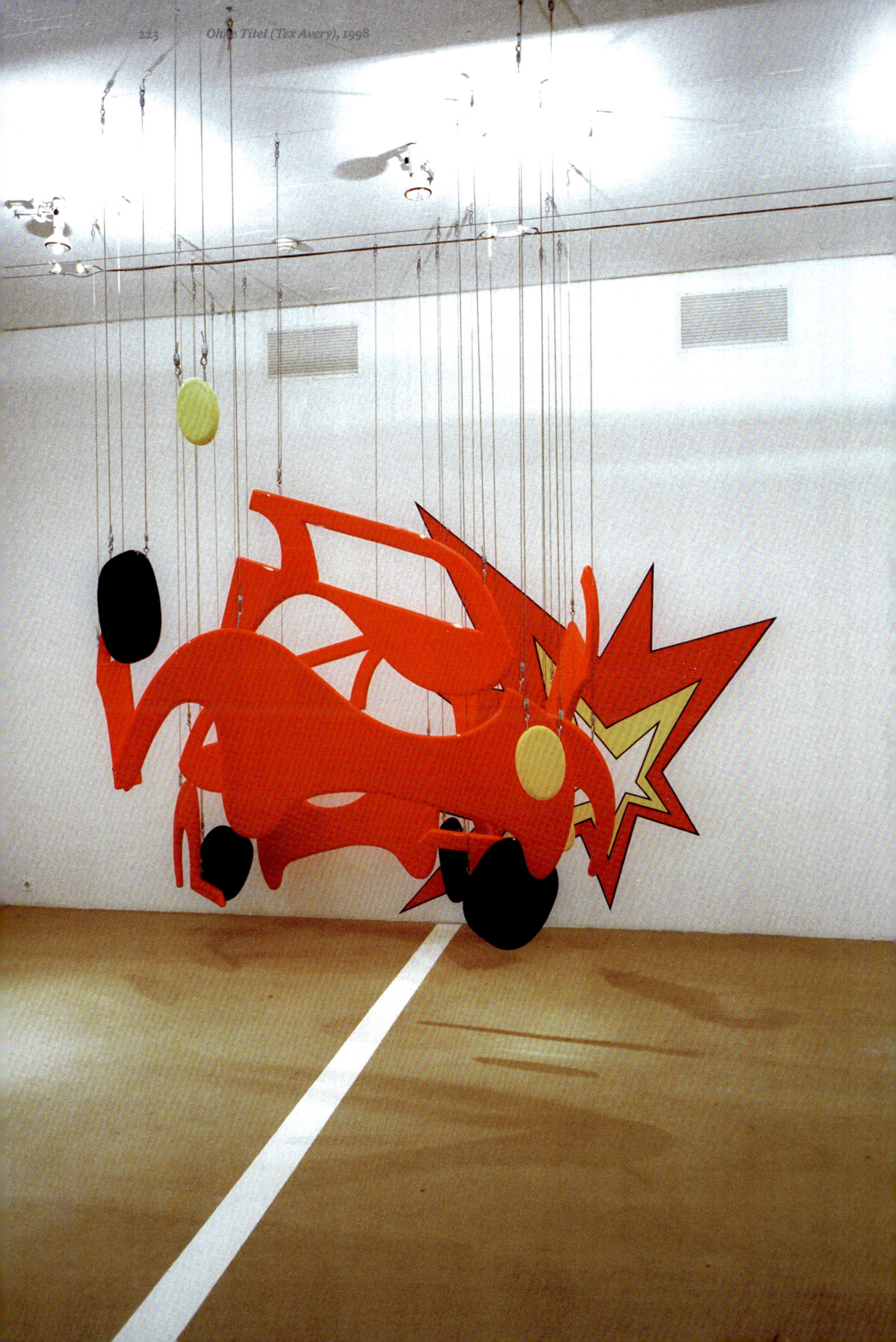

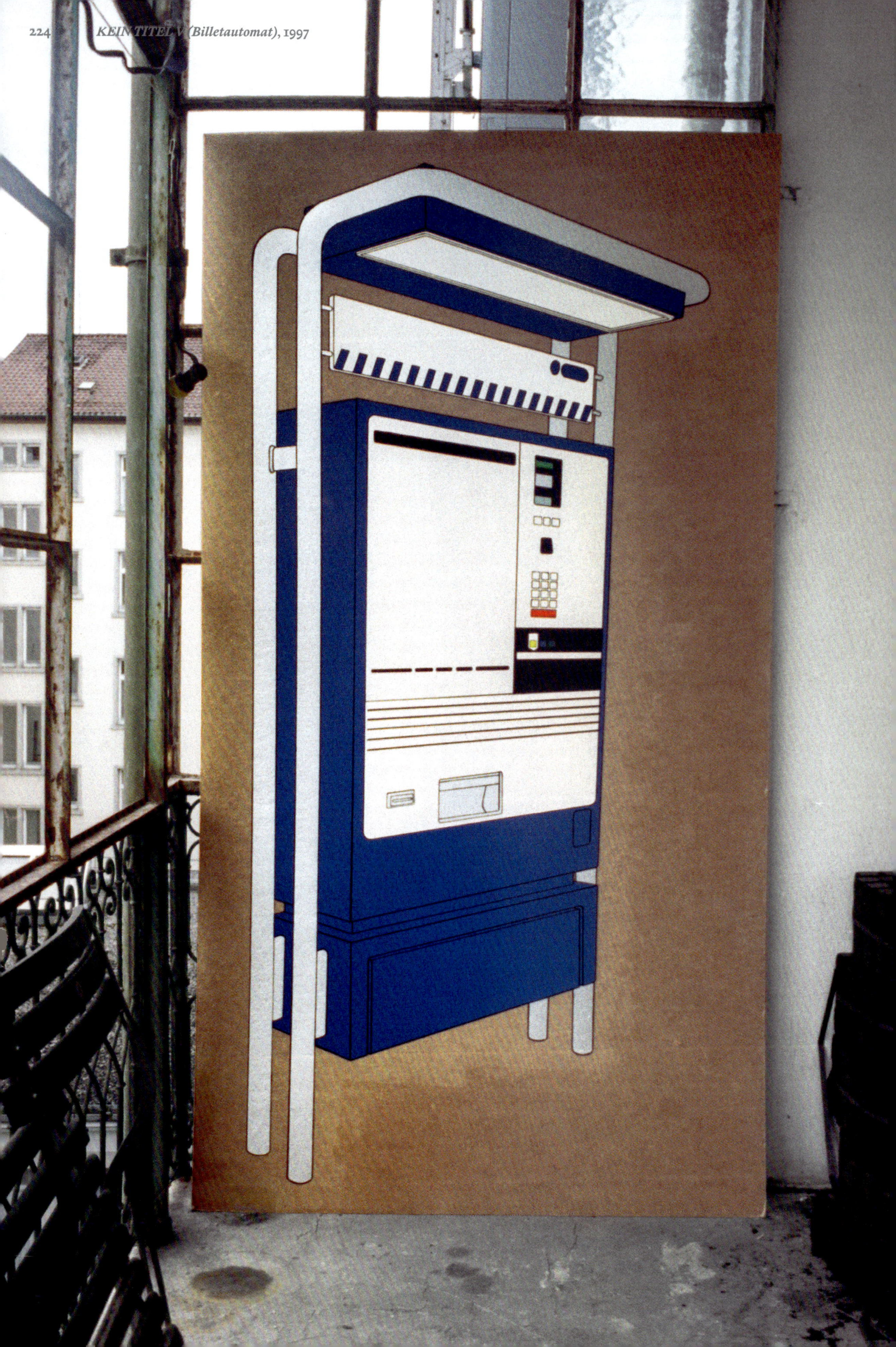

KEIN TITEL V (*Billetautomat*), 1997